John Clare in 1820, from the portrait by William Hilton, R.A.,
(National Portrait Gallery)

John Clare

A Life

J. W. & Anne Tibble

London
Michael Joseph

This edition first published in Great Britain by Michael Joseph Ltd, 52 Bedford Square, London, W.C.1.
First published 1932 by R. Cobden-Sanderson Ltd.
New edition completely revised by Anne Tibble 1972

7181 0828 0

Set and printed in Great Britain by Ebenezer Baylis & Son Limited, The Trinity Press, Worcester, and London in Bell eleven on twelve point on paper supplied by P. F. Bingham Ltd., and bound by James Burn at Esher on material specially printed by Arborfield Products Ltd.

To Edmund Blunden

Contents

Illustrations

Acknowledgements

I cannot sufficiently say how much I am indebted to the Hon. Anthea Joseph and Evan Owen for their percipience in regard to the subject of this book. Nor can I sufficiently thank its two editors. To the librarians of the Central Library, Northampton, and Judith Levin, curator of the Peterborough Museum, I am deeply grateful for all their help in making accessible manuscripts and photostat copies in each of the two biggest collections of Clare papers. I must also record my thanks to Dr James Harper, the Medical Director of St Andrew's Hospital, Northampton, for his patient answers to queries. I am indebted to the staff of the British Museum Music Room; and to Margaret Grainger for the use of her manuscript index in dealing with the Peterborough Manuscripts. Finally I am grateful to Heinemann Educational Books Ltd, for permission to quote from *John Keats* by Robert Gittings.

Anne Tibble

Foreword

In 1820, with *Poems Descriptive of Rural Life and Scenery*, John Clare became known to the London literary world as the "peasant poet" of Northamptonshire. Born in 1793, he had lived twenty-seven years in the poverty and obscurity which were the natural lot of one born into the agricultural stratum of English society of his time. The swift turn of fortune's wheel which carried Clare to a very brief, dizzy success was in turn followed by a slow descent on the other side which condemned him to twenty-seven years of grimmer obscurity in places for the insane.

His after-fame is as full of paradox as his life. His death in 1864 revived memories, often condescending, of the "peasant poet" of 1820. In that year Macmillan contemplated a Life and two volumes of his Collected Poems, but nothing emerged. In 1865, thirty years after the appearance of the last of his five volumes, a *Life* of him was published by Frederick Martin. In 1873 J. L. Cherry's *Life and Remains of John Clare* carried a selection from Clare's Asylum poems. In 1893, after a Centenary exhibition, some ninety manuscripts, ranging from rough drafts scribbled on the backs of letters and bills, to neatly written, finely bound books, our largest collection, was housed in Peterborough Museum. A second collection, equally important, of seventy-two manuscripts, has gradually been built up by the Northampton Public Library. Six volumes of letters to Clare were bought by the British Museum in 1873. Since then, manuscripts of this most English of poets have gone to America: some to the Pforzheimer Library, Yale University Library, Harvard University Library and the University of California Library. Others are owned by the Pierpont Morgan Library and the Henry E. Huntington Library; there are some in the Berg Collection in the New York Public Library. Here in Britain the Bodleian houses a small number of manuscripts.

In 1901 a selection from Clare's published poems was made

by Norman Gale; in 1908 Arthur Symons edited another selection, including some previously unpublished poems, with a usefully perceptive introduction.

During these years anthologists had not wholly neglected Clare, and the story of his life had been told briefly in newspaper articles and encyclopaedias, almost always with emphasis on the "peasant poet" or "poor Clare" aspects which Clare himself had abetted by speaking of himself as a "clown".

Frederick Martin yielded to none in enthusiastic Victorian appreciation of Clare. Martin had access to all, or most of, the manuscripts mentioned above. He used them as a novelist rather than a biographer, inventing thoughts, people, emotions, conversations and tears. But he was on the spot and closer in time. A drinker himself, he sympathized with Clare's drinking, and perhaps fellow-feeling made him careless of exact evidence about Clare's drinking capacity. The few who mistrusted his "bastard-Carlylese" were sometimes led to belittle Clare as well. Among these, Charles Dickens wrote indignantly of "such preposterous exaggeration of small claims". A second edition of Martin's *Life* (1964) corrected a few of its inaccuracies.

J. L. Cherry's brief account of Clare in his *Life and Remains* gave quotations from the Journal and letters and expressed doubts of Martin's accuracy. But Cherry was unable to consult some already scattered manuscripts.

Except for Arthur Symons's work, it was Edmund Blunden and Alan Porter who in 1920, in *Poems Chiefly from Manuscript*, offered a selection of Clare's work and an assessment totally free from condescension, of both poet and poems to this century. A hundred years after Clare's success with his first volume, they printed in their selection a large number of hitherto unpublished poems, many of them among Clare's best work; they revealed the stores of autobiographical material among the manuscripts at Peterborough and Northampton. After Alan Porter's untimely death, Edmund Blunden printed more unpublished poems in *Madrigals and Chronicles* (1924), and, in 1931, in *Sketches in the Life of John Clare Written by Himself*, gave Clare's pen-portraits of the poets, writers and painters he met in London together with the sketch of his early life which Clare sent up to his publishers Taylor and Hessey in March 1821. This had remained among Taylor's papers for over a century.

The sketches of the *Londoners* are printed again in the present book. Clare's second "autobiography", which he brought up to 1824, was sent probably to H. F. Cary and Mrs Eliza Louisa Emmerson, and then presumably lost sight of; it contains fragments from among the Peterborough manuscripts which are different from the account sent to Taylor in 1821. Among these are the extracts used in the present book. In the first edition of *John Clare: A Life* we too youthfully and blithely followed Clare's first instructions to his first editors: "Print just what suits you and in any form whatever." We supplied punctuation, regularized spelling, and were sometimes ignorant transcribers often unwitting of the complexities of Clare transcription. By 1951, in the *Letters* and *Prose*,[1] we sought to reproduce his occasional dashes and even more occasional stops, his unorthodox and often inconsistent spellings. He is presented thus in this edition, I hope with far greater accuracy. Readers in general maintain that lack of punctuation offers no great difficulty.

Illegible passages, doubtful or debatable words or sequences —and there are many—are noted and marked, usually with alternative possibilities, thus, "black [*blank*]". Where possible he is given the benefit of the doubt, as with his often indistinguishable "then" and "than", his "–l" and "–ll", his "–ies" and "–ys". If Clare's "were" for "where" increases difficulty of comprehension, "w[h]ere" is given.

The greatest editorial problem arises from Clare's method of making three, four, five, sometimes six drafts of a poem. He seems to have done this from memory, with variant words and phrases; it is often impossible to know which draft he meant for the final one. In his autobiographical fragments there are sometimes two versions of the same incident, again probably jotted down from memory, but each is different from the other, difficult to combine. Where there is no manuscript of a poem other than the one punctuated by Taylor, or Taylor's copyist, that punctuation has been given. The "W. F. Knight Transcripts" —though there are in fact two other transcribers—were acquired by the Northampton Library in 1938. There are also two later sets of transcripts of the St Andrew's poems and in some instances of individual poems these transcribers may have had access to

[1] Both published by Routledge & Kegan Paul.

manuscript scraps which have disappeared. Quotations from Knight, his successors, or the two other transcribers, are given with their punctuation.

We have tried to let Clare speak for himself where possible. Although he described himself as "far from a close reasoner in prose", and called Priscian's art of grammar, the *Grammatici*, black magic, his native idioms give freshness and individuality. There are also passages of moving beauty.

Edmund Blunden called the contradictions and divergencies of opinion on Clare and his poetry a "puzzling profusion of good and bad critiques". The traditional, condescending view dies hard. Since 1920, one writer thinks he is too well read in the poets of the eighteenth century, and imitates them continually; another notes the immense gulf which divides him from these same poets. To one his poetry is "mere picturesque description"; another sees in him always "a poet of the spirit". One finds "no principle of inner growth"; another comments on the "continuous growth of the poet's mind, strangely crowned in the Asylum period". We read of the "pure imagination of a hundred enchanting phrases", and of "not one startling felicity, one concentrated ray in the whole body of his work". In his life some see a miserable record of failure due to weakness of character, lack of business acumen, and dissipation sexual and otherwise; others see a struggle against great, almost impossible, odds and a life of achievement despite outward failure and lack of practical success.

With these contradictions of estimate in mind, we have tried to give in this book a record of Clare's life in which the reader may, if he wishes, disregard our interpretations and occasional judgments, and base his own conclusions on first-hand evidence. New evidence since 1932 throws more light on Clare's mind, character and achievements. The self he himself strove with such integrity to clarify and which he would have wished to be remembered by may emerge. For the rest—a remark he made in a letter to a friend: "If life had a second edition, how I would correct the proofs!"

Anne Tibble
1972

Introduction

The point of discovering John Clare, at any rate of reading about him, is not the pathos of his life. No doubt many people who end their days mentally sick and under care are as pathetic, deserving as much to be cherished and loved; but they remain in the private realm, they are not what Clare was, a great man, a great poet. The pathos, though, mixes with his greatness: terrible it seems that such crystalline ability, such lucidity, such incandescence of mental substance and response, had to consort with deprivation and failure, and with hardness from the world.

One reads of him, in a way, with fascinated shame. Wait till you reach the page where Dr Fenwick Skrimshire (who himself was given to authorship) signs the paper committing Clare to that final asylum in which he was to write his greatest lyrics.

There is no reason to think this country and infirmary doctor was anything but kind or sympathetic; to believe that, with his long knowledge of Clare and his own predilection for so much that also gave pleasure to Clare, he acted except as he should have done. Clare was mad.

But then consider the words he wrote on the printed form—that Clare's madness had been preceded—by what? "By years addicted to Poetical prosings."

We are better placed, we know much of these "poetical prosings", we know the lyrics in which Clare forgave his fate, and the world:

Hesperus! thy twinkling ray
Beams in the blue of heaven,
And tells the traveller on his way
That Earth shall be forgiven!

Or—

I loved but woman fell away,
I hid me from her faded fame,

I snatch'd the sun's eternal ray
And wrote till earth was but a name.

In every language upon earth.
On every shore, o'er every sea,
I gave my name immortal birth
And kept my spirit with the free.

It must be supposed that Fenwick Skrimshire M.D. was faced with something which still seems to worry a few readers, though it should exhilarate them: that an unlettered son of penniless labouring parents—in a somewhat dismal countryside, moreover—should have pre-empted their own privilege of literacy and education. It is as if Dr Skrimshire was complaining that Clare did not know his place, and couldn't spell, and had been giving himself cultured airs; and no wonder, seeing that he was now mad;—which he was, beyond argument. (Now-a-days this Skrimshire attitude is also reversed quite often: there are partisans of Clare as working man who think that his poems should be printed in every edition and selection, not as he heard them to himself, in their making and completion, but exactly as he wrote them out, misspelt and nearly unpunctuated, and indistinctly divided into stanzas; which would serve Clare and his readers badly. All that must be preserved is Clare in his exact words, grammar or no, not the inexact, inconsistent spelling of his words, which he would have regretted.)

The tragedy of Clare, all the same, involves far more than how individuals behaved to him. If some of the Londoners and the *haute monde* he came to know, acted towards him with incomprehension and with the conceit of class, others got him right, as far as the evidence allowed (they had no collected poems as we have; no such biography as this one). He was, in short, both cherished, up to a point, and rejected, regarded and disregarded. And many who stood by him must also have been baffled into a dying regard, and so into a final indifference or forgetfulness by the special difficulties of Clare's situation, and his character. The benevolent, all-seeing, all-powerful *deus ex machina* is a rare bird, and seldom descends on to the stage to put everything right.

So we read of his life between London and the country, between well-meaning ladies and fellow authors, between exploiting publishers and exploiting journalists, and we are wrung by the contemplation of such rarity, such delicacy, for which there is no durable relief, and no home, as Clare so often said in his poems. He was the heart without a home; for whom, in spite of his wife and children, a home was impossible.

In this cold world without a home
Disconsolate I go,
The summer looks as cold to me
As winter's frost and snow.

True and untrue, for there is another consideration. Wrung as we may be, we don't, after reading this biography and when we have accepted Clare into ourselves as an influence which stays alive, warm and active, feel disconcerted. Is it too much to claim that after all happiness predominates? At least the happiness revealed, bubbling up and up after falling away, has to be set against the desolation. Each intensifies the other; the mental desolation of Clare poignantly intensifies the happiness; the element, I find, which works most in my own ineradicable experience of this marvellous man. I think of particular moments whether enshrined in or out of his poems, in the life or in his tone and rhythm.

For instance, I always remember, in this addition sum of happiness, Clare going into Stamford and buying one of the first two books of verse which he owned (Thomson's *Seasons*), how on the way home, through the lime trees in Burghley Park, he composed his first poem—aged thirteen:

There the stinking bryony weaves
Round the hazel her scallopt leaves, etc.

I think of Clare again losing—or finding?—his own identity by entering into other life. One or two other English poets have had an equal power of creative empathy, but I think none have used it so much (or only Shakespeare, and Tennyson?). Clare in this may not always achieve perfect form to match the degree of empathy and happiness, but consider an example or two of Clare standing and entering life, or absorbing it. He watches a cuckoo singing on an oak tree—

Until its quick eye noticed me
And then it whewed away.
Its mouth when open shone as red
As hips upon the briar.

He writes down the exact singing of a nightingale (in "The Progress of Rhyme"), which he makes both the bird of his Northamptonshire summer and the bird of all western literature. He sees a frog in the early sunshine—"His bright sides scatter dew"—then he notes

The jetty snail creep from the mossy thorn,
In earnest heed and tremulous intent,
Frail brother of the morn,
That from the tiny bents and misted leaves
Withdraws his timid horn,
And fearful vision weaves.

For a last, I think less celebrated example, the ageing Clare, no longer the small built, fair-headed boy with blue eyes and delicate hands, but short, stocky Clare of the asylum, or rather out of it for the day in the fields round Northampton, still watching, still taking life, and entering it, and—yes—conferring it as well:

Green solitude, his prison, pleasure yields,
The bitch fox heeds him not—birds seem to laugh.
He lives the Crusoe of his lonely fields
Which dark green oaks his noontide leisure shields.

Perhaps to suggest even then that happiness predominates with Clare is to use the wrong word. Certainly *being* predominates. Clare is in the heart of being, where being is most healthy. For that we must value him, and reverence him. I think Pasternak spoke of the duty of poets—or all of us—towards existence who has been our host; whose hospitality we must, if we can, be grateful for.

That expresses our transcience.

But it is better still to be able to speak of Clare as himself a portion of the hospitality he celebrates. Also he is love of that being—love, he says, which lives in itself as the wild flower lives in its own scent. Even then, beyond the utmost that a poem can say,

> Language has not the power to speak what love indites:
> The Soul lies buried in the ink that writes.

—to quote two lines which survive by themselves in the asylum poetry.

It is still necessary to make more people understand the piercingness of Clare's greater verse and to ensure that he has the right place in the canon of English poets (here I recall—a little mischievously I won't deny—Keats's view that Clare described too much at the expense of the 'prevailing idea'; and Clare's counter-criticism of the cockneyism of Keats too given to dryads and fauns, too given to placing a Venus behind every rose bush and "under every laurel a thrumming Apollo", and to a faking of nature. Each criticism applies, but which of these two writers exhibited the greater freedom and purity of style?). Finding room for uncanonized greatness inside a closed circle—that is a long, slow business; but this present biography, a work of devotion, now strengthened and revised, has been serving that end for nearly forty years. We should not know Clare without it.

Geoffrey Grigson

Spring

CHAPTER ONE

Jumping Time Away: 1793-1805

What may be called the "Clare country" is that north-east corner of Northamptonshire which lies between the curving valley of the river Welland on the north and that of the river Nene to the south. Here, as in Tennyson's Lincolnshire, are two distinct types of country—the dyke-sown, treeless fen, and the wooded midland with sunny eventful field-corners.

A glance at the modern Ordnance map will show that the dividing-line between the two types of country is sharp and clear. The main road from Peterborough to Lincoln seems to define a boundary between fen and midland scarp country. Once, the division may have been the Roman road of King Street. On the east, in years past, sea marshes crept up as far as this; for the land on the fen side retains still an indefinable likeness to the sea itself. As late as 1810 the Peterborough Great Fen lay between Peterborough and Crowland Abbey. A tract of level land of six or seven thousand acres and capable of the highest output of crops, it was up to then undivided and uncultivated. Writing after the drainage, Charles Kingsley lingered in fancy "over the shining meres, the golden reed-beds, the countless waterfowl, the strange and gaudy insects, the wild nature ... where the coot clanked, and the bittern boomed, and the sedge-bird, not content with its own sweet song, mocked the notes of all the birds around."

Round the small town of Market Deeping, eight miles north of Peterborough, the fenland penetrates westwards to the main line of what, before the advent of British Rail, was the London and North-Eastern Railway, laid down in the 1820s. On the south-west side of the railroad, only fifty feet above sea-level and just outside the bounds of the fen, some seven miles from Peterborough, is the small village of Helpston. Here, on July

13th, 1793, John Clare was born. To the west and south of the village lies the district that Clare was later so untiringly to wander in, with its woods and heathy common-land. To the east and north the fen "spreads its faint shadow of immensity". Clare wrote of both these kinds of country: again and again he described "the flaggy forest and the flood"; but that which he loved and clung to, as Michel loved and clung to the plain of Montmartre, was the wooded, softly swelling midland, with its many grey spires, to the south and west of his home.

Helpston[1] has not altered greatly in the last hundred years until the 1960s. It is a long, spacious village, with big gardens, and picturesque because of the Northamptonshire yellowstone, Ketton stone, or Barnack Rag, of most of its houses. The parish adjoins that of Barnack, for some years Charles Kingsley's home, and the birthplace, in 1830, of Henry Kingsley. In 1793 Helpston had accommodation for sixty families. On the right-hand side of the village street, running south, the cottage where Clare was born stands, made of stone, and reed-thatched, like the rest of the older dwellings. Originally it must have been one well-proportioned, detached house, but in the 1780 to 1790 population increases other parts were added to make it two, then three; by 1970 it was modernized as one. When Clare was born the two cottages both belonged to a book-loving retired farmer named Gee, a good landlord. There were elm trees near by, one so huge and thick that it "turned a whole days' rain",

> Where ring-doves from their nest would call
> And the grey-veined ivy grew

Each of the two cottages probably had four rooms, two up and two down. The ladder which led to the rooms above was, in the 1930s, used instead of a staircase. The cottage, Clare records in his autobiographical fragments,

> was as roomy & comfortable as any of our neighbours & we had it for forty shillings [a year] while an old apple tree in the garden generally made the rent the garden was

[1] As was the custom a century and a half ago, Clare always spelt it "Helpstone". The first element is the O.E. personal name, Helpric or Helparic: Professor Frank Stenton, *Place-names of Northamptonshire* (Cambridge University Press, 1933).

> large for a poor man & my father managed to dig it night & morning before the hours of labour & lost no time He then did well but the young farmer that succeeded our old landlord raised the rent & the next year made four tenements of the house leaving us a corner of one room on a floor for three guineas a year & a little slip of the garden which was divided into four parts but as my father had been an old tenant he gave him the choice of his share & he retained our old apple tree Tho the ground was good for nothing yet the tree still befriended us & made shift to make up the greater part of our rent

Clare's father was Parker Clare. The name was common in the district and throughout the county. Perhaps residence in or near the small town of Clare in Suffolk originated the surname, though its corruption from "Clayer", meaning clay worker or agriculturist, sounds most feasible when the strong Anglo-Saxon farming bent of eastern England is recalled. Clare himself knew and cared little about it:

> I cannot trace my name to any remote period a Century & a half is the utmost & in this I have found no great ancestors to boast in the breed—all I can make out is that they were Gardeners Parish Clerks & fiddlers & from these has sprung a large family of the name still increasing w[h]ere kindred has forgotten its claims & 2nd & 3rd cousins are worn out

Parker Clare, born on January 14th, 1765, was "one of fate's chancelings who drop into the world without the honour of matrimony". His second name was that of his mother, doubtless the daughter of the "John Clare, Clark" whose flowing signature in the Helpston parish registers is now all the trace that can be found of him. Parker was the name of the child's fiddler father, John Donald Parker, a Scotsman who stayed for a while at Helpston as schoolmaster. He disappeared at the inconvenient rumour of his child.

Parker Clare was in his youth a man of great strength, whose means of livelihood was day-labouring among the farmers round about. He was noted at the village feasts and among his acquaintances as a wrestler, and he liked in later years to show his scars. This traditional rustic wrestling included kicking, the feet shod with heavy country boots studded with sharp nails. According to his son, Parker Clare's conversation, like that of many who work close to the soil, was full of pith, virility and aptly coloured phrases. His memory was stored with ballads and old songs, and his son records that he could sing or recite over a hundred. He was in social demand because of this, too. Because of his strength, threshing with a flail became his chief labour. While he was hale and strong his living, if meagre, was regular and assured.

He married Ann, the daughter of John and Elizabeth Stimson,[1] daughter of a shepherd of the neighbouring village of Castor. She was eight years older than her husband, having been born on April 14th, 1757.[2] Unlike Parker, who could read a little in the Bible, Ann did not know her letters. Like him, she could sing and recite ballads and songs in plenty. A prudent woman and a loving mother, she showed courage and endurance under the dropsy with which she became afflicted a few years after John's birth. The bond of understanding between her and her only son was strong.

"There was five of us", he tells. He was the elder of twins. The other child was a "bouncing girl", while John "might have gone into a pint pot";[3] but the younger, more promising, child died soon after birth, as we know from a sonnet of Clare's, published in the *London Magazine* for August, 1821, "To a Twin Sister Who Died in Infancy". Though Clare apostrophized her as "Bessey", there is record of neither her baptism nor her death, so it is probable that she was given the unceremonious burial then, as now, accorded to unbaptized babies. Clare himself was small and slight, with startlingly blue eyes.

The cottage at Helpston contained one of those closely-knit, unassuming families of which there are more than is sometimes suspected. Before the more dire poverty overtook them and

[1] Or *Stimpson*.

[2] Clare's Journal for Thursday, April 14th, 1825: "My mother is 67 years old this day . . ." From the baptismal registers at Castor she was baptized on April 17th, 1757. She was therefore thirty-five when her marriage to Parker took place, not eighteen as Frederick Martin says.

[3] *Quarterly Review*, May 1820.

Parker Clare was unable to work through rheumatism, they managed without too much difficulty. The children were decently if meanly, clad: "And housewife's care in many a patch was seen". Later, and not infrequently, the "sad fiend" necessity was at their backs, while the farmer, like Stephen Duck's employer, was not friend but an enemy to the hireling whop-straw. In spite of all this, times without number after Clare grew up he recalled his childhood's Eden of happiness:

O I could tell for aye & never tire
The simple trifles infancy supplies
O I could view for ever & admire
The gilded prospects of its painted skies

When he was five, the line where those painted skies met the earth so stirred his fancy that he set out to explore:

To the worlds end I thought I'd go
And oer the brink just peep adown
To see the mighty depths below

He records this attempt to outwit distance in his fragmentary autobiography:

I lovd this solitary disposition from a boy & felt a curosity to wander about spots w[h]ere I had never been before I remember one incident of this feeling when I was very young it cost my parents some anxiety it was in summer & I started off in the morning to get rotten sticks from the woods but I had a feeling to wander about the fields & I indulgd it I had often seen the large heath calld Emmonsales stretching its yellow furze from my eye into unknown solitudes when I went with the mere openers & my curosity urgd me to steal an oppertunity to explore it that morning I had imagind that the worlds end was at the orizon & that a days journey was able to find it so I went on with my heart full of hopes pleasures & discoverys expecting when I got to the brink of the world that I coud look down like looking into a large pit & see into its secrets the same as I believd I coud see heaven by looking

> into the water So I eagerly wanderd on & rambled along the furze the whole day till I got out of my knowledge when the very wild flowers & birds seemd to forget me & I imagind they were the inhabitants of new countrys the very sun seemd to be a new one & shining in a different quarter of the sky still I felt no fear my wonder seeking happiness had no room for it I was finding new wonders every minute & was walking in a new world & expected the worlds end bye and bye but it never came often wondering to myself that I had not found the edge of the old one the sky still touchd the ground in the distance as usual & my childish wisdom was puzzld in perplexitys night crept on before I had time to fancy the morning was bye which made me hasten to seek home I knew not which way to turn but chance put me in the right track & when I got back into my own fields I did not know them everything seemd so different the church peeping over the woods coud hardly reconsile me when I got home I found my parents in the greatest distress & half the village about hunting me as one of the woodmen in the woods had been killd by the fall of a tree & it seemd to strengthen their terrors that some accident had befallen myself as they often leave the oaks half cut down till the barkmen come up to pill[1] them which if a wind happens will fall down unexpected[2]

Although Clare might, writing later, in certain moods remember himself as a lonely boy with little relish for the games and rivalry of companions, it seems clear that this love of solitude did not greatly distinguish him till after the first boisterous discovery of the countryside as a playground. No small child with an imagination, turned loose in all seasons among lanes and meadows and woods, could keep all the adventure and inventions to himself. He and his nameless companions played the kind of game that unconfined country children have played for three or four thousand years. In summer they cut the stalks from mushrooms and floated them for mimic boats down streams; in days when rumours of war reached their heedless

[1] "Peel" or "strip", particularly of oaks felled in spring.
[2] Peterborough MSS.

ears, they waded through the farmers' wheat to get the blue corn-cockle for a "wild cockade", tore through the woods to pull hollow-stemmed "kecks"[1] for bugles; when they were hungry they stole peas from the fields, and ate crab-apples and hazelnuts, "shells, pith and all". Sometimes imagination supplied the feasts; they made houses of clay, sticks and stones, hoarded bits of broken pot for pottery, spread on a "table-stone" their burdock leaf of a tablecloth, had mallow seeds for cheeses and henbane seedboxes for loaves of bread; flowers of the greater bindweed made drinking-horns.

Their most serious employment was taking their fathers' dinners to the hayfield and refilling the empty water-bottles at one of the springs. Then they ran behind the loaded hay-wain "just for the joy of riding back again".

Their games were those that have not staled from the time when the boys of Ancient Greece played them—leap-frog, nine-peg Morris, "nicked upon the green", hopscotch, and

> Chucking up the bouncing ball
> By bee-haunted cottage wall[2]

Langley Bush, formerly the meeting-place of the old Hundred Court of Nassaburgh, was a rendezvous. Round it the boys played clink-and-bandy and chock-and-taw. When cowslip time came, they went with baskets to gather the flowers for tea and for wine, and garlanded the village street on feast days with branches, berries or blossom.

Clare remembered those jubilant days with regret, could not recall them often or vividly enough:

> Time writes them with a golden pen
> But never lives them back again[3]

Yet as early as this, gleams of that rarer fancy, which was to be his torment but also his comfort for so many years, are evident. Like most children then, he believed in fairies; but when, with most, the very sympathy with these beliefs is fading, Clare was remembering

[1] Or *kecksie*, the hollow-stemmed hogweed, *Heracleum sphondylium*.
[2] Peterborough MSS.
[3] *Ibid.*

Stave acres little yellow weeds
The wheat fields constant blooms
That ripen into prickly seeds
For fairy curry combs[1]

The grey lichens among the creeping thyme at Swordy Well were fairy forests; like the maturer Blake he discerned foot-marks in the dark rings among the molehills, "where plough-shares never come to hurt the things antiquity hath charge of". Although he kept his fancies to himself, in an unlettered spot such as Helpston was a hundred and seventy years ago, when the existence of witches, will-o'-the-wisps and fairies was an open question in the minds of many grown-ups, there was plenty of this kind of goblin-food for a child's imagination:

> The sallow palms were called when I was a boy Geese and Goslings & cats and kitlings—I asked an old cow woman or herd woman[2] the reason & she said it might be from their being known to belong to the fairys who changed them into wild Geese & Goslings & Cats & kitlings at their pleasure or anything else when they feasted on the rings in a pasture in summer nights[3]

He often listened to the tales of other old dames as they sat down on summer noons to take their snuff. Stories of Jack the Giant-Killer and Hickathrift filled him with "fearful ecstasy". His mother knew all the superstitions of the village, about the ghosts that haunted the spot where, in her youth, the gibbet stood, about all the will-o'-the-wisps and witches. On winter nights, as he tells in *The Shepherd's Calendar*, she regaled them with tales until the silent children trembled. Then she would break off, promising to finish her stories the next night:

The children cringe away to bed
And up the ladder softly tread

[1] Peterborough MSS.
[2] Clare himself has no mention of the Granny Bains of whom Frederick Martin speaks.
[3] Peterborough MSS.

Scarce daring from their fearful joys
To look behind or make a noise
. . . . . .
While yet to fancys sleepless eye
Witches on sheep trays gallop bye

The minds of Parker and Ann Clare were uncorrupted by the idea being thrust at, or creeping upon, a few of the adult poor about this time as a result of the industrial system—the exploitation of children. The Clares did not regard their surviving son or daughter as means of making money. If Ann occasionally suspected the higher learning might be witchcraft, she was anxious that John should have the best education that the village and their circumstances could give. Parker, always the kindliest of fathers, backed her ambition against often great odds. Never less than three months out of the twelve were spared for schooling. The child went first to a dame school[1] in the village, where he learnt to write a little and to read from the Bible. From the age of about seven to twelve he attended, but intermittently, a school at Glinton. To obtain money for this he helped his father at threshing, with a small flail his father made for the purpose; or he worked for the farmers himself, tending sheep and cows and bird-scaring in the fields. The wages for eight weeks' work paid for one month's schooling at fourpence a week. His sister Sophy, too, must have gone to school, since in 1820 she wrote a very fair hand. At Glinton, under a master named Seaton, Clare learned to read and write and understand the rudiments of arithmetic. At first he had a boy's usual attitude to school, hating the nine and one o'clock bells which called him from play, disliking the imprisonment, and mourning over his thumb-soiled hornbook for liberty. In time, though, the cottage table of an evening became littered with pens and paper. At her spinning-wheel Ann regarded them with awe but silent delight, her son records.

Still Clare had not that seriousness with which he later regarded study. There were occasions when he played truant, fishing for struttle and gudgeon, seeking "painted

[1] Clare does not mention the name of the school mistress. Martin gives her as Mrs Bullimore.

pooties"[1] by the dyke-sides, or following the landrail or corn-crake's call for hours in the vain hope of finding her nest.

In school, under Seaton, the children were sternly disciplined. He was an old white-haired man and he died before Clare reached the age of twelve; his peeled switch hung over the smoke-stained chimney-piece. His school was held in the vestry of the church; the graveyard was the children's playground. The day-school room was perhaps that in which the Sunday-school was held, to which Clare went as well, both his parents belonging to the Church of England. When he had mastered the "three Rs" Seaton encouraged him to go further, with the hope of qualifying for the position of usher in a village school. Sometimes the boy received from the master as much as threepence a week, reward for well-learnt work. There is a family story that once he earned sixpence for repeating, from memory, the third chapter of *Job.* Inspired by Seaton's praise, he started on such books of mathematics as Bonnycastle's and Fenning's; a love of learning was beginning to set him apart from other boys.

Yet, in spite of what he tells us later—that he "had little relish for the pastimes of youth"—Clare had pleasure, up to the age of eleven or twelve at least, in most of the enjoyments which village life had to offer. Helpston prided itself on the upkeep of its feast-days. In *The Village Minstrel* Clare tells in detail how, at Martinmas, neighbours met to drink warm, nutmegged ale, to roast apples, and to play Dusty Miller, Scotch Pedlar, charades and games. One was bid to shut his eyes and open his mouth to taste what gifts were sent him—when he received, no doubt amid peals of laughter, a handful of ashes on his tongue. Hodge was often baited, and that none too gently: invited to sit between two girls on a sheet thrown over a tub of water, as he sat they rose and "let him swearing in". Fortunes were told, while "poor beguilèd Kate", silent in her corner, listened eagerly and hoped for the sweetheart whom by her "lapse" she had forfeited. When tired of "fortunes" the revellers made music with warming-pans and muffled combs, and danced. About midnight they all went home, with lanterns gleaming through rain or snow.

Weddings and house-warmings and harvest-homes were

[1] Pooties: snails.

occasions for festivities; but Statute time, the labourers' holiday week, was to the villagers of Helpston the most uproarious time of all. To this May or Michaelmas Quarter-day feast people came from surrounding villages; and, besides hiring or rehiring themselves for the coming twelve months, they often spent all their past year's savings. They amused themselves with such sports as hunting a "soapt and larded pig", cock-fighting, badger-baiting, racing and wrestling,

> Where wrestlers join to tug each other down
> And thrust and kick with hard revengeful toe.

Though his father had local fame at this pastime, Clare says he himself did not care to look on at the rougher sports. Though he enjoyed watching many of the games he perhaps did not often actually join the "rude revelry". In the evening the dancing was to the tunes of the gipsy's fiddle, when cotton drabs, worsted hose and heavily clouted shoes were put away; or there was ale drinking in the public-houses, where the rattling tongue of the landlady could barely keep peace among the brawlers, especially if there happened to be a sergeant or two recruiting for the Militia: these would ogle the girls from their lovers and rouse the mettle of the men till they either fought among themselves or enlisted to fight shoulder to shoulder against Napoleon. Clare's *The Village Minstrel* supplies these pictures in its panorama of a country poet's childhood.

For all his slight frame and acknowledged diffidence, Clare was evidently not lacking in prowess—climbing trees, vaulting walls or fences and jumping streams. He records one or two adventures:

> What a many such escapes from death doth a boys heedless life meet with I met with many in mine once when wading in the meadow pits a lot of cow tending boys we byd [*tryd*] to do each others tasks we had gone several times & it was my turn to attempt again when I unconsciously got beside a gravel ledge into deep water when my heels slipt up & I siled down to the bottom I felt the water choke me & the thunder in my ears & I thought all was past but some of the boys coud swim & so I escapd another time we were swim-

ming [*sweeing*] on bundles of bulrushes when mine getting to one end suddenly bounced from under me like a cork & I made shift to struggle to a sallow bush—catching hold of the branches I got out but how I did it I know not for the water was very deep—yet we had dabbld there sunday after sunday without the least fear of danger once when bird nesting in the woods of which I was very fond we found a large tree on which was a buzzards nest it was a very hard tree to climb there was no twigs to take hold of & it was too thick to swarm so we consulted for a while some proposing one thing & some another till it was decided that a hook tyd to the end of a long pole that woud reach to the collar of the tree woud be the best to get up by in taking hold of it & swarming several attempted to no purpose & at last I tryd tho I was rather loath to try the experiment I succeeded at getting up to the collar which swelld in such a projection from the tree that I coud not make a landing without hazarding the dangerous attempt of clinging with my hands to the grain & flinging my feet over it I attempted it & faild so there I hung with my hands & my feet dangling in the air I expected every moment to drop & be pashd to pieces for I was a great height but some of my companions below while some ran away had the shrewdness to put the pole under me & by that means I got on the grain just in time before I was quite exhausted.[1]

Another autobiographical fragment tells how he slowly grew beyond these escapades and amusements:

I never had much relish for the pastimes of youth instead of going out on the green at the town end on winter Sundays to play football I stuck to my corner stool poring over a book in fact I grew so fond of being alone at last that my mother was feign to force me into company for the neighbours had assurd her mind into the fact that I was no better than crazy at length my schooldays was to be at an end as I was thought learned enough for my intended trade which was to be a shoemaker

[1] Peterborough MSS.

But there usd to be "crookhorn" in those days I usd to like & "duck under water" on May eve or to toss the cowslip balls over the garland that hung from chimney to chimney across the street[1] & there was going to Eastwell on a Sunday to drink sugar & water at the spring head but enclosure came & drove these from the village I usd to be very fond of fishing & of a Sunday morning I have been out before the sun delving for worms on some old weed blanketed dunghill & sliving off across the wet grass that overhung the narrow path then I usd to stop to wring my wet trouser bottoms now & then & off agen beating the heavy drops off the grass with my pole end till I came to the flood washd meadow stream my tackle was eagerly fastend on & my heart woud thrill with hopes of success as I saw a sizable gudgeon twinkle round the glossy pebbles or a fish leap after a flye or a floating something on the deeper water Where is the angler that hath not felt these delights in his young days and where is the angler that doth not feel taken with their memory when he is old

I usd also to be very fond of poking about the hedges in spring to hunt pootys & I was no less fond of robbing the poor birds nests or searching among the prickly furze on the heath poking sticks into the rabbit holes & carefully observing when I took it out if there was down at the end which was a sign of a nest with young then in went the arm up to the shoulder & fear came upon us that a snake might be concealed in the hole our bloods ran cold within us & started us off to other sports we usd to chase the squirrels in the woods from grain to grain that would sit washing their faces on the other side & then peep at us again we usd to get boughs from the trees to beat a wasps nest till some of us were stung & then we ran away to other amusements

& then the year usd to be crownd with its holidays as thick as the boughs on a harvest-home there was the long-wishd-for Christmas the celebrated week with two Sundays when we usd to watch the clerk return with his bundle of

[1] Very ancient May-games, introduced either by the Romans with their Floralia, games in honour of the goddess Flora, or else played previous to the Roman conquest. See appendix to Anne Elizabeth Baker's *Glossary of Northamptonshire Words and Phrases.*

evergreens & run for our bunch to stick [in] the windows & empty candlesticks hanging in the corner or hasten to the woods to get ivy branches with their jocolat berries which our parents usd to color with whiting & the bluebag sticking the branches behind the pictures on the walls

Then came valentine though young we were not without loves we had our favourites in the village & we listend the expected noises of creeping feet & the tinkling latch as eagerly as upgrown loves wether they came or not it made no matter disappointment was nothing in those matters then the pleasure was all then came the first of April O how we talkd & hoiped of it ere it came of how we woud make April fools of others & take care not to be caught ourselves when as soon as the day came we were the first to be taken in by running on errands for pigeons milk & glass eyed needles or some such April fool when we were undeceivd we blushd for shame & took care not to be taken in again till the day returned when the old deceptions were so far forgotten as to deceive us again Then there was the first of May We were too young to be claimants in the upgrown sports but we joind our little interferences with them & ran under the extended handkerchiefs with the rest unmolested Then came the feast[1] when the Cross was throngd round with stalls of toys & many colord sugar plums & sweets horses on wheels with their flowing manes lambs with their red necklaces & box-cuckoos we lookd on these fineries till the imagination almost coaxd our itching fingers to steal & seemd to upbraid our fears for not daring to do it the sweetmeats were unbounded there was barley sugar candied lemon candied horehound & candied peppermint with swarms of colord sugar plums & tins of lollipops our mouths watered at such luxurys we had our penny but we knew not how to lay it out there were ginger-bread coaches & gingerbread milkmaids & to gratifye two propensitys the taste & the fancy together we bought one of those gilded toys & thought we had husbanded our

[1] Statute Sessions were established in 1351 for sheriffs, and, later, magistrates, to regulate in every shire in England farm-servants' wages and allot work to all. By 1824 "statute" had become only the agricultural holiday-feast for re-hiring at Michaelmas.

pennies well till they were gone & then we went away to coax our parents for more thinking of making better bargains when we got money again[1]

& then came the sheep-sheering w[h]ere we was sure of frumity from the old shepherds if we sought the clipping pens & lastly came the harvest-home & its cross-skittles Ah what a paradise begins with life & what a wilderness the knowledge of the world discloses surely the Garden of Eden was nothing more than our first parents entrance upon life & the loss of it their knowledge of the world[2]

[1] Clare repeats himself: "then there was Eastwell spring famous in those days for its spaws & its brough at the fountain w[h]ere we usd to meet of a Sunday & have sugard drink".

[2] Peterborough MSS.

CHAPTER TWO

A Happy and a Lonely Boy: 1805–1809

From early days Clare had that need to be alone which is a necessity in achieving poetry or art of any kind. He inherited, or had by nature, or else rapidly developed, a nervous capacity for overwork and the barometric up-and-down of feelings and mood consequent upon mental and nervous exertion. In spite of the many social recreations of village life, from the age of about ten onwards his liking for rambles with one companion increased. Richard Turnill was the younger son of a neighbouring farmer for whom Parker Clare sometimes worked:

> Among all the friendships I have made in life those of schoolfriends & childish acquaintance are the sweetest to remember there is no deseption among them there is nothing of regret in them but the loss they are the fairest sunniest pages memory ever doubles down in the checkerd volume of life to refer to there is no blotches upon them—they are not found[ed] [*formed*] like bargains on matters of interest nor broken for selfish ends—
>
> One of my first friendships was with Richard the brother of John Turnill it began with infancy from playing at feasts by the cottage wall with broken pots & gathering the crumpled seeds of the mallow for cheeses making houses & fires of sticks stones & clay to the second stage of hunting birds nests & painted pooty shells among the dewy boughs & busy growing grass in the spring & the partnerships of labours toils & sunday leisures but death came when we were growing up into each others pleasures like twin flowers & took him away before our budding friendship coud blossom—yet it was the mirage [*image*] of happiness—what numberless hopes of successes did we

> whisper over as we hunted among the short snubby bushes of the heath or hedgerows or crept among the blackthorn sprays after the nest of the nightingales & what happy discourses of planning pleasures did we talk over as we lay on the soft summer grass gazing into the blue sky shaping the passing clouds to things familiar with our memorys & dreaming of the days to come when we shoud mix with the world & be men ... [1]

Richard died of typhus fever. Clare thought him "all goodness centred in one piece". He grieved in at least two poems years afterwards: "Thou art gone the dark journey" was probably on this friend;[2] and

> O Turnill Turnill dear should thou
> To this fond mourner be
> By being so much troubled now
> From just a naming thee

In a still later, unfinished prose tale, "The Two Soldiers", one character reminds his companion: "These days Richard are all over & our happiness gone after them for some other boys to pick up & lose again as we did."

Although affection for, and the early death of, Richard Turnill laid hold on Clare's childish emotions, there began about this time another friendship which was to have a far greater influence on him. This was with Mary, fair-haired, blue-eyed daughter of James Joyce, a Glinton farmer. It began as a preference among school-mates. In "Sketches" of his life sent to John Taylor in 1821 Clare calls her "the stillest and most good-natured girl in the school"; but "she knew nothing of my fondness for her, no more than I did of her inclinations". Mary Joyce, four years younger than he, was born in January, 1797, and towards the end of his year under Seaton, perhaps after Turnill's death, Clare and Mary worked and played together. He now enjoyed the old church school under "the spire where pellitory dangled & grew" too well to play truant:

[1] Two fragments, Peterborough MSS.
[2] Published by Tom Hood in his Annual *The Gem*, 1829.

... I was a lover very early in life my first attachment being a school boy affection but Mary—who cost me more ballads than sighs was belovd with a romantic or platonic sort of feeling if I coud but gaze on her face or fancy a smile on her countenance it was sufficient I went away satisfied we played with each other but named nothing of love yet I fancyd her eyes told me her affections we walkd together as school companions in leisure hours but our talk was of play & our actions the wanton innosense of childern yet young as my heart was it woud turn chill when I touchd her hand & tremble & I fancyd her feelings were the same for as I gazd earnestly in her face a tear woud hang in her smiling eye & she woud turn to wipe it away her heart was as tender as a birds ... I cannot forget her little playful fairy form & witching smile even now ...

I remember an accident that roused my best intentions & hurt my affection into the rude feelings of imaginary cruelty when playing one day in the churchyard I threw a green walnut that hit her on the eye she wept & I hid my sorrow & my affection together under the shame of not showing regret lest others might laugh it into love[1]

Sometimes he in his "patcht coat" and the farmer's daughter may have wandered in the fields:

A clownish silent haguish boy
Who even felt ashamed of joy
So dirty ragged & so low
With nought to reccomend or show
That I was worthy een a smile
—Had I but felt amid my toil
That I in days to come should be
A little light in minstrelsy
& in the blush of after days
Win beautys smile & beautys praise
My heart with lonely fancy warm
Had even bursted with the charm[2]

[1] The last paragraph is a Peterborough fragment entirely by itself, but almost certainly it refers to Mary Joyce.

[2] Peterborough MSS.

When Clare stopped going to Glinton day school three country miles separated them. They did not see each other. He became more and more attached to "woodland peace & privacy", longing for spring and the first primrose, shunning the gangs of lads and their "unpleasing" play. The village "gossips" began to say he was "half a ninny" and prophesied no good for him. "In fact I grew so fond of being alone at last that my mother was fain to force me into company for the neighbours had assured her mind into the fact that I was no better than crazy—"[1]

But from "friendships I gatherd an acquaintance with books" besides broadsheets and the "sixpenny romances" sold by chapmen and hawkers:

> The first books I got hold of besides the Bible & the Prayer Book were an old book of Essays with no title & another large one on Farming *Robin Hoods Garland* & *the Scotch Rogue*[2] the old book on farming belongd to old Mr Gee who had been a farmer & who livd in a part of our house which once was his own he had had a good bringing up & was a decent scholar & he was always pleasd to lend me them even before I coud read without so much spelling as guesses at words so as to be able to make much of them or understand them
>
> I became acquainted with *Robinson Crusoe* very early in life having borroed it of a boy in Glinton school of the name of Stimson who only dare lend it to me for a few days for fear of his uncles knowing of it to whom it belonged yet I had it a sufficient time to fill my fancys with hero Crusoes & adventures[3]

About this time the boy who spent hours among the matted thorn-bushes to watch the nightingale feed her young began to pass the winter evenings on his corner stool beside the cottage inglenook "reading poems not too long". Wordsworth's "We are Seven", hawked about among the villages as a penny

[1] *Ibid.*

[2] There were innumerable editions of the *Complete History of all the Notable and Merry Exploits performed by Robin Hood and his Men*. I have failed to trace *The Scotch Rogue*.

[3] Peterborough MSS.

ballad, was a favourite. "Jessie, the Flower o' Dumblane", one of the most popular, if not one of the best, achievements of the Scottish song-writer, Robert Tannahill, also sold on penny sheets, was among the first Clare read. Years after his childhood, he recalled his father's reading him some stanzas from John Pomfret's "Love Triumphant over Reason" a poem well known among the so-called vulgar peasantry. The rhythm "haunted" Clare; and his father and mother sometimes whiled away the long dark winter evenings singing ballads—"Nelson and the Nile", "The Red Red Rose", "Love's Riddle", "Maid of Ocram", "Fare Thee Well", "The Banks of Ivory" [Inverye] "Barbara Allen" and "Peggy Band".

But Parker Clare was earning less and less money by flail-threshing. Less and less could John help earn money for schooling with the small flail made by his father to his measure. The idea of John's qualifying for the post of usher in a school became a castle in the air. He was now thought schooled enough for a shoemaker. On the exhortation of the day-school master, he was to continue his studies at a night-school at Glinton. For some time after his leaving the day-school there had been no suitable work at hand. He was slight of frame, probably because of protracted under-nourishment rather than from an inherited lack of constitution, and he was not particularly fitted for outdoor labour. But in place of anything better, he continued to work for the neighbouring farmers as he had done for his education up to then. In the winter he attended a night-school kept by James Merrishaw. Seaton died in 1805 or 1806, so that Merrishaw was perhaps both day- and evening-school master by that time.

Perhaps because Clare's parents were so interested in what he was doing, his "cypher-book", with dates for 1803 and 1806, has escaped time's demolitions. It contains sums in addition, multiplication and rule-of-three. Like Seaton, Merrishaw was an old, white-haired man. He died in November, 1809, but not before he had fostered Clare's love of learning. No lack of books afterwards could quite kill enthusiasm. While Merrishaw lived, Clare had the run of his small library, and years later in 1822, he sought out and visited Merrishaw's neglected grave, when he paid tribute in a long poem of gratitude. James Merrishaw, a true scholar, died poor and lonely.

But meanwhile Clare had become team-leader (rider of a lead-horse in ploughing, sowing or reaping teams) probably on the farm of Mr Turnill, for whom we know he worked at weeding and at haytime. Here, one day, when he saw the loader fall from the top of his wagon and break his neck, he suffered an attack which, though only epileptiform and not epileptic, recurred every spring and autumn for some years afterward. He tells how the accident affected both his imagination and his physical self:

> The ghastly paleness of death struck such a terror on me that I could not forget it for years, and my dreams was constantly wanderings in churchyards, digging graves, seeing spirits in charnel houses, &c., &c.
>
> In my fits I swooned away without a struggle, and felt nothing more than if I'd been in a dreamless sleep after I came to myself; but I was always warn'd of their coming by a chillness and dithering, that seemed to creep from one's toe ends till it got up to one's head, when I turned senseless and fell. Sparks as of fire often flashed from my eyes, or seemed to do so, when I dropt; which I laid to the fall. These fits was stopt by a Mr. Arnold, M.D., of Stamford, of some notoriety as a medical gentleman, and one whom I respect with grateful remembrances; for he certainly did me great benefit, tho' every spring and autumn since the accident happened my fears are agitated to an extreme degree, and the dread of death involves me in a stupor of chilling indisposition as usual, tho' I have had but one or two swoonings since they first left me.[1]

Night-school, solitary musing, as well as work, went on. Since Richard Turnill was dead and Clare's leaving day-school had separated him from Mary Joyce, he made two new confidants. One was John, elder brother of Richard, a boy who had been educated at boarding-school and was now at home working for his father and carrying on his enquiries energetically if erratically by himself. Clare's ambition at the moment

[1] *Sketches in the Life of John Clare*, ed. Edmund Blunden (Cobden-Sanderson, 1931). The punctuation given there has been followed.

was to write "copper-plate" and to continue with mathematics. John Turnill's interests were more varied:

> John's acquaintance began with learning me on winter nights to write & sum he was of a studious musing turn of mind & fond of books always carry[ing] one of some sort or other in his pocket to read between toils at leisure hours ... they were somtimes sixpenny books of storys & at other times the books which he usd at school for he had been [to] boarding school & read in books there that are unknown in a village school I remember being often delighted with one which he repeated by heart in ryhme a story of a young lady being killd in battle by a speed [shard] ball while seeking her lover & another tale in prose of the old man & his ass which was a favourite & he contrivd to bring the Newspaper in his pocket in weeding time which I was always very anxious to read his father was a farmer & I usd to work for them in the weeding & haymaking season his mind was always anxious after knowledge & too restless to stick to anything long so he had a superficial knowledge of many things & a solid information with none one season he woud be occupied with Mathematics working problems (he was also ambitious of stirring in the almanack diarys & attempted to unriddle the puzzles for the prizes & to ryhme new charades riddles & rebuses) of algebra & Geometry on a slate fitted to his pocket & making dials on a board & fixing them on the top of his weedhook shaft to enquire the hour of the day then before he had formed half an acquaintance with them he woud be with the assistance of a book which he had purchasd a cheap pennyworth at some secondhand bookstall once he happend in with Lily's astrology[1] at Deeping fair & then his head was forever after Nativitys & fortunetelling by the stars his mother was skilld in huswife phisics Culpepper's *Herbal*[2]

[1] Perhaps *Christian Astrology* (1647), one of William Lilly's many works; for two centuries Lilly was an authority in astrological literature.

[2] Nicholas Culpepper's *Herbal*, or complete "Family Physician", "a botanical and astrological practice of physic", contained, as well as the "Herbal", the "London Dispensatory" and "Astrological Judgments of all the diseases of the Human Body".

> & she usd to be up after getting herbs at the proper time of the planets that was said to rule them expecting they woud perform Miracles I remember the last things which he was busy after were studying a book on bees & a restless desire after glass hives ...
>
> But in the midst of all his inventions & thirst for knowledge a couzin came down from London who had a power of getting him a place in the excise his present occupation so his friends [parents] hopes were ripend & he was sent to school & then to the excise & all his hopes anxietys & crowds of schemes were left unfinished behind him to make way for new ones[1]

There is a family tradition that the vastness of the night sky seen through Turnill's telescope sent Clare home aghast. Whether that is true or not, the departure of this friend again left him without congenial companionship. It deprived him too, of his source of books and information: the elder boy patiently sought to teach the younger what he himself knew. The two kept in touch until at least 1822. In September of that year Turnill wrote him a long rhyming letter from Manchester, but though it expresses appreciation of Clare, Turnill sounds swallowed up in the business of earning a living and it contains no detail or news. Among Clare's manuscripts are two poems to this friend, the better of which is printed:

> Turnill we toiled together all the day
> & lived like hermits from the boys at play ...

Yet Clare managed to find, not far from Helpston where, he afterwards wrote, "useless Ignorance slumbers life away", another boy interested in books, flowers and insects. His spare time was once more occupied to his satisfaction:

> I found another boy acquaintance which grew up with a few breaks in it to manhood with Tom Porter who lives in a lone cottage on Ashton green he had a fondness for flowers & possesd a few old Books old "heirlongs" in the family

[1] Peterborough MSS. Three fragments.

> one belonging to his great grandfather who had been steward to the Noells at Walcott Hall two which I usd to be most pleasd with were Sandys *Travels*[1] & Parkinsons Herbal[2] I usd often to make Sunday visits to read them his fondness for books were those of gardening & he bought & buys still all the secondhand ones that treat upon that subject which chance lays his hands on we usd to go out on sundays in the field to hunt curious wild flowers to plant in the garden such as the orchises

George Sandys, Gibbon's "judicious traveller", had become a well known writer. But it is eye-opening to find these "peasant" boys of the early nineteenth century turning with the delight Clare records to authors such as Sandys and Parkinson for recreation. Up to this time Clare had not, beyond his school books, a volume of his own. In this year, when he was thirteen, he managed to acquire two of note. One was a copy of Watt's *Hymns and Spiritual Songs*, purchased of "J. T. Drakard, Printer, Bookseller, Stationer, Binder, Music Seller, Dealer in Genuine Patient Medicines, Perfumery, Umbrellas, Hat Cases, Bonnet Boxes, Trinkets, etc.," of Stamford. The book contains a neat signature and the date 1806, but it is not certain whether Clare bought it with his own money or not. In that year either Tom Porter or another young man in the village showed him Thomson's *Seasons*. During a whole day he had time to dip into the book by stealth, when he ought to have been working. Thomson's book had penetrated into almost every obscure country alehouse. Its author could, Coleridge said, "carry his fellow-men along with him into nature". *The Seasons* and its reputation so impressed Clare that he managed to "teaze" one and sixpence out of his father, and to walk to Stamford the next Sunday morning to buy the book for himself. The Stamford shop was shut. He had to give one of his work-companions twopence to tend his horses for him, while he stole away again to Stamford one day the following week. This time he got his book, and for sixpence less than he anticipated. As he

[1] *The Travels* of George Sandys (1578–1644), colonist and poet, first appeared in *The Relation of a Journey*, begun in 1610 in Four Books (1615).

[2] The *Theatrum Botanicum*, or "Herbal of large extent", by John Parkinson (1567–1650), King's herbalist, was first issued in 1640.

walked home, he says, through the grove of lindens in Burghley Park, his "itching after rhyme" which up to this time had shown itself only in scribbled stanzas in exercise books, grew into what he afterwards said was his first poem. This was "The Morning Walk". Even if he re-wrote it two or three times later, this fragment deserves a hearing at this point in his life. Though the *Seasons* had urged his pencil, he used not Thomson's blank verse but a rhyming stanza, and his contact with nature was not got through Thomson:

> Look yonder see the rising sun
> His daily course has just begun
> Lets lightly beat the dewy grass
> & mark each object as we pass
> There the unheeded daisy grows
> There the golden kingcup blows
> There the stinking bryony weaves
> Round the hazel her scallopt leaves
> Here the woodbine & the rose
> All their blushing sweets disclose
> Ah lovely Lucy to describe
> The different flowrets tribe by tribe
> Would be too much for me or you
> Or any shepherd lad to do
> Nay had I Darwins prying thought
> Or all the learning Ray has taught
> How soon description would exhaust
> & in sweet Flora's lap be lost ... [1]

The metre might be direct from Isaac Watts; the poem reminds us of Parnell's "Hymn to Contentment"; and "blushing sweets", "Flora's lap", "prying thought" of Erasmus Darwin whom he had read. All this is undeniably eighteenth-century. Yet the "stinking bryony" and her "scallopt leaves" throw a hint, however small, of what this boy of thirteen might do for survival. Now, though very tentatively, he found that poetry had power to give

[1] Peterborough MSS.

joy in most delicious ways
& rest my spirit after weary days

As he worked in the fields he watched with glee when the south grew black with rain. Then he could hasten home "to feed on books". For the time he kept his attempts at poetry secret from his parents. He told his aspirations to the older boy, Tom Porter, but Porter discouragingly placed greater value on grammar and learning than on verse. Borrowing a book from him, Clare battled with spelling and syntax, to come at last to the conclusion that if he made himself understood he might do without grammar. He discarded the spelling-book and went on with poetry:

> I cannot say what led me to dabble in Ryhme or at what age I began to write it but my first [were imitations of][1] my fathers Songs for he knew & sung a great many I made a many things before I venturd to commit them to writing for I felt ashamd to expose them on paper & after I venturd to write them down my second thoughts blushd over them & burnt them for a long while but as my feelings grew into song I felt a desire to preserve some & usd to correct them over & over till the last copy had lost all kindred to the first even in the title I went on some years in this way wearing it in my memory as a secret to all tho my parents usd to know that my leisure was occupyd in writing yet they had no knowledge of what I coud be doing for they never dreamd of me writing poetry at length I venturd to divulge the secret a little by reading imitations of some popular song floating among the vulgar at the markets & fairs till they were common to all but these imitations they only laughd at & told me I need never hope to make songs like them this mortified me often & almost made me desist for I knew that the excelling such doggerel woud be but a poor fame if I coud do nothing better but I hit upon a harmless deception by repeating my poems over a book as tho I was reading it this had the desird effect they often praisd them & said if I coud write as good I shoud do I

[1] MS. torn.

> hugd myself over this deception & often repeated it & those which they praisd as superior to others I tryd to preserve in a hole in the wall but my mother found out the hoard & unconsciously took them for kettle holders & fire lighters when ever she wanted paper not knowing that they were anything further then attempts at learning to write for they were writing upon shop paper of all colors & between the lines of old copy-books & on any paper I coud get at for I was often wanting tho I saved almost every penny I had given me on Sundays & holidays to buy it instead of sweetmeats & fruit I usd to feel a little mortified after I discoverd it but I dare not reveal the secret by owning to it & wishing her to desist for[1] [ ] I feared if I did she woud have shown them to some one to judge of their value which woud have put me to shame so I kept the secret dissapointment to myself & wrote on suffering her to destroy them as she pleasd but when I wrote anything which I imagined better then others I preservd it in my pocket till the paper was chafd thro & destroyd by a different & full as vain preservation[2]

His parents were patient with his ineptitude for any kind of trade, but they distrusted rhyming. Ann Clare is reported to have said: "When he was fourteen or fifteen he would shew me a piece of paper printed sometimes on one side & scrawled all over on the other & he would say Mother this is worth *so* much & I used to say to him Aye boy it looks as if it warr—but I thought he was wasting his time."[3]

But, in spite of seeming mistrust she respected his leanings as far as poverty allowed:

> My mother brought me a pictured pocket hankerchief from Deeping may fair as a fairing on which was a picture of Chatterton & his Verses on Resignation chance had the choice of it she was mentioning the singular circumstance to me yesterday by asking me wether I remembered it & saying that she little thought I shoud be a poet then

[1] Clare has repeated "if".
[2] Peterborough MSS.
[3] *Quarterly Review*, 1820.

Chatterton's name was clouded in mellancholly memorys [while][1] his extraordinary Genius was scarcely know[n] the common people knew he was a poet & that was all they know the name of Shakespear as one but the ballad monger who supplys hawkers with their ware as poets with them & they imagine one as great as the other so much for that envied eminence of common fame I was fond of imitating every thing I met with & therefore it was impossible to resist the oppertunity which this beautiful poem gave me I am not certain that this is the name of the poem my memory was freshend some years ago to believe so by reading the life of Chatterton by (I think) someone of the name of Davey as I have the poem by me I will insert it[2]

The verses on Chatterton were composed a little later than this. Chatterton's tragic story was often depicted on handkerchiefs, as well as extracts from poems. Clare says he came to know Shakespeare as "a great playwright" through seeing his name on the bills of strolling players who visited the village in his boyhood.

For some months he continued threshing with his father when his father could work, cow-tending for John Turnill's father or other farmers, attending Merrishaw's night-school at Glinton, and using his spare time writing verse or reading. What he wrote about this time and destroyed was mostly "descriptive of local spots about the Lordship & favourite trees & flowers". "The Fate of Amy", printed in his first volume in 1820, was, he says, begun when he was fourteen. It was a village story which he put into stanzas after reading David Mallet's "true and tragic" "Ballad of Edwin and Emma" which John Turnill had once read him while they sheltered from rain whilst weeding.

Clare was encouraged to begin, as many greater and less than he have been, because of some similarity between his own

[1] Clare has written "which".

[2] The MS. does not give the poem; but it must have been "The Resignation", which James Montgomery admired, not "Resignation", on the Duke of Grafton's resigning the premiership. John Davis's *Life of Thomas Chatterton* was published in 1806.

experience and another poet's work he had read and admired. But perception of bird and insect, flower and plant and animal was from his earliest days as vivid in him as if he drank mescal every day of his life: this was what gave him initial urge and individual bent. "The Fate of Amy", "Noon", Helpstone", "Address to a Lark", "The Gipsies' Evening blaze", were all begun "when I was 14". "The Lost Greyhound", another very early poem, was made, he says, when "I saw one lie quaking under a haystack in the snow". "Evening", also published in his first volume, although "altered from a very early one of great length", is perhaps the first poem in which he directly translated his sense of the *life* in creatures into appropriate words:

> ... the heedless beetle bangs
> Against the cow boys dinner tin
> That oer his shoulder hangs
>
> The owls mope out & scouting bats
> Begin their giddy round
> While countless swarms of dancing gnats
> Each water pudge surround

Clare was sure that the result would be poetry if he could only set down the intensity of sight and feeling. This was as far as he had advanced, by the age of about fourteen or fifteen, in assumptions about poetry.

Meanwhile, in more childish moods, he could still throw up his hat when he saw the creature in the dusk and bawl, "Bat, bat, come under my hat & I'll give you a slice of bacon." He and Tom Porter made long expeditions after the rarer orchises of the district: spider orchis in Ashton stone pits, one of the then disused quarries of the neighbourhood, bee orchis at Swordy Well[1] (after the Second World War a refuse dump, now a re-opened gravel pit), fly orchis in Hilly Snow. A later list in his friend Henderson's writing has notes also of fragrant orchis, green man, dwarf orchis and frog orchis. Moth mullein was common and pasque flower grew on Barnack Sinnoms. Clare was not yet too grown up to creep among blackthorn thickets

[1] Swordy Well, Swardy Well, or Swoddy Well locally.

and down hedge sides seeking "painted pootys", as soon as the sun was warm on the hedges. He tried to classify these snail-shells according to colour.

A boy who sought the nest of the wryneck to find her hissing over seventeen eggs was almost sure to have pets. But he heard sorrow in the song of the caged linnet and redcap (goldfinch), not joy. He was before his time in believing the daily habits of birds could be more intimately learnt without confining them:

> I kept a tamed cock sparrow 3 years it was so tame that it woud come when calld & flew where it pleasd when I first had the sparrow I was fearful of the cat killing it so I usd to hold the bird in my hand toward her & when she attempted to smell of it I beat her she at last woud take no notice of it & I venturd to let it loose in the house they were both very shoy at each other at first & when the sparrow venturd to chirp the cat woud brighten up as if she intended to seize it but she went no further than a look or smell at length she had kittens & when they were taken away she grew so fond of the sparrow as to attempt to caress it the sparrow was startled at first but came to by degrees & venturd so far at last to perch upon her back puss would call for it when out of sight like a kitten & woud lay mice before it the same as she woud for her own young & they always livd in harmony so much the sparrow woud often take away bits of bread from under the cat's nose & even put itself in a posture of resistance when offended as if it reckoned her no more than one of its kind In winter when we coud not bear the door open to let the sparrow come out & in I was alowd to take a pane out of the window but in the spring of the third year my poor tom Sparrow for that was the name he was calld by went out & never returnd I went day after day calling out for tom & eagerly eying every sparrow on the house but none answered the name for he woud come down in a moment to the call & perch upon my hand to be fed I gave it out that some cat which it mistook for its old favourite betrayed its confidence & destroyed it[1]

[1] Peterborough MSS.

There was a robin which perched on his finger and ate from his hands:

> it woud never stay in the house at night tho it woud attempt to perch on the chair spindles & clean its bill & ruffle its feathers & put its head under its wing as if it had made up its mind to stay but something or other always molested it when it suddenly sought its old broken pane & departed when it was sure to be the first riser in the morning[1]

Though he might labour with zeal to excel John Turnill in writing, and although he had written, secretly, verses of some slight merit, yet the problem of a trade for him was acute. There was talk of shoemaking, as there had been for Linnaeus, not because Clare was considered a dunce, as the great naturalist was thought to be, but because of his unfitness for heavier work. The boy showed no willingness or special leaning which might have rewarded his parents' patience. By this time he was fourteen:

> After I had done with going to school it was proposed that I shoud be bound apprentice to a shoemaker but I rather dislikd this bondage my scholarship was to extend no further then to qualify me for the business of a shoemaker or stonemason so I learnt cross multiplication for the one & bills of account for the other but I was not to be either at last a man of the name of Mowbray of Glinton woud have taken me for a trifle & another at home was desirous of taking me merely out of kindness to my father but the trifle they wanted coud not be found & I did not much relish the confinement of apprenticeship
>
> this Will Farrow was a village wit a very droll fellow a sort of Æsop his shop usd to be a place for the amusement for the young ploughmen & labourers on winter evenings he was famous for a joke & a droll story & had a peculiar knack at making up laughable anecdotes on any curious "bull" which happend in the village & a satirical turn for

[1] *Ibid.*

applying nicknames to people who were almost sure to be calld by the one given till the day they dyd & remembered by it afterwards when their own was forgotten many of his names are now afloat in the village he had a brother living who was a sailor 21 years & who kept a Journal of his life which he got me to copy out in part there was nothing particular in it expect a mention of Lord Byron who saild in the same ship & was known among the sailors not as a poet but as a traveller

George Shelton a stonemason woud have taken me but I dislikd this too & shoyd off[1] with the excuse of not liking to climb tho I had clomb trees in rapture after the nests of kites & magpies this fondness for climbing trees after birds nests went against me but I whimperd & turnd a sullen eye upon every occasion till they gave me my will my parents hopes were almost gone as they thought I had been born with a dislike to work & a view to have my liberty & remain idle but the fact was I felt timid & fearful of undertaking the first trial in everything they woud not urge me to anything against my will so I livd on at home taking work as it fell

I went weeding wheat in the spring with old women listening to their songs & stories which shortened the day in summer I joined the haymakers in the meadow or helpd upon the stacks when I was out of work I went to the woods gathering rotten sticks or picking up dried cow dung in the pasture which we call cazons for firing[2]

In days before the old village organization was swept away by enclosure, the pleasures of shepherds and herdboys, often thought dull, mean, backward, Clare remembered afterwards for their quiet enjoyment. When the bells rang from Northamptonshire's "steeples shining round", and farmers and gentry were nodding over prayer-books, he and other boys sat on the heath and

in snug nooks their huts beside
The gipsy blazes they provide

[1] Shied off. Clare spells it as he pronounced it.
[2] Peterborough MSS.

Shaking the rotten from the trees
While some sit round & shell the peas
Or pick from hedges pilfer wood
To boil on props their stolen food ...

In 1970 boys who steal peas or other property in towns can be put on probation. "Nature's niggard hand"—and man's—are barely discernible over Clare's childhood scenes. Nor does he, a peasant himself, and deeply concerned with accuracy, later record much about the "boobies broil" which Crabbe so repeatedly observed to be the end of the pleasures of the poor. Though Crabbe's pictures helped to dispel Arcadian, sentimental illusion and showed up misery among the industrious classes, they were grimly unrelieved. Crabbe's description of the inside of a cottage was, as Hazlitt said, like that of "a person sent there to distrain for rent". Clare does not, even later in the harshly satirical "The Parish", stress the miseries and shames of poverty more than the ignorance and arrogance of those who escaped. His descriptions in prose and verse of the life of the agricultural poor of his day give a balanced account of the often-untutored genuineness of village life in the early nineteenth century. They are a useful antidote to Crabbe's.

But meanwhile he had himself been bitten by a need for something other than irregular work at home. His narrative continues:

> Thus I livd a season spending the intervals of play along with shepherders or herdboys in lone spots out of sight for I had grown big enough to be ashamed of it & I felt a sort of hopeless prospect around me of not being able to meet manhood as I coud wish I always had that feeling of ambition about me that wishes to gain notice or to rise above my fellows
>
> after I had been left to my idle leisures awhile doing jobs as I coud catch them I was then sent for to drive plough at Woodcroft Castle of Oliver Cromwell memory,[1]

[1] This fortified and moated manor-house was held for the Royalists in the Civil Wars by Dr Michael Hudson, chaplain to the King. Trying to escape, Hudson had his hands hacked off as he hung from the battlement and was later killed by a Stamford soldier as he struggled out of the moat.

tho Mrs. Bellairs the mistress was a good kind woman & the place was a very good one for living my mind was set against it from the first & I was uneasily at rest one of the disagreeable things was getting up so soon in the morning as they are much earlier in some places then in others & another was getting wetshod in my feet every morning & night for in wet weather the moat woud overflow the causeway that led to the porch & as there was but one way to the house we was obliged to wade up to the knees to get in & out excepting when the headman carried the boys over on his back as he somtimes woud I staid here one month & then on coming home to see my parents they coud not persuade me to return they now gave up all hopes of doing anything with me & fancyd that I shoud make nothing but a soldier[1]

An opportunity lost: Mrs Bellars, however, overlooking this childish defaulting, became a good friend who lightened the burden of poverty in the Clare household with occasional gifts. Next there was hope of a situation for Clare which fostered his ambitions to be something different from his fellows. His uncle, Morris Stimson, was footman for a lawyer named Bellamy at Wisbech. There was a vacancy in Bellamy's office for a writer, or clerk, and Morris Stimson promised to do his best to get the boy the place. He was certain that Clare was "scholar good enough", but, though his father and mother were "full as certain", Clare himself was timid and doubted his abilities very strongly. Counsellor Bellamy wished to see the aspirant for the post, at Wisbech. To get there, Clare would have to walk some seven miles to Peterborough, and then go, as Hazlitt went in *his* youth to see the farm where his mother was born, down the river Nene by one of the two packet-boats. Peterborough, in the days before the railways a small city of about five thousand inhabitants, depended a great deal for communications on its river. The city stood on rising ground above the Nene, which, at this point, separates the county from Huntingdonshire. The more important town of Stamford had the only local newspaper of the time, the *Stamford Mercury*, and on Stamford

[1] Peterborough MSS.

Peterborough depended for the coach to London. In his walk Clare would go down the narrow street to the fairground and the old Peterborough Brig, beside which the packet lay. He would "hear the hoarse murmur of the bargemen ... come up from the willowy stream, sounding low and underground like the voice of the bittern"; see, from the rising ground above the Brig, "the fresh marshes stretching out in endless level perspective (as if Paul Potter had painted them) with cattle windmills and red-tiled cottages gleaming in the sun to the verge of the far horizon."

Clare himself describes his feelings during this first journey of his life:

> I started for Wisbeach with a timid sort of pleasure & when I got to Glinton turnpike I turnd back to look on the old church as if I was going into another country Wisbeach was a foreign land to me for I had never been above eight miles from home in my life I coud not fancy England much larger than the part I knew At Peterborough brig I got into the boat that carrys passengers to Wisbeach once a week & returns the third day a distance of twenty-one miles for eighteenpence I kept thinking all the way in the boat what answers I shoud make to the questions askd & then put questions to myself & shapd proper replys as I thought woud succeed & then my heart burnt within me at the hopes of success I thought of the figure I shoud make afterwards when I went to see my friends dressd up as a writer in a lawyers office I coud scarcely contain myself at times & even broke out into a tittering laugh but I was dampd quickly when I thought of the impossibilitys of success for I had no prepossessing appearance to win favours for such a place my mother trimmd me up as smart as she coud she had found me a white neckcloth & got me a pair of gloves to hide my coarse hands but I had outgrown my coat & almost left my sleeves at the elbows & all my other garments betrayed too old an acquaintance with me to make me as genteel as coud have been wishd but I had got my fathers & mothers blessings & encouragements & my own hopes in the bargain made me altogether stout in the dreams of success

> At length the end of my journey approachd when the passengers lookd out to see Wisbeach brig that stretches over the river in one arch my heart swooned within me at the near approach of my destiny "To be or not to be" I kept working my wits up how to make the best use of my tongue while the boatmen were steering for the shore & when I was landed my thoughts were so busy that I had almost forgot the method of finding out the house by enquiring for Counselor Bellamy people stared at me & paused before they pointed down the street as if they thought I was mistaken in the name "& are you sure it is Counselor Bellamy you want?" said another "I am sure of it" I said & they showed me the house in a reluctant way when I got up to the house I was puzzled as I often have been in finding but one entrance w[h]ere a fine garden gate with a "Ring the bell" seemd to frown upon me as upon one too mean to be admitted I paused & felt fearful to ring[1]

A diffident boy like that would do himself little justice in an interview on which his own expectations and his parents' had founded such hopes:

> I was puzzld what to do & wish[ed] myself a thousand times over in my old corner at home at length my hand trembld & pulld the bell it wrang & to my great satisfaction my uncle came being the only man servant & bade me welcome I have told Master about your coming said he you must not hang your head but look up boldly & tell him what you can do—so I went into the kitchen as bold as I coud & sat down to tea but I ate nothing I had filld my stomach with thoughts by the way at length the counsellor appeard & I held up my head as well as I coud but it was like my hat almost under my arm "Aye aye so this is your Nephew Morris is he" said the Counsellor "Yes Sir" said my uncle "Aye aye so this is your Nephew" repeated the Counsellor rubbing his hands as he left the room "well I shall see him again"—but he never saw me agen to this

[1] Peterborough MSS.

day—I felt happily mortified for the trial was over I was not much dissappointed for I thought all the way that I cut but a poor figure for a lawers clerk so far it seems I was right the next morning my uncle said that his mistress had bade him to make me welcome & to keep me till sunday morning when the boat returned to Peterbro so I spent Saturday looking about the town after amusements I was fond of peeping into booksellers windows & I found one full of paintings as specimens of a painter who was taking portraits & teaching drawing in the town they was the early travels after fame of a name well known with the world now—Rippingille[1]—I remember one of them was the "Village ale house" another was a pencil sketch of the Letter carrier of the town whose face seemd to be familiar with everyone that passd by the rest I have forgotten— I little thought when I was looking at these things that I shoud be a poet & become a familiar acquaintance with that painter who had blinded the windows with his attempts for fame—Poets & painters grow ashamd of their early productions & perhaps my friend Rippingill will not thank me for bringing up this association of his early days yet I dont see what occasion they have to feel so for all things have a beginning & surely it is a pleasure in happiness to review the rough road of anxietys & trouble in gaining it—On Sunday morning my uncle saw me to the boat & I left Wisbeach & my disapointment behind me with an earnest tho melancholy feeling of satisfaction & I made up for my lost ambition by the thoughts of once more seeing home & its snug fireside my parents welcomd me home with a mellancholy smile that bespoke their feelings of dissapointment as I sat upon my corner stool & related my adventures[2]

Soon after this rebuff, Francis Gregory, the proprietor of The Blue Bell, an inn a few yards from the cottage, offered to hire the boy for one year. Gregory, an ageing man, in poor

[1] See Chapter 10 for Clare's later friendship with, and pen-portrait of, E. V. Rippingille, self-taught painter of rural and domestic life. Rippingille eventually became a champion of orthodoxy against the Pre-Raphaelites.

[2] Peterborough MSS.

health, lived unmarried, with his mother as housekeeper. He was, Clare says: "fond of amusement & a singer tho his notes were not more varied then those of the cuckoo he had but 2 songs for all companys one calld 'The milking pail' and the other 'Jack with his broom' his jokes too were like a pack of cards they were always the same but told in a different form"

Gregory kept a horse and a cow or two, and needed a boy to attend to these and to plough his six or eight acres of land. Chastened perhaps after his visit to Wisbech,

> I was glad and readily agreed it was a good place & they treated me more like a son than a servant & I believe this place was the nursery for that lonely & solitary musing which ended in rhyme I usd to be generally left alone to my toils for the master was a very weak man & always ailing my labours were not very burthensome being horse or cow tending weeding etc. when I made up for the loss of company by talking to myself & engaging my thoughts with any subject that came uppermost in my mind one of my worst labours was a journey to a distant village name Maxey in winter afternoons to fetch flour once & somtimes twice every week in these journeys I had hanted spots to pass & as the often heard tales of ghosts & hobgobblings had made me very fearful to pass such places at night it being often nearly dark ere I got there I usd to employ my mind as well as I was able to put them out of my head so I usd to imagine tales & mutter them over as I went on making myself the hero somtimes making myself a soldier & tracing the valorous history onwards through various successes till I became a great man somtimes it was a love story not fraught with many incidents of knight errantry but full of successes as uncommon & out of the way as a romance travelling about in foreign lands & indulging in a variety of adventures till a fair lady was found with a great fortune that made me a gentleman & my mind woud be so bent on the reveries somtimes that I have got to the town unawares& felt a sort of dissappointment in not being able to finish my story tho I was glad of the escape from the hanted places I know not what made me write poetry but these journeys & my toiling in the fields by myself gave me

> such a habit for thinking that I never forgot it & always mutterd & talkd to myself afterwards I have often felt ashamed at being overheard by people that overtook me it made my thoughts so active that they became troublesome to me in company & I felt the most happy to be alone[1]

If Francis Gregory hired Clare on Mayday 1809, the boy would be nearly sixteen. When the superstitions enfolding the last century are remembered, his terrors along the road to Maxey mill, his invention of a tale "without a ghost in it", his fear of the "midnight morrice dance of hell", "will o' the whisps", a cade-foal wandering after him at dead of night, are not surprising. Reason and common sense won him to a disbelief in goblin and ghost but childhood had made its impression and whenever his nervous health failed him morbid fears returned. Dark walks, solitary toils for Gregory, while they strengthened imagination and made him a more sensitive observer, had a corresponding effect in heightening already tightly-strung nervous apprehensions. He disliked taking animals to grass on the heath in the January dusk because of the "horrible squealing noise" from badger or vixen. Perhaps development of his imaginative drive could be gained only by these experiences. He follows up the account of his night terrors with an account of how—divided again from former companions—every creature and individual plant in nature began to affect him:

> On sundays I usd to feel a pleasure to hide in the woods instead of going to church to nestle among the leaves & lye upon a mossy bank where the fir like fern its under forest keeps
>
> "In a strange stillness"
>
> watching for hours the little insects climb up & down the tall stems of the wood grass oer the smooth plantain leaf a spacious plain or reading the often thumbd books which I possesd till fancy "made them living things" I lovd the lonely nooks in the fields & woods & my favourite spots

[1] Peterborough MSS. Two fragments.

had lasting places in my Memory "the boughs that when a schoolboy screend my head" before enclosure destroyd them all ...

I lovd to employ leisure when a boy in wandering about the fields watching the habits of birds to see "the woodpecker sweeing away in its ups & downs & the jay-bird chattering by the woodside its restless warnings of passing clowns & the travels of insects w[h]ere the black beetle mumbled along & the opening of field flowers such amusements gave me the greatest of pleasures but I coud not account for the reason they did so a lonely brook a rude bridge or woodland style with ivy growing around the posts delighted me & made lasting impressions on my feelings but I knew nothing of poetry then yet I noticd everything as anxious as I do now & everything pleasd me as much I thought the gipseys camp by the green wood side a picturesque & an adoring object in nature & I lovd the gipseys for the beautys which they added to the landscape I heard the cuckoos "wandering voice" & the restless song of the Nightingale & was delighted while I pausd & [it] utterd its sweet jug jug as I passd its blackthorn bower I often pulld my hat over my eyes to watch the rising of the lark or to see the hawk hang in the summer sky & the kite take its circles round the wood I often lingerd a minute on the woodland stile to hear the woodpigeons clapping their wings among the dark oaks I hunted curious flowers in raptures & mutterd thoughts in their praise I lovd the pasture with its rushes & thistles & sheep tracks I adord the wild marshy fen with its solitary hernshaw[1] sweeing along in its mellancholy sky I wanderd the heath in raptures among the rabbit burrows & golden blossomd furze I dropt down on a thymy mole hill or mossy eminence to survey the summer landscape as full of rapture as now I markd the varied colors in flat spreading fields checkered with closes of different tinted grain like the colors in a map the copper tinted colors of clover in blossom the sun tanned green of the ripening hay the lighter hues of wheat & barley intermixed with the sunny glare of the yellow carlock & the

[1] Grey heron.

sunset imitation of the scarlet headaches[1] with the blue corn bottles[2] crowding their splendid colors in large sheets over the land & troubling the cornfields with destroying beauty the different greens of the woodland trees the dark oak the paler ash the mellow lime the white poplar peeping above the rest like leafy steeples the grey willow shining chilly in the sun as if the morning mist still lingered in its cool green I felt the beauty of these with eager delight the gadflys noonday hum the fainter murmur of the beefly "spinning in the evening ray" the dragonflys in spangled coats darting like winged arrows down the thin stream the swallow darting through its one archd brig the shepherd hiding from the thunder shower in a hollow dotterel the wild geese skudding along & making all the letters of the alphabet as they flew the motley clouds the whispering wind that mutterd to the leaves & summer grass as it flitted among them like things at play I observed all this with the same rapture as I have done since but I knew nothing of poetry it was felt & not utterd most of my sundays was spent in this manner about the fields

I noticd the cracking of the stubbs in the increasing sun while I gazed among them I lovd to see the heaving grasshopper in his coat of delicate green bounce from stub to stub I listend the hedgecricket with raptures

the evening call of the partridge the misterious spring sound of the landrail that cometh with the green corn

I lovd the meadow lake with its flags & long purples[3] crowding the waters edge I listend with delight to hear the wind whisper among the feather topt reeds & to see the taper bulrush nodding in gentle curves to the rippling water & I watchd with delight on haymaking evenings the setting sun drop behind the brigs & peep agen through the half circle of the arches as if he longd to stay

With such merry company I heard the black & the brown beetle sing their evening songs with rapture & lovd to see the black snail steal out again upon its dewy baulks I saw the nimble horse bee at noon "spinning" on

[1] Poppy, *Papaver rhoeas.*
[2] *Centaurea cyanus.*
[3] Purple loosestrife, *Lythrum salicaria.*

wanton wing I lovd to meet the woodman whistling away to his toils & to see the shepherd bending oer his hook on the thistly green chatting love storys to the listening maiden while she milked her brindld cow[1]

Spenser, Pope, even Thomson, wrote of this kind of rusticity from behind town comforts and the pastoral convention which has come down to us from Theocritus, through Virgil. Clare lived the country life and put it into the most accurate words he knew.

Twice in the above extract he has said he knew nothing of poetry. But he had certainly begun "The Morning Walk" and "The Evening Walk", "The Fate of Amy" and "Helpstone"—though he may not have completed these last two until some years later. He had tried the sonnet form in "The Gipsies' Evening blaze" and (according to Gilchrist in his *Quarterly* article) in "The Primrose". Besides these there were other verses on village stories and scenes which had been destroyed. Evidence of quotation and the imitation of metre in the poem "Noon", which was probably written in 1808, must mean that he had already read some of the "Pastorals" of John Cunningham, and had appreciated occasional exactitudes of description to be found there. He had perhaps read a little of *The Deserted Village*, or seen it in extract. *The Seasons* we know he had read many times. Some unnamed friend had presented him with Milton's poems and Percy's ballads "for keeping Sunday well and going to church"—a gift, no doubt, made before the defaulting he has told of. Chatterton's well-known story and his "Resignation" to fate before the tragic August 24th, 1770, had impressed and inspired him more than any of the poet's other work which he read; with the opportunities for leisure which work for Gregory gave, he wrote the lines "(supposed to be) Written by the Unfortunate Chatterton just before he took the deadly Draught that put a Period to his Existence". These lines, which are the first instance of those imitations which Clare afterwards deliberately practised, display more realisation of Chatterton's loneliness and anguish than poetic merit of Clare's. Chatterton's indomitable resolve helped Clare at this time. He

[1] Peterborough MSS.

had not Chatterton's pride and capacity for reckless challenge. He found his parents' continued discouragement and the villagers' ridicule hard to support. Except for Francis Gregory's fatherly indulgence in the matter of his leisure there was not a single person with whom he could discuss poetry. John Turnill had left the village, and Tom Porter offered no sympathy on the subject of authorship. Even in these early days of his apprenticeship, Clare began to feel that mental loneliness which was always one of his problems. His poems were very uncertain of their title, yet he went on with a kind of strained resolution. Other poems of this date are "To a Violet", published later in his second volume, *The Village Minstrel*, "The Robin", no doubt in praise of the pet he had had, "Reflection in Autumn", and "The Universal Epitaph". Other verses are "The Lodge House", a long narrative of midnight mystery concerning an old ruin where "the wild cat used to hide and raise its kittens", and a collection of verses, which he recast later, on Dobbin, "an old cart-horse [which] was in great fame in the village for his gentleness and strength and readiness for all sorts of jobs." About this time Clare had enough spare money to buy another volume from the bookshop at Stamford—Izaak Walton's *The Compleat Angler*.

One thing is clear. Books, much as he treasured them and gained from them ideas for work of his own, remained rather the encouragement of aspiration than the urge itself. From the beginning his surroundings were the source and meaning of poetry for him. "I always wrote my poems in the fields & when I was out of work I usd to go out of the village to particular spots which I was fond of ... " Again and again he tells how "I grew so much into the quiet love of nature['s] presence that I was never easy but when I was in the fields."

CHAPTER THREE

Sons of Poverty: 1809-1813

While Clare was at Francis Gregory's, perhaps in the autumn of that year, his acquaintance with Mary Joyce, broken off when he left day-school at Glinton, may have been renewed. If what he himself says is fact and not fancy, they met again at a village party on Martinmas night. Mary, by some token during the games of forfeits, betrayed preference for him. After that she blushed and "paid with joy a kiss for every fine".

The childish companionship ripened suddenly. How long it prospered is not clear. They probably met—he sixteen, she twelve—frequently during the winter of 1809 and the early spring of 1810, renewing their enthusiasm for flowers and fields. Clare's mind, already rich with observation, expanded under the new charm. Perhaps they parted in the following May-time, which would account for Clare's restlessness then and his refusal to re-hire himself with Gregory for a second year. Perhaps it was only after Clare had been absent from the village at his next situation, from which he returned penniless, that they became estranged. Blame for separating the boy and girl lovers rested, according to the earliest biographer, Martin, with the father of Mary. There is no evidence in any of Clare's writing known to date for this. It was Mary herself who realized the difference between her social position and that of the labourer's son who had no prospects. Clare says the world

> choaked the hopes I had of thee
> & made thee haughty Mary

He was evidently too sensitive about his poverty to make any attempt to overcome the influence:

> ... when she grew to womanhood she felt her station above mine at least I felt that she thought so for her parents were farmers & farmers had great pretensions to something then ... I felt the disparagement in my situation & fearing to meet a denial I carried it on in my own fancies to every extreme writing songs in her praise & making her mine with every indulgence of the fancy[1]

Before he declared his love they parted, but during the years which followed, before the publication of his first book, he kept a half-smothered hope that he would one day be her equal and dream become reality.

Meanwhile, the term of his hiring with Francis Gregory up, he was no nearer permanent employ than he had been a year ago.

> I left with the restless hope of being something better than a ploughman my little ambitions kept burning about me every now & then to make a better figure in the world I knew not what to be at
>
> A bragging fellow namd Manton from Market Deeping usd to frequent the public house when I livd there he was a stone cutter & sign painter he usd to pretend to discover something in me deserving encouragement & wanted to take me apprentice to learn the misterys of his art but then he wanted the trifle with me that had dissapointed my former prosperitys he usd to talk of his abilitys in sculpture & painting over his beer till I was almost mad with anxiety to be a sign painter & stone cutter but it was useless & such things made my mind restless[2]

In the guise of luck, another chance of a situation came. Clare heard from Tom Porter, whom he still visited on Sundays, that the head gardener of the Marquis of Exeter at Burghley House needed an apprentice. His health, no more robust than it had been, decided his mother and father that he would never be fitted for hard land work. An opportunity at such a place seemed the very thing.

[1] Peterborough MSS.
[2] Two fragments, Peterborough MSS.

The "fretted Gothic windows" of Burghley House look across a wooded park towards the many spires of Stamford. And Stamford, one of the centres of medieval learning, honoured by Saxon, Dane, and Norman, and the scene of Cecil pomp in Elizabeth's time, was perhaps at its most prosperous in those days just before the coming of railways. Mentioned by E. V. Lucas as possibly the original home of Charles Lamb's family, it lay on the Great North Road, a day's post from London. Coaches rattled down its streets, and its inns were always full of travellers. Though after the making of railroads it settled down into the sleepy respectability of a small market-town and watched Peterborough rapidly outstrip it in importance, in those days Clare would think of it as of a metropolis, imagining life so near it in the gardens of Burghley:

> so off my father took me it was a fine Sabbath morning & when we arrived he mistaking everybody for gentlemen that wore white stockings pulld off his hat to the gardener as if it had been the Marquis himself I often thought afterwards how the fellow felt his consequence at the sight for he was an ignorant proud fellow he took me & I was to stop three years my work for the time I staid was taking vegetables & fruit down to the Hall twice a day as requird & go on errands to Stamford as requird
>
> After I had been there a few weeks I savd my money to purchase Abercrombies *Gardening*[1] which became my chief study the gardens was very large & I remember finding some curious flowers which I had never seen before growing wild among the vegetables one was a yellow headache[2] perrenial & another was a blue one anual I never saw none like them before or since

But the head gardener, Clare says, "was of so harsh a temper that none liked him":

> I was often sent to Stamford at all hours in the night for one thing or other somtimes for liquors & somtimes to

[1] Perhaps the most widely read of John Abercrombie's popular manuals were *Every Man his own Gardener* and *The Gardener's Pocket Journal*.

[2] Greater celandine, *Chelidonium majus*?

seek him by the mistresses orders but I dare not seek him & as I was of a timid disposition I [was] very often fearful of going & instead of seeking him I usd to lye down under a tree in the Park & fall asleep & in the autumn nights the ryhme usd to fall & cover me on one side like a sheet which affected my side with a numbness & I have felt it ever since at spring & fall & I oftentimes think that the illness which oppresses me now while I write this narative proceeds from the like cause tho I have often made the fields a bed since then when I have been at merry makings & stopt out when all were[1] abed & at other times when I had taken too much of Sir John Barleycorn & coud get no further

Clare was the youngest among the Burghley gardening staff and:

I learnt irregular habbits at this place which I had been a stranger too had I kept at home tho I had no money to spend yet my elder companions woud treat me we was far from a town yet confinement sweetens liberty & we stole every oppertunity to get over to Stamford on summer evenings & when I had no money to spend my elder companions woud offer to treat me for the sake of my company there & back agen & to keep me from divulging the secret to my master by making me a partner in their midnight revels we usd to get out of the window & climb over the high wall of the extensive gardens for we slept in the garden house & was lockd in every night to keep us from robbing the fruit I expect—our place of rendevoux was a public house calld "The Hole in the Wall" famous for strong ale & midnight merriment kept by a hearty sort of fellow calld Tant Baker (I suppose the short name for Antony) he had formerly been a servant at Burghley & his house in consequence was a favourite place with the burghley servants always he dyd last year 1822 very rich—I wrote a long poem in praise of his ale in the favourite scotch metre of Ramsay & Burns it was not good but there are parts of it worthy as I think of a better fate than being

[1] Clare has repeated "all were".

> utterly lost it has long been out of my possesion my friend Gilchrist told me after I had shown it to him that the house had been long celebrated by drunken Barnaby & that he himself had gaind a niche of imortality for Tant Baker in a new Edition of that work[1]

Writing in 1823, Clare does not mean that his long poem on Tant Baker's ale was composed while he was at Burghley. It was more probably written in 1814 or 1815, about the time when he used Allan Ramsay's metre for his "Address to a Lark". His judgment on "Ale" is right. Where Burns's lines on "Scotch Drink" are national, Clare's on "Ale" are local and even personal. He praises ale as a kill-care for the labourer because of his "water-porridge fate", for himself because of his "damps" or melancholy. But for both only a tenpenny quart at a time, at feast or inn. More is "brutish".

During the nine months of his apprenticeship in the gardens of the Marquis of Exeter he was not in the mood for poetry, and he soon grew to dislike the situation which had seemed so advantageous at first. The only one among the gardening staff with whom he had anything in common was the foreman, George Cousins, who had introduced Abercrombie's *Gardening* to him. Cousins was a man of the "most simple mind". But his culture extended beyond Abercrombie to the Bible, from which he could repeat whole chapters by heart.

Like Clare he was weary of the place, but their agreements prevented them from leaving openly:

> So we got up early one morning in the autumn & started for Grantham which we reached the first night a distance of 21 miles & I thought to be sure I was out of the world we slept at an alehouse calld the crown & anchor & I wishd myself at home often enough before morning but it was too

[1] A twentieth edition of *Drunken Barnaby's Four Journeys to the North of England*, the original of which was *Barnabae Itinerarium* (1638), was published in 1822—presumably Gilchrist's edition. In this facetious, topographical, Latin-English rhyme of the supposed Barnaby Harrington (Richard Brathwait) we find reference to the deserted halls and kitchens of Burghley's "vast brick house", to the many beggars of Stamford, and a bawdy description of the "Hole of Sarah", the "drunkard's cave". This must have been Tant Baker's "Hole in the Wall". The "Hole in the Wall" test was a medieval means of testing virginity.

late then our enquirys not meeting work there we travelld on to Newark on trent & there we got work at a Nurserymans of the name of Withers we lodged at a lame mans house of the name of Brown whose son was a carpenter & celebrated for making fiddles I felt quite lost when I was here tho it was a very livly town but I had never been from home before scarcely further than out of sight of the steeple I became so ignorant in this far land that I coud not tell which quarter the wind blew from & I even was foolish enough to think the suns course was alterd & that it rose in the west & set in the east I often puzzld at it to set myself right but I still thought so the fine old castle stands bye the river & I stood upon the bridge I remember one night to look at it by moonlight & if I remember rightly there is a brick mansion bound up in its ruins which are uninhabited & the light of the windows glowing through the ruins gave it an awful appearance at night something akin to the old ruind castles inhabited by banditti in romances we did not stay here long for the master did not give us wages sufficient paying us one part & promising us the rest if we suited him by a further trial[1]

It was early autumn when Clare and Cousins arrived at Newark, and the ground was baked hard with the summer sun. Clare found the heavy digging and hoeing too much for his strength, though the strength of his companion was "stubborn enough for any toil". Moreover, Clare's mind, like his body, was "strange & unfit with the world". He grew restless and unhappy.

They seem to have stayed some months at Newark; while they were there, Clare made his first attempt to join the Militia. This was, in those years, cursory enough in its methods of obtaining recruits. He and Cousins went to the village feast at Baldwick, there "got fresh", and Clare, though only seventeen, offered himself for service. Fortunately for him, as he himself felt afterwards, he was found "too short" when he went to Nottingham to be sworn in.

All this was done without the knowledge of Withers the

[1] Peterborough MSS.

nurseryman; although they were heartily tired of his dalliance with wages, they were still in his service. In the winter, however,

> We got up earlier than usual one morning & as we were not burthened with luggage we easily stole away undetected & left our credit with our host ninepence halfpenny in debt we travelled from Newark to Stamford the same night but dare not show ourselves in a public house so we went through & lay under a tree in the Park the rime fell thick & we were covrd as white as a sheet when we got up[1]

Clare records the melancholy smiles with which his parents received him again at Helpston, penniless and out of work once more. Doubtless they bore their troubles with that "dangerous patience" which men and women often have who work in the peace of the country. In the spring of 1811, nearly eighteen, there was now far less chance of work for him than there had been before. In 1809, even before he left the village to work in the gardens of Burghley, an Act of Parliament had been passed[2] "for enclosing lands in the parishes of Maxey with Deepingate, Northborough, Glinton with Peakirk, Etton, and Helpstone"; and, although the Award of Land bears the date 1820, already in 1811 those changes were afoot which altered the very structure of the place, slowly obliterated long-established customs, swept away the independence and freedom of the old community, and according to Clare put an end to the "innocent pleasure of the old days". Before this, Helpston, like many another village before 1800, was under the open field system: it was surrounded by common pasture, ploughland of individual strips for corn, and the common heath. Barbarous and uneconomic as the common heaths had become to the eye of the eighteenth century, Clare could see in these scenes only the delights of independence and youth. He looked on Enclosure disturbance with distaste and rebellion and his indignation and regrets did not lessen as they mixed with adult nostalgia for the past:

[1] Peterborough MSS.
[2] 49 Geo. III: from a copy of the Helpstone Extract of the Award.

There once were springs where daisies silver studs
Like sheets of snow on every pasture spread
There once were summers when the crow flower buds
Like golden sunbeams brightest lustre shed

He makes Swordy Well, whose flowers people came for miles to praise, tell the tale of its desolation:

& save his Lordships woods that past
The day of danger dwell
Of all the fields I am the last
That my own face can tell
Yet what with stone pits delving holes
& strife to buy & sell
My name will quickly be the whole
Thats left of Swordy Well

In the years of his early manhood, ploughs turned up the Green at Helpston, Cowper Green was levelled, and "the very moles were hung for traitors". Nearly all the hollow trees which had made his favourite seats were cut down. Round Oak, above the ancient spring, and the

... old Ivied Oak in Oxey wood w[h]ere I twisted a sallow stoven into an arbour which grew into the crampd way in which I had made it ... all my favourite places have met with misfortunes the old ivied tree was cut down when the wood was cut down & my tower was destroyed the woodmen fancied it a resort for robbers & some thought the crampd way in which the thing [*twigs*] grew were witch knotts & that the spot was a haunt w[h]ere witches met ... Lee Close Oak was cut down in the inclosure & Langley bush was broken up by some wanton fellows while kindling [*kidding*][1] furze on the heath the carpenter that bought Lee Close oak hearing it was a favourite tree of mine made me two rulers & sent me & I preservd a piece of the old Ivy the thickest I have ever seen[2]

[1] Dialect verb for "cutting".
[2] Peterborough MSS.

Whatever of ultimate good the land received through enclosure, Clare could see none of it. He regarded the countryside as the habitation and the birthright of the rustic, and he rejoiced in it for the home of creatures and the English garden that it was. The villages and cottages were part of it; the "stately homes" possessed, for him, a doubtful, certainly an alien, beauty. Everyone had been free to wander in the country, to gather sticks, and to cut furze on the common: these were rights they had had since any could remember. When game-preserving was extended and these freedoms denied to the villager, Clare, with many more, resented the upstart game-keepers who warned men out of their old haunts.

From the obscurity which, until it was revealed by J. L. and Barbara Hammond in 1927, and later Royston Pyke and Edward Thompson, had closed round the records of the poor in those days, Clare's voice rises to certify to distress. In spite of the growth of luxury among farmers and the better classes after this alteration in the land, the class to which Clare belonged sank for a time into penury. At a time when so many farm labourers lost their strips of land, and even their privilege of keeping a cow, what the Clares and their like lost was the chance of near and permanent work for father and son. Farmers bought up land from those who could not afford to keep it, enclosed their farms, and hired bailiffs to work them as economically as possible. While the labourer lost his independence and his cow, at the same time he frequently lost his work as well. Since there was not enough labour for all villagers, "catch-work" men, under gang gaffers, congregated and tramped to any farmer, near or distant, who required them.

Clare does not say whether his father resorted to these gangs to help him towards employment at this period, nor does he mention whether his father had yet become incapacitated by his rheumatism. For himself, his return to the village in 1811 marked the beginning of a change in his outlook. Though it is important to remember that the results of enclosure were seen only very gradually, yet, when he came back, he found himself irrevocably cut off. It was the shepherd-boy who had played on the heaths and sat in his wattled shelter, "piping as though he should never be old", suddenly thrust out of youth. Since land was being enclosed, not only in the immediate vicinity of

Helpston by the Act of 1809, but also in other parts of the district, he drifted into one of the "catch-work" gangs before many months had passed: no more listening to the tales of old cow-tending women, and no more quiet Sunday pastimes with shepherds and herdboys while he waited for better employ. The familiar figures of pinder and hayward were gone from the village. Bailiffs and game-keepers took their places. In the general disruption, morals were loosened and self-respect lost. Clare himself put aside his poetry and again forgot his readings. "As I grew up a man I mixed more in company ... for the sake of meeting with the lasses."

> My fondness for study began to decline on mixing more into company [with] young chaps loose habits that began by force & growing into a custom was continued by choice till it became wild & irregular Poetry was for a season thrown by these habits were gotten when the fields were enclosed mixing among a motley set of labourers that always follow the news of such employments I usd to work at setting down fencing & planting quick-lines[1] with partners whose whole study was continual striving how to get beer & the bottle was the general theme from week-end to week-end such as had got drunk the oftenest fancied themselves the best fellows & made a boast of it as a fame but I was not such a drinker as to make a boast of it though I joined my sixpence towards the bottle as often as the rest I often missed the tot that was handed round for my constitution would not have borne it Saturday nights usd to be what they calld randy nights which was all meeting together at the public house to drink & sing & every new beginner had to spend a larger portion than the rest which they calld "colting" a thing common in all sorts of labour
>
> Once in these midnight revels we escaped a great danger very narrowly on going for ale at the dancing a quarrel ensued when one of the party determind on cheating the others by running off with the beer I was with him & we got into an old barn which had been open to the weather for years & had been falling a long time We saw no danger &

[1] Young hawthorns.

hugd ourselves over our bottle till we had finishd it when we started the next day when I passed the gable end we had sat under was down a heap of rubbish[1]

Despite this, there is a hint that "nature in all her shows and forms" did not cease to engage Clare's deeper attention. Copied up years later, in 1828 perhaps, there is a jotting for July 2nd, 1811: "Found a snake with a large frog in the belly of it"; there are other entries made on the same sheet concerning a primrose of January and a blackbird in that month "singing as earnest as if it was April".

Though he was at Helpston in 1811, he was probably not at home very long. There was little present hope of permanent employ for the gangs of labourers. To his restlessness the Militia offered a solution a second time. Under Castlereagh's reforms, each infantry regiment of the line was attached to one of the counties. It consisted of two battalions, the first for the Line itself, the second, or Regular Militia, for defence at home. These second battalions, to be raised by annual ballot for a term of service of seven years, were the local Militia. They were to be balloted from a foundation, or Army of Reserve, of two hundred thousand men between the ages of eighteen and thirty, who were to be called up and trained for one month every year. It was under this national training scheme for the local Militia that Clare enlisted. In spite of his short stature,[2] he was sworn in Peterborough. Thence he was marched to Oundle, where at that time the Northamptonshire Militia was stationed; his own story tells what a rough regiment of village Lotharios, runaway youths, and unemployed labourers like himself, had been attracted by the lavish bounty of two guineas:

When the country was chin deep in the fears of invasion & every month was filld with the terrors which Bonaparte had spread in other countrys a national scheme was set on foot to raise a raw army of volunteers & to make the matter plausible a letter was circulated said to be written by the prince regent I forget how many was demanded from our

[1] Peterborough MSS., two fragments.

[2] The enlistment papers which J. L. Cherry saw in 1872 or '73, which would have given Clare's exact height and other details, have been lost.

parish but I remember the panic which it created was very great—no great name rises in the world without creating a crowd of little mimics that glitter in borrowed rays & no great lye was ever yet put in circulation with[out] a herd of little lyes multiply[ing] by instinct as it were & crowding under its wings the papers that were circulated assured the people of england that the French were on the eve of invading it & that it was deemd nessesary by the regent that an army from 18 to 45 shoud be raised immediatly this was the great lye & then the little lyes was soon at its heels which assurd the people of Helpstone that the French had invaded & got to London & some of these little lyes had the impudence to swear that the french had even reachd northampton—the people got at their doors in the evening to talk over the rebellion of 45 when the rebels reached Derby & even listend at intervals to fancy they heard the french rebels at Northampton knocking it down with there cannon I never gave much credit to popular storys of any sort so I felt no concern at these storys though I coud not say much for my valour if the tale had provd true We had a cross graind sort of choice left us which was to be forced to be drawn & go for nothing or take on as Volunteers for the bounty of 2 guineas I accepted the latter & went with a neighbours son W. Clarke to Peterbro to be swore on & prepard to join the regiment at Oundle the morning we left home our mothers parted with us as if we was going to Botany Bay & people got at their doors to bid us farewell & greet us with a Jobs comfort that they doubted we should see helpstone no more I confess I wished myself out of the matter by times [turns] when we got to Oundle the place of quartering we were drawn out into the fields & a more motly multitude of lawless fellows was never seen in oundle before & hardly out of it there were 1300 of us we was drawn up into a line & sorted out into companys I was one of the shortest & therefore my station is evident I was in that mixd multitude calld the batallion which they nicknamed "bum-tools" for what reason I cannot tell the light company was calld "light bobs" & the grenadiers "bacon bolters" these were names given to each other who felt as great an enmity against each other as ever they all felt for the french some took lodgings but lodgings were very expensive the people took advantage of the tide & chargd high so I was obligd to be content with the quarters alloted me which was at the Rose & Crown Inn kept by a widow woman & her 2 daughters which happend to be a good place the girls were modestly good naturd & the mother a kind hearted woman behaving well to all that returnd it our company was the 5th & the Captain was a good sort of fellow using his authority in the language of a friend advising our ignorance when wrong of what we ought to do to be right & not in the severity of a petty tyrent who is fond of abusing those beneath him merely for the sake of showing authority I was never wonderful clean in my dress at least not clean enough for a soldier for I thought I took more than nessesary pains to be so I was not very apt at learning my exercise for I then was a ryhmer & my thoughts were often absent when the word of command was given & for this fault I was terribly teazd by a little louse looking corporal who took a delight in finding fault with me & loading me with bad jests on my awkardness as a soldier as if he had been a soldier all his life I felt very vext at the scurrilous coxcomb & retorted which only added more authority in his language he found fault with me when it belongd to others merely to vex me & if I venturd to tamper with his mistake he woud threaten me with the awkard squad for speaking I grew so mad at last with this fool that I realy think I shoud have felt satisfaction in shooting him & I was almost fit to desert home agen then I though[t] my companions woud laugh at me so I screwd up my resolution to the point at last & determind if he accusd me wrongfully for the time to come I woud certainly fall out of the ranks & address him be the consequence what it woud I had no great heart to boxing but I saw little fear in him for he was much less in strength than I was & the dread of the dark hole or awkard squad was but little in comparison to the teasing insults which this fellow daily inflicted so I was determind to act up to my vengance be the consequence what it might & I soon found an oppertunity for he was presently at his pert jests & sneering meddling again madness flushd my cheeks in a moment &

when he saw it he rapt me over my knees in a sneering sort of way & said that he woud learn me how such fellows as I was dealt with by soldiers I coud stand it no longer but threw my gun aside & seizing him by the throat I hurld [thrusted] him down & kickd him when he was down which got the fellow fame for those that had been against him before lifted him up & calld him a good fellow & calld me a coward ...

I was threatend with the black hole by one & even the tying up to the halberd by others who said that drummers were exercising themselves & very able to use the whip with punishment I thought I possesd commonsense in a superior degree as not to feel fear at threatend surmises of any sort for I had always lookt on such things as mere trumpery for children but I confess my commonsense was overcome & I felt fearful that somthing was in the wind till it blew over & got too stale the Captain enquired into the fray & the black hole was dispensd with I serving an addition on guard in its stead the fellow threw a mortified eye on me ever after & never found his tongue to tell me of a fault even when I was in one[1]

Clare was evidently not balloted for the local Militia. He went home again and was, he says, called up a second time. On this last occasion he took a further bounty for service abroad. Five shillings of this was paid him on the spot, and the rest was to be handed over when he was wanted. But he heard no further about it. Soon after the peace declaration in May 1814 the Northamptonshire Militia was disbanded.

[1] Peterborough MSS., three fragments.

CHAPTER FOUR

Itching after Rhyme: 1813–1816

At home again in the changed village in May 1813, on the same sheet as for 1811 Clare has an entry for May of the later year: "Some men digging stone on Copper Green[1] found several bones of the human species lying all their length in one grave." The incident was the one which furnished him with some fragments of verse afterwards gathered into the long poem published in *The Rural Muse*, "On Seeing a Skull on Cowper Green".

> Wert thou a Poet who in fancys dream
> Saw Immortality throw by her veil
> & all thy labours in Fames temple gleam
> In the proud glory of an after tale

Whether or not in his dreams "Immortality" had already showed him her face he was hard at it, as soon as he was home from the Militia, writing verse again. Almost twenty by this time, thin and slight and not much taller than Keats or Hartley Coleridge, his eyes were blue, bright, keen; his hair, a pale chestnut, fell over a wide brow. Though he had a reputation as a scholar, he had no better prospect in manhood than occasional labour in the fields. Plenty of verses, including some written on his twentieth birthday in July of this year, still eighteenth-century enough in flavour, disclose his sense of almost hopeless odds.

He might write despondently, reviewing his affairs on the threshold of manhood, but he did not throw aside either writing or reading. He resumed both with greater seriousness. In 1814 he went to a bookseller named Henson of Market Deeping and

[1] He usually wrote it Cowper Green; it is now Copy Green.

bought a book for copying those of his poems which he thought worth keeping. Into this folio he began to transcribe the best of what had escaped his mother's fire. Up to now his reading had been chiefly of poetry and his inability to write "a common letter" did not please him. In spite of Tom Porter, "I never saw a book in grammar before I was twenty or knew anything of the proper construction of sentences." Books were an inexcusable luxury while work was intermittent: "yet," he adds, "I was so far benefitted from reading an old newspaper now & then as to write pretty correctly & never any otherwise then to be intelligable." A later, unaddressed draft letter testified that someone, perhaps Henson, allowed him to have books on credit, "when no one else woud have trusted me for a halfpenny Ballad".

Youth was over and circumstances obdurate. Ambitions and dreams would not fade. Since farm labour was not forthcoming except in haytime and harvest, he used his experience at Burghley and Newark:

> I now followd gardening for a while in the Farmers Gardens about the village & workd in the fields when I had no other employment to go too poetry was a troublesomly pleasant companion anoying & cheering me at my toils I coud not stop my thoughts & often faild to keep them till night so when I fancyd I had hit upon a good image or natural description I usd to steal into a corner of the garden & clap it down but the appearance of my employers often put my fancys to flight & made me loose the thought & the music together for I always felt anxiety to conseal my scribbling & woud as leave have confessd to be a robber as a ryhmer when I workd in the fields I had more oppertunitys to set down my thoughts & for this reason I liked to work in the fields & bye & bye forsook gardening all together till I resumd it at Casterton I usd to drop down behind a hedge bush or dyke & write down my things upon the crown of my hat & when I was more in a kip for thinking then usual I usd to stop later at night to make up my lost time in the day thus I went on writing my thoughts down & correcting them at leisure spending my Sundays in the woods or heaths to be alone for that purpose & I got a bad name among the

weekly church goers forsaking the "churchgoing bell" & seeking the religion of the fields tho I did it for no dislike to church for I felt uncomfortable very often but my heart burnt over the pleasures of solitude & the restless revels of ryhme that was eternaly sapping my memorys like the summer sun over the tinkling brook till it one day shoud leave them dry & unconsious of the thrilling joys burning anxiety & restlessness which it had created & the praises & censures which I shall leave behind me I knew nothing of the poets experience then or I shoud have remaind a labourer & not livd to envy the ignorance of my old companions & fellow clowns I wish I had never known any other tho I was not known as a poet my odd habits did not escape notice they fancyd I kept aloof from company for some sort of study others believd me crazd & some put more criminal interpretations to my rambles & said I was night walking associating with the gipseys robbing the woods of the hares & pheasants because I was often in their company & I must confess I found them far more honest than their calumniators[1]

The sequence of events from 1814 to 1817 is far from clear. Probably Clare tried gardening for the Helpston farmers in 1814 and 1815 and then gave it up until he went to Casterton in the spring of 1817. His acquaintance with the gipsies extended over the whole of this period and his preference for their society became more marked the further he fell into disrepute among the farmers. He had friends in the village; but to the average mind which

> Views new knowledge with suspicious eyes
> & thinks it blasphemy to be so wise

he was suspect. He might stay at night and make up time lost through writing: some employers came readily to believe that since he was a dreamer and a poet he was no good for manual labour.

The corner of Helpston Heath round Langley Bush was a

[1] Peterborough MSS.

traditional camping-ground of the gipsies. The scene is desolate of the ancient whitethorn now; "its scarred trunk and grey mossy bough" were first struck by lightning, and then finally demolished by furze-burners. During Clare's childhood gipsies were seen at every village feast and merrymaking. He thought the "quiet, pilfering, unprotected race" graced the landscape with their camps. Their liberty and their disregard of "parsons fetters" attracted him; their neighbours, the hare and the fox, he would have liked for *his* neighbours.

> No matter where they go or where they dwell
> They dally with the winds & laugh at hell

As a child he had pitied the gipsies for the blame they often took for thefts they had not committed. He loved to listen to their "gibberish talk" as they smoked the tainted flesh of hedgehog or "purloined cat" for their meal. Sometimes he had wealth and good fortune predicted him by the sibyl; but as he grew more sensible and refused her a coin she prophesied he should

> Of not a hoarded farthing be possest
> & when all's done be shovd to hell at last

He knew best the Boswells, whose name is well known with the Romany, who were then a popular tribe famous for their fiddlers. On summer evenings and Sundays he sang and fiddled with them, pastimes which for some years afforded him great enjoyment. Like Lamb's friend, George Dyer, he wished to know more of the language and life of these wandering people, and he was often tempted, when they told him of the money to be made by fiddling at fairs and on the Kentish hop-fields, to join them for good. He does not seem to have aroused the hatred of any of them, as George Borrow aroused that of old Mrs Herne. On the contrary, both the Boswells and the Smiths allowed him to join in their talk and amusements, so that he became "as ready as themselves" to converse in their language. He has left a long account of the humour and habits of this cunning, "untamable animal" and awards the gipsy a fairer name than he is given by common repute:

... I had often heard of the mistic language and black arts which the gipseys possesd but on familiar acquaintance with them I found that their mystic language was nothing more then things calld by slang names like village provincialisms & that no two tribes spoke the same dialect exactly their black arts were nothing more of witchcraft than the knowledge of village gossips & the petty deceptions playd off on believing ignorance

but every thing that is bad is thrown upon the gipseys their name has grown into an ill omen & when any of the tribe are guilty of a petty theft the odium is thrown upon the whole tribe An ignorant iron hearted Justice of the Peace at —— Sessions whose name may perish with his cruelty sitting as judge in absence of a wise & kinder associate mixd up this malicious sentence in his condemnation of 2 Gipseys for horse-stealing "This atrocious tribe of wandering vagabonds ought to be made outlaws in every civilized kingdom & exterminated from the face of the earth!" (& this persecuting unfeeling man was a clergyman)

I usd to spend my Sundays & summer evenings among them learning to play the fiddle in their manner by the ear & joining in their pastimes of jumping dancing & other amusements I became so instructed in their ways & habits that I was often tempted to join them[1] They are very ignorant in the ways of the world & very loose in their morals they seem by their actions to be ignorant of any forms of faith in religion & if they are questiond by a confidant for they will reveal nothing to strangers they will admit the existance of a God & say that a belief that there in a God is sufficient without any more trouble to get to heaven They keep the Sabbath[2] by indulging in all manner of sports & pastimes but they show a knowledge of how it ought to be kept by desisting from them when a stranger or suspicious person dressd in the color of a parson passes bye I never met with a scholar amongst them nor with one who had a reflecting mind they are susceptible of insult & even fall into sudden passions without a seeming cause their

[1] Twelve words crossed out.
[2] One line indecipherable.

friendships are warm & their passions of short duration but their closest friendships are not to be relied on The men are very hot in their tempers & loose in their discourse delighting to run over smutty ribaldry but the women have not lost the modesty that belongs to them so far as to sit & hear it without blushing the young girls are reserved & silent-seeming in the company of men & their love affections are cold & careless of return they sometimes marry with the villagers but it is very rarely & if they do so they often take to their wandering courses again village clowns are oftener known to go away with the gipsy girls which happens very frequently

They are decietful generaly & have a strong propensity to lying yet they are not such dangerous characters as some in civilized life one hardly ever hears of a Gipsey committing murder their common thefts are trifling depredations taking anything that huswifes forget to secure at night killing game in the woods with their dogs but some of them are honest …[1]

they eat the flesh of badgers & hedgehogs which are far from bad food for I have eaten of it in my evening merry-makings with them they never eat dead meat but in times of scarcity which they cut into thin slices & throw on to a brisk fire till it is scorchd black when it loses its putrid smell & does very well for a makeshift providence when they can afford it they wash the meat in vinegar which takes the smell out of it & makes it eat as well as fresh meat they are more fond of vegetables then meat & seldom miss having tea in an afternoon when they can afford it they are fond of smoking to excess both men & women their common talk is of horses asses dogs & sport …

In my first acquaintance with them I had often noticd that the men had a crooked finger on one hand nor woud they satisfy my enquireys till confidence made them more familiar when I found the secret was that their parents disabled the finger of every male child in wartime when infants to keep them from being drawn for Militia or being sent for soldiers for any petty theft they might commit

[1] Very confused for two lines.

which woud invariably be the case if they had been able men when taken before a magistrate as they lay under the lash of the law with the curse of a bad name ...

Clare might have found a girl to go gipsying with, but he had not their iron health, impervious to the severest weather, or their restless longing after change of scene. His sympathy for them might in time have marked him in the eyes of authority; his tale of the harshness of the J.P. is of a piece with what is known of one or two of the new officials of the Crown who, since the passing of the old manor courts, had much power in rural districts.

Clare made other friends as well during this period who were not calculated to put him in the highest repute either. At the wakes and fairs where he had met the gipsies, he tells that he lost that lonely feeling which had been his in later childhood and most of boyhood. He "grew dissipated".

When gipsy company was not available

I usd to spend many of my winter nights & sabbath leisure when I grew up in the world at a neighbours house of the name of Billings it was a sort of meeting-house for the young fellows of the town w[h]ere the[y] usd to join for ale & tobacco & sing & drink the night away the occupiers were two Bachelors & the cottage was calld "bachelors hall" it is an old ruinous hut & hath needed repairs ever since I knew it for they neither mend up the walls nor thatch the roof being negligent men but quiet & innofensive neighbours I still frequent their house it has more the appearance of a deserted hermitage than an inhabited dwelling I have sat talking of witch & ghost storys over our cups on winter nights till I felt fearful of going home John Billings the elder had a very haunted mind for such things & had scarce been out on a journey with the night without seeing a gost a will o wisp or some such shadowy mystery & such reccolections of midnight wanderings furnishd him with storys for a whole winters fireside

We usd to go often to the woods to pill oaks & sometimes to shoot crows in the winters evening or in fact anything chance started & once we went on a sabbath day there was three of us & James Billings was the gunner for I had no eye to kill any thing even if I was close to it though my will perhaps was as good as the rest & on rustling about among the bushes we started a hare which hopd on a little way & stood to listen when my companion lifted his old gun to take aim & a sudden shock tingld in my ears like the sound of broken glasses we was astounded & looked on each others faces with vacancy—the gun had bursted & all the barrel was caried away to the lock & part of the lock likewise we saw danger in each others faces & dare not make enquiry what was the matter as all of us expected we were wounded but as soon as the fright was over we found none of us was hurt what became of the gun we coud not tell for we coud not find a fragment but that which he held in his hand was not this an alarm to tell our consciences that we were doing wrong & whether it was chance or providence that interfered it was a narrow escape I felt the warning for me & never was caught on the same errand again

John Billings was an inoffensive man he believes everything that he sees in print as true & had a cupboard full of penny books The King & the Cobler Seven Sleepers[1] accounts of People being buried so many days & then dug up alive Of bells in churches ringing in the middle of the night Of spirits warning men when they were to die he had never read Thomson or Cowper or Wordsworth or perhaps heard of their names yet nature gives everyone a natural simplicity of heart to read her language & the gross interferences of the world adulterate them He often usd to carry a curious old book *The Pleasant Art of Money Catching*[2] & another whose title was *Laugh & be Fat* there was a tale of *Juggler Percy & the Butchers Dog* several rules & receipts for saving & cheap living a collection of proverbs & a long poem of forty or fifty verses I fancied some of the verses good & I think they were written by a poet perhaps Randolph[3] he felt as happy over these as we whiled away the impatience of a days bad fishing under a green

[1] Folk tales; *Seven Sleepers* is known in African folk lore.
[2] An anonymous publication (1816–51).
[3] Thomas Randolph (1605–35). His sketch on ale and sack was popular.

> willow or an old thorn as I did over Thomson Cowper & Walton which I often took in my pocket to read
>
> he is fond of getting "cuckoos"[1] Bluebells Primroses & my favourite flowers from the fields & woods to set in his garden his Sundays best leisure is when the weather & seasons permit him to ramble by the river sides a fishing & we have spent many sundays together in that diversion[2]

At a time when the inhumanity of English game-preserving permitted laws of such severity that one of them, at least, as Romilly the philanthropic law-reformer said, had no parallel in any country in the world, Clare was wise when he decided to go no more to the woods with firearms. Once, while writing in some nook, more than half a day's journey from home, he was nearly discovered by the keepers of the Marquis of Exeter and he sat in fear of being taken for a poacher. But among all his records there is no further indication than the incident just recounted that he permitted himself any poaching, so easy for a man who spent a great deal of time alone in the woods. Even Isaac Bawcombe, that "good shepherd" and most admirable of men, eked out his poverty in this way and held himself innocent. Clare's dislike of violence grew stronger as he grew older. He had a contract with the boys of the village to bring all birds which they caught to him. He purchased them for some trifle, and, courting ridicule, gave the boys

> a fee
> To buy the captive sparrow's liberty

Poaching with sticks and snares, which, in spite or because of all its attendant dangers, still held a fascination as a sport among many men, was not likely to attract him.

On another occasion he records an experience of a different kind in the woods. He does not say whether his companions this time were the Billings brothers or not. While he was gathering acorns, the branch on which he was sitting broke with him, and he fell fourteen or fifteen feet to the ground.

[1] *Ranunculus acris* or meadow crowfoot, *Cardamine pratensis* or bitter cress, *Lychnis dioica* or red campion and *Arum maculatum* or lords and ladies, are all called cuckoo-flower. Clare probably here meant the last.

[2] Peterborough MSS.

" ... On coming to myself I crawled up & saw that the large grain had lodged above me I could not catch my breath unless by deep groans but I got over that."

"Bachelors Hall", for some years to come, provided entertainment with occasional solace for loneliness and comfort for melancholy. Once he had been drunk he drank again, he says, to stifle self-reproach over the folly that was past. Besides, he could keep his talents and his sense of learning to himself no longer. Conviviality at "Bachelors Hall" became an outlet. There, at least, was a little appreciation of his powers:

> I had got the fame of being a good scholar & in fact I had vanity enough to fancy I was far from a bad one myself while I coud puzzle the village schoolmasters over my quart for I had no tongue to brag with till I was inspired with ale with solving algebra questions for I had once struggled hard to get fame in that crabbed wilderness but my brain was not made for it & it woud not reach it tho it was a mystery only half unveild to my capacity yet I made enough of it to astonish their ignorance for a village schoolmaster is one of the most pretending & most ignorant of men—& their fame is often of the sort which that droll genius Peter Pindar[1] describes

There are drinking songs, such as the unpublished "Fill the foaming glass again", referring to this period, which show a very different aspect of him from that of the solitary youth he had been until lately. But like Lamb, Clare could "carry" little ale. At any time, a quart was enough to loosen his tongue and unsteady his legs. But that did not prevent his spending a good deal of time in the congenial company at the Billings's house where for the moment anxieties and responsibilities were lightened and ambition took on a fairer form.

Clare has already related how he and John Billings, the elder brother, had more tastes in common than carousing. They took long walks to seek flowers and transplant them to their gardens. Probably from John Billings Clare acquired the habit of planting

[1] John Walcot (1738–1819), satirist and physician, was author of *The Lousiad* (1785), a popular, coarsely humorous diatribe ridiculing the King, Pitt and other ministers.

wild flowers from field and wood beside garden ones. Not that he preferred those which "pranked the garden" in splendour to "retired flowers": "never was there a garden like the meadow." He set wild flowers beside cultivated without preference or precedence.

But sometime in these three or four years before 1817, another interest appeared which drew him a little from the society at "Bachelors Hall" and from the company of the gipsies. He fell in love a second time. We do not know when he first met Elizabeth Newbon. A definite date during this period, when his time was divided among work, fiddling with the gipsies, at the Billings's house, and courting Elizabeth, would be welcome. Apparently Elizabeth revealed her affections in rustic fashion one Sunday by writing "an unfinished sentence with chalk on the table in an old ruined cottage where young people used to meet". Writing of "rejected addresses to someone whom I felt a sudden affection for & who on my disclosing it woud affect to snear & despise me", Clare added:

> my first love in reallity was with a girl of Ashton whose name was Elizabeth Newbon She was no beauty but I fancyd she was every thing & our courtship was a long one I usd to meet her on Sundays at a lodge[1] house on Ashton Green at first & then went to her home her father was a Wheelwright & an old man who professd to be learned in the bible he was always trying my wisdom w[h]ere such & such passages might be found my silence generaly spoke my lack of religion & he shook his head at my ignorance he thought that religion consisted of learning such scraps as a sort of necesity [curiosity] by heart he knew the book in the bible in which God was not once mentiond it was Ezra & he knew the name of the Mountain w[h]ere noahs ark rested & other bible curosities he read it to search for these things & to be able to talk about them & thought himself a religious man tho he never went to church & he was so for he was happy & harmless he possesd a Large bible with notes which he took in Numbers when a young man it was Wrights Bible & he spoke of the pleasure he felt in reading

[1] Farm.

the first number one sunday night in a terrible thunderstorm he had another book on which he set great value it was Lord Napeirs Key to the revelations[1] he believd the explanations there given as the essence of truth & every newspaper occurrence that happend in war & political government he fancyd he coud find there ... he believd in Moors Almanack too with great reverence & unlockd its mystical hierogliphic with his revelation key yearly though it was not so suitable a key as Moors who waited the events of the year & explained it afterwards[2]

From the space which Clare devotes to recollections of Elizabeth's father, it seems to have been he as well as his daughter who attracted Clare to the cottage at Ashton. He has no more to say of his courtship of Elizabeth than that it "went on for years with petty jealouses on both sides at length giving ear to the world she charged me with sins of changing affection & random fancys I felt the accusations as insults & my temper mastered".[3] Events between them were not closed till some time near 1817, the short period when Clare had hopes of Mary Joyce again. The lines "To a Cold Beauty", in *Poems Descriptive*, probably refer to Elizabeth. But he pays a much higher tribute to old Mr Newbon; the far better poem "The Cottager", first printed in the Stamford *Bee*, was inspired by him:

> The "Pilgrim's Progress" & the "Death of Abel"
> Are seldom missing from his Sunday table
> & prime old Tusser[4] in his homely trim
> The first of bards in all the world with him
> & only poet which his leisure knows ...

If Elizabeth's jealousies and accusations about Clare's rambling affections were justified, there were causes. He was restless for more reasons than one. His father's rheumatism had gradually

[1] "*A Plaine Discovery of the whole Revelation of Saint John*", *set forth by John Napeir of Marchistoun. Whereto are annexed certain Oracles of Sibylla* (1593). The D.N.B. has Napier [*sic*] John (1550–1617) as the inventor of logarithms.

[2] Peterborough MSS.

[3] End of fragment torn off. Peterborough MSS.

[4] Thomas Tusser's *Hundreth good pointes of husbandrie* was published in 1557.

grown worse, till he was, by 1815 or 1816, unable to work anything like regularly, even if work were there. For some years he had earned five shillings a week by road-mending. In some way Lord Milton,[1] eldest son of Earl Fitzwilliam of Milton, had heard of his illness and difficulties, and had sent him to the Sea-bathing Infirmary at Scarborough. The treatment there gave him relief, but, to save expense, he made part of the journey home on foot, so aggravating his disease that he became worse than before. Ann Clare, troubled with dropsy, could do no extra work to supply the deficiency of money caused by her husband's illness. The whole responsibility of providing for father, mother, and sister, fell on John, and, by a poem "Addressd to my Lame Father" we realise how bitterly he felt his helplessness to give the comforts needed at home. Parker Clare was now forced from independence for the first time to ask for the hated "parish bounty".

These considerations were enough to make Clare restless and dissatisfied. But, besides this, he knew himself capable of more than casual labour in the fields. By "frequent trials" his verses were now much better than they had been: "I always wrote my poems in the fields", "in great haste"; and yet another note: "what corrections I made I always made them while writing the poems & could never do anything with them afterwards". Their numbers grew steadily. Schemes began to form in his mind as to what he might do with them. His friends at "Bachelors Hall" and

> The neighbours believing my learning to be great thought it a folly in me to continue at hard work when they fancyd I might easily better myself by my learning & as Lord Milton was a great friend to my father they persuaded me to go to Milton to see what he woud do for me the parish clerk a man of busy merits who taught the sunday school offerd to go with me as he knew his Lordship better then I did by seeing him at the Sunday school often I accepted the proposal & started once more upon ambitions hitherto fruitless errands I remember the morning we saw two crows as soon as we got into the fields & harpd on good

[1] After 1833 the 5th Earl.

luck & success & my companion gave me advice with the authority of a patron as well as a friend as soon as we got there on making the necessary enquiries we was told that his Lordship woud see us bye & bye hour passd after hour till night came & told us we was dissapointed & the porter comforted us by saying we shoud call again tomorrow but my friend the Clerk had more wits in the way & we met his Lordship the next day at the heath farm near home which he was in the habit of visiting often as soon as we came up to his Lordship my companion began to descant on my merrits in a way that made me hang my head & begd his Lordship to do somthing for me but I found he had a double errand for before he had finishd his tale of my [learning?] he pulled an antique box out of his pocket which he had found in leveling some headlands near eastwell spring a spot famous for summer sunday revels it was in the form of an apple pye & containd several farthings of King Charles the first or seconds reign his Lordship reachd & took it & gave him a good exchange for his curiosity which raisd the clerks voice in the conclusion of his story of me when his Lordship heard to whom I belongd he promisd to do somthing for me but such trifling things are soon shovd out of the memory of such people who have plenty of other things to think of I heard no more of it & worked on at my employment as usual[1]

Despite Lord Milton's forgotten promise Clare's plans, indeed, his whole life, had begun to centre round poetry and reading. He was no longer ashamed of "ryhming"; and though his methods had not yet begun to be anything like wholly formulated, his aim is clear. An invocation to the "Muse of youth's fairy themes" reveals the nineteenth-century romantic outgrowing the imitator of eighteenth-century poets.

> ... Look on thy votary like the clouds of even
> & let a portion of thy spell be given
> If one so mean as I may merit aught of heaven

[1] Peterborough MSS.

Although he wrote the following long after his theory of poetry was articulate, his method and aim remained much the same from the time he consciously formulated it.

> I usd to drop down under a bush & scribble the fresh thoughts on the crown of my hat as I found nature then so I made her if an old pond with its pendant sallows fringing its mossy sides happend to be in the pleasant nook where I sat concealed among the blackthorns drawing its picture I calld it a pond & so my feelings were stirred into praise & my praises were mutterd in prose or ryhme as the mood might suit at the moment[1]

The poems completed and copied fair during this period are numerous, but definite dates for any of them are scarce. He tried his hand at satire, and wrote the "Elegy on the Death of a Quack" on a certain "Doctor Touch" who came to Deeping and gave out that he could cure diseases by laying his hands on the sufferers. Credulous people flocked to him, and Parker Clare went or was taken in hopes of having his rheumatism cured. But, Clare says, "the fellow did not cure them by touch but by blisters which he laid on in unmercifull sizes at half a guinea a blister". When Parker heard that the "Doctor" required his fee "to be paid down before he did his work", his faith was shaken and he returned home as he had gone. His recital of the story and "Doctor Touch's" decamping in the night stirred Clare to record the incident in prose and to write the first of his satirical poems.

There is one clear date belonging to this period. He wrote "The Village Funeral" in 1815. However tonally still eighteenth-century in its overall impact, it carries a growing surety of phrase that is interesting when his reading of poetry, as of subjects other than poetry, was obviously still so haphazard:

> As to my learning I am not wonderfully deep in sience nor so wonderfully ignorant as many may have fancied from reading the accounts which my friends gave of me if I was to brag of it I might like the village schoolmaster boast of

[1] Peterborough MSS.

> knowing a little of every thing a jack of all trades & master of none I puzzled over every thing in any hours of leisure that came in my way Mathematics Astronomy Botany & other things with a restless curiosity that was ever on the enquirey & never satisfied & when I got set fast with one thing I did not tire but tryed at another tho with the same success in the end it never sickened me I still pursued[?] Knowledge in a new path & tho I never came off victor I was never conquered[1]

He had "gotten together by saving a quantity of old books of motley merits". Among these were books on mathematics, land-surveying, astrology, electricity, travel and botany. To "Sir" John Hill's *British Herbal* he acknowledged a debt for much of his wild flower lore. Lee confused him:

> I have puzzled wasted hours over Lees Botany to understand a shadow of the system so as to be able to class the wild flowers peculiar to my own neighbourhood for I find it would require a second Adam to find names for them in my way & a second Solomon to understand them in Linauses system—moder[n] works are so mystified by systematic symbols that one cannot understand them till the wrong end of ones lifetime & when one turns to the works of Ray Parkinson & Gerrard w[h]ere there is more of nature & less of Art it is like meeting the fresh air & balmy summer of a dewy morning after the troubled dreams of a nightmare[2]

and: "I always had a thirst after knowledge in everything & by that restless desire have only acquired a very superficial knowledge of many things that serves no other purpose than to make me feel my real ignorance of everything so much the more". Poetry was carefully if unmethodically garnered, dependent as he was on a chance book in an out-of-the-way bookshop and on his own sacrifice or the sacrifice of his parents to find the requisite spare shilling with which to buy a book

[1] Two variant drafts, Peterborough MSS.
[2] Peterborough MSS.

when he saw it. Hadn't his father once given more than a day's wage to allow him to buy his treasured Thomson's *Seasons*? Among the books he possessed at this time—all of which, later, "Drury got for a little or nothing"—were some now obscure names and some still well known ones. Besides Cobb's,[1] Fawkes's,[2] Broome's,[3] and Mrs Hoole's[4] poems, there are Cowley's works, Milton's *Paradise Lost*, Samuel Wesley's *Maggots*,[5] Waller's, Parnell's, and Carew's poems; and of course there are his great favourites, Walton's prose-poem and Bloomfield's poems. For some years now Bloomfield's example and his many-editioned *Farmer's Boy* had been an encouragement. Among his notes, too, there are names now unfamiliar; Sturm's *Reflections*[6] is side by side with stories such as *The Female Shipwright*, and *The Father's Legacy*, L'Estrange's *Fables of Æsop*, *Tom Jones*, and the story which "charmed all Europe", *The Vicar of Wakefield*.

Dissatisfied with his undisciplined mode of reading he could not change it:

> My acquaintance of books is not so good as late oppertunitys might have made it for I cannot & never coud plod thro every book in a regular mecanical way as I meet with I dip into it here & there & if it does not suit I lay it down & seldom take it up again but in the same manner I read Thompsons [*sic*] Seasons & Milton's Paradise Lost thro when I was a boy & they are the only books of Poetry that I have regularly read thro yet as to history I never met with the chance of getting at yet & in novels my taste is very limited Tom Jones Robinson Crusoe & the Vicar of Wakefield are all that I am acquainted with they are old acquaintances & I care not to make new ones tho I have

[1] James Cobb (1756–1818).
[2] Francis Fawkes (1720–77).
[3] William Broome (1689–1745).
[4] Mrs Hoole (1610–67).
[5] Or *Poems on Several Subjects never before Handled* by Samuel Westley (Wesley) (1662–1735), containing "To my Gingerbread Mistress", "The Lyar" and "A King turn'd Thresher", all of which may have had some small influence on Clare's early metres.
[6] On *The Evidence of God and His Providence Throughout all Nature for Every Day of the Year*, translated from the German in 1788.

often been offerd the perusal of the Waverly Novels I declind it & the readily remaining in ignorance of them is no trouble yet my taste may be doubted for I hear much in their praise & believe them good – I read The Vicar of Wakefield over every Winter & am delighted tho I always feel dissapointed at the end of it[1] with the partings my mind cannot feel that it ends happily[2] ...

He had already introduced himself to some of the classical authors in translation.

About the end of 1816 he saw Mary Joyce. He saw her only once that we know of after this.[3] Mary gave Elizabeth Newbon no cause for jealousy. Clare may have had hopes in his heart and poems in his folio; but neither in the sounding years ahead gave him Mary. From this time he had to content himself with the memory of how at sunset they once hastened with eager feet to each other. That memory changed curiously as years passed—"such tricks hath strong imagination." In 1816, while he did not know it, that link with his happy boyhood snapped too. The burdens of maturity began to accumulate:

> There is nothing but poetry about the existence of childhood real simple soul moving poetry the laughter & joy of poetry & not its philosophy & there is nothing of poetry about manhood but the reflection & the remembrance of what has been nothing more
>
> Surely our play prolonging moons on spring evenings shed a richer lustre then the midday sun that surrounds us now in manhood for its poetical sunshine hath left us it is the same identical sun & we have learned to know that—for when boys every new day brought a new sun we knew no better & we was happy in our ignorance there is nothing of the new & refreshing sunshine upon the picture now it

[1] Clare has written "happily" after "it" as well as in the next line.

[2] Peterborough MSS.

[3] In a letter to John Taylor, for August 11th, 1821, he wrote: "I have not had dossity about me to answer your last till now—but you'll excuse me I have had the horrors once agen upon me seeing devoted Mary & have written the last doggerel that shall ever sully her name & her remembrance any more tis reflection of the past & not of the present that torments me." This seems to contradict the evidence that Mary herself caused their separation, leaving the matter a puzzle.

shines from the heavens upon real matter of fact existences
& weary occupations[1]

The experiences of his manhood often appeared to him thus—until he discovered a refuge from the world in which he found himself. Though his "Eden" of youth, as he came later to call it, had neither spiritual nor physical cosiness, he revisited—relived almost—again and again in memory, his lost childhood. He wrote many poems to Mary—before and after 1821. More than that, he linked her with creature and flower; and an ability to consider the lily, that defenceless wisdom which worldly calculation and brilliance may assail with scorn or cynicism but never quite subdue, stayed with him until the end of a long life.

[1] Peterborough MSS.

CHAPTER FIVE

A Poet in his Joy: 1817

In the spring of 1817 Clare was nearly twenty-four. By disposition he was thoughtful and silent (except after a quart of ale) with what Geoffrey Grigson has called an individual "integrity". Knowledge of what he called his own failings led him often into too frequent apologies and acute self-condemnation that was hampering. He wrote an excellent hand when he was paying heed and copying poems carefully. At other times it was strong, bold and fly-away. He was beginning to have decided opinions on the writing of poetry. When he was a child nothing in the world of plant and animal failed to interest him: "Leaves from eternity are simple things." When he sought expression in poetry nothing was too trivial to be praised—a shaped stone, a weed, a shell, a path that seemed to go nowhere, but always went somewhere. This traditional English concept of Nature, of which he is one of our chief exponents in poetry, has, by today, shrunk to "something quaint and marginal in the eyes of the rest of the world".[1]

Neither in gardening nor field-labour had Helpston enough employment. He and the brother of a friend, Stephen Gordon by name, obtained work, in the spring of 1817, lime-burning for a man called Wilders at Bridge Casterton in Rutland. Clare has a description of the quiet village, the peace of which was broken only by the rattle of the daily Stage along Ermine Street. Amid these "dear vallies" he wrote and read with an impatient energy during most of the next two years:

It was pleasant livly town consisting of a row of houses on

[1] Bernard Bergonzi: "The ideology of being English" in *The Situation of the Novel* (Macmillan, 1970).

each side the turnpike about a furlong long the river gwash ran its crooked course at the back of them on the south side & washd the foot of the gardens till it crossd the turnpike under a modern looking bridge & wound along a sloping meadow northward loosing its name and its waters into stranger stones there is some beautiful spots on its banks towards the little village of Tickencoat southward w[h]ere the bank on the field side rises very stunt in some places from the edge of the river & may by a fancy usd to a flat country be easily imagind into mountains the whole prospect is diversified by gently swelling slopes & easy swimming valleys

The reaches of the Gwash rivulet gave him shelter for contemplation and writing. But during the first few weeks he worked long hours at the kiln to cover the expenses his change of situation had involved:

we worked at first from light to dark (& in some emergencys all night) to get some money to appear a little descent in a strange place having arrivd penniless with but a shabby appearance in the bargain we got lodgings at a house of scant fame a professd lodging-house kept by a man & his wife of the name of Cole & we was troubled at night with threble fares in each bed an inconvenience which I had never been usd to they took in men of all descriptions the more the merrier for their profits when they were all assembled round the evening fire the motley countenances of many characters lookd like an assemblage of robbers in the rude hut dimly & mysteriously lighted by the domestic savings of a farthing taper

When we first went we workd hard to save money & tryd to be saving in which we succeeded for a time & I got about 50 shillings in about 6 weeks with which I intended to purchase a new olive-green coat a color which I had long aimd at & for which I was measurd already ere I left home expecting to be able to pay for it in a very short time but an accident happend in the way which prevented me.[1]

[1] Peterborough MSS. Two fragments.

Clare's employer, Wilders, who kept the New Inn at Casterton, had a kiln in that village, another at the neighbouring village of Ryhall, and was about to open a third at the more distant village of Pickworth, some four miles away. Clare had not been employed at the Casterton kiln very long when Wilders, hearing that he had worked in the gardens of Burghley, offered him work in his own garden at the New Inn. Here the labour was easier, but temptation nearer. In the autumn Clare went, with his companion, Stephen Gordon, to burn lime at the Pickworth kiln. The village of Pickworth he calls "a place of other days", and adds that the piece of ground where they "dug the kiln was full of foundations and human bones".

Here Clare wrote the "Elegy on the Ruins of Pickworth". Although lime-burning was more laborious than gardening, he preferred to work out there rather than at the inn, because he was more alone. Not that, in those days, he invariably chose solitude. On Sundays he and his companions took long walks in field and lane, usually ending up at the Flower-Pot public-house at Tickencote; and

> ... on one of these excursions I first saw Patty going across the fields towards her home I was in love at first sight & not knowing who she was or w[h]ere she came from I felt very ill at rest & clomb on the top of a dotterel[1] to see which way she went till she got out of sight but chance quickly thru her again in my way a few weeks after one evening when I was going to fiddle at Stamford I then venturd to speak to her & succeeded so far as to have the liberty to go home with her to her cottage about 4 Miles off & it became the introduction to some of the happiest & unhappiest days my life has met with after I left her to return home I had taken such a heedless observance of the way that lead over a cow-pasture with its thousand paths & dallied so long over pleasant shapings of the future after I left her that twilight with its doubtful guidance overtook my musings & led me down a wrong track in crossing the common & as I coud not correct myself I got over a hedge

[1] In his glossary to *The Village Minstrel* (vol. 2) Clare gives *dotterel* as "Old stumping trees in hedge-rows, that are headed every ten or twelve years for firewood".

> & sat down on a baulk between a wheatfield w[h]ere my ryhming feelings again returnd & I composd while sitting there the ballad[1] inserted in the village minstrel & the song of all the days &c when the moon got up I started agen & on trying to get over the same hedge again as I thought to cross the common I saw somthing shine very bright on the other side I fancyd it to be bare ground beaten by the cows & sheep in hot weather but doubting I stoopd down to feel & to my terrord supprise I found it was water & while in that stooping posture I saw by the lengthy silver line that stretchd from me that it was the river if I had take[n] a step without this caution my love [ ] I was frighted & sat under the hedge till daylight ...[2]

The courtship was the more fervent because, although Patty favoured Clare, a rival was before him. "When John came," she would recall long afterwards, "I'd run and get my gingham dress from the hedge where it was airing, and put it on whether dry or not." But her parents, who had known better days, and whose friends still enjoyed comparative prosperity, considered a lime-burner a very unfitting match for their daughter, and did their utmost to encourage Clare's rival. He records how

> A young shoemaker paid his addresses to her whose visits were approved of more by her parents than herself when I had disinherited him of [her] affections they encouraged him to come on & urgd & tried to win her mind over to his & their wishes such was the tide that bore strongly against us on our first acquaintance[3]

Since Patty returned his love, neither her parents nor the shoemaker proved physical hindrances. He rejoiced in the seclusion round Walkherd and when he was not with her, rambling there to write he formed, he says, a resolution of publishing "Sketches Poems Songs Ballads & Sonnets by John

[1] There are five "ballads" in *The Village Minstrel*. Two mention "Mary". Any of the other three could be the one Clare means.

[2] Peterborough MSS.

[3] *Ibid.*

Clare a Northamptonshire Pheasant", for: "I was over head & ears in embarassments & knew not which way to get out":

> Casterton cow pasture where I usd to pass on my visits to Patty was a very favourite spot & I planned & wrote some of the best poems in my first volume among its solitudes my love rambles then made me acquainted with many of the privacies of night which she seemed wishing to keep as secrets I was then the companion of the evening & very often the morning star Patty's Lodge stood in a lone spot & the very path seemed to lose itself in the solitudes & was glad to take the direction of rabbit-tracks ere it led one to the door Nature revelled in security
>
> I usd to go on evenings in the week & every Sunday to the Lodge not at all times on love-errands merely but to get out of the way for the lodging house was generally cumberd with inmates & the Inn was continually troubling one with new jobs the solitude round the Lodge was plentiful & there were places w[h]ere the foot of man had not printed for years perhaps the scenery all round w[h]ere beautiful heaths & woods swelld their wild & free varieties to the edges of the orizon[1] I usd to wander about them with my artless & interesting companion in more then happiness A large wood in summer usd to be coverd with Lillys of the valley of which she usd to gather handfuls for her flower pots & I helpd her to gather them in the woods were large caverns calld swallow pits by the woodmen of an immense depth so that if a stone was thrown in one might count awhile before one heard it echo[2]

[1] This word is very unclear in the MS. It might be "vision".
[2] Peterborough MSS.

CHAPTER SIX

The Struggles Young Ambition Made: 1817–1819

When in 1814 Clare purchased the manuscript book from Henson of Market Deeping, to preserve poems hitherto jotted on scraps of paper, the book's cost, eight shillings (a week's wages) was paid for in instalments. On its first page is neatly printed, in imitation of the title page of a book, *A Rustic's Pastime/in Leisure hours;/ J, Clare;/* 1814.[1]

J. B. Henson "was a religious man belonging to the congregational dissenters or Independents", whom Clare had met at the chapel at Helpston, where he was fond of hearing the Independents at that time. At the time of Clare's acquaintance with him, Henson was doing tolerably well as a bookseller and printer in a small way, but eventually his business declined; according to Clare he "did some dirty doings with sathan, was turned off from his profession of clerk to the Independents", and left Deeping in search of better fortune.

Clare's purchase of the book aroused Henson's curiosity. "He urged many side-wind enquiries ... but I had kept the secret too long to be so easily persuaded to let it go." The name of poet was still

> A title that I dared not claim
> I hid it like a private shame

However, one Fair-day, flushed with a pint of ale, Clare let slip some hints about dabbling in rhyme and later showed Henson some of his earliest poems. One of these, "On the Death of Chatterton", "he wanted to print in a penny book to sell to hawkers but I was very doubtful of its merits & not covetous of such fame."

[1] Northampton MSS.

Clare was working at Pickworth toward the autumn of 1817 and as "a poor man's meeting with a wife is reckond but little improvement to his condition" he next showed the "Sonnet to the Setting Sun" and "To the Primrose" to Henson.

> ... these two he approvd of very much & ... he seemd very anxious to publish the poems he said he woud write to his London booksellers & we proposd to do it by subscription & as soon as an hundred subscribers was gotten (I forget their names) he was to begin to print it & on our starting he was to print 300 prospectuses for one Pound & I wishd him to write the thing but he declind & urgd me to it I was very loath & had a worse opinion of my prose abilitys then my poetry for I had never written a letter excepting the silly love epistles aluded [to] but I tryd what I coud do we lodgd at a public house still if a mellancholy sign swinging in the wind by a solitary clump of some five or six houses coud give it a licence to be calld so that stood as if no passenger coud ever be supposd to find it & as tho the road had forgotten the few fragments of the town that remaind [?] it seemd to stand out of the worlds eye yet there was occasional droppers in that made it anything but a place fit for study so I usd to think over it in my morning & night journeys too & from work in one of the mellancholy mornings I wrote the two first verses of What is life having another limekiln at Royal[1] about 2 miles off & at this place I sat down one day on a coal skuttle & wrote my address to the Public on a piece of paper which I kept for the purpose it gave me a deal of trouble & I was ill satisfied with what I had written but I wanted to do something to get out of debt so I wrote it & directed it with a pencil[2]

This pencilled letter, on paper "crumpled and grizzled", and sealed with pitch and for which Clare could not produce the penny demanded as late-postage fee, contained his "Proposals for publishing by Subscription, a Collection of Original Trifles, on miscellaneous Subjects, religious and moral, in Verse, by John

[1] Ryhall.
[2] Peterborough MSS.

Clare, of Helpstone." A quotation from Ramsay was followed by the conditions of publication; the book was to cost three shillings and sixpence, and be printed "on a superfine yellow wove foolscap paper, in octavo size." Then came the Address to the Public:

> The Public are requested to observe, that the Trifles humbly offered for their candid perusal can lay no claim to eloquence of poetical composition, (whoever thinks so will be deceived,) the greater part of them being *Juvenile* productions; and those of a later date offsprings of those leisure intervals which the short remittance from hard and manual labour sparingly afforded to compose them. It is hoped that the humble situation which distinguishes their author will be some excuse in their favour, and serve to make an atonement for the many inaccuracies and imperfections that will be found in them. The least touch from the iron hand of *Criticism* is able to crush them to nothing, and sink them at once to utter oblivion. May they be allowd to live their little day, and give satisfaction to those who may choose to honour them with a perusal, they will gain the end for which they were designed, and their author's wishes will be gratified. Meeting with this encouragement, it will induce him to publish a similar collection, of which this is offered as a specimen.[1]

This specimen poem was the earliest "Sonnet to the Setting Sun". A letter arrived from Henson, arranging to meet Clare at the Dolphin Inn at Stamford. "I accordingly went & for the first time saw a sonnet of mine in print & I scarcely knew it in its new dress & felt a prouder confidence than I had hitherto done thinking it got merit by its dress." He found Henson, less enthusiastic about the scheme, demanding five or six shillings more than the sum agreed on and three hundred subscribers instead of one hundred. As they were drinking together, "a dull-looking fellow in a genteelish dress" came in, and Henson gave him one of the papers; "but the fellow just threw his eyes over it then looked at me and walked out of the room without

[1] Punctuated by Henson or the printer.

saying a word." However, the next arrival read the paper, praised the sonnet, asked Clare to drink with him, wished him success, and bade Henson set his name down as a subscriber. "This gave me heart and did me more good than all I ever met with before or after. I felt deeply and never forgot the name of the Rev. Mr. Mounsey." Clare's first subscriber, Thomas Mounsey, was second master, which meant acting headmaster, of the Stamford Free Grammar School, where he taught "the Greek and Latin Languages and every branch of Commercial and Mathematical Learning".

For a while the hopes aroused by the Rev. Thomas Mounsey seemed likely to be realized. Clare wrote to Henson enclosing a list of subscribers, one of whom was a baronet: "Good God, how great are my Expectations. What hopes do I cherish as great as the unfortunate Chatterton's were on his first entrance into London which is now pictured in my mind & undoubtedly like him, I may be building 'Castles in the Air'; but Time will prove it." He urged Henson to procure subscribers, and considered that the printing might begin when a hundred names had been obtained. But though Clare distributed prospectuses few responded to the invitation: "I found not one subscriber." This must be an exaggeration due to gloom. A draft-note from Clare to Henson offered names of "principal subscribers". The final number probably was seven, but names are lost.

> I hardly knew what course to take I had got no work to go to & I hardly dare show my face to seek for any everybody seemed to jeer me at my foolish pretensions & seemd shoy at my fallen hopes & I felt ashamed as I went down the street scarcely daring to look anyone in the face for the prospectuses had filled everybodys mouth with my name & prospects enquiry stood on tiptoe with questions go where I woud & I hated to hear them I evaded them as well as I coud I felt uncommonly uneasy & knew not what to do I sometimes thought of running away & leaving home were I might be at peace among strangers for my dissapointment was fast growing into a byword I went to Stamford twice to enlist in the artillery which was recruiting there but my variety of minds prevented me besides my love matters &c were a strong tether that I coud not easily break I went so

> far at one time to take the money for a recruit but the sergeant was a better man then such usually are & said he took no advantage of a man in liquor for I was fresh at the time & let me off with paying the expenses of the drink but I was wanting in height which might be a better plea then the sergeant's honesty—[1]

Despite the "tethered perplexity" which inspired this, his third, attempt to enlist, Clare went on preparing poems. Henson now wanted £15 before he would begin printing them, and as Clare could not borrow even fifteen shillings, his hopes sank still lower. Soon he received a bill for that sum from Thompson, a Stamford bookseller, with a demand for immediate payment. Clare wrote a brief explanation of his situation, promising to pay the bill as soon as he was able, and his old, once-sceptical friend, Tom Porter of Ashton, took the letter with a few prospectuses to Thompson's shop. The bookseller treated the letter with contempt and abused the messenger. But a man named Drury entered Thompson's shop before Tom Porter departed with the rejected prospectuses. Drury read one of them and paid the fifteen shillings for Clare, with a promise to enquire further about him.

Edward Bell Drury prided himself on being a descendant of the Elizabethan family in whose honour Drury Lane was named. He was the son of John Drury, a Lincoln printer, whose sister was the mother of John Taylor, a London bookseller and publisher. Edward Drury, having served his apprenticeship, came to Stamford in 1818, took a shop opposite the post-office, and became a bookseller and "agent for Twining's Tea and Antiscorbutic Drops". He was a keen young businessman, and perceived in his discovery of Clare a possibility of making use of his connection with a London publisher. He lost no time: in December 1818, accompanied by his friend, Robert Newcomb, proprietor of the *Stamford Mercury*, he visited a farmer named Clark to enquire about Clare's character and merits as a poet.

> The former [Clare wrote] was open to every meddler but the latter was a secret so they came to enquire more about

[1] Peterborough MSS.

it with me I was at a neighbour's house when they came (at Billings's, the "Bachelors Hall") & my sister ran for me & on telling me two gentlemen wanted to see me I felt hopeful & hurriedly went home where I found them talking to my parents Drury said little or nothing but Newcomb askd some questions as to how my writings were disposd of when I told him that I had made proposals for Henson to print them he said they did not wish to take them out of his hands but that instead of desiring money to print them they woud let me have money for my necessitys so I thought the difference of advantage a good one & readily engaged to get my MSS from Henson Mr Newcomb invited me to dine with him on the Monday as he prepard to start but cautiously opend the door again to remind me that unless I brought the MSS I need not come I felt insulted with his kindness & never accepted the invitation tho I took some of them the next day when Drury looked over them & gave me a guinea as a sort of earnest I suppose & promisd to pay my debts I remaind with him the whole day & he gave me a poem in my hands to read of Lord Byrons – I think it was "The Giaour" – the first time I had ever seen any of them[1]

Clare's next concern was to retrieve the poems sent to Henson who now became anxious to retain them, holding that Clare had incurred responsibility by agreeing to let him publish them. Clare replied that he considered the engagement broken by the request for £15 which he could not obtain and asked him to give up the poems. This Henson did with some reluctance. Clare took them to Stamford, Drury stating that he was prepared either to purchase them or to conclude an agreement which would leave Clare independent of his proceedings.

To obtain an estimate of the literary value of his find, Drury showed the poems to "the Revd. Mr. Twopenny, of Little Casterton who sent them back with a cold note stating that he had no objection to assist in raising the poor man a small subscription tho the poems appeard to him to possess no merit". Clare took the criticism hardly. "As I fancyd all men in a station superior to mine as learned & more wise especially

[1] *Ibid.*

parsons I felt my fortunes as lost & my hopes gone". He wrote a verse punning on Twopenny's name[1] and a letter, "which I never sent".

Drury soon found a less adverse critic in Sir John English Dolben[2] who left his name as a subscriber. During the winter of 1818–19, at home and out of work, Clare wrote many poems and completed and corrected others, some of those which had been begun as early as 1807.

With the spring of 1819 he returned to Casterton to work in Wilders's garden at the New Inn, his life there widened by new prospects:

> I usd to seize the leisure that every wet day brought me to go to Drury's shop to read books & to get new tunes for my fiddle which was a pleasure of no freshness whenever I wrote a new thing I usd to take it to Drury very often on Sunday morning to breakfast with him in one of these visits I got acquainted with Dr. Bell a man of odd taste but a pleasant acquaintance he was fond of books & had edited a droll one entitled *The Banisher of the Blue Devils* a jest book he usd to cut all the curious & odd paragraphs out of newspapers & paste them on sheets of pasteboard he had a great many of these things which he had collected for many years he had been a doctor in the army & in the east or west Indies became acquainted with Peter Pindar then in the same capacity some of whose early poems he possesd which had never been publishd[3]

While at Casterton, Clare first had attentions from curious visitors which his acute shyness turned into a misery he did not outgrow. "My mistress wished to see some of my pieces & usd to be anxious to introduce me to strangers whom she would talk to about me & who would express a curiosity to see me but I used to get out of the way whenever I could."

His return to Casterton and better prospects had brought

[1] Twopenny his word out is & twopenny his fame is
Twopenny his merit is & twopenny his name is.

[2] John English Dolben, of Finedon Place, Northamptonshire, was an ancestor of the poet—a friend of Robert Bridges—D. M. Dolben.

[3] Peterborough MSS.

about a renewal of his acquaintance with Patty which ripened with the year into strong affection. Patty's relatives, the Turners, whose opposition to her connection with a lime-burner had hitherto harassed the lovers, now began to look more favourably on the match and even courted Clare's company. He was not disposed to trim his sails so suddenly: "I felt myself on advantage ground & determind to take my revenge & neglected to go or but slightly heeded their urgent invitations." Hopes of success with his poems, as well as Patty's pregnancy, made him obstinate:

> while I was at home in the winter I renewd my acquaintance with a former love I had made a foolish confidence with a young girl at Southorp & though it began in a heedless [frolic][1] at Stamford fair from accompanying her home it grew up into an affection that made my heart ach[e] to think it must be broken for patty was then in a situation that marriage coud only remedy I felt awkardly situated & knew not which way to proceed I had a variety of minds [maids] about me & all of them unsetteld my long smotherd affections for Mary revivd with my hopes & as I expected to be on a level with her bye & bye I thought then I might have a chance of success in renewing my former affections amid these delays pattys emergencys became urgent she had reveald her situation to her parents when she was unable to conseal it any longer who upbraided her with not heeding their advice & told her as she had made her bed hard she shoud lie on it [...][2] when I reflected on these things I felt stubbornly disposd to leave them the risk of her misfortunes but when she complaind of their [ ] I coud stand out no longer & promisd that my prosperity shoud make me her friend & to prove that I was in earnest I gave her money [ ] till we shoud be married This behaviour pacifyd them & left her at peace

The girl of Southorpe, whom Clare met at Stamford Fair, was

[1] There are gaps in the manuscript, of which this is one.

[2] Clare has here repeated himself word for word: see passage on p. 82, "A young shoemaker ... their wishes".

Betty Sell.[1] She was sixteen and worked in the fields. Clare wrote several songs to her, some as late as 1835, remembering her black ringlets and hazel eyes and the freshness of the mornings when they met. This is the girl, mentioned by Martin, of whom Edward Drury wrote to John Taylor's partner, Hessey, concerning Clare's connection with her, that she was a "Cyprian". Of Clare in 1819, in 1968 Robert Gittings has concluded: "Clare liked drink and women, one of whom was a local whore, while another was with child by him; he also had had venereal disease."[2] There is no precise evidence that Betty Sell was a whore. About venereal disease direct evidence is in the autobiographical sketch Clare sent to his London publisher in 1821:

> not only my health but my life has often been on the eve of its sacrifice, by an illness too well known, and too disgusting to mention. But mercy spared me to be schooled by experience who learned me better.[3]

This can equally well mean that he was "spared" venereal disease as that he caught it.

Poems to Patty bear traces of the conflicting emotions of 1819. In "The Adieu" he bids farewell to his "Stain'd Rosebud", though by a poetic licence he appears to attribute the stain to the dealings of some rival lover. In a verse-letter "To Patty under a Cloud" he deplores the storm brewing round his rosebud and the beauties "all despoiled by luckless amorous Johnny". He assured her of his love, despite his "many failings". In verses "An After Repentance", in a second Peterborough draft titled "A half repentance of past folly":

> I seek the house thats full of noise
> Where signs in gay temptations hing
> I join the ranting roaring boys
> To blunt old memorys hornet sting
> Past is my honey mooning nights
> & bitter dregs the sweets succeed

[1] Clare has noted "Met E. Sells at Stamford fair." Peterborough MSS. A draft of a poem in the Fitzwilliam Museum, Cambridge, has "Sell".

[2] *John Keats* (Heinemann, 1968).

[3] *Sketches in the Life of John Clare by himself*, edited by Edmund Blunden, *op. cit.*

How hard it is i' these delights
    Loves sweetest charm should be a deed

The parsons lessons fools decieve
    Their pocket fees their lessons suit
& ere we're wed theyd makes believe
    To taste of loves forbidden fruit
Effeth I tremble at the crime
    A sinful sad unruley lout
I quake I quake at gossip time
    Whose tongue blabs every secret out[1]

Belonging also to 1819 are "Patty of the Vale" and "To a Rosebud in Humble Life", besides still unprinted "ballads" with a modern touch:

Wi my hair down my back & bib'd up to ones chin
Mam had made me a child all the days of my life
Hadnt love seen thro the disguise I was in
& wisperd bob Rottle to take me to wife
He made me surprisd when I heard what he said
& I felt that hour like a bird that is free
Childish thoughts for ever went out of my head
& I 'greed robbin rottle shoud come & court me

& when I grew sick of mams whimseys & fashions
Ty'd a bow gainst her will feth or shifted a pin
She little might guess tho she fell in her pashions
Twas done robbin rottle the ploughman to win
& vain had she made me conceit Id been younger
She might as well sed snow in harvest woud be
As Id bin a child at her apronstring longer
When rob offerd making a woman o me[2]

There was a scheme, of one of Clare's friends, in the winter of 1819–20 to train him for two months in London as a usher in a school. There is a note among the Peterborough MSS, a reminder for a letter perhaps: "I hope you have not forgot

[1] Two variant drafts, Peterborough MSS. Second version in *Poems*, 1935.
[2] Peterborough MSS.

your promise of sending me to some School—I shall certainly reap great benefit." The cautious friend did forget. The scheme came to nothing.

These months saw the earliest of Clare's many poems about Mary Joyce: simple love-poems, touched with regret for hopes which cannot be realized, not yet quickened by the accepted yearning and despair of later days, not etherealized by any metaphysical symbols. He employs his regret for Mary's lost love to point the already familiar theme of autumnal melancholy and winter dearth, or pleads that with the sanction of Saint Valentine he may call her his love for that day only. A more practical mood accepts the fate that has parted them, and regards their love as of a dead past. In his conflict of hope and resignation there was only a hint of the sea-change which was later to transform his love for Mary Joyce "into something rich and strange". During the winter of 1819–20 Patty Turner remained at Walkherd whilst Clare was at Helpston still obstinately free.

CHAPTER SEVEN

Travel into Day: 1819-1820

The autumn of 1819, despite troubles, had brought compensations.

> ... Drury told me now that my poems was crownd with the utmost success I coud wish for as they were in the hands & met the favourable opinion of a gentleman who coud & woud do them justice but he woud not tell me his name & a painter of profiles was in the town whom he engagd to take my likeness these things were trifle[s] to remember but they were great at their beginings they made me all life & spirits & nothing but hopes & prosperity was before me—

The "person of talent" superintending the printing of the poems in London was Drury's cousin, John Taylor, of the firm of Taylor and Hessey. But Drury continued to write as if he were in full control of the publishing. Clare sent Drury all his poems as he wrote them, and received in return various small sums of money to pay debts or buy necessities. Drury wrote frequently in this vein: "I consider myself to be the purchaser of your MSS. and to sustain all risks ... you will receive from me every encouragement to induce you to dispose of future productions to me." Clare took the precaution of obtaining the opinion of a trusted friend upon his new acquaintance. Isaiah Knowles Holland, a Nonconformist minister of Deeping—

> Whose tongue did ne'er belie its good intent,
> Preacher as well in practice as in trade—

had given Clare encouragement and criticism at a time when there was no one else to perform that friendly office; he remained a sympathetic adviser until he left Deeping for St Ives. In October 1819 he called on Drury, and wrote to Clare after the visit that, as far as he could judge, Drury was his friend and would promote his interests.

In November, Clare finally ceased working for Wilders at Casterton.

> I workd on at the New Inn till the winter & then returned home on a disagreement in the wages as he promised me nine shillings a week the year round & then wanted to put me off with seven he was an odd man but a good Master & the place on the whole was one of the best I ever met with I left it with regret & rather wishd to return as I liked the town & the fields & solitudes were wild & far better than the fenny flats &c that I had been usd to
>
> I left Casterton on the Bullring [*Bull-running*] day at Stamford & on calling on Drury I fell in with John Taylor whom I found was the Editor of my poems then in the press & nearly ready for publishing he was visiting at Mr Gilchrists & in the evening they sent one of the servant maids to Drurys to invite me to go I felt loath but on his persuasion I started & he showd me the door I felt very irksome while I stayd Mr Gilchrist read an account of Woodcroft Castle from Woods *Historys*[1] & Taylor talkd over some sayings & doings of the living authors ...

John Taylor, born in 1781 at Retford, was the son of a publisher of Scottish extraction. A writer of poems himself, he went to London in 1803, and, after some years in the service, first of Lackington at the famous "Temple of the Muses", then of Vernor and Hood, he formed a partnership with James Augustus Hessey to open a publishing and bookselling business at 93 Fleet Street. By 1819 they had built up a sound and progressive business; not content merely to meet the demands of the general reading public, they had already published for Keats, Hazlitt, Cary and Reynolds, and were soon to add Lamb, De Quincey and Landor to the list. By their honesty and liberality the firm

[1] Scott used the historical story of Dr Michael Hudson's tragic end at the hands of the Roundheads at Woodcroft in *Woodstock*.

gained the respect of all who had dealings with them; their friendship and generosity towards Keats is well known. "For a man of very thoughtful and quiet temperament," wrote Taylor's friend Augustus De Morgan, "he had a curious turn for vexed questions. But he reflected very long and very patiently before he published: and all his works are valuable for their accurate learning ..." The identification of Junius[1] with Sir Philip Francis, first made by Taylor in 1813, is still considered to be accurate. He was also an authority on currency and in later years became a student of theology and evolved theories about the Great Pyramid. According to his early friends, the ruling features of his mind were "order, precision, exactness, and fact".

Clare's poetry, and the circumstances under which it had been written, had aroused considerable interest in the publisher and champion of Keats. He realized that the story of the "peasant-poet" would be an excellent advertisement for the poems, and he did everything he could to ensure a favourable reception of Clare's first book by the critics and the public. In this he found a useful ally in Octavius Graham Gilchrist, for among Gilchrist's friends was William Gifford. So it came about that the *Quarterly*, which with *Blackwood's* had damned Keats, gave hearty and influential blessing to Clare. Gilchrist, some years older than Clare, owned a grocery business at Stamford. In his leisure time he indulged his tastes for scholarship and criticism; he had published a volume of verses in 1805, edited Bishop Corbet's poems in 1807, was an authority on the Elizabethan dramatists, and contributed freely to Leigh Hunt's *Reflector*, the *Quarterly Review*, and other periodicals. He was a man of catholic tastes and lively humour, no shirker of controversy, whether political or literary. Gilchrist's house soon became a regular port of call where Clare could always be sure of a hearty meal, cheerful company, good advice, music and poetry, usually followed by a visit to the theatre.

The review of Clare's poems in the *Quarterly* for May 1820 was not the only outcome of Gilchrist's influence and advocacy. A more immediate result of the meeting at Stamford was his article in the *London Magazine* for January 1820, the first

[1] The pseudonymous writer of letters to the *Public Advertiser* between 1769 and 1771. The letters contained personal but shrewd political invective and were for many years a source of public discussion.

number of that journal and Clare's introduction to the literary world. John Scott, editor of the *London,* was another of Gilchrist's friends; Scott had edited the *Stamford News,* which he took to town in 1813 as *Drakard's London Paper*, later re-named the *Champion*. In the *London* article Gilchrist described Clare's visit to his house:

> Clare announced his arrival by a hesitating knock at the door—'between a single and a double rap,'—and immediately upon his introduction he dropped into a chair. Nothing could exceed the meekness and simplicity and diffidence with which he answered the various inquiries concerning his life and habits, which we mingled with subjects calculated or designed to put him much at his ease. Nothing, certainly, could less resemble splendour than the room into which Clare was shown; but there was a carpet, upon which it is likely he never previously set foot; and wine, of which assuredly he had never tasted before. Of music he expressed himself passionately fond, and had learned to play a little on the violin, in the humble hope of obtaining a trifle at the annual feasts in the neighbourhood, and at Christmas.

Clare's music-books disclose that he collected some hundred-and-fifty tunes, chiefly old country-dances and folk-songs, with annotations for the dances themselves—eighteenth-century hornpipes and jigs, and a sprinkling of waltzes, polkas, marches, and songs by Dibdin.

At home in the December of 1819, Clare needed all his hopes for the success of his book. The family fortunes were at a very low ebb. Parker Clare, now entirely disabled by rheumatism, had depended for some time on an allowance of five shillings a week from the parish. When Drury found Clare, two years' rent was owing, the cottage was to be given up and Clare's parents were to move to the workhouse. The town officer had branded the paupers' goods and set them down in the parish books, an indignity Clare did not forget, which earned the officer a place in the bitter satire written in 1823, "The Parish". The dawn of better days came in January 1820, when his "poems was publishd after a long waiting anxiety of nearly two years & all the reviews except Philips waste paper Mag spoke in my favour". His excessive nervous expectation he had expressed just before in a letter to John Taylor: "My soul is in a Lethargy my warmth for ryhming has left me my poetical spirit is no more—Get the Book out as soon as you can I long to know my doom—" Nothing, he says, gave him more happiness in the prosperity the book's reception promised than being able to remove from his parents' lives the shadow of pauperdom and to keep on the old house.

The new year found him already preparing a second volume of poems, cheered by the promise of better days; nor had he to wait long for a fulfilment which exceeded his wildest dreams. "*Poems Descriptive of Rural Life and Scenery*, by John Clare, a Northamptonshire Peasant", was published by Taylor and Hessey, and E. Drury, on January 16th, 1820. A second edition of a thousand copies was soon called for, and in May a third followed; before the end of the year a fourth was printed. The first news of his success was brought to Clare by his good friend Holland. "He came over as soon as the book was published & before I was aware of its fate but I instantly read success on his countenance for he opened the door eagerly & laughed as he shook me by the hand, saying 'Well, am I not a good prophet?' " ... good luck began to smile from all quarters & my success made me almost beside myself ... "

Clare found himself whirled from a backwater into a turbulent stream. In the months which followed events crowded. In February he was requested to present himself at Milton and Burghley, which he had visited before in humbler capacity. On the publication of *Poems Descriptive* Clare sent a copy by his mother to Milton and she returned with a request for ten copies and the invitation for Clare. Drury sent one of his own shirts, and advised Clare not to pay the visit in his Sunday clothes, "which are more suitable to a Squire of high degree than humble John Clare".

> On the following Sunday I went & after sitting awhile in the servants hall where I could eat or drink nothing for thought his Lordship sent for me & instantly explaind the reason why he did not answer my letter in a quiet unaffected manner which set me at rest he told me he had heard of my

poems by Parson Mossop [Vicar of Helpston] who I have since heard took hold of every opportunity to speak against my success or poetical abilitys before the book was publishd & then when it came out & others praisd it instantly turnd round to the other side Lady Milton also asked me several questions & wished me to name any book that was a favourite expressing at the same time a desire to give me one but I was confounded & coud think of nothing & so I lost the present in fact I did not like to pick out a book for fear of seeming over reaching on her kindness or else Shakespeare lay at my tongue end Lord Fitzwilliam & Lady Fitzwilliam too talkd to me & noticd me kindly & his Lordship gave me some advice which I had done well perhaps to have noticed better than I have he bade me beware of booksellers & warnd me not to be fed with promises on my departure they gave me a handful of money the most that I had ever possesd in my life together & I felt almost sure I should be poor no more there was seventeen pounds

Clare sent the news of his reception at Milton to all his friends, one of whom passed on the story to the *Morning Post*, which was assiduously booming the sensation of the "peasant-poet".

Some weeks later the Hon. Henry Manvers Pierrepont[1] brought an invitation for Clare to visit Burghley on the following Sunday.

But when Sunday came it began to snow too unmercifully for a traveller ever to venture thus far so I declind going tho it was not the weather prevented me I felt fearful that my shoes would be in a dirty condition for so fine a place when I got there the porter asked me the reason why I did not come before & when I spoke of the weather he said 'they expected you & you shoud stand for no weathers tho it raind knives and forks with the tynes downward we have been suspected of sending you away' this was a lesson which I afterwards took care to remember after awhile his Lordship sent for me I went upstairs & thro winding passages after

[1] Brother-in-law to the Marquis of Exeter.

> the footman as fast as I could hobble almost fit to quarrel with my hard nailed shoes at the noise they made on the marble & boarded floors & cursing them to myself as I set my feet down in the lightest steps I was able to utter his Lordship recieved me kindly askd me some questions & requested to look at the MSS. which Mr Pierrepoint wishd me to bring in my pocket He expressed a regret that Lady Sophia his sister could not see me being very ill & having sat up too long the day before on expecting my coming I felt vexed I did not go but it was no use Her Ladyship gave me the *Pleasures of Hope* after I had been about half an hour eyeing the door & now & then looking at my dirty shoes and wishing myself out of danger of soiling such grandeur he saw my embarrassment as I suspect & said I shoud lose my dinner in the servants hall & had better go but it was no use starting for I was lost & could not stir a foot I told his Lordship & he kindly opend the door & showd me the way when he suddenly made a stop in one of the long passages and told me that he had no room in his gardens for work at present but that he woud alow me 15 guineas a year for life

Meanwhile the publicity given by magazines and newspapers had brought a host of visitors and correspondents, some moved by a desire to help, others by a passing curiosity which tickled condescension to know more about a "peasant-poet". Among the former was Mrs Emmerson, of 4 Berners Street, London, who began her long friendship with Clare in a letter of February 7th, praising his poems and sending a copy of Young's *Night Thoughts*. On the 12th Taylor enclosed a letter from Lord Radstock with a copy of Blair's *Sermons*. Admiral the Hon. William Waldegrave, second son of the third Earl Waldegrave, became the first Baron Radstock after an active and successful career in the Navy. He had been a friend of Nelson's, and as Naval Governor of Newfoundland quelled a mutiny on board H.M.S. *Latona* at the time of the mutiny of the Nore, nicely mingling threats to blow the ship out of the water with exhortations to prayer and repentance. "This fire-eating old Admiral was sincerely religious and in private life a kind and benevolent man; he looked carefully after the food and comfort of the soldiers and sailors, and organized a society for the relief of the poor in St. John's".[1] The titles of two books by Lord Radstock sufficiently reveal his interests: "*The Cottager's Friend*, or a word in Season to him who is so fortunate as to possess a Bible or New Testament and a Book of Common Prayer", which was in its twentieth edition in 1816; and "*The British Flag Triumphant* ... being copies of the London *Gazette* containing the accounts of the victories ... of the British Fleets during the last and present war". Having made enquiries of Taylor and written to the Vicar of Helpston, Radstock, satisfied that Clare deserved help, took up his cause with characteristic energy.

The first letter of congratulation Clare received was from Dawson Turner, botanist and antiquary, and friend of J. S. Cotman. Seeing in Clare the herald of a cultivated peasantry, he warned him against any temptation to escape from his "humble station". Another correspondent was Captain M. E. Sherwill, who knew Walter Scott and brought Clare's poems to his notice. He hoped to do something more when Scott came to London in March. A third whose visit Clare records was a young poetaster, Edward Bailey Preston.

The zeal of Lord Radstock won friends for Clare nearer home —Herbert Marsh, Bishop of Peterborough, not hale but a fiery controversialist, and his wife Marianne. In spite of his official pugnacity, in private life Bishop Marsh was a kindly person, and Clare saw only the amiable side of his character. Marianne Marsh, German by birth, was a woman of kindliness and tact, and her notes to Clare, accompanying comforts, medicine, books, or invitations to the palace, were entirely free from prevailing patronage. She came to see him for the first time early in the spring. Not all his visitors were as welcome as Marianne Marsh.

> The first publication of my poems brought many visitors to my house out of a mere curosity I expect to know wether I realy was the son of a thresher & a labouring rustic as had been stated & when they found it realy was so they lookd at each other as a matter of satisfied supprise askd some

[1] D. W. Prouse, *A History of Newfoundland* (1896).

gossiping questions & on finding me a vulgar fellow that mimickd at no pretensions but spoke in the rough way of a thorough bred clown they soon turnd to the door & dropping their heads in a goodmorning attitude they departed—I was often annoyed by such visits & got out of the way whenever I coud ...

... I was now wearing into the sunshine & the villagers that saw carriages now & then come to the house filld with gossiping gentry that was tempted by curosity more then any thing else to seek me from these I got invitations to corespond & was swarmed with promises of books till my mother was troubld & fancied that the house woud not hold them but her trouble was soon set aside for the books never came ...[1]

Or letters would arrive,

... worded with extravagant praise courting a quick reply I replied warmly & there the matter ended I had nothing but my dissapointment in return but I soon felt experience growing over these deceptions & when such matters was palmd on me again I never answerd them I had two or three of these things nay more from parsons—

... Envy was up at my success with all the lyes it could muster some said that I never wrote the poems & that Drury gave me money to father them with my name others said that I had stole them out of books & that Parson this & Squire tother knew the books from which they were stolen Pretending scholars said that I had never been to a grammar school & therefore it was impossible for me to write anything our parson industriously found out the wonderful discovery that I coud not spell & of course his opinion was busily distributed in all companies which he visited that I was but a middling promise of success but his opinion got its knuckles rapt & then he excusd the mistake by saying he did not read poetry & consequently knew little about it there he was right[2]

[1] Peterborough MSS.
[2] *Ibid.*

Yet new friends near home compensated. He had another invitation to visit Milton Hall:[1]

> not to visit Lord Milton but his servants but they were first rate of the house & well informed men not unacquainted with books & I never met with a party of more happy & heartier fellows in my life there was Artis up to the neck in the old Norman coins & broken pots of the Romans & Henderson never wearied with hunting after the emperor butterfly & the Hornet Sphinx in the Hanglands wood & the Orchises on the Heath & West an upright honest man tho his delight in reading extended little further then the prices that fat sheep & bullocks fetchd & the rise of corn each week in the newspaper – 'the mans the man for a' that' & Roberts who sung a song of Moors [*sic*] & admired his poetry as clever & as stoutly as most amateurs & 'Grill' the Cook he was a frenchman & possesd a fund of patient good humour & a countenance unmatchable in England his visage was a Ciracatire [caricature?] in good earnest & woud heartily repay Cruikshank a journey from London to take it Artis drew an outline often of his countenance but they want the spirit of the original they are only outlines – & there was Hague the wine Butler whose library consisted of one solitary book Browns[2] Reflections on a Summer Day he was an odd good sort of fellow – there were two young maidens Mrs Procter & Mrs Byron who had not the womanly affectation about them of even attempting to show me some affinity of kindred from the coincidences of their names with two popular poets they were above pardonable vanitys & one of them was a lover of poesy[3]

With Henderson the naturalist and Artis the archeologist, Clare enjoyed many a country excursion during these years. His friendship with these men of kindred tastes and ready sympathies often relieved him when isolation weighed.

[1] Clare's visit to Milton which began his friendship with Artis and Henderson may have preceded his visit to Holywell in April 1820, or even Townshend's visit of March.

[2] *Britannia's Pastorals* by Coleridge's "William Browne of Ottery" seems to have been the book Hague had.

[3] Peterborough MSS.

Any attempt to account for the popularity of Clare's first volume—3,000 copies sold within a year—must look beyond the book as well as at it. In his able and sympathetic, only slightly condescending, Introduction, John Taylor gave reviewers a cue: "The following poems will probably attract some notice by their intrinsic merit; but they are also entitled to attention from the circumstances under which they were written." He went on to give an account, a trifle exaggerated, perhaps, of this poet, "the least favoured by circumstances, and the most destitute of friends, of any that ever existed." Having done his best to arouse sympathy and interest he proceeded to disarm criticism: Clare, he suggested, was in the position of early poets who had no traditions to guide them. His innovations followed that "rational mode of procedure, by which all languages have been formed and perfected". Taylor, in actual fact, was right. Clare's unfamiliar expressions were not new. They are among the oldest in the language, preserved by that strong, cool, hard, oral tradition which in the eleventh and twelfth centuries saved the English tongue from a Norman-French takeover. Then Taylor extolled Clare as a child of nature: "No poet has more completely devoted himself to her service, studied her more closely, or exhibited so many sketches of her under new and interesting appearances." Concluding with a renewed appeal for sympathy, Taylor quoted from one of Clare's letters, nicely punctuated. Taylor knew perfectly well that readers of the time would not stand for "illiteracy":

> If my hopes don't succeed, the hazard is not of much consequence: if I fall, I am advanced at no great distance from my low conditions: if I sink for want of friends, my old friend Necessity is ready to help me as before. It was never my fortune as yet to meet advancement from friendship: my fate has ever been hard labour among the most vulgar and lowest conditions of men; and very small is the pittance hard labour allows me, though I always toiled even beyond my strength to obtain it.

Most of the reviewers followed this lead. The article in the *Quarterly* for May 1820, prepared by Gilchrist but rounded off by Gifford himself, gave generous praise to the poems and the poet. Considering the discouraging circumstances under which most of the poems were written, the writers were astonished "that so few examples should be found of querulousness and impatience, none of envy or despair". The *London Magazine* printed a second article in March, with a further account of the poet and a full review of the poems. The *Gentleman's Magazine*, the *New Monthly* and the *Monthly Magazine* gave Clare welcome, willing to pass over the "vulgarisms". A reviewer in the April number of the *Eclectic Review*, the organ of the protestant dissenters, saw danger in this social condescension towards him. "If, instead of thinking the poems 'very clever considering they are by a day-labourer', our readers agree with us in conceding to them a high degree of poetical merit quite independent of the circumstances of their author, they will be prepared to enter with the requisite sympathy into the details of his history." Clare was also honoured by the *Annual Register* for 1820. Newspapers followed suit; in the *Morning Post*, poems, news of Clare, and letters from admirers, appeared almost daily for some time. His fame spread to America, where the *Analectic Magazine* of Philadelphia reviewed his book.

The story of the "peasant-poet", thus broadcast by most of the influential periodicals of the day, was sympathetically received by readers. Some, no doubt, were more interested in a sensation than in the poetry; yet there existed in 1820 a more considerable poetry-reading public than is often estimated. During fifty years of rapidly developing social conditions, a new reading public—and not only of the middle classes—had grown steadily, nourished by an almost inevitably widening system of education, by new circulating libraries, book-clubs, debating and mutual benefit societies, and encouraged by enterprising publishers such as Harrison, Bell, Cooke and Lackington, who set out to provide cheap books of all kinds. Village readers Clare himself has told of, those who, by hook or crook, bought copies of, and, by means of an often hard-got literacy, read Chaucer, the Bible, the Robin Hood and other ballads, Milton, Jeremy Taylor, Tusser, Erasmus Darwin, Wordsworth and many authors now totally forgotten. The genius of Scott and Byron captured people's imagination and the genius of Constable and Murray exploited it to the full. In the short flush of that popularity astonishing prices began to be given for copyrights, a host of periodicals appeared to guide the public, a fresh era began for men of letters, poetry became a fashion and a middle-class rage, and a popular poet could become the hero of a day.

It is not surprising that this demand for poetry should be erratic and distribution and supply uneven. The Press gave Scott and Byron full measure of attention; but it failed to recognize as great or greater poets and it applauded many less. Taylor wrote to Clare in August 1820, of Keats's *Lamia* volume, "We have some trouble to get through 500 copies of his work, though it is highly spoken of in the periodical works." Shelley's circle of admirers was lamentably small. The 500 copies of Wordsworth's *Excursion*, 1814, were not sold out until 1820. Southey said he would be surprised if 500 copies of his oriental tale, *The Curse of Kehama* (1810), sold within seven years. Yet many beside Scott, Byron, Moore and Campbell reaped rich rewards. Murray could give Crabbe £3,000 for his copyrights in 1819; 10,000 copies of Rogers's *Pleasures of Memory* sold between 1801 and 1816; Bloomfield's and Kirke White's poems ran into many editions; Milman had 500 guineas for his *Fall of Jerusalem*. "In 1822," wrote R. P. Gillies, with some justice, "the fortunes of literary men from high to low wore *couleur de rose* ... even minor authors were paid and encouraged then."

Clare's own correspondence testifies to the widespread interest in poetry in 1820. He had letters from men of all ranks and conditions, who, inspired by his success, hoped to win fame or money by verse. The success of *Poems Descriptive* was largely due to this interest in poetry among new readers in society. Unfortunately for Clare the book appeared towards the end of a first flush of enthusiasm when poetry of all kinds and degrees of excellence was seized upon. As Cyrus Redding later noted, "Clare's first works were read because they were published about the culminating point of the true and false in the popular taste." Financial failures among publishers in 1825 marked the end of the boom. During the next decade popular taste could rise little higher than the album verses offered by the Annuals, the *Magnet*, the *Anniversary*, the *Gem*, the *Amulet;* and the best of the popular poets were James Montgomery, Bernard Barton, L. E. L.[1] and Barry Cornwall. Clare

[1] Letitia Elizabeth Landon (1802–38).

found his public only to lose it. Those who applauded *Poems Descriptive* in 1820, either had no ear for, or did not hear of through poor distribution, *The Shepherd's Calender* of 1827.

The poems of Clare's first book were arranged in three sections— forty descriptive and narrative poems, twelve songs and ballads and twenty-one sonnets. The earliest had been written in 1806 when he was thirteen, the latest in 1819 when he was twenty-six. The book represents the achievements of a long apprenticeship.

Although his life to date had afforded few facilities for systematic reading and experiment in poetry, he had browsed over Milton, Walton, Goldsmith, Cowper, Chatterton, Beattie, Bloomfield and Ramsay. He was presently re-reading Chaucer and Shakespeare. "Crazy Nell", a very early poem, he says "was taken from a narative in the *Stamford Mercury* nearly in the manner it was related"—almost what is now called a "found" poem. "Helpstone", the first poem in his book and one of the earliest written, was intended, Clare says, for a poem in the manner of Goldsmith. Aware about accusations of plagiarism, yet clear that poets owe much to previous poetry, he sent it to Drury—

> I hinted to you that I had seen the Deserted Village you may think I imitated it I saw it as I have seen a many dipping into it here & there I perhaps may have read a hundred lines the Parish Priest was what struck me therefore to clear this & let you see it I am not a plagarist I beg you to compare them together & then the difference will be seen my imitations I may be proud of I have never taken a single line or sentence from any but what I owned to

The influence of slightly older poets on Clare's early writing was of this kind. Goldsmith's poem suggested the idea of "Helpstone"; the subject was so individually his own, the decline of the closely-knit life of a village so nearly concerned him, that the finished poem was the story of his own boyhood. Some 1820 critics spoke of Clare's debt to Burns in the poems "Address to a Lark" and "Familiar Epistle". Of "Address to a Lark", "When doing well—Content cant please us/What fools we are", written when he was twenty, Clare said: "The fact is that when my first poems were written I knew nothing of Burns not even by name for the fens are not a literary part of England ... I had an odd volume of Ramsay a long while & if I imitated any it should be him to which I am ready to acknowledge a great deal."

His early reading was chiefly among eighteenth-century books easiest to come by, but his own first draft of "What is life?" shows a still earlier affinity which he was soon to explore:

& what is Life?
An hour glass in the sun
A mist retreating from the morning sun
A busy bustling still repeated dream
—Its Length?
—A minutes pause—a moments thought
& happiness?
A Bubble on the stream
That in the act of seizing shrinks to nought[1]

The influence most clearly discernible in *Poems Descriptive* is John Cunningham's delicate scene-painting and quiet meditative mood. Clare found in these much to his taste. As *The Deserted Village* suggested "Helpstone", so Cunningham's "Morning", "Noon", "Evening", "An Elegy on a Pile of Ruins", may have offered to Clare the idea of "Summer Morning", "Noon", "Evening", "Elegy on the Ruins of Pickworth". There is more than a similarity of subject, as may be seen by putting a verse from "Summer Morning"—

As slow the hazy mists retire
Crampt circles more distinctly seen
Thin scatterd huts & neighbouring spire—
Drop in to stretch the bounded scene

beside the last verse of Cunningham's "Landscape":

Hamlets—villages and spires
Scatter'd on the Landscape lie,

[1] Peterborough MSS.

Till the distant scene retires
Closing in an azure sky.

Clare's "Noon" has a quotation from Cunningham's "Evening" —the line "Verges in successive rings". Cunningham's songs and his miscellaneous stanzas, epigrams and fables also gave Clare hints for numerous poems of a similar kind in his apprentice period.

But rapidly he was familiarizing himself with a variety of stanza forms. Yet from the first his devotion to the theme of what men since tribal days have called Nature, the ambience Anglo-Saxons are particularly aware of, guided his experiments. Friends urged him to court popularity by following fashionable themes of the moment. But Clare was not persuaded, as Stephen Duck and Robert Bloomfield were persuaded, to forsake the pursuit of the subject he knew integrally. He sold no pass. As a high intelligence entirely lacking in all characteristics of intellectualism, his own early remarks on poetry show that he was already conscious of what he was about: "to look on nature with a poetic eye magnifys the pleasure she herself being the very essence & soul of poesy." And the corollary to that not negligible but often overlooked creed:

> I think an able essay on subjects in nature that would beautify descriptive poetry might be entertaining & useful to form a right taste in pastoral poems that are full of nothing but the old thread bare epithets of "sweet singing cuckoo" "love lorn nightingale" "fond turtles" "sparkling brooks" "green meadows" "leafy woods" &c &c these make up the creation of Pastoral & descriptive poesy & everything else is reckond low & vulgar in fact they are too rustic for the fashionable or prevailing system of ryhme till some bold inovating genius rises with a real love for nature & then they will no doubt be considerd as great beautys which they really are

Classical pastoral and "rich Antiquity" were not for him. The two aims, to regard all nature, bloody or beautiful, with the eye of a poet, and poetry with the acutely realistic eye of a naturalist, both these tenets understood in their essential relationship, define Clare's contribution to English country poetry. He was in revolt against old, fast-clinging conventions, classical and artificially intellectual, which cut poetry off from its traditional source. He would not let go of his sense of a natural delight in being alive. If Wordsworth expressed his vision more richly and with wider and more articulate learning than Clare, he did not do this more clearly or more directly. Nor did Clare forget how continually poetry must be brought to this touchstone of accuracy. The reality of accuracy in question already concerned his belief in innocence of sexual love: childhood and adolescent happiness in love—he called both Eden—a wide, overall, time-aware vision illumined by what he also persisted in regarding as "common sense". The very intensity and directness of Clare's insight prevented it from fading with the years. Unlike that of the greater poet, it remained keen and penetrating. Though Clare sacrificed a part of his mind, he did not forego as he aged his essential steadfastness of outlook.

His first book is to be valued for the glimpses of that village world which were later to grow into our completest picture of pre-Enclosure England in poetry. In descriptive poems he was already travelling away from pastoral-conventional. Themes might be similar, even some forms, but an original eye sees the scene; and a fresh voice, refusing yesterday's words and all cliché, describes what the eye sees. Old forms themselves are quickened by an intimate knowledge acquired by years of patient, delighted, minute observation. Instead of the soft tones and sentimentally selected grouping of classical or pastoral poem or water-colour are the vigorous lines and detail of an etching. Clare did not yet paint the seasonally rounded yet vanishing scene, but after a swift glance he exploits his quite astonishing addiction to turning into words the underworld of plants, animal and insect life, noting the adventures of beetle, slow-pacing slug, stinging, dancing gnat and now-almost-extinct chirruping field cricket. He translates directly the sight and sounds of a harvester with a now-nearly-obsolete scythe:

His scythe the mower oer his shoulder leans
    & whetting jars with sharp & tinkling sounds

Then sweeps again mong corn & crackling beans
& swath by swath flops lengthening oer the ground

Strict frugality with epithets, vigour of verbs, give strength to this directness. Significant that among the dialect words in the glossary of *Poems Descriptive* verbs outnumber adjectives by more than three to one; and few of Clare's dialect words, being practically all onomatopoeic, really need a gloss. His attitude at this time toward "provincialisms" was explained in his first instructions to his publishers about the editing of his text:

Bad spelling may be corrected by the Amenuensis but no word is to be altered

"Eggs on" in the "Address to a Lark"—whether provincial or not I cannot tell but it is common with the vulgar (I am of that class) & I heartily desire no word of mine to be altered

The word "twit-a-twit" (if a word it can be called) you will undoubtedly smile at but I wish you to print it as it is for it is the Language of Nature & that can never be disgusting

He retracted meekly later, gave in too much and too often perhaps—in the unequal struggle to get his poems published—to emendators and advisers.

He was not concerned with the pictorial or decorative values only of natural things but more with their inner life and individual, transient uniqueness. It is the characteristic essence of plant, no less than insect and bird, which catches his ear or eye. From "Noon", written, he says, when he was about seventeen:

All how silent and how still
Nothing heard but yonder mill
While the dazzel'd eyes surveys
All around a liquid blaze
And amid the scorching gleams
If we earnest look it seems
As if crooked bits of glass
Seem'd repeatedley to pass
O! for a puffing breeze to blow

But breezes all are strangers now
Not a twig is seen to shake
Nor the smallest bent to quake ...
Shepherds with their panting sheep
In the swailiest corners creep
And from the tormenting heat
All are wishing to retreat
Huddel'd up in grass and flowers
Mowers wait for cooler hours
And the Cow boy seeks the sedge
Ramping in the woodland hedge
While his cattle oer the vales
Scamper with uplifted tails
Others not so wild and mad
That can better bear the gad
Underneath the hedge row lunge
Or if nigh in waters plunge ...
Ragged-robins once so pink
Now are turnd as black as ink
And their leaves being scorch'd so much
Even crumble at the touch
Drowking lies the Meadowsweet
Flopping down beneath ones feet[1] ...

Descriptions of the inert and the inorganic are from the same vital point of view:

Nay een a post old standard or a stone
Mossd oer by Age & branded as her own
Would in my mind a strong attachment gain

From this perception of the individuality of every natural thing sprang Clare's hatred of the violent and the cruel especially the kind inflicted by sentient man. In the poem "On Cruelty" he lists the beaten horse, dumb cringing dogs, whipped asses, trapped birds and mice. An instinctive recoil was strengthened by conclusions based on observations as a naturalist. Already, a century and a half ago, he saw that smallness, frailty and

[1] Peterborough MSS.

quietness can, and often does, outlast size, strength, force – an insight which our present obsession with the coolly technical, the huge and the violent often overlooks. Already he saw that man's wholesale destruction of species among so-called weed, pest and vermin was often arrogant and perverse, sometimes positively mischievous; he deplored a short-sightedness we are now being driven to re-think:

> Hardy clowns grudge not the wheat
> Which hunger forces birds to eat
> Your blinded eyes worst foes to you
> Can't see the good which sparrows do
> Did not poor birds with watching rounds
> Pick up the insects from your grounds
> Did they not tend the rising grain
> You then might sow to reap in vain

In the sonnets of *Poems Descriptive* Clare adapted form to his needs; he realized its value for expressing moods of quiet touched with melancholy: "I began to write Sonnets," he noted "from seeing two very pretty ones in an old newspaper I think they were by Charlotte Smith."[1]

[1] Peterborough MSS. Charlotte Smith (1749–1806) was the author of *The Old Manor House* (1793).

Summer

E*

CHAPTER EIGHT

Public Praise's Hue and Cry: 1820

The crowding excitements of the new year culminated in Clare's first visit to London. He left Stamford at six in the morning in company with Octavius Gilchrist, travelling by the Regent coach, which conveyed passengers to the George and Blue Boar, Holborn, within fourteen hours:

> Mr Gilchrist often asked me if I shoud like to see London & as I felt an anxiety he said I shoud go up with him the next time he went which was early in March & I started with him in the old Stamford Coach but I felt very awkward in my dress my mind was full of expectations all the way about the wonders of the town which I had often heard my parents tell storys about by the winter fire & when I turnd to the reccolections of the past by seeing people at my old occupations of ploughing & ditching in the fields by the road side while I was lolling in a coach the novelty created such strange feelings that I coud almost fancy that my identity as well as my occupations had changd that I was not the same John Clare but that some stranger soul had jumpd into my skin—when we passed thro Huntington [*sic*] Mr G. shewd me the House at this end of the town w[h]ere Oliver Cromwell was born & the parsonage with its mellancholy looking garden at the other w[h]ere Cowper had lived which was far the most interesting remembrance to me tho both were great men in the annals of fame I thought of his tame hares & Johnny Gilpin as we glided along in the heavy sweeing coach I amusd myself with catching the varying features of scenery—I remember the road about Royston was very dreary the white chalk like hills opend [*spread*] all round the circle & not a tree

was to be seen on[e] mellancholy thorn bush by the road side with a bench beneath it was all that my eye caught for miles as we approached nearer London the coachman pointed out 3 large round hills close by the road side & told a superstition about them which I forget ... the roads were lined with lamps that diminished in the distance to stars 'This is London!' I exclaimed he laughed at my ignorance & only increased my wonder by saying we were yet several miles from it ... on the night we got into London it was announced in the Play Bills that a song of mine was to be sung at Covent Garden by Madame Vestris & we was to have gone but it was too late I felt uncommonly pleasd at the circumstance we took a walk in the town by moonlight & went to westminster bridge to see the river thames I had heard large wonders about its width of water but when I saw it I was dissapointed thinking I shoud have seen a freshwater sea & when I saw it was less in my eye then Whittlesea Meer I was uncommonly astonished to see so many ladys as I thought them walking about the streets I expressd my suprise and was told they were girls of the town as a modest woman rarely venturd out by her self at night fall ... the next morning everything was so uncommon to what I had been used to that the excess of novelty confounded my instinct everything hung round my confused imagination like riddles unsolved while I was there I rarely knew what I was seeing & when I got home my remembrance of objects seemed in a mass one mingled in another like the mosaic squares in a Roman pavement[1]

The song which Madame Vestris sang was "The Meeting", set to music by Haydn Corri, and the success of this led to some small demand for Clare's songs by the music-setters.[2] Clare stayed, during his visit, with Gilchrist's brother-in-law, a jeweller named Burkhardt. They took him sight-seeing:

[1] Peterborough MSS. The above is a combination of three draft-fragments.

[2] In his *Life of Clare* (1865) Frederick Martin wrote that a song of Clare's was set to music by Rossini. This statement remains in the 1964 reprint of the *Life*. The extensive Rossini music index in the British Museum has been searched but no trace can be found of this song.

> Octave took [me] to see most of the curiosities we went to Westminster Abbey to see the poets corner & to both Playhouses w[h]ere I saw Kean & Macready & Knight & Munden & Emery the two latter pleased me most of all but the plays were bad ones[1] ... Burkhardt took me to Vauxhall & made me shut my eyes till I got in the midst of the place & when I opened them I almost fancied myself in a fairy land but the repitition of the roundabout walk soon put romance out of my head & made it a faded reality these were the scenes that he delighted in & he wished to take me sometime to see the Beggars Opera[2] a public house so called the resort of [gap of one word in MS.] but we had no time I had had a romantic sort of notion about authors & an anxious desire to see them fancying they were beings different to other men but the spell was soon broken when I became acquainted with them[3]

Clare has a note about the solemn warnings given him by one of his neighbours concerning dangers which beset the countryman in London. A shopping expedition gave him justification for some of his less lurid apprehensions.

> ... On my last visit to London I wanted to take somthing home for Patty & thinking that Waithman[4] had been a great stickler for freedom & fair dealing among the citizens his newspaper notoriety reccomended me to his shop at the corner of Bridge Street as the hope that I might come in for a fair bargain but here I was more decieved then ever for they kept the best articles aside & reccomended the worst as soon as they found out their customer was of the country when I took the things home I found that they were a bad bargain still & a great deal dearer than they might have been bought for at home—so much

[1] Kean was at Drury Lane in *The Hebrew*, a drama based on *Ivanhoe*; Macready was at Covent Garden in *Ivanhoe, or The Jewess*, a musical drama. Emery and the others appeared in farces accompanying these productions.

[2] The Beggar's Bush, properly the Hare and Hounds, a wild music-hall inn demolished about 1844 with the rest of the Rookery in Holborn.

[3] Peterborough MSS.

[4] Robert Waithman, linendraper and vociferous political reformer, M.P. for the City of London for several years and Lord Mayor in 1823.

for Patrons of Liberty & newspaper passports for honest men—[1]

During his week in London, Clare dined several times at John Taylor's, where, the publisher wrote to his brother, he "pleased us all by his simple, manly, and sensible conduct and conversation". Here he first met Lord Radstock who

at first sight appears to be of a stern & haughty character but the moment he speaks his countenance kindles up into a free blunt good hearted man one whom you expect to hear speak exactly as he thinks he has no notion of either offending or pleasing by his talk & cares as little for the consequences of either there is a good deal of the bluntness & openheartedness of the sailor about him & there is nothing of pride or fashion he is as plain in manner & dress as the old country squire a stranger would never guess that he was speaking to a Lord though his is one of the noblest familys in England ... His Lordship is a large man of a commanding figure[2]

Radstock's interest in Clare was strengthened by their meeting and soon revealed itself in practical form by various schemes to better the poet's condition:

Lord Radstock introduced me to Mrs Emmerson she has been & is a warm kind friend of tastes feelings & manners almost romantic she has been a very pretty woman & is not amiss still & a womans pretty face is often very dangerous to her common sense for the notice she recieved in her young days threw affectations about her feelings which she has not got shut of yet for she fancies that her friends are admirers of her person as a matter of course & acts accordingly which appears in the eyes of a stranger ridiculous enough but the grotesque wears off on becoming acquainted with better qualities & better qualities she certainly has to counterbalance them she at one word is the best friend I

[1] Peterborough MSS.
[2] *Ibid.*

found & my expectations are looking no further her correspondence with me began early in my public life & grew pretty thick as it went on I fancied it a fine thing to correspond with a lady & by degrees grew up into an admirer sometimes writing as I felt sometimes as I fancied & sometimes foolishly when I could not account for why I did it[1]

Clare's letters to Mrs Emmerson, which would have offered information on his conflict between ideal and actual love, have not come to light, although she kept them carefully, intending to publish them. Her letters to him, to the number of over three hundred, are preserved among the Clare correspondence in the British Museum. The opinion of them expressed by J. L. Cherry, editor of Clare's *Life and Remains*, is that

> The Editor, having read the whole of them, feels constrained, a different version of the relationship having been given [by Frederick Martin] to state his conviction that no poor struggling genius was ever blessed with a tenderer or a truer friend. No man of feeling could rise from the perusal of them without the deepest respect and admiration for the writer. The style is effusive, and the language in which the lady writes of Clare's poetry is occasionally eulogistic to the point of extravagance, and was to that extent injudicious; but all the blemishes are forgotten in the presence of overwhelming evidences of pure and disinterested friendship.

The friendship lasted for more than fifteen years, and was shared by her husband, Thomas Emmerson, who was always ready to help in such business matters as Clare's distance from London made it difficult for him to transact. They spread his name and copies of his books among their friends. Mrs Emmerson had a large circle of literary acquaintances, and befriended several young writers beside Clare. She herself contributed to the periodicals, and her letters are thickly sprinkled with her own verses. She understood that much of

[1] *Ibid.*

Clare's illness was of nervous origin, for she herself suffered in the same way. Her advice was therefore inspired by sympathy and, on occasion, frankly worded. Nor was her friendship limited to advice and encouragement; gifts of money, clothing, and books, for Clare and his family, accompanied her letters.

Clare also became acquainted with Taylor's partner, J. A. Hessey, whom Keats used to call "Mistessy",[1] and whom J. H. Reynolds remembered as "a very respectable person". Most of the other writers who mention Hessey seem to have agreed with Reynolds, and were content to leave it at that. We find no account of him among Clare's papers. Expressing surprise at his failure in business in 1829, Clare remarked that he had always thought of him as "a sort of miserly, cautious, and monied man". In this paucity of information, John Taylor's pen-portrait of Hessey, written in the early days of their partnership, is welcome:

> James Augustus Hessey is thin, dresses principally in black, his face is round and good-humoured when he does not frown—when he does, *it has the contrary expression.* He is about 22, but retains a boyish appearance about the head. His application is good—his conversation and manners lively. He has a readiness of droll quotation, and humorous allusion—is somewhat witty but had rather be considered a man of strong sense. His enunciation is not very distinct, but rapid, and when he wishes to utter his opinion in a serious manner, he hesitates or stutters a little, as if in doubt what words to select next. His reading has been various, but not *very* deep or extensive. He can speak with propriety on all subjects because his good sense teaches him how far he is qualified to speak. He is a great favourite wherever he goes, particularly with young ladies, who like him for his great cheerfulness, and because he sings a little, plays a little, and dances well ... [2]

Hessey's first letter to Clare on March 14th was accompanied by the gift of a violin of some value, a Cremona, which he

[1] Possibly imitating Taylor's porter's way of saying the words, but also conveying Keats's idea of Hessey's primness.

[2] Quoted from *Keats's Publisher* by Edmund Blunden (Jonathan Cape, 1936).

himself used to play; the last phrase suggests that Hessey, now married, had renounced those youthful gaieties which won him favour with young women. Indeed, we find in his many letters to Clare little of the lively wit and humorous allusion with which Taylor credited him, but much of the cautious sense.

Other friendships with men whom Clare came to know on his second and longer London visit had their beginnings at Taylor's house during this week. H. F. Cary, the translator of Dante, wrote to his brother-in-law, Thomas Price, on March 8th, asking him to review *Poems Descriptive*,

> which, remember that you have told me, you find *surprising* and *beautiful* ... I spent an evening lately with him [Clare] at our common bookseller's ... He has the appearance rather of a big boy who has never been used to company, than of a clown, though his dialect is clownish enough; and like *all true geniuses*, he was longing to be at home again, and is now there.

The second edition of Cary's translation had been published by Taylor and Hessey in 1819, and Cary had been agreeably surprised by the liberality of the firm, and pleased by Taylor's keen interest in the work. Clare and Cary did not begin to correspond until after the second visit to London.

Clare also made the acquaintance of John Hamilton Reynolds, and enjoyed both his humour and his poetry; Taylor gave Clare a copy of Reynolds's *The Naiad*, and, on the publication of *The Fancy* in the summer of 1820, sent a copy. We know from Clare's journal that he read these books and Reynolds's *The Garden of Florence*, 1821, with critical attention. Brilliant but temperamental, in 1819 J. H. Reynolds wrote, and Taylor and Hessey published, a parody on Wordsworth's advertised *Peter Bell*. In the stanza of "The Idiot Boy" this came out before Wordsworth's poem and was much applauded. "Simon Pure", otherwise "Peter Corcoran" and "Edward Herbert" of the *London Magazine*, J. H. Reynolds had been bracketed, by Leigh Hunt, with Shelley and Keats as "destined to carry forward the torch of English Poetry". In 1825 Reynolds collaborated with Thomas Hood in the successful *Odes and*

Addresses to Great People. He was one of the first proprietors of the *Athenaeum* in 1828. Yet, becoming a lawyer, he faded out, to die in 1852 a tragic, disappointed alcoholic.

Taylor's letter of March 16th is interesting for its reference to the friend whom Reynolds freely and generously acknowledged to be greater than himself:

> Keats came to dine with me the Day before yesterday for the first Time since his Illness—He was very sorry he did not see you—When I read Solitude to him he observed that the Description too much prevailed over the Sentiment—But never mind that—it is a good fault.[1]

Thus Clare seems to have missed his only opportunity of meeting Keats, who left for Italy in September 1821. It would have been an interesting meeting between these two, to whom illness, misunderstanding and neglect came in such different guises.[2] No less different were their attitudes toward their common loves, nature and poetry, as may be exemplified by placing Clare's opinion of *Endymion* beside Keats's criticism of "Solitude".

> He keeps up a constant alusion or illusion to the Grecian mythology & there I cannot follow yet when he speaks of woods Dryads & Fauns & Satyrs are sure to follow & the brook looks alone without her naiads to his mind yet the frequency of such classical accompaniment makes it wearisome to the reader where behind every rose bush he looks for a Venus & under every laurel a thrumming Appollo but as far as I can judge his descriptions of scenery are often very fine but as it is the case with other inhabitants of great citys he often described nature as she appeared to his fancys & not as he would have described her had he witnessed the things he describes thus it is he has often undergone the Blackwood stigma of Cockneyism & what appears as beautys in the eyes of a pent up citizen are

[1] Letters, British Museum.

[2] Points of contact—and divergences—between them have been noted by John Middleton Murry in "The Poetry of John Clare", *Countries of the Mind* (First Series), 1922.

> looked upon as conceits by those who live in the country—these are merely his errors but even here they are the errors of no common mind & of no common man he is often mistical but such poetical liscences have been looked on as beautys in Wordsworth & Shelley & in Keats they may be forgiven—to read thro him page by page we shall find is impossible to follow or understand the vagueness [?] of his fancy ...[1]

In Taylor's company Clare visited the painter, William Hilton, and sat for his portrait. Hilton, who shared a house in London with Peter De Wint, and whom Robert Gittings calls "a plodding traditional technician", was elected R.A. in 1819. He was perhaps more highly esteemed by the Academy, of which he became Keeper in 1826, than by the public. He suffered from ill health; according to his friend and fellow-student, Benjamin Haydon, "A more amiable creature never lived, nor a kinder heart; but there was an intellectual and physical feebleness in everything he did." The boisterous Haydon was not among those who considered Hilton "the first historical painter of the age".

His picture of Clare once kept company with his portrait of Keats in the National Portrait Gallery. It is an impression of Clare in an inspired moment: "C in alt." Lamb called it. The face, with its balanced features and fresh colouring, wears an eager, candid expression; far-seeing blue eyes look out beneath the high forehead and light-brown wavy hair; the nose is well moulded, the mouth tranquil yet sensitive. Hilton sloughed away any peasant in Clare and left the poet.

We do not know whether Clare appreciated Hilton's historical painting, but he was keenly interested in another branch of the art, and held decided views about it. In Peter De Wint, the landscape painter, Hilton's brother-in-law, he recognized an artist who had achieved in his own medium the very effects which Clare sought in his. De Wint's Dutch ancestry made the level stretches of fen country around Peterborough especially attractive to him, and in his frequent visits to the district he

[1] Peterborough MSS: from two drafts of a letter to the editor of the *Champion* to whom Clare was giving a copy of *Endymion*.

painted Whittlesey Mere and other scenes familiar to Clare. He was never so happy as when in the fields, and painted direct from nature. His water-colours, faithful renderings of typical English scenes, are notable for their realism, simplicity, and breadth of light and shade. Clare's appreciation of De Wint's work appears again and again, both in his letters and in notes for an "Essay on Landscape":

> there is no nice trickery in effect disposing of lights & shadows to catch the eye from object to object with excessive fractions of diminishings untill the eye rest upon a last pinspoint effect that makes a tree appear a mile high & the neighbouring background a mile off—these beautifull extravagances of false effects have produced such beautiful imagings that many have clomb into fame & profit by their creations but Dewint has none of these minute gradations these atom stipplings by which beautiful effective compositions are produced but not paintings from Nature as they profess to be ... look at his sketches his studies there is the simplest touches possible giving the most natural possible effects the eye is led over the Landscape as far as a sunbeam can reach & there sky & earth blends into an humanity of greetings a beautiful harmony & mystery [symmetry] of pleasant imaginings—there is no harsh stoppage no bounds to space or any outline further then there is in nature—if we could possibly walk into the picture we fancy we might pursue the landscape beyond those mysterys (not bounds) [bonds] assigned it so as we can in the fields ... look at them they are the very copys of nature—& she rewards the faith of her worshipers by revealing such beautys in her settings [as the][1] fanciful never meet with ... —the dewy morning is not more fresh in her features than the air & the sky & the sunny grass of the pictures—tis summer the very air breathes hot in ones face ... [2]

The "Essay on Landscape" was never published, probably

[1] Clare has "that that".
[2] Peterborough MSS.

never finished; but in a sonnet to De Wint, included in *The Rural Muse*, Clare paid as eloquent a tribute to the painter:

> Dewint I would not flatter nor would I
> Pretend to critic skill in this thine art
> Yet in thy landscapes I can well descry
> Thy breathing lines as natures counterpart
> —No painted freaks—no wild romantic sky
> No rocks or mountains as the rich sublime
> Hath made thee famous—but the sunny truth
> Of nature that doth mark thee for all time
> Found on our level pastures spots forsooth
> Where common skill sees nothing deemed divine
> Yet here a worshipper was found in thee
> Where thy young pencil worked such rich surprise
> That rushy flats befringed with willow tree
> Rival'd the beauties of Italian skies

He returned home at the end of the first week in March, and, belatedly, on the 16th his marriage with Patty took place at Casterton Magna: "I held out as long as I coud & then married her at Casterton Church her uncle John Turner was father and gave us the wedding dinner." John Turner and Sophy Clare signed as witnesses, and Martha Turner made her mark. Patty could read but she could not write. There was no room for another family in the part of the cottage which the Clares then inhabited, and there was a scheme to provide a new home for John and his wife. Radstock had already written to Lord Milton to ask for a cottage and land, rent free for life. Gilchrist wrote on March 28th: "Surely Patty and you would be more 'snug and canny' in a room together, till the cottage was ready, than two counties asunder as at present."

The poem "Proposals for Building a Cottage", written at this time, describes the kind of dwelling Clare wanted. It was to be built beside a runnel, with a thatch which he might pull out here and there to make hiding-places for the sparrows, and with holes within the chimney-top for the swallows' nests. There were to be grass plots by the door and "a little garden, not too fine" with woodbines, spindling sedge and what Edward Thomas, too, called "old man's beard"—traveller's joy.[1] Inside Clare wanted shelves and cupboards in all the corners for his books. In April, Lord Milton sent for Clare to meet him in the fields to choose a piece of ground; but they missed each other. Clare grew impatient, and wrote to Milton on his own account, against the advice of his friends; but nothing came of that. Finally, part of the tenement next to the Clares became vacant: John took it and brought Patty there. His later comments show that he was not sorry to remain under the old roof:

> I have often been urged & advised to leave it & get a more roomey & better looking house by visitors who gave me no better encouragement then their words & whom I did not expect woud be of any service to me in case their advice happened to lead me into greater inconvenience in the end so I took no notice of them & lived on in the same house & in the same way as I had always done following my old occupations & keeping my old neighbours as friends without being troubled or dissapointed with climbing ambitions that shine as fine as they may only tempt the restless mind to climb so that he may be made dizzy with a mockery of splendor & topple down headlong into a lower degradation then he left behind him[2]

Settlement at Helpston with Patty did not take place until perhaps near the birth of their first daughter; meanwhile Clare was enjoying his short springtime of good fortune. In the "Address to Plenty", written in December 1817, he interrupted his passionate plea for the "Sad sons of Poverty", whose sufferings were his own, to give a vivid picture of the life he would lead if Plenty smiled on him: how he would shut out the blast and take his ease before a roaring fire, a pitcher and barrel near at hand, his chimney corner well supplied with coal or wood, his cupboard lined with victuals. He would loll in an elbow-chair, reading a page in a book, peeping at the news, or taking a nap. After his return from London, Clare came briefly near to realizing his dream, revelling in the favours of the new

[1] *Clematis vitalba.*
[2] Peterborough MSS.

plenty. Reviewers who urged him not to desert his field labours certainly meant well; the gulf fixed in those days between a pauper peasantry and the other classes of society was too vast to be bridged by a few poems. But, while they wished to see Clare's poverty relieved, they were unable to sympathize with his expressed desire to escape from the estate to which a wise providence had called him; nor did they accept him as an advocate for his fellow-peasants. He must be helped, not because he was a peasant to whom, as such, the conditions of the time denied a livelihood, but because he was, by some God's miracle, a peasant-poet. The term represents the age's solution of a very awkward problem and an even more awkward reality. As poet, Clare ought to be encouraged in his ambition; as peasant, clearly discouraged. So he became a "peasant-poet" and was half-helped, often with condescension.

But only the lightest shadow of difficulties to come yet rested on him. His letters to Gilchrist give glimpses of his enjoyment of the period of respite. He is reading Pope, Dryden, and Johnson's *Dictionary*, gifts from Lord Milton; he returns Wordsworth and asks for the loan of a Byron. He is writing, and requests "a good fair jar of ink"; he is quite set up now as to money matters, and will not be much friendly with work (field-work) for a time. He must write an ode to the Marquis of Exeter as his Laureate. Flattering verses teem in, accompanied by gifts of money (usually small) but he is busy saying thank you for them and writing anecdotes of his early life for Gilchrist. A guest from Trinity Hall, Cambridge, has paid him a special visit. The pitcher and barrel of the "Address to Plenty" have their place in these celebrations, though he found them a less pure joy in reality than in fantasy. Gilchrist writes on March 28th: "Is not the headache the denunciation threatened in Scripture—'Woe unto them that drink strong drink'? When will you leave off these sad doings, John Clare, John Clare?" And thus began a long hyperbole of Clare's capacity for drink.

Unwonted excitements, suddenly succeeding years of borderline poverty soon threatened more serious trouble than headaches. On April 22nd, Hessey wrote to Gilchrist in some alarm because Drury, who was in town, had heard that Clare had been attacked by "a fit on the 19th or 20th of a dangerous kind". Perhaps, for once, rumour did not exaggerate. Clare's letter of the 19th reported that he was indeed "worse in health than you can conjecture or than myself am aware of"; yet he was in good spirits still. There is no firm evidence that this illness of 1820 was other than one of the epileptiform attacks he mentioned in the sketch of his life sent to Taylor and dated 1821 – the swoonings he had endured since as a boy he saw the loader fall from his wagon and break his neck. From this time onward, Taylor, Hessey, Drury, Gilchrist, Mrs Emmerson and Lord Radstock showered advice on Clare's ethics and habits. A letter conjecturally dated January 1821 but more likely belonging to 1820 from Clare to Hessey says: "the information you got respecting me no doubt has magnified your ideas & made mountains of molehills I am not bad in body but in mind Tis an old complaint perhaps 8 or 9 years ..."[1] Another letter to Taylor and Hessey postmarked 1820 has a postscript. "I coud not help smiling when O. G. [Gilchrist] told me Mr Hessey had heard fearfull news of my having had a appolectic fit – tis wonderful how such things get out ..."

The visitor from Cambridge of whom Clare wrote was Chauncy Hare Townshend, then twenty years old and a student at Trinity Hall. In his account, written some years later, Clare mis-dated the visit; it took place in March, 1820.

> Chauncy Hare Townsend[2] came to see me it was one evening in summer & askd me if John Clare lived there I told him I was he & he seemd supprised & askd agen to be satisfied for I was shabby & dirty he askd freely & was dissapointed I dare say at finding I had little or nothing to say for I always had a natural depression of spirits in the presence of strangers that took from me all power of freedom or familiarity & made me dull & silent for [when] I attempted to say anything I coud not reccolect it & made so many hums & hahs in the story that I was obliged to leave it unfinished at last I often tryd to master this confusion by trying to talk over reasonings & arguments as I went about in my rambles which I thought I did pretty well but as soon as I got before anybody I was as much to seek

[1] Northampton MSS.
[2] The original spelling of the name; Townshend himself changed it.

as ever—C H T was a little affecting with dandyism & he mimicked a lisp in his speech which he owd to affectation rather then habit otherwise he was a feeling & sensible young man he talked about Poets & poetry & the fine scenery of the lakes & other matters for a good while & when he left me he put a folded paper in my hand which I found after he was gone was a sonnet & a pound bill He promised & sent me Beatties Minstrel some letters passd between us & I sent him a present of my Village Minstrel when I never heard of him afterwards he has since published a Volume of Poems[1]

Townshend's sonnet to Clare was published in the *Morning Post*; he sent Beattie's *Minstrel* in April; in May Clare replied:

The Minstrel is a sweet poem & (as) far as I have read a many thoughts occur which are in my "Peasant Boy" I doubt the world will think them plagarisms therefore I must alter them or cut them out altogether but nature is the same here at Helpstone as it is elsewhere—I am now employed in writing songs for a music seller in Town If I succeed it may perhaps be to my advancement If I dont there is not much risk to run—so I am careless as to these matters ... I shall be happy to see you agen at Helpstone likewise your first visit found me in a gloomy [*glowering*] desponding condition that often gets the sway but when I have been inspired with a pint of 'John Barleycorn' & in one of my sunshiny moments you would not know me I am a new man & have too many tongues though your visit did not find it still I can be cheery but in my sullen fits I am defiled with the old silence of rusticity that always characterized me among my neighbours before I was known to the world I was reckoned a "glumpy half sort of fool" amongst em you will excuse all this it is only to make apology for the ill behaviour that might seem predominent at our first interview— ... [2]

[1] Peterborough MSS.
[2] *The Letters of John Clare*, edited by J. W. and Anne Tibble (Routledge and Kegan Paul, 1951).

As late as 1865, after the publication of Martin's *Life of Clare*, Townshend recalled with pleasure his visit to Helpston, remembered no glumness but the "fine intellectual countenance, the paleness of which gave the impression of weak health", and criticized the absurd story which Martin made from Clare's account of the visit, where among other inventions Townshend is said to have mistaken Clare for a highwayman.

Early in April, Clare paid a visit to Holywell Hall, the seat of the Reynardson family, descendants of a Jacob Reynardson who was Lord Mayor of London in 1649 and suffered imprisonment for his adherence to the cause of Charles I. This is Clare's story of the visit:

> It was a pleasant day for the season & I found the scenery of Holywell very beautiful ... He showed me his library ... after looking about the gardens & the library I was sent to dinner in the Servants Hall [two lines scored through] & when it was over the housekeeper invited me into her room w[h]ere the governess came & chatted in a free manner & asking me to correspond with her gave me her address the housekeeper wished me to write an address to her son in imitation of Cowper's lines on his mother's picture—the governess was a pretty impertinent girl & mischeviously familiar to a mind less romantic than my own I felt startled into sudden supprises at her manner & in the evening on my return home I was more supprisd still when on getting out of the park into the fields I found her lingering in my path & on coming up to her she smiled & told me plainly she was waiting to go a little way home with me I felt evil apprehensions as to her meaning but I was clownish & slow in smiles & advantages to interpret it she chatted about my poems & resumed the discourse of asking me to correspond with her which I promised I woud when we came to the brink of the heath that stands in view of Patty's cottage I made a stop to get rid of her but she lingered & chatterd on till it grew very late when a man on horseback suddenly came up & askd the road we had come from when she thinking it was the General hastily retreated but on finding her mistake she returned & resumed her discourse till it grew between the late & early when I wishd her goodnight

> & abruptly started without using the courage of shaking her by the hand—I felt excessively awkward all the way home & my mind was filld with guesses & imaginings at her strange manner & meanings—I wrote one letter to her & intended to be very warm & very gallant in it but fancying [?] that she only wanted me to write love letters to have the pleasure to talk about them & laugh at them so my second mind wrote a very cold one in which I inserted the second address to a Rosebud in humble life in which I requested no answer nor hinted a second advance so there the matter or mystery ended for I never unriddeled its meaning tho it was one of the oddest adventures my poetical life met with it made me rather consieted as I fancied the young lady had fallen in love with me—She came from Birmingham I shall not mention her name here.[1]

Soon after this visit to Holywell there came definite news from London that Lord Radstock's efforts were bearing fruit. A subscription list had been opened for a fund to provide Clare with a settled income, and, by the end of April Radstock had collected about £100. To this was added £100 which had been sent to Taylor by Earl Fitzwilliam in February, and a further £100 advanced by the publishers themselves. In a letter of April 18th, Taylor called this last sum a gift, and as such it appeared in the subscription list. But the gift was taken back out of the profits on *Poems Descriptive*; the policy of generosity for which the firm was at this time renowned underwent drastic changes in the next few years. On April 28th, £250 was invested in Navy 5 per cents., and on June 7th a further £125 was added. The investment was held in trust to Clare by Taylor, who took Richard Woodhouse to whom he entrusted the editing of Keats's poems as joint trustee in September, and the half-yearly dividend of £9 7*s.* 6*d.*, which fell to £7 17*s.* 6*d.* in 1823, was paid through the publisher. Clare was not consulted in this transaction, but, if he had been, he was too amazed by his good fortune and too aware of his ignorance of business affairs to question the wisdom of his

[1] Peterborough MSS., from two fragments.

benefactors. In May came a further addition to his income through his friend Dr Bell of Stamford, who had pleaded his cause with Earl Spencer.[1] The earl promised an annuity of £10, which was also paid through Taylor and Hessey. Thus, with the £15 from the Marquis of Exeter, Clare now had a yearly income of £43 15*s*. Relating these facts in the Introduction to *The Village Minstrel*, Taylor added, "His means of living, it is hoped, will be increased still further by the publication of the present work, and by the profit which may arise from the continued sale of his first production."

With his assured and regular income, and with every prospect of increasing it by an occupation which was no labour to him but his chief delight, Clare might well feel that the spring of 1820 had fulfilled the new year's promise.

[1] The Right Honourable George John Spencer, 2nd Earl Spencer and Viscount Althorpe, Privy Councillor, Trustee of the British Museum and collector of one of the finest libraries in Europe.

CHAPTER NINE

Books are Out and Books are Read: 1820–1822

As spring passed into summer, and Clare settled down in his part of the old cottage with Patty, he gradually became aware of the importance of those profits of which Taylor spoke. The "small fortune" which the benevolence of his patrons had assured to him was in fact just a little more than the £30 a year he might have earned by full-time work as a day labourer; and the earnings of a day labourer in 1820, in view of the cost of living at that time, were no longer sufficient for barest needs; from the first Clare had to support his parents as well as his own family; and a little more was swallowed by those necessary expenses, unknown to the peasant, which he incurred as a writer. It is true that his patrons thought that he could easily add to his income by part-time work at his old occupations; his letters from London friends often contained idyllic pictures of the happy life he was supposed to be leading, composing poems or working in the fields just as it pleased him, free from care. They do not seem to have considered what employer would hire a labourer on those terms. Clare did in fact work in the fields in the busy harvest months whenever he was able; but at other times there was little enough work for the full-time labourer. Knowing from experience the difficulties and uncertainties of the peasant's lot, Clare naturally turned his hopes toward his new profession rather than his old. It was by his writing that he trusted to win freedom from the struggle with poverty; hence his business relationship with his publishers becomes a matter of first importance.

That relationship was complicated from the very beginning by the fact that the poems had been published by Taylor and Hessey in partnership with Drury, and the partnership was not a happy one. Drury had discovered Clare, had received and copied his poems, decided to print them, advanced a little money on them, and therefore considered himself prime mover in the affair, and copyright of some poems as belonging to him. Taylor, with experience and resources Drury lacked, had edited and published the poems, introduced Clare to the literary world, and had seen the venture crowned with success. He was by no means content to be regarded merely as his cousin's agent in the business. It is certain that he, too, regarded himself as owning some copyright. Realising this, Drury had taken steps to strengthen his claims before Clare visited London. Clare made this memorandum in one of his note-books:

> Drury has persuaded me to write down in his account book & under my accounts with him that I have sold him my first Vol for £20 which is to be deducted from my account as he only wishes to have a check against Taylor & Hessey who he strongly thinks will cheat him

In the Introduction to *The Village Minstrel*, referring to *Poems Descriptive*, Taylor wrote, "The present Publishers gave Clare twenty pounds for his Poems." Yet in fact Clare was neither given £20 by Taylor and Hessey nor was it deducted from Drury's account, which was presented and paid in full later; for it appears as an item in the expenses for the publishing of *Poems Descriptive*, the account of which Clare did not receive until 1829: "Cash paid Mr. Clare for copyright p. Drury." To this Clare added a note: "How can this be? I never sold the Poems for any price. What money I had of Drury was given me on account of profits to be received; but here it seems I have got nothing and am brought in minus twenty pounds of which I never received a sixpence."

Drury was not satisfied with this claim on the copyright. He wanted an agreement; but he evidently feared that Clare's caution, even in his then ignorance of publishing matters, would defeat his plans. Clare also recorded:

> I once signed an agreement of Drurys which alowd me a quarters profit I was fresh at the time but it got wind & others heard of it that knew better then I did who calld it a villainous trick so he sent it up to London to be des-

troyed as they say I know nothing tho I know that I have never signd an agreement of any kind since & never will[1]

What seems clear is that Clare *did* lose £20 through putting his signature to Drury's note. It is not surprising, therefore, to find that by March 1820 the partnership between Drury and Taylor had become very strained; their letters to Clare show them skirmishing for position. "Have you any Letters of his wherein he Speaks of the Share I took in bringing out the Poems? or any later letters referring to the agreement?" Taylor inquired on the 28th. On the same date Drury wrote that he could not consent to give up the MS. book for which Clare had sent: "It is so importantly useful to me towards clearing up a mischievous misunderstanding between me and Mr. Jn. Taylor of London ... " This book contained Clare's receipt for the £20. But at no time had Clare any intention to sell the copyright as both Taylor and Drury assumed. In April Drury commented on the "dilatory twaddling habits of J. T." and announced his intention of going to London to clear up the disagreement between them. The result of that visit was the destruction of the agreement, which marked a temporary truce to discord. Taylor explained what had been decided at that meeting:

> We have settled to give E.D., on condition that he sends up the agreement for us to destroy it, one half of whatever profit we may derive from the present or future Poems, retaining in our own Hands the sole management, and perfectly uncontrolled in what we think proper to give the Author. E. D. has been repaid the Copyright and all the other Expenses and I have charged nothing for my Trouble as Editor so far ... You shall have at least half of all the profits, and he shall sustain no loss by our advancing any sums we may deem right to you. These Things I state for your Information, for I have no Disguise.[2]

[1] Peterborough MSS.
[2] Letters, British Museum.

For a while affairs ran more smoothly. Drury continued to receive and copy poems for a new volume; but he was by no means satisfied with his position, and disapproved of Taylor's management of Clare's affairs. His letters later in the year were full of complaints about the publisher's reticence and reserve; he would give them no information about the profits on the first book or about the progress of the new one. Drury's view of the situation was very different from Taylor's:

> However useful their services may have been both to you and myself, I humbly apprehend that, as they were volunteered, and, moreover, as Lord R. observes, they have been amply repaid—they have no title, no consideration nor any plea for monopolizing your Poems as they now do ... What moral or gentlemanly feeling can they possess?—if they continue thus to abuse the confidence I have reposed in them; in return for which they abstract entirely from my control or even approval the undertaking which to all intents and purposes is an affair entrusted by you to me alone—They are in the situation of individuals with whom I have associated in order to accomplish your views.[1]

Edward Drury was not an unbiased judge, but he had a shrewd eye for his cousin's character. Taylor was indeed capable of exceptional reticence and procrastination in conducting his business affairs. But, to do him justice, in this instance he was deliberately limiting Drury's share in the business, and during 1820 he was facing continual difficulties because of his generosity to John Keats. In September the firm was £130 out of pocket over *Endymion*, and *Lamia* had not yet paid the expenses of publishing. In an unsent letter to Keats, Taylor wrote: "If I were rich enough to do without the whole sum that you might want, I would gladly give it to you, but if I wanted it I know nobody who would let me have it." Here, no doubt, is the explanation of those gifts to Clare which were later retracted by the firm.

The dispute between Taylor and Drury, with its atmosphere

[1] Letters, British Museum.

of distrust and uncertainty, disturbed Clare by placing him in an unpleasant position. Drury wrote to Clare that Taylor was behaving in a "dastardly manner". Both men appealed where they knew he was vulnerable—to his loyalty and friendship; he was asked to choose between the publisher upon whom depended the success of his books and the earlier friend who had set his feet on the road to fame. There could be little doubt about the issue: Taylor had the stronger hand and played it skilfully; but Clare did his best to keep both friends. A note, dated July 1820, and scribbled in the front of the MS. book *A Rustic's Pastime*, testifies clearly enough that he was sensible of his debt to Drury: "These leaves of scribbling that ... certainly woud have been obliterated by the flames had not friendships warm atachments interposed to retrieve them from so just a fate are left to E. Drury as desired."[1]

As the year wore on, Clare was discovering that the problems and difficulties of the writer are no less real than those of the peasant. Moreover, he had to consider not only his publishers, but also his patrons, whose zeal on his behalf sometimes led to unpleasant situations. A correspondent of Clare's, Captain M. E. Sherwill, knew Scott. When Scott came to London in April to be made a baronet, Captain Sherwill, according to his promise to Clare, visited him and spoke about Clare. In Sherwill's words, his "spoils of victory" were a copy of *The Lady of the Lake* and £2 to be laid out in books. Clare chose Currie's *Life and Works*. *The Lady of the Lake* was to be sent, at Scott's own desire, from Scotland, but after three months' delay it was forwarded by Sherwill himself with this comment:

> All my endeavours, all my efforts of persuasion, proved fruitless in the anxious desire I had expressed to Him, that He would address a few lines to you in the blank leaf. Sir W. seemed bound hand and head, not from any disapprobation of your talent or taste, but occasioned by the high path in which He strides in the literary field of the present day.

Clare's reply shows what he felt:

[1] Northampton MSS.

> I thought Sir Walter a different person his omitting to write his name in the book shows a stiffness of pride too much affected with little things There was a day when as a poet he shone little above his humble servant. He has patronized the 'Ettrick Shepherd' and some others but—I was going on, but murmurs are useless.[1]

It is possible that Scott disliked being importuned by Sherwill, who evidently expected some large benefit to accrue to Clare from this connection. As a leader of the new profession of letters, Scott may have disapproved, as did Dickens, of any attempt to revive the almost defunct system of patronage. Radstock had been urging him to use his influence with Lockhart for an article in *Blackwood's*. The article appeared, its illiberality not redeemed by perceptiveness. It recommended Clare to remain a "happy" peasant rather than become a mediocre poet. As usual—anxious to judge nobody unjustly Clare commented further that the incident was

> wrongly & sadly misstated in the gossip that appeard in the London Mag. entitld a Visit &c. ... C. S. made apology for the omission by saying that Walter Scott enjoyed such a high literary character that he did not wish to hazard an opinion & insert his name in the Vol ... but ... he remembered the time when the author of the Lady of the Lake hazarded his reputation ... by courting the favour of the critics in stating that his livelihood consisted in his writings ... wether this is true or false it rests on my mistake for Octave Gilchrist was the man that told me[2]

In Lord Radstock, Clare had found a patron who was untiring in his efforts to improve the poet's circumstances and widen his reputation; but, with his autocratic character and decided views, the old admiral was not content to confine his energies. As early as February there were signs of friction between Clare's publisher and his chief patron. Taylor had written to his father on the 15th:

[1] Peterborough MSS.
[2] *Ibid.*

Lord Radstock still exerts his utmost interest to sell the Book and did I not hate Patronage for its Selfishness (for such it is too frequently) I could not but admire the pains he takes. He is now proposing by broad Hints a better Bargain as he thinks for Clare's next Vol. viz. for us to publish and divide the Profits with the Author. This I would willingly consent to, if anybody would do the office of Editor *gratis*. It is amusing to think how different an Estimate would have been formed of these Poems in any other person's hands. I should be interested to see Gifford and Murray attempt to decypher and publish them, and should have no objection at all if the latter would make an offer of £500 or £1,000 for the next Volume[1]

About the same time Taylor informed Clare that Radstock disapproved of some of the poems in *Poems Descriptive* and wished them to be omitted in the next edition. The poems were "Dolly's Mistake", a rollicking ballad about a Wake and how the too-trusting Dolly was deceived by Young Ralph, and "My Mary", a love poem. Mary, a rough, hard-working servant-girl, is described with vigorous realism yet delicate sympathy; this lover's eye does not see "Helen's beauty in a brow of Egypt"; it accepts the brow of Egypt and loves none the less. But it was not Lord Radstock's idea of a love poem. There were other passages in the book which aroused even greater disapproval: one was in "Dawnings of Genius", where Clare described the ploughman as

> That necessary tool of wealth and pride;

the other in "Helpstone":

> Accursed wealth o'er-bounding human laws
> Of every evil thou remain'st the cause
> Victims of want those wretches such as me
> Too truly lay their wretchedness to thee
> Thou art the bar that keeps from being fed

[1] John Taylor's letters are in the possession of Messrs Brooke-Taylor, Bakewell.

& thine our loss of labour & of bread
Thou art the cause that levels every tree
& woods bow down to clear a way for thee[1]

In May, when the third edition was to be published, Mrs Emmerson wrote urging Clare to agree to the omission of these "highly objectionable" passages and quoting Lord Radstock: "Tell Clare if he has still a recollection of what I have done, and am still doing for him, he must give me unquestionable *proofs* of being that Man I would have him to be—he must expunge—expunge!" The lines were held to contain "radical and ungrateful sentiments".

But Clare considered that the kindness shown to him had not rescued the English peasantry from their evil plight; nor had it absolved the promoters of Enclosure from all responsibility for the disasters Enclosure brought on the poor. He resented interference in a matter which concerned himself and his publisher, and was for leaving the lines as they stood. No prude, Taylor approved of Clare's feelings; he disliked Radstock's encroachment into his own domain in this and other matters. He wrote to his brother on May 31st:

> We have published the 3rd edition of Clare which seems likely to go off with as much spirit as its predecessors. I am much annoyed by Lord R.'s Puffing in the *Post* and *New Times* and am determined to put an end to it, for I cannot but think it is disgraceful to me and injurious to Clare's fame as well as feelings ...

However, he thought it best to give way for the moment and the offending lines were omitted from the fourth edition toward the close of 1820. Taylor gave this explanation to Clare: "Lord R. has expressed his Intentions of disowning you in such strong terms ... that I conceived it would be deemed improper in me as your friend to hold out any longer ... When the Follies of the Day are past ... we can restore the Poems according to the earlier Editions." Clare did not write to Radstock for some time; he had refused to have anything to do

[1] Peterborough MSS., an early draft.

with the alteration of the poems, and left the matter in Taylor's hands. Since the subscription list was not yet closed, and Radstock was still busy collecting money, Taylor decided to propitiate him for the moment. But he had not changed his views about patronage, and merely awaited a more favourable opportunity to join issue with Radstock for the control of Clare's affairs.

When on June 1st or 2nd, Clare's first child, Anna Maria, was born, he celebrated the occasion by writing verses in the Burns stanza, "To an Infant Daughter", Hessey liked them, but added prudently: "There are Reasons why they should not be made public just yet." According to Taylor, Clare was finding Patty a termagant, but their lack of a home and their unsettled condition in those early months must have been unfavourable to harmony. The birth of the child, followed by their settlement in the cottage at Helpston, relieved the strain. Mrs Emmerson wondered if Clare read her letters aloud to "dear Patty", as she read his to her husband and Lord Radstock. "I've ever addressed you in your own very affectionate language—for we may unblushingly acknowledge ourselves lovers in poetry." She sent him a portrait of herself, and wished him to put it in a private drawer.[1] If in the nature of things Patty could claim only the more domestic part of Clare's affection, it was not for Mrs Emmerson that he reserved the rest, and they soon outgrew the mild literary flirtation of their early relationship.

In the summer, Clare returned to work in the fields, which he continued during the harvest months; he did not find the laborious employment very congenial after his burst of freedom, but the Fund brought him no dividend until December, and he received nothing directly in the way of profits on *Poems Descriptive*, of which the third edition was selling fast. Taylor had promised him half-profits, but as they were used to pay back the £100 which stood in the publishers' name in the subscription list, he got no benefit from them for the moment. Despite his good fortune, he lacked ready money when he most needed it.

[1] This was the portrait by Behnes. Later Clare notes (Peterborough MSS.) "she took to patronizing one of Coleridges [sons] ... & ... she then wisht for her picture agen & I readily agreed to part with it ... "

This, besides sending him back to field labour, made him glad to fall in with Drury's scheme to gain a few pounds by having songs set to music. One of these music setters was Crouch. Clare's London friends all disapproved of this side-line, which, indeed, seems to have profited Drury more than Clare. His friendship with Drury was not closed by the discord between Drury and Taylor.

Clare continued to receive many visitors, and after his return to field labour he found their visits often untimely and troublesome. He was sometimes sent for several times a day to satisfy the curiosity of strangers:

> Among the many that came to see me there was a dandified gentleman of unconscious odditys of character that not only borderd on the ridicilous but was absurdly smotherd in it he made pretentions to great learning & knew nothing on his first coming he began in a very dignified manner to examine the fruits of experience in books & said he hoped I had a fondness for reading as he wished to have the pleasure to make me a present of some he then begd my walking stick & after he had got it he wanted me to write my name on the crook I really thought the fellow was mad he then asked some insulting libertys respecting my first acquaintance with Patty & said he understood that in this country the lower orders made their courtship in barns & pigstyes & asked wether I did I felt very vext & said that it might be the custom of high orders for aught I knew as experience made fools wise in most matters but I assured him he was very wrong respecting that custom among the lower orders here his wife said he was fond of a joke & hoped I shoud not be offended but I saw naught of a joke in it & found afterwards that he was but a scant remove from the low order himself as his wife was a grocers daughter After he had gossiped an hour he said well I promised to give you a book but after examining your library I dont see that you want anything as you have a great many more than I expected to find still I shoud make you an offer of somthing have you got a Bible I said nothing but it was exactly what my Father had long wanted & he instantly spoke for me & said we have a bible sir but

> I cannot read it the print is so small so I shoud thank you for one the man looked very confused & explained by his manner that he had mentioned the very book which he thought we had to escape giving it[1]

Hopkinson, a magistrate, invited him to his house at Morton and roused Clare's anger by behaving with unbelievably absurd pretentiousness. According to Drury, Clare's mind was also harassed and oppressed by the laborious correspondence which he was obliged to support. But whatever his other occupations, he continued to write poems assiduously. In January, Taylor had suggested as a subject, "A Week in a Village", to consist of a story about village life for each day. Clare took up the suggestion, and the result appears in a bound quarto MS. volume, entitled "Village Scenes and Subjects on Rural Occupations", dated August 21st, 1820. The volume contains sixteen poems, written in Clare's hastiest handwriting, but fairly legible and evidently intended for the press. Six of them were included in *The Village Minstrel*, three in *The Shepherd's Calendar*, and the rest remained unpublished. Of this series of bucolics Mr Blunden has written:

> The collection as a whole is a painting of life in an English village a hundred years since in most of its common manifestations. The artist knew his theme, and was gifted with extraordinary freshness of outlook upon the familiar spectacle. In this respect he differed from many who like himself were born tillers of the soil; the shrewd enthusiasm of the best of them was not unaccompanied by his sweet intensity and universality of feeling. What he saw, that he was. His pity through all the delineation reminds one of Lamb's great words, 'feeling, which seems to resolve itself into the elements which it contemplates,' ...
>
> Rustic in form these poems certainly are, and, judged by the polish of other poets and by not a little of Clare's own later work, they have many flaws. His conception of poetry, at this time, appears on the title page of his

[1] Peterborough MSS.

> *Village Minstrel* in Spenser's verse, 'I play to please myself,' and that has something to do with this raggedness ... He lacked form a little, but what poet ever made up for that with greater riches of material? Even these early writings display that careless variety of rapture; and it is of course true that they have a hardy energy which is not so clear in later work, as he became aware of hues and tones at first unknown.

The writing and copying of these poems fully occupied Clare's leisure of 1820's spring and summer months. In July came a letter from Bloomfield, his "brother bard and fellow-labourer", to whom Drury had sent a copy of *Poems Descriptive*. The letters of both Taylor and Hessey frequently contained news of Keats. Taylor had written on April 27th, "I have got all Keats's MSS. in my hands now to make a Selection out of them for another Volume, as I did of yours; and I should like to write an Introduction too, as Editor, to speak about the unfair Reception he has met with from the Critics, & especially from the *Quarterly Review*; but perhaps I had better not." During the preparation of the *Lamia* volume, when Keats frequently visited Taylor to correct proofs and make emendations, they sometimes talked of Clare. There exists a postscript sheet torn from a letter of Clare's to Taylor, dated June 5th, on which is written in Keats's writing a couplet of *Lamia*, an emendation of the earlier MS. reading.

On June 6th, Taylor sent a number of extracts from *Lamia*, which was to appear in about three weeks. On the 27th, Hessey wrote that Keats was very ill again, and three days later he sent a copy of the book with further news:

> A Blood Vessel in his Lungs broke last week and he has been under Dr. Darling's Care ever since. By copious bleedings and active medicines the evil is at present reduced, but the prospect of its return & the evidence it affords of the state of his Constitution make me feel the greatest concern for him. I think the simplicity of 'Isabella' will please you much. 'Hyperion' is full of the most sublime poetical Images & the small Poems delight me very much ...

On August 19th, 1820, Taylor wrote that Keats would have to spend the winter in Italy.

> You are now a richer Man than poor K. and how much more fortunate – We have some trouble to get through 500 Copies of his work, though it is highly spoken of in the periodical Works, but what is most against him, it has been thought necessary in the leading Review, the *Quarterly*, to damn his (Poems) for (imputed) political Opinions – Damn them (I say) who could act in so cruel a way to a young man of undoubted Genius – I hate Criticism at all Times except when it is of that enlarged kind that takes entire Surveys of a Subject, and conceiving old writers to be new and new ones to be old awards to each his proper Share of Commendation. Besides in Poetry I think Praise should be given where it is due, and that Silence is sufficient Dispraise –

On September 27th, he told Clare that Keats was on the way to Italy.

> If he recovers his Strength he will write to you. I think he wishes to say to you that your Images from Nature are too much introduced without being called for by a particular Sentiment – To meddle with this Subject is bad policy when I am in haste, but perhaps you conceive what it is he means: his remark is only applicable now and then when he feels as if the Description overlaid and stifled that which ought to be the prevailing Idea – He likes your first pastoral which E. D. copied and sent very much indeed.

Keats's criticism was pertinent enough; Clare's revolt from poetry in which images were so overlaid by sentiment that they lost their freshness and truth to nature sometimes tempted him to the opposite extreme.

Impatient for the publication of his new book, Clare was under the impression that the poems he had sent up were ready for the press. He now heard from Sherwill that Taylor had not yet begun to select them, and was going out of town shortly.

He intended, he said, to visit Helpston and take Clare back with him to help in the editing. In the meantime, Clare turned to his Stamford friends for companionship. During one of his visits in September an incident occurred which caused him to write to Gilchrist:

> I went to Drurys agen & now comes the d——d hobble that vexes me after I had been there a few minutes a gentleman came in & asked me how I did I very bluntly answered "Very well thank you Sir" he stard [at] me very hard & asked the prentice if it was not Clare & told me that he came to hear if my book was out—"no Sir"—(with my hat on)—was the answer he went out without saying a word more & he had not gone 2 minutes when the disclosure of the secret came out D——n it twas a thunderbolt to my ignorance & I stood gauping like an idiot to hear the man say it was no worse a person than the marquis—what the marquis will think of me I dont know but I wish very much I had been the length of London out of the matter—but if there is anything to disadvantage the poor devil your humble servant is sure to get over head and ears in it ... [1]

Gilchrist informed Clare later that he had seen Mr Pierrepont and explained the mistake, so that the matter was now set right.

Taylor's policy of reticence during the autumn of 1820 brought the truce between Lord Radstock and himself to an end. By December a wordy conflict, into which Drury and Mrs Emmerson were drawn, was again being waged for the control of Clare's affairs. Radstock's interest had not ceased with the closing of the subscription fund. He often sent messages through Mrs Emmerson, and sometimes wrote himself, in an almost unreadable hand, letters of admonition and concern for Clare's mental and spiritual development. He sent books frequently, many of them on religious subjects, and among the others the works of Akenside, Beattie, Coleridge, and Cowper, volumes of the *Idler* and *Rambler*, and Johnson's *Lives of the Poets*.

[1] *The Letters of John Clare*, edited by J. W. and Anne Tibble, *op. cit.*

In September we hear of a scheme of Radstock's whereby Clare was to visit a clergyman who would improve his external conduct and make it accord with his "inner delicacy". November foreshadowed a crisis: Mrs Emmerson passed on Radstock's complaints about Taylor's secrecy and lack of respect to him; he was going to look into the matter on his return to town. Events then moved quickly. Radstock wrote to Taylor, stressing the need for a written agreement between Clare and his publisher. In his reply, dated December 11th, Taylor stated that he was actually benefiting Clare more than he would have been bound to do under the terms of the obligation suggested by Radstock in a conversation of the previous April, namely, that the publishers should defray the expenses and share the profits with the author. "But my Lord, if you think your arbitration will be advantageous to Clare—I as a Publisher can have no objection to it; in the meantime I shall suspend those labours which are not within the province of a publisher." To this Radstock replied immediately. He did not doubt the publisher's goodwill,

> but still I apprehend that in matters of real business, no man's word, however well established his integrity, would be considered sufficiently binding, unless accompanied by some written document. As the case now stands between you and Clare, I understand that no terms whatever have been offered, he would therefore I think be to blame to resign his manuscript to any Publisher whatever, without a specified security for his labours.[1]

As to the labours of editing, if "no Lord Radstock had stepped forth in support of the Work, my own private opinion is, that a second edition of the Poems would not yet have shewed itself. That your labours were great respecting the little volume in question, I most willingly allow, but that you were amply remunerated I am equally convinced."

On Taylor's own showing, he had no real objection to the proposed written agreement. But he was not one of those who suffer criticism gladly; his next move was to deliver an

[1] Letters, British Museum.

ultimatum to Lord Radstock: "I will write to Clare to know whether I am to treat with him or your Lordship for the Copyright of his next Volume; and upon his answer will depend whether I shall again have the Honour of addressing your Lordship." Then he turned his attention to Clare. In a letter written on December 16th he described Radstock's criticisms as the meddling interferences of a patron anxious for notoriety.

> Unless you commission Lord R. to interfere in this Matter I know of no Right that he has to write to me on the Subject, and if he possessed ever so good a Right the observations he has allowed himself to make on my Conduct would disincline me to have any further Communication with him ... I would resign the MSS. rather than acknowledge his agency after what he has said ... [1]

If, however, Clare wished to go on as heretofore, he must insist on an agreement being executed between them on a basis of half profits, as the only way to keep meddlers out. On the 17th, Mrs Emmerson wrote that Lord Radstock had broken with Taylor, whose impetuosity had done Clare real injury. She urged him to press for a written agreement, but advised him not to withdraw his manuscripts, since that would delay the new book and derange his affairs generally. This consideration placed Taylor in a very strong position, as he well realized. On December 24th he consolidated that position by informing Clare that he was busy selecting poems, and intended to publish two volumes under the title "Ways of a Village". He also sent the first half-yearly dividend several days before it was due—in the future it usually arrived several days late—and suggested how pleasant it was to receive £20 a year free from obligation to anyone. Of Radstock he said, "I fear he will not be content till he is acknowledged your supreme Friend, and pre-eminent Patron." Clare was to ask Drury to show him the story of Sinbad, who also had relations with "an old Gentleman who belonged to the Sea-service". Mrs Emmerson wrote again on December 20th, promising to do her best to smooth things over; she believed Taylor's intentions were honourable, but

[1] Letters, British Museum.

he had not been candid and liberal in his communications. Clare was to send up a copy of the agreement to Lord Radstock. Taylor's letter of January 1st marked his victory, won on his own terms, or lack of terms. Clare expressed his confidence in his publishers; he was willing not only to sign an agreement for the forthcoming book, but one binding him for future publications. Taylor thanked him, but could not accept the latter proposal. "I know we cannot be more secure of your Goodwill than we are without any such Bond, and should a Difference arise between us ... it would be unjust to tie you fast ... That foolish Lord R. has no Conception of such Sentiments as these; what a wretched world he moves in, to have learnt no better at his time of life than thus to estimate his Friends as he pretends to call them—" Clare felt that these last remarks were uncalled-for, and commented "very unjust" in the margin of the letter.

Meanwhile Drury had been carrying on a guerrilla warfare on his own account. He expressed grave concern to Clare about Taylor's conduct, advising him to apply to Radstock to get an exact statement of his position, but warning him not to become too friendly with his patron. Then we hear that Radstock had written to Drury a "flaming appeal" about Taylor's reserved and disingenuous ways. Whereupon, since "hawks mustn't peck out hawks' eyes", he wrote back to persuade Radstock he was mistaken about Taylor, setting his private dudgeon aside, and in the process taking some blame on himself and scattering a few spots on Clare. In his opinion, he explained to Radstock, the published and forthcoming works were entirely Clare's property, and he would be justified in demanding the whole profits on them if he felt inclined.

Here for the time the matter rested. The agreement, suggested by Radstock to save Clare from Taylor, then insisted upon by Taylor to save Clare from Radstock, then accepted by Clare but refused by Taylor to save Clare from himself, remained still unsigned. Writing of this business Clare commented:

> Lord Radstock was my best friend it was owing to him that the first Poems succeeded he introduced them into all places w[h]ere he had connections got them noticed in

> newspapers & other [periodicals] & if it did nothing more it made them known—he kindly undertook to settle my affairs with my Publishers which they kindly enough on their parts deffered [deferred] & its not settld yet—he wrote Taylor a letter wishing him to draw up an agreement in "black & white" as his Lordship expressd it as faiths in men was not to be trusted Taylor pretended to be insulted at this & wrote his Lordship a genteel saucey one that settld the affair in the present confusion of no settlings at all Nay they will neither publish my poems or give them up[1]

During December and January Clare was troubled by "nervous fears", and suffered agitation of mind about the fate of his forthcoming book. Anything approaching the fine self-confidence that is often a part of genius was not part of his. The odds were too great. At times he thought he would not recover, and received a will-form from Woodhouse. Meanwhile, the fourth edition of *Poems Descriptive* had been printed in December, and progress was made with the new volumes. On January 23rd, 1821, Taylor sent the first proofs, and proof correction went on steadily during February and March. The choice of a title gave some trouble. "Ways of a Village" had been dropped, and "The Village Minstrel" was finally chosen, but with some reluctance because of its resemblance to Beattie's *The Minstrel*.

It was about this time that Clare, an innocent spectator, received a stray shot from the Battle of the Pamphlets which had been raging for some years between the Rev. W. Lisle Bowles on the one side and Thomas Campbell, Gilchrist and Byron on the other. It began in 1806, with Bowles's criticisms of Pope in his edition of that poet's *Works*, to which reference was made by Byron in *English Bards and Scotch Reviewers*. Ten years later, Campbell, in his *Essay on English Poetry*, championed Pope, and was answered by Bowles in a pamphlet. Then in the *Quarterly Review*, 1820, appeared an article supporting Campbell, ridiculing Bowles, and bringing Byron's

[1] From a crossed-through fragment (which means it is fair-copied elsewhere). Peterborough MSS.

name into the conflict. Byron took up the cudgels in Pope's defence, and wrote two *Letters to John Murray*, attacking Bowles, who replied in 1821 with two *Letters to Byron*. But Bowles had also replied to the *Quarterly* article of 1820, and, because he knew that Gilchrist had already defended Pope's character in the *London Magazine*, February 1820, and had written the review of Clare's poems in the *Quarterly*, he attributed to Gilchrist the *Quarterly* article on Pope, which was really from the pen of Isaac Disraeli. Thus, in his reply, Bowles assumed that his antagonist was the critic who had written about "certain productions of a 'poet of nature'. If so, his praise or blame may be held in equal contempt." Gilchrist made capital out of Bowles's mistake and his supposed slight on Clare, quoting two of Clare's sonnets to show that he was a better poet than Bowles in the only branch of the art in which the latter was noteworthy. In his next counterblast, Bowles made some amends to Clare and contended that his remarks applied only to the critic, "whose pompous and pedantic criticism rather injured than promoted the cause of him it was intended to serve." Byron took up this reply in his second *Letter*.

> In my humble opinion, the passage referred to both ... 'A certain poet of nature' is not the style of commendation ... Had he felt a spark of kindling kindness for John Clare, he would have named him. There is a sneer in the sentence as it stands. How a favourable review of a deserving poet can 'rather injure than promote his cause' is difficult to comprehend. The article denounced is able and amiable and it has 'served' the poet, as far as poetry can be served by judicious and honest criticism.

This is an incidental, though sincere, tribute; there could be few greater contrasts than between these two poets' fortunes, characters and poetry. Clare's first acquaintance with Byron's poetry had been made in 1819, but he had heard of Byron many years before that. In reminiscences of his boyhood, Clare tells how he copied out the journal of one of the villagers who had been an able seaman on board the *Fox* cutter, when Lord Byron sailed in her. The sailor remembered him as an odd young man "of a resolute temper, fond of bathing in the sea and going ashore to see ruins in a rough sea when it required six hands to manage the boat. This teased the sailors so much that his name became a by-word in the ship for unnecessary trouble." After 1820 there is abundant evidence of Clare's interest in Byron, both as man and as poet, and the interest grew, assuming strange guise as each year increased the contrast between their fames and fortunes.

In February 1821 came news of an event which was to have a great influence on John Taylor's plans and bring Clare into close contact with some of the writers of the day. John Scott, whose ability had placed the *London* among the foremost magazines of the time, had been shot in his unfortunate duel with Christie. In the same letter, Taylor said that he had just heard again of Keats, who could not live a fortnight longer. He thought of writing Keats's life to do justice to his memory. On March 9th Taylor wrote again: "We heard yesterday of Keats; he was still alive, though very weak—but calmer than he had been. It was not considered that he could last many Days longer— Probably at the very Time Scott died, he also died. In this last Letter we are told that Keats desires to have this Line put upon his Tombstone 'Here lies one whose name was writ on Water.' " On March 26th he sent news of Keats's death, and suggested that Clare might write some lines to his memory. "Poor Keats, you know how I reverence him," Clare wrote in reply, with a tirade on the dead poet's critics. He treated this theme allegorically in one of his long poems, and a sonnet was written just in time to be included in *The Village Minstrel*.

When Rancours aims have past in nought away
    Enlarging specks discernd in more than thee
And beauties minishing which few display
    When these are past true child of Poesy
Thou shalt survive[1]

Clare read the *Lamia* volume and copied into one of his note-books a number of its finest lines and phrases. On his cottage wall, beside his fiddle, hung a reproduction of one of the portraits of Keats; his children used to call it "the miserable man".

[1] Peterborough MSS.

By the end of March, Clare was again restored to health. His nervous disorder—so often the result of mental overwork and fatigue— had been accentuated by the threatened destruction of some elm-trees which had sheltered the cottage and murmured in the chimney-top long before his earliest memory. He wrote to Taylor:

> My two favourite elm trees at the back of the hut are condemned to die—it shocks me to relate it but 'tis true the savage who owns them thinks they have done their best & now he wants to make use of the benefits he can get from selling them O was this country Egypt & was I but a caliph the owner should lose his ears for his arrogant presumption & the first wretch that buried his axe in their roots should hang on their branches as a terror to the rest I have been several mornings to bid them farewell had I one hundred pounds to spare I would buy them reprieves—but they must die yet this mourning over trees is all foolishness—they feel no pains—they are but wood, cut up or not a second thought tells me I am a fool were people all to feel as I do the world coud not be carried on—a green woud not be ploughed—a tree or bush woud not be cut for firing or furniture & everything they found when boys woud remain in that state till they died this is my indisposition & you will laugh at it

Clare's feeling for trees, symbols of slow, steadfast lastingness, and his anger against the ruthless destruction which Enclosure brought, were expressed in "The Fallen Elm". For a time, through the intervention of Gilchrist and Drury, the elms were spared.

About this time, Clare's visits to Stamford gave his London friends some concern. Taylor was "grieved" to hear of his "late fit of drinking", and wrote, "One of the very very few poets of this day is gone—let another beware of Stamford. I wish you may keep to your resolution of shunning that Place for it will do you immense injury if you do not." Drury, on the other hand, thought he would not get well until he left Helpston and his "low-minded companions".

On April 7th, Taylor acknowledged the receipt of some poems

and an account of Clare's early life which he was to use in his Introduction to *The Village Minstrel.* Taylor remarked that he had never had such strong proof of what Clare was capable of producing in prose, and asked him to send accounts of the origins of his poems, his opinions of books, or passages from his novel of low life.[1] Thus encouraged, Clare's achievements in this, for him, much more difficult art, though fragmentary, are by no means negligible. He had already sent Taylor a long descriptive passage, "The Woodman, or the Beauties of a Winter Forest", and the publisher had been so surprised by its correctness that he had enquired if it was his own composition. Clare was soon busy with a number of projects, some of which never passed the experimental stage. Lack of training in the orderly exposition of ideas was an obstacle which he did not entirely overcome, but in the descriptive and personal prose the gifts of exact observation and clear expression notable in his poetry were ample compensation. Drury, impressed by Clare's progress with prose, advised him to write for some magazine, as Hogg did for *Blackwood's.* On May 1st, Taylor wrote that he would like Clare to try his hand at an article for the *London Magazine*, and would tell him why in his next letter. The reason was that Taylor was on the point of buying the *London* for his firm. Since Scott's death in February, both Hazlitt and Cary had been approached with regard to the editorship, and Cary was quite willing to take the post, should a definite offer be made.

On May 11th Taylor wrote to Clare that they had bought the *London* and there would be a chance of his writing articles for it as well as poetry. There is little doubt that Taylor had already decided to edit it himself; he wrote to Cary on the 18th asking for contributions, but making no mention of the editorship. On the 31st he informed his family that his editorial duties began that day; he looked forward to them with confidence and enthusiasm. The new venture began well; all the old contributors promised their support; and Cary, who had just cause of complaint in Taylor's treatment of the editorship problem, was won over.

With these new duties on his hands, Taylor could find no time for *The Village Minstrel*; yet the season was slipping by;

[1] Probably " 'Cares & Comforts' or 'Notes from the Memoirs of Uncle Barnaby & Family as written by himself' ". Letter to Taylor of January 31st, 1822. Northampton MSS.

within a month, Mrs Emmerson wrote, all the families of consequence who had patronized the first book would be out of Town. In the midst of Clare's anxiety for the fate of his book a second daughter was born on June 2nd, but died soon after. On the 23rd, Hessey wrote apologizing for delay; the book was now ready for the Introduction, which Taylor was too busy to write. On July 5th Hessey sent three copies for the Marquis of Exeter, lacking the Introduction, which was still unfinished. It had been decided to omit a print of Clare's cottage from a drawing by De Wint, intended as a frontispiece to the second volume; the drawing was unsatisfactory. On August 7th, Taylor found time to write; he was still attempting to complete the Introduction. He thought that as the season was now past it was of little consequence whether the book came out then or a month later. On the 29th he wrote that the Introduction was at last completed. It had taken him four months to write it. "I am overworked, and have much more reason than you to think of dying," he commented. He wanted to delay publication until November, but, in view of Clare's distress, decided to issue the book at once. He dwelt on the difficulties of the work; he would have given £100 to anyone who would have taken the editing off his hands. He bade Clare be satisfied: "You have now £45 a year, and reckoning one page monthly in the *London*, £57." Two poems had already been printed in the July and August numbers, and Clare was to have a guinea a page for them. Although thirty poems appeared in the *London* in the next three years, there was no sign of the promised guineas. Clare made a note some time later in his memorandum book: "This year I commenced writing for the *London Magazine* and was to have £12 in addition to my income, but I have not had anything allowed me as yet." In fact, Taylor, business interests multiplying, entirely forgot his promise. There was no mention of this money in the accounts presented in 1829, and Clare had to call Taylor's attention to the omission. The publisher was already finding his new duties a heavy burden; *The Village Minstrel*, a prior obligation, was practically ready for issue before Taylor bought the magazine. Had Clare known that his third book would suffer a delay of as many years as his second had months, he might not have shown the restraint which marks his letter of August 20th:

Your cousin D. fancies I believe that you & I are confederate in dark mysteries about the publication for he grumbled like a bear with a sore head last Friday when I called on him & seemed discomforted I told him I was going to write for the *London* a short while before & I dare say that's what gravels him at all events it will be as beneficial as writing his songs for I've got nought yet either by dedications or music save a small sum which I borrowed at times with the intention of never paying again I will begin a series of Village Sketches for the Mag. as Hessey hinted a while back and you may insert those you have got when you please upon that head.

Your delay makes me swear cursedly at times— that is, grumbling to oneself—for I say little elsewhere. Still I am yours sincerely & affectionately & ever shall be

During the summer months Clare had been busy as usual with harvesting work, but there were respites. Bishop Marsh and Mrs Marsh paid him a visit in July, and in August he visited Whittlebury Forest as the guest of Joseph Bunney, Lieutenant, K.O.S.M., of Silverstone. At last, on September 22nd, he received a dozen copies of *The Village Minstrel*. "The season is sadly against the sale," Mrs Emmerson wrote. Taylor had printed 2,000 copies; by December 1821, 800 had been sold. In March 1822 Hessey wrote, "I am happy to tell you that the *Village Minstrel* continues to sell as well as we could expect"; Taylor was less cheerful: "It is certain that the last work does not take like the first."

It was natural enough that those who had been attracted in 1820 chiefly by the novelty of a peasant-poet should be less interested in Clare now that he was "possessed of a small fortune", "passing rich with forty pounds a years," as one reviewer quoted, forgetting that Goldsmith's preacher would have been much less rich in 1820. Yet the sale of 800 copies in three months—Keats's last book had sold only 500 in eighteen months—seems to indicate that Clare had a public genuinely interested in his poetry; had Taylor been able to publish books as often as Clare could write them, he might well have established himself with his own public, as Wordsworth did with his

between 1820 and 1830. *The Village Minstrel* was less widely reviewed than *Poems Descriptive*, but the reviews were favourable, if more critical. It was recognized by all that Clare had fulfilled promise, had improved on his first book. Reviews appeared in the *New Monthly*, *Literary Chronicle*, *Literary Gazette*, *Gentleman's Magazine*, *European Magazine*, and *Eclectic Review*. The adverse criticism was chiefly of the poet's use of provincialisms, "low and insignificant" words. The *Literary Gazette* also thought that the kind of scenery Clare described—"the rushes, sedges, willow groves and sluggish rivulets of Northamptonshire"—would not excite general interest, and advised him to turn his attention to "landscape of a more sublime and beautiful order".

One reader's critical opinion of *The Village Minstrel* in 1821, a review intended for the *London Magazine* but rejected, Taylor sent to Clare, saying that he had thought that the genius and taste of the poet to whom he had entrusted the task would have had better results. He did not name the writer, but the hand-writing and style identify Allan Cunningham. He found much that was extraordinary and beautiful in the book, but noted obscurity and wordiness in some of the poems, and thought the imagery too confined. He disliked the glossary, assuming that the words in it were the poet's coinings, and suggesting that Burns and Ramsay furnished no excuse, for they were using their native tongue. He was evidently unaware that Clare was doing the same thing. He wished to see in Clare's poetry more human situations and events, more pruning and selection, more action and incident greater elegance and wider use of the established language of poetry.

At the end of this manuscript Clare's comment reveals his ability to distinguish between sound criticism and the abundant irrelevant.

> There are a many just faults found in this Criticism among some trifling—the censures are generaly just & the praises in one or two instances more than I dare or can believe I deserve—his observation that Poets should conform their thoughts or style to the taste of the country by which he means fashion—is humbug & shows that he has no founda-

> tion of judgment for a critic that might be relyed on his lights lead astray[1]

Taylor's Introduction to *The Village Minstrel* was ably written. He quoted freely from Clare's own story of the events which led to the publication of the first book and the raising of the subscription fund, adding, "Money is still a desirable accompaniment, and for want of it our Poets' finances are somewhat too much straitened to support his family with comfort." He also gave Clare's notes on some of the old country sports and customs mentioned in the poems. He put forward a plea for fair criticism rather than indulgence: "the critic is not the poet's superior, though he often affects to be so, on the strength of having had, probably, a better education." There followed a courageous if guarded reference to Keats: "Clare has created more of these never-dying forms, in the personification of things inanimate and abstract—he has scattered them more profusely about our paths, than perhaps any poet of the age except one." He explained in a letter: "I will alter that mention of Keats, for I am not very certain whether it be correct, but if not of him it is not of anyone—[we] will say 'except one,' and leave every man to [suppose] it means his own peculiar favourite." Taylor went on to deplore the illiberal spirit of criticism in late years, which had "let slip the dogs of war in the flowery fields of poesy".

Of the title-poem, begun in the autumn of 1819, Clare has left the following note:

> The encouragement my first volume met with lifted me up into heartsome feelings & rhyming was continually with me night & day I began the "Village Minstrel" a long while before attempting to describe my own feelings & love of rural objects I then began in good earnest with it after the trial of my first poems was made and completed it ... but I was still unsatisfied with it I am now & often feel sorry that I did not withhold it a little longer for revision the reason why I dislike it is that it does not describe the feelings of a rhyming peasant strongly or locally enough ...[2]

[1] Peterborough MSS.
[2] *Ibid.*

Though Clare himself was not satisfied with the vigilance of his eye and the vigour of his descriptions, this long poem on the pleasures, trials, and aspirations of the poetically inclined village boy betrays few of the faults which he found with it in these respects. The whole of this second book was written chiefly "to please myself", Clare indicated on the title-page. He was definitely concerned with the development of his art, as well as with making some money. Contemptuous of conventional phrasing and pen-flourishings, he was concerned to use only the "genuine word", enforced by keen and what he saw as truthful observation, reinforced by passionate necessity to speak. More than once in *The Village Minstrel*, the word he used was so genuine that his editor winced at it, and changed it to one less startling for the age and more vague.

The two books of James Beattie's unfinished epic on a poet's development, *The Minstrel*, had appeared in 1771 and 1774. Beattie's use of the Spenserian stanza influenced Byron's *Childe Harold*, as Beattie's subject influenced Clare. But compared with Beattie's eighteenth-century rhetorical flow and *The Minstrel*'s moral and philosophical undertones, Clare's poem is remarkable for these very characteristics which he was not satisfied about—strength of local colouring, detailed observation in nineteenth-century English country custom and landscape, and integrity of emotional description. There were, of course, suggestions that he copied Beattie, but, except that he used the Spenserian stanza, there is nothing in the two poems to compare. Clare's poetic achievement in his *Village Minstrel* was very much his own.

His creed was by no means yet entire, or entirely his own. Among the shorter poems of the book there are reminders of John Dyer's "Grongar Hill", of Kirke White's "Solitude", faint echoes of Samuel Wesley's metres and fainter still, of Smart's versions of the Psalms, which had been reviewed side by side with *Poems Descriptive* in the *London Magazine*. Many of *The Village Minstrel* poems were written before his first book was published and belong to his apprenticeship period.

Among the poems of the second volume of *The Village Minstrel* are sixty sonnets. We may fall foul of the academician by using the term. Clare knew nothing of octave and sestet, and only a little about presentation and application of idea, pause and continuity. In these sixty sonnets he used thirty-six different rhyme-schemes, ranging from rhymed couplets through the Spenserian and Shakespearian forms to combinations as intricate as the Petrarch model. He did not always discipline himself within fourteen lines; some of his later "sonnets" had twelve or sixteen. Do Clare's sonnets lack "adequacy of sonnet-motive", as William Sharp noted in his *Sonnets of this Century*? Sharp did not seek the best, where there *is* adequacy.

Clare was not using the sonnet form chiefly for its principle of emotional compression. He was experimenting with fourteen lines, linked into a stanza by some system of rhyme which served as a frame for a scene—of "Hillywood", "Summer Tints", "A Lair at Noon", "Pleasures Past", or "A Wild Nosegay". He was using the form pictorially; yet it would be misleading to say that the pictures have no emotional significance. In the best of these sonnets there are pen-paintings, finished, richly coloured, conceived and given with impassioned selection and clarity for "most innocent enjoyment". Their "realism", so different from Dyer's, Beattie's or Crabbe's, was individual in the day's verse.

While Clare was trying his hand at these sonnet experiments, or at a kind of poem which Smart had composed almost inimitably before him, he was working out another part of his contribution toward the poetry of his day. Besides the characteristics already mentioned concerning the poem "The Village Minstrel", there glows in all the poems in this volume a delight in every hour, however commonplace to the countryman's mind, however trivial or gloomy to the townsman's, in the four seasons. A world crowded with creature-loves and full of united sources of joy was revealed: cowslips are "bowing adorers of the gale"; habits of a butterfly:

> Oft Ive seen thy little leg
> Soft as glass oer velvet slides
> Smoothen down thy silken sides[1]

Burns, Thomson or Cowper had not seen the thousand and one things Clare saw. He was determined that neither "cant" nor "conceit" in his art nor any artifice should stand between his vision and the reader. The world he had introduced to the

[1] Peterborough MSS.

poetry-reading public in his first book was more accurately and more deliberately disclosed in *The Village Minstrel*. This is what was new.

In October John Taylor, returning to London after a visit to his family, spent a day with Clare at Helpston. Taylor wrote an account of this visit for the November *London Magazine*, in the form of a letter to the editor, headed "Wansford, October 12th, 1821". He combined a picture of Clare at home and observations on his character with a notice of *The Village Minstrel*, from which he quoted extensively.

Taylor tells how he met Clare, who was not aware of his coming, on the Roman road, King Street, about a mile from the village. He was going with Patty and her sister to a Michaelmas reunion of the Turner family at Casterton, intending to call first at Burghley House for his quarter's salary. Clare turned back with his guest, but, before returning to the village, they paid a visit to Lolham Bridges, where King Street crosses the flood-meadows and marshes of the Welland. Taylor was interested to look on the scene of the poem "The Last of March", and noted with wonder what Clare's eye and imagination had revealed in this "dull line of ponds, or rather one continued marsh, over which a succession of arches carries the narrow highway". Retracing their steps, they saw in the distance Langley Bush, that ancient landmark which had sheltered so many generations of shepherds and gipsies. Referring to Clare's poem on this old whitethorn, Taylor wrote:

> The discretion which makes Clare hesitate to receive as canonical all the accounts he has heard of the former honours of Langley Bush, is in singular contrast with the enthusiasm of his poetical faith. As a man, he cannot bear to be imposed upon—his good sense revolts at the least attempt to abuse it;—but as a poet, he surrenders his imagination with most happy ease to the illusions which crowd upon it from stories of fairies and ghosts. The effect of this distinction is soon felt in a conversation with him. From not considering it, many persons express their surprise that Clare should be so weak on some topics and so wise on others. But a willing indulgence of what they term weakness is the evidence of a strong mind. He feels safe there, and luxuriates in the

> abandonment of the sober sense for a time, to be the sport of all the tricks and fantasies that have been attributed to preternatural agency. Let them address him on other subjects, and unless they entrench themselves in forms of language to which he is unaccustomed, or take no pains to understand him according to the sense rather than the letter of his speech, they will confess, that to keep fairly on a level with him in the depth and tenour of their remarks, is an exercise requiring more than common effort. He may not have read the books which they are familiar with, but let them try him on such as he has read, (and the number is not few, especially of the modern poets,) and they will find no reason to undervalue his judgment. His language, it is true, is provincial, and his choice of words in ordinary conversation is indifferent, because Clare is an unpretending man, and he speaks in the idiom of his neighbours, who would ridicule and despise him for using more or better terms than they are familiar with. But the philosophic mind will strive to read his thoughts, rather than catch at the manner of their utterance; and will delight to trace the native nobleness, strength, and beauty of his conceptions, under the tattered garb of what may, perhaps, be deemed uncouth and scanty expressions.

On the white-washed wall of the cottage living-room Taylor noticed the water-colour of Clare's portrait by Hilton which the artist had copied and sent as a present to Parker Clare. Parker was in the garden, hobbling on two sticks, too crippled to kneel or stoop. While Taylor talked to him, Clare prepared a meal of bread and cheese, with beer from the Blue Bell.

> In the midst of our operations, his little girl awoke, a fine lively pretty creature, with a forehead like her father's, of ample promise. She tottered along the floor and ... her father looked after her with the fondest affection, and with a careful twitch of his eyebrow when she seemed in danger.

They next examined Clare's library, where Taylor noticed the works of Burns, Cowper, Wordsworth, Coleridge, Keats, Crabbe, and about twenty of Cooke's poets. Most were presentation volumes, and their handsome bindings and gilded letters made a brave show in the cottage, which "except in cleanliness" was "no whit superior to the habitations of the poorest of the peasantry".

Taylor and Clare walked together as far as Barnack, pausing on the way before several of the scenes described in *The Village Minstrel*. They parted at the top of Barnack Hill, Clare going on on foot to Casterton and Taylor to Wansford to await the London coach.

Early in November, Taylor sent news of some of the *Londoners*—Cary, Reynolds, and Allan Cunningham. Cunningham was one of Taylor's closest friends at this time, but Clare had not yet met him. Following the custom of Murray, Blackwood and other publishers of the day, Taylor had already instituted those dinner-parties at which the contributors of the *London Magazine* met to drink, talk and jest together. Richard Woodhouse, in his "Notes of Conversations with Thomas De Quincey", mentions dinners at Taylor's and De Wint's in November and December, attended by De Quincey, Reynolds, Lamb, Cunningham, Rice, Hood, Wainewright, Talfourd, Dr Darling and others. On December 8th Taylor read to his visitors part of a letter from Clare, to whom he had sent Wordsworth's poems. "I like Wordsworth better than Crabbe," wrote Clare. "I can read the one a second time over with added pleasure, but I am disgusted with the other after it has been once read. Still Wordsworth's nursery ballads inspire me with an uncontrollable itch of parodying them; I did ease myself by burlesquing one, which you shall have in my next." De Quincey wondered at the comparison between Wordsworth and Crabbe, who had nothing in common; Crabbe was no poet at all, and Wordsworth's apparent simplicity was subtle, deep insight. Clare referred to his itch for parody in a later letter:[1]

> Do you mistake my imitation of W. W. as a serious attempt in his manner—twas written in ridicule of his affectations of simplicity— & I had thoughts of imitating the styles of all the living poets as I got hold of them to read them nor has the thought left me yet—Southey & Crabb I fancy I can do to a tittle the ones affectation in mouthing over big

[1] February 21st, 1822.

> words & the others tedious prosing over trifles often border on the ridiculous tho they are both great men & geniuses as I venerate & esteem[1]

Toward the end of the year Clare asked Taylor if he could advance his dividend money. After some delay, Taylor sent the £10 on December 17th, and promised Earl Spencer's £5 and 6 guineas for the magazine poems in a few days. The former arrived on January 30th, the latter not at all. The comparative failure of *The Village Minstrel* was now apparent enough; the news merely stirred Clare to renewed activity; he was "determined in the teeth of vexation to surmount disappointment by unwearied struggles". "I am all madness for writing," he wrote in January, "but how long it's to last I don't know." He was then busy with a love-tale in the measure of Spenser, a novel of village life, a dramatic pastoral, and several long poems for the *London Magazine*.

Clare continued to feel the need for congenial company as relief from writing and solitary rambles. He sometimes went over to Stamford, where the Gilchrists were always glad to see him. He visited the Simpson family, Mrs Gilchrist's relatives, and became very friendly with her nephews, Frank and Octavius Simpson, both young art students at this time. Clare did not go to Drury's as often as formerly. In January 1822 he spent three pleasant days with Artis at Milton, inspecting the remains of a Roman bath and pavement which he had recently unearthed. These visits could not entirely compensate for the lack of congenial society at Helpston; isolation had become much more marked since his success.

> I live here among the ignorant like a lost man in fact like one whom the rest seems careless of having anything to do with—they hardly dare talk in my company for fear I shoud mention them in my writings & I find more pleasure in wandering the fields then in mixing among my silent neighbours who are insensible of everything but toiling & talking of it & that to no purpose[2]

[1] *The Letters of John Clare, op. cit.*
[2] *Ibid.*

On one occasion he evidently tried to break down the barriers between himself and his neighbours, with not very happy results. Mrs Emmerson wrote:

> You tell me by an act of inebriety you have made yourself 'ridiculous and have been suffering for it this week past.' Why suffer the goodness of your heart to mislead your understanding by taking you into society no longer suited to your situation and pursuits in life? Why not, (if they were your once fellow-labourers), give them a trifle to enjoy themselves in their own way—they would feel equally grateful to you for it.

Clare had certainly realized by this time that a draught of "John Barleycorn" was for him a poor remedy for an overdose of solitude, but he could not have followed this condescending advice. Occasions when he sought release in conviviality were followed by remorse, which, like Bunyan's, were out of all proportion to the gravity of the offence. There is a glimpse of the effect of such a mood in the poem "The Dream", written for the February *London* and included later in *The Shepherd's Calendar*. It gives a picture of the world dissolving into chaos amid the fury of the elements, and of the poet's terror as hell yawned for his damned soul.[1]

Clare's extraordinary literary activity during December 1821 and January 1822 was partly inspired by his desire to raise some money to help his old acquaintances, the jovial brothers Billings, who had had to mortgage their property, "Bachelors Hall" with its seven-acre farm, to a Jew, and they could not pay the interest. Clare wanted to take over the mortgage and set up a "Poet's Hall". He could not use his Fund money for the purpose, so he proposed to sell his interest in his poems for five years for £200. Taylor refused the offer, and pointed out the risky nature of the proposed transaction, which could benefit Clare little at the

[1] It is a macabre poem, describing such a burning up of all life as might be supposed to happen in nuclear war: "lightnings", "purple flame", "leaving earth as desolate as hell". "The Nightmare", not printed until 1935, is a similar poem: "A nightmare mystery of a sealing doom/ A feeble picture of the dread to come." For an understanding of Clare's imagination these can be read with his dream in prose of 1832.

best. Clare's disappointment was eased when Lord Milton came to the rescue and *lent* £20 to pay off interest on the debt.

The urgent need of his old friends and the excitement of a creative mood had as usual tempted Clare to overwork. With the passing of the mood he suffered inevitable reaction. "I mustn't do no more terrible things yet," he wrote to Taylor in February, referring to "The Dream";[1]

> they stir me up to such a pitch that leaves a disrelish for my old accustomd wanderings after nature ... the Muse is a fickle Hussey with me she sometimes stilts me up to Madness & then leaves me as a beggar by the way side with no more life then whats mortal & that nearly extinguishd by mellancholy forbodings.

This mood persisted throughout February and March, and his dissatisfaction at his idleness did not improve it. On March 16th, 1822, he wrote of the

> confounded lethargy of low spirits that presses on me to such a degree that at times makes me feel as if my senses had a mind to leave me Spring & Fall such feelings it seems are doomd to be my companions but it shall not overpower me as formerly with such weak & terrible dreads & fears of dropping off when death comes he will come & while lifes mine I'll make the best of it[2]

Realizing that he needed a change of scene and company as well as a rest, he wished London were nearer. In April Mrs Emmerson wrote entreating him to pay them a visit; she had recently moved to a house in Stratford Place, and he should have "the most elevated spot in the house"—his "sky-chamber", they later called it. Clare was only too eager to accept, and when Hessey also wrote assuring him that they would be glad to see him, and enclosing £5 for his expenses, Clare set out on his second visit to London.

[1] *The Letters of John Clare, op. cit.*
[2] *Ibid.*

CHAPTER TEN

The Wits: 1822-1824

Clare travelled up alone to London toward the end of the third week in May. Gilchrist had been ill for some time and could not accompany him. Clare's first visit had been too brief to give him assurance in the whirl of the metropolis and allay his country suspicions; on arriving this second time he was said to have denied himself to the messenger sent by Taylor to conduct him to Fleet Street. Here he remained for the first few days, and became more familiar with his surroundings.

> On my second visit things became more distinct or separate on the memory and one of my greatest wonders then was the continual stream of life passing up and down the principal streets all the day long and even the night one of my most entertaining amusements was to sit by Taylors window in Fleet Street to see the constant successions throng this way and that way[1]

Further acquaintance with the methods of London tradesmen did not allay his suspicions of them.

> I observed it was always a custom in most shops that when you went in to ask for an article the thing they first shewed you was always put on one side and another recommended as superior which I found was always to the contrary so experience taught me always in future to take the one thing they did not recommend[2]

He did not forget to send home presents for the family,

[1] Peterborough MSS.
[2] *Ibid.*

ome dress material for Patty and Sophy, "two very
atures on that point, as I have before experienced."
r to take care of the Doves," he added in his letter.
hrist was well enough to join him in London, they
ng together.

> ... he took me to see Gifford who the first time we went up was too ill to see us but this time he was rather getting near neighbour to health & gave me welcome with a hearty shake of the hand & congratulated me on my last poems (the Village Minstrel, just published) which he said were far better then my first he also bade me beware of the booksellers & repeated it several times he was sitting on his sofa surrounded with books & papers of all sorts He chatted awhile to Gilchrist about Books and Authors and Pope & lent him a New Satire to read called the "Mohawks"[1] in which he said he was mentioned he supposed Lady Morgan was the Author & after Gilchrist had dipped into it here & there he pronounced it worthless—the next day we went to call on Murray in Albemarle Street who flatterd me with some compliments on my success & hoped that I woud always call on him whenever I came to London he is a very pleasant man he showed us the English Bards & Scotch Reviewers illustrated with Portraits which we turned over & departed & as we got at the door Giffords carriage drove up & on leaving the shop he gave each of us a copy of his Translations of Persius[2]

Gifford's warning about booksellers was no doubt directed against Taylor in particular; there was no love lost between the editor of the *Quarterly* and the publisher of Keats's poems.

When Clare had been at Fleet Street a few days, he heard from Mrs Emmerson, who begged him to go and stay with her, adding that Rippingille was there. Edward Villiers Rippingille

[1] Mohawks, or Mohocks, were aristocratic, lawless young men who infested London's theatres and streets in the eighteenth century; Mohocks was also the name given to Blackwood's writers. Lady Sydney Morgan (1783?–1859), or Sydney Owenson, wrote her *Book without a Name* about her travels in France. Her satirical poem, "The Mohawks", was published in 1822.

[2] Peterborough MSS. Gifford translated Juvenal (1802) and Persius (1821).

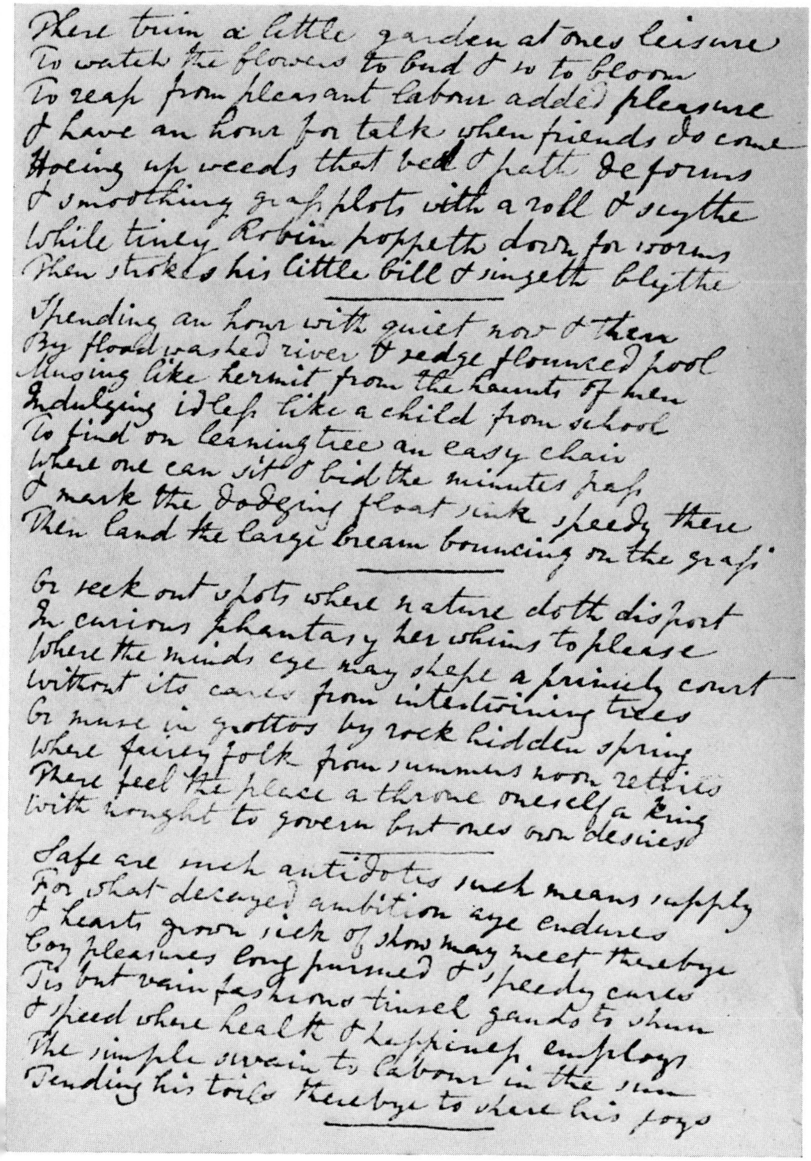
There trim a little garden at ones leisure
To watch the flowers to bud & so to bloom
To reap from pleasant labour added pleasure
& have an hour for talk when friends do come
Hoeing up weeds that bed & path deforms
& smoothing grassplots with a roll & scythe
While tiney Robin poppeth down for worms
Then strokes his little bill & singeth blythe

Spending an hour with quiet now & then
By flood washed river & sedge flounced pool
Musing like hermit from the haunts of men
Indulging idless like a child from school
To find on leaning tree an easy chair
Where one can sit & bid the minutes pass
& mark the dodging float sink speedy there
Then land the large bream bouncing on the grass

Or seek out spots where nature doth disport
In curious phantasy her whims to please
Where the minds eye may shape a princely court
Without its cares from intertwining trees
Or muse in grottos by rock hidden spring
Where fairey folk from summers noon retires
There feel the place a throne oneself a king
With nought to govern but ones own desires

Safe are such antidotes such means supply
For what decayed ambition aye endures
& hearts grown sick of show may meet thereby
Coy pleasures long pursued & speedy cures
Tis but vain fashions tinsel gauds to shun
& speed where health & happiness employs
The simple swain to labour in the sun
Tending his toils thereby to share his joys

page from one of Clare's fair copies of the 1820s (By kind permission of the Peterborough Museum Society)

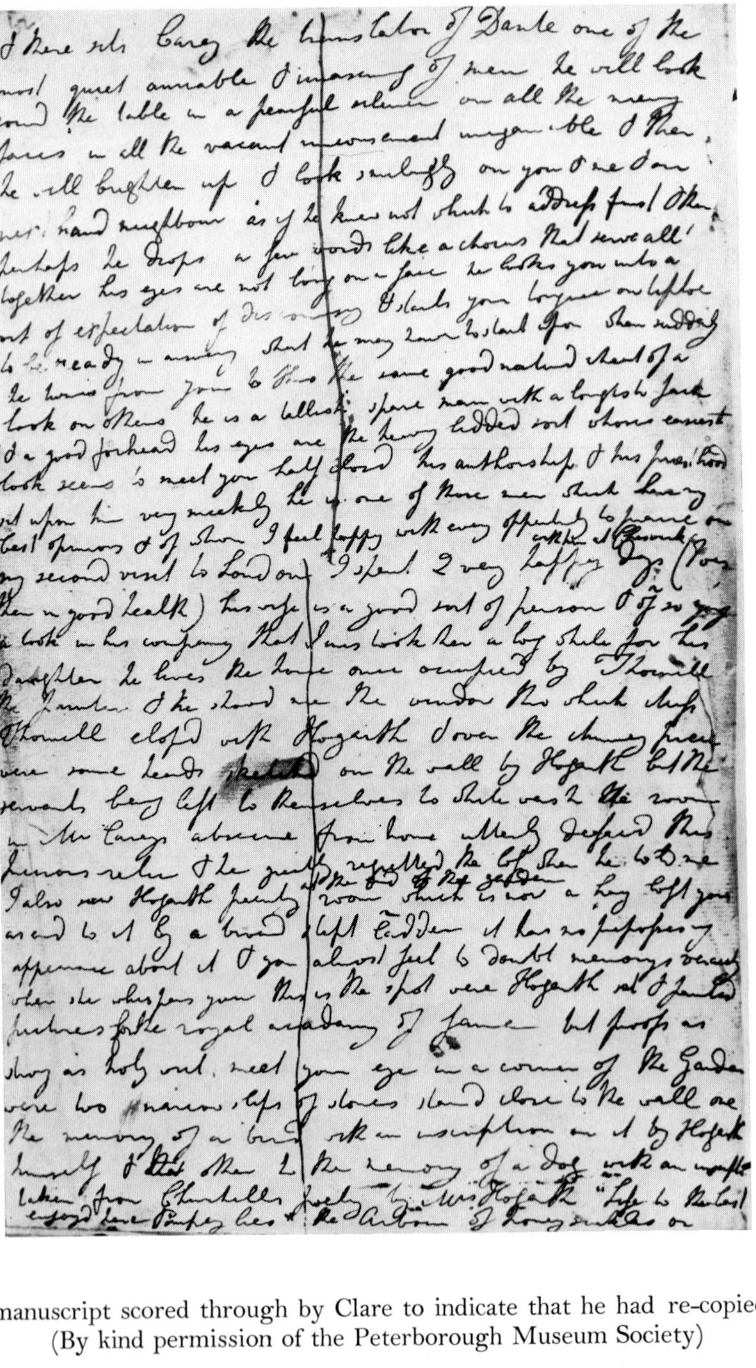
& there sits Cary the translator of Dante one of the
most quiet amiable & unassuming of men he will look
round the table in a fearful silence on all the merry
faces in all the vacant unconcernd unyealdable & then
he will brighten up & look smilingly on you & me & one
near hand neighbour as if he knew not which to address first & then
perhaps he drops a few words like a chorus that serves all
together his eyes are not long on a face he looks you into a
sort of expectation of discoursing & starts your tongue on tiptoe
to be ready in answering what he may have to start upon when suddenly
he turns from you to throw the same good naturd start of a
look on others he is a tallish spare man with a longish face
& a good forehead his eyes are the heavy lidded sort whose earnest
look seems to meet you half closed his authorship & his priesthood
sit upon him very meekly he is one of those men which heavy
best opinions & of whom I feel happy with every opportunity to praise on
my second visit to London I spent 2 very happy days (I was
then in good health) with him at Chiswick his wife is a good sort of person & of so gay
a look in his company that I was took her a long while for his
daughter he lives the house once occupied by Thornhill
the painter & he showd me the window thro which Miss
Thornhill eloped with Hogarth & over the chimney piece
were some heads sketched on the wall by Hogarth but the
servants being left to themselves to white wash the room
in Mr Carys absence from home utterly defaced this
precious relic & he greatly regretted the loss when he told me
I also saw Hogarth painting room at the end of the garden which is now a hay loft you
ascend to it by a broad step ladder it has no pretensions of
appearance about it & you almost feel to doubt memorys veracity
when she whispers you this is the spot were Hogarth sat & painted
pictures for the royal academy of fame but proofs as
strong as holy writ meet your eye in a corner of the Garden
were two narrow slips of stones stand close to the wall one
the memory of a bird with an inscription on it by Hogarth
himself & that other 2 the memory of a dog with an inscription
taken from Churchills poetry by Mrs Hogarth "Life to the last
enjoyd here Pompey lies" & the arbour of honeysuckles on

A manuscript scored through by Clare to indicate that he had re-copied
(By kind permission of the Peterborough Museum Society)

was a native of King's Lynn, son of a farmer, and a self-taught artist. His pictures of rural and domestic life, "Scene in a Gaming House", "Country Post Office", "Going to the Fair", "The Recruiting Party", brought him some renown as a reward for his early struggles. Mrs Emmerson had met him in Bristol, where he lived at this time, and he had visited her in 1821. She could not persuade him at first that Clare's poetry was as worthy of admiration as that of Burns. Then he had been won over and sought all over London for a book to send to Clare, the *Remains of Nithsdale and Galloway Song*, for which Allan Cunningham had been partly responsible. Clare had, as has been told, seen some of Rippingille's pictures years before. In his account of his visit to Wisbech, he tells of a shop-window full of the pictures of a painter then teaching drawing in that town.

Clare and Rippingille struck up a friendship, and on this second, as on Clare's third, visit to London, in each other's company they visited playhouses, inns, and boxing-booths, as well as the picture galleries and houses of Rippingille's fellow-artists. Clare liked the man for his lively and generous temperament, was amused by his affectations as the artist and man-about-town, and admired his paintings.

> He is a rattling sort of odd fellow with a desire to be thought one & often affects to be so for the sake of singularity ... he is a man of great genius as a painter & what is better he has not been puffed into notice like thousands of farthing rush lights (like myself perhaps) in all professions that have glimmered their day & are dead I spent many pleasant hours with him while in London his greatest rellish is punning over a bottle of ale for he is a strong dealer in puns we acted a many of lifes farces & crackt a many jokes together many of them bad ones perhaps & without kernels & we once spent a whole night at Offleys the Burton ale house & sat till morning he has some pretensions to ryhme & wrote An Address to Eccho which was inserted in the London Mag[1] most of his "Trifles" in that way are satirical I was to have gone over to Bristol to see

[1] In the August number, 1824—an ingenious piece of punning.

> him but illness prevented me he affected to be little taen with worldly applause & was always fishing for it—he was very careless of money & squandered it away as a thing of no other use but to spend[1]

Several times Clare couples Rippingille's name with De Wint's in his esteem of their painting, praising the "grouping of peasantry" of the one and the landscape of the other for their realism. "Nobody has such a true English conception of real pastoral life and reality of English manners and English beauty as Rippingille, and the poesy of painting is breathing in every story he shadows on the canvas."

They corresponded for some years; Rippingilles' lively, fly-away letters are typical of the man. He lectured and wrote on art in later years, started the *Artists' and Amateurs' Magazine* in 1843, and became a champion of orthodoxy against Pre-Raphaelitism and the author of *Modern Painters*.

When Clare could not find a conductor, his excursions were necessarily more limited.

> I did not know the way to any place for a long while but the royal academy & here I used to go almost every day as Rippingille the painter had told the ticket keeper who I was & he let me come in when ever I chose which I often made use of from nessesity altho I had conquered the old notion of kidnappers or menstealers being common[2]

But the most memorable events of his stay in London were his meetings with "those former wonders of Poets, Painters, and Authors of all denominations", the contributors to the *London Magazine*. The early months of 1822 marked the zenith of the *Magazine* under Taylor's editorship. Foremost among the regular contributors were Lamb, Hazlitt, Cary, Allan Cunningham, Thomas Hood, Hartley Coleridge, Charles Abraham Elton and Clare himself. There were also occasional poems or essays by John Hamilton ("Peter Corcoran") Reynolds, Brian Walker Procter, Thomas Noon Talfourd, James Montgomery,

[1] Peterborough MSS.
[2] *Ibid.*

and a poem or two of John Taylor's own, one at least to Isabella Jones who had also been a friend of Keats's. Of the more famous names we miss only De Quincey's: his first contribution for the year was in December.

Most of these contributors attended the monthly dinners at Waterloo Place, where, as Barry Cornwall has chronicled, "all the fences and restraints of authorship were cast off, and the natural human being was disclosed." Clare, of course, was one of the guests when he was in London, and he met some of his fellow-contributors on other occasions. He visited Hilton and Lamb, dined at Wainewright's, and spent two days with Cary at Chiswick; there were doubtless other visits not recorded. After his third visit in 1824, Clare jotted down his impressions of the *Londoners* he had met, and these jottings, rough and fragmentary as they are, give vivid and intimate pictures of some of that band of writers who talked and jested together round the dinner-table at Waterloo Place.

> One of my greatest amusements while in London was reading the booksellers windows—I was always fond of this from a boy—& my next greatest amusement was the curiosity of seeing literary men of these ... I shall give a few pictures just as they struck me at the time some of them I went purposely to see others I met in literary parties that is the confused[1] contributors dinners at Taylor and Hesseys I had no means of meeting the constellations of Genius in one mass They were mingld parties some few were fixd stars in the Worlds hemisphere others glimmered every month in the Magazine some were little vapours that were content to shine by the light of others I mean dabbling critics that cut monthly morsels from genius whose works are on the waters free for all to catch at that chuses These bye the bye I coud observe had a selfsatisfaction about them that magnifyd molehills to mountains I mean that little self was in its own eye a giant & that every other object was mere nothing I shall not mention names here but it is evident I do not allude to friends[2]

[1] The word might be "confounded".
[2] Peterborough MSS.

This introduction is followed by a description of J. H. Reynolds, who, despite his prudent but oft-regretted "Farewell to the Muses" in 1818, continued to express his versatility in verse and prose. Clare's richly detailed picture may be compared with those of other observers. Barry Cornwall recorded that Reynold's "Good temper and vivacity were like condiments at the feast", and Keats's friend Woodhouse wrote, "Reynolds when in fine cue, and amongst friends, is equally ready and lavish in his wit, sporting it extempore on every subject and with astonishing good humour and freedom from acrimony and personality." Clare recorded:

> Reynolds was always the soul of these dinner partys he was the most good natured fellow I ever met with his face was the three-in-one of fun wit & punning personified he woud punch you with his puns without ever hurting your feelings for if you lookd in his face you coud not be offended & you might retort as you pleasd nothing coud put him out of humour either with himself or others if all his jokes & puns & witticisms were written down which were utterd at two or three of these dinner partys they woud make one of the best Joe Millers[1] that have ever passd under that title he sits as a carless listener at table looking on with quick knaping sort of eye that turns towards you as quick as lightning when he has a pun joke or story to give you they are never made up or studied they are the flashes of the moment & mostly happy he is a slim sort of make somthing as you may conceive of an unpretending sort of fashionable fellow without the desire of being one he has a plump round face a nose somthing puggish & a forehead that betrays more of fun then poetry his teeth are always looking through a laugh that sits as easy on his unpuckerd lips as if he was born laughing he is a man of genius & if his talents were properly applied he woud do somthing I verily believe that he might win the favours of fame with a pun—but be as it will wether she is inclined to smile or frown upon him he is quite at home wi content the present is all with him he carrys none

[1] *Joe Miller's Jests* was compiled by John Mottley, and published in 1739. The original Joe Miller (1684–1738) was an actor in the Drury Lane company, a humorist of repute.

> of the Author about him a hearty laugh which there is no resisting at his jokes & puns seems to be more reccompense then he expected & he seems startld into wonder by it & muses a moment as if he turnd the joke over agen in his mind to find the "merry thought" which made the laughter they drop as it were spontaneously from his mouth & turn agen upon him before he has had time to consider wether they are good or bad he sits in a sort of surprise till another joke drops & makes him himself again ... he is one of the best fellows living & ought to be a poet of the first order—himself is his only hindrance at present[1]

Reynolds's impression of Clare was written with a sonnet in a copy of *The Rural Muse*, which he gave to a niece in 1843:

> I knew Clare well, and from the first hour of his escape from oppression, poverty and ignorance (except through the inspiration and observation of nature) he was a quiet and worthy yet enthusiastic man; ... a guileless yet suspicious man; ... a true observer of nature in her generous earth-work and waterwork, but a man alive to more ... than town apprehensions ...

Clare also had his place in that quip of Reynolds's, "The Literary Police Office, Bow Street", which appeared as an "Edward Herbert" letter in the *London* for February 1823. Writers of the day were described as appearing before the magistrate, charged with various extravagant offences:

> John Clare (a comely country-looking man, in a smock frock, and a face to match) appeared to resist an order of filiation, made on the affidavit of one of the Muses with whom he had kept company, and who appeared to have been too liberal of her favours to him. The oath being persisted in, his innocence stood him in no stead; and he was ordered to set apart half-a-crown, out of sixpence a day, to support the child. He pleaded poverty; but the magistrates explained

[1] Peterborough MSS.: two of three fragments in *The Prose of John Clare*, edited by J. W. and Anne Tibble (Routledge and Kegan Paul, 1951).

> to him that a poor soldier had been known to have managed such an allowance, and therefore they resisted his plea. Clare is said to have a wife, and ten little children all under the age of four years, which makes his case more reprehensible.

Clare's friend, Gilchrist, was also in court and "gave information of having been shot at while playing a game at Bowles, in his garden at Stamford".

Struck by the contrast between the two men, Clare followed his account of Reynolds with a sketch of Hazlitt, who must have attended one of the dinners during Clare's visit. Hazlitt was in London for a week towards the end of May, correcting the second volume of *Table Talk* for the press; his habitual shyness and his silence at the dinners, noted by Barry Cornwall, may well have been accentuated by the distressing experiences he was passing through at this period.

> Hazlitt is the very reverse of this he sits a silent picture of severity if you was to watch his face for a month you woud not catch a smile there his eyes are always turnd towards the ground except when one is turnd up now & then with a sneer that cuts a bad pun & a young authors maiden table talk to atoms w[h]erever it is directed I look upon it that it carries the conviction with it of a look to the wise & a nodd to the foolish he seems full of the Author too & I verily believe that his pockets are crambd with it he seems to look upon Mr This & Mr Tother names that are only living on Cards of Morning Calls & Dinner Invitations as upon empty chairs as the guests in Macbeth did on the vacancy w[h]ere Banquos ghost presided they appear in his eye as nothings too thin for sight & when he enters a room he comes stooping with his eyes in his hands as it were throwing under gazes round at every corner as if he smelt a dun or thief ready to seize him by the colar & demand his money or his life he is a middle sizd dark looking man & his face is deeply lined with a satirical character his eyes are bright but they are rather buried under his brows he is a walking satire & you woud wonder w[h]ere his poetry came from that is scatterd so thickly over his

writings for the blood of me I coud not find him out that is I shoud have had no guess at him of his ever being a scribbler much more a genius they say she is an odd lady & sure enough in him her odditys are strongly personified ...[1]

Leaving the enigma of Hazlitt, Clare passed, by way of another contrast, to a *Londoner* with whom he felt much more at ease. 1822 was a busy year for Charles Lamb; it was the last of the three years which produced such a remarkable harvest of essays. Lamb was beginning to tire and to think seriously of leaving the India House, yet the essays continued to grace the pages of the *London*. At the time of Clare's visit Charles and Mary were on the eve of their journey to France, which Lamb mentions in his letter to Clare. They saw each other several times during the month; meetings at Taylor's, Wainewright's, Cary's, and Lamb's are recorded.[2]

Of Lamb Clare wrote:

... then there is Charles Lamb a long remove from his friend Hazlitt in ways & manners he is very fond of snuff which seems to sharpen up his wit every time he dips his plentiful finger into his large bronze colourd box & then he sharpens up his head thros himself backwards in his chair & stammers at a joke or pun with an inward sort of utterance ere he can give it speech till his tongue becomes a sort of Packman's strop[3] turning it over & over till at last it comes out wetted as keen as a razor & expectation when she knows him wakens into a sort of danger as bad as cutting your throat but he is a good sort of fellow & if he offends it is innosently done who is not acquainted with Elia & who woud believe him otherwise as soon as the cloath is drawn the wine & he become comfortable his talk now doubles & threbles into a combination a repetition urging the same thing over & over again till at last he leaves off with

[1] *The Prose of John Clare*, edited by J. W. and Anne Tibble, *op. cit.*

[2] Lamb's earliest recorded reference to Clare is in a letter to B. W. Procter in the spring of 1821: "*The Wits* (as Clare calls us) assemble at my Cell ... this evening at ¼ before 7."

[3] Charles Johnson's suggestion that Clare meant to write "Packwood's" (Packwood being then famous for the poetical advertisements of his strops) is perhaps right.

> scarcely a 'goodnight' in his mouth & dissapears leaving his memory like a pleasant ghost hanging about his vacant chair & there is his sister Bridget a good sort of woman tho her kind cautions & tender admonitions are nearly lost upon Charles who like an undermined river bank leans carelessly over his jollity & recieves the gentle lappings of the waves of womans tongue unheedingly till it ebbs & then in the same careless posture sits & recieves it again tho it is all lost upon Charles she is a good woman & her cautions are very commendable for the New River runs very near his house & the path for a dark night is but very precarious to make the best of it & he hearty fellow is not always blind to dangers so I hope the advice of his sister Bridget will be often taken in time to retire with the cloth & see home by daylight[1]

It is clear from Clare's last remarks here that he had his third visit to London (1824) in mind; the Lambs did not move from Great Russell Street to Colebrooke Cottage until 1823. Thomas Hood has left a lively picture of Clare and Lamb hobnobbing at a *London Magazine* dinner:

> On the right hand of the Editor sits Elia, of the pleasant smile, and the quick eyes – Procter said of them that 'they looked as if they could pick up pins and needles,' – and a wit as quick as his eyes, and sure, as Hazlitt described, to stammer out the best pun and the best remark in the course of the evening. Next to him, shining verdantly out from the grave-coloured suits of the literati, like a patch of turnips amidst stubble and fallow, behold our Jack i' the Green – John Clare! In his bright, grass-coloured coat, and yellow waistcoat (there are greenish stalks too, under the table), he looks a very Cowslip, and blooms amongst us as Goldsmith must have done in his peach-blossom. No wonder the door-keeper of the Soho-bazaar, seeing that *very countrified* suit, linked arm-in-arm with the Editorial sables, made a boggle at admitting them into his repository, having seen, perchance, such a made up Peasant 'playing at playing,' at

[1] *The Prose of John Clare, op. cit.* Peterborough MSS.

thimble-rig about the Square. No wonder the gentleman's gentleman, in the drab coat and sealing-wax smalls, at W——'s [Wainewright's] was for cutting off our Green Man, who was modestly the last in ascending the stairs, as an interloper, though he made amends afterwards by waiting almost exclusively on the Peasant, perfectly convinced that he was some eccentric Notable of the Corinthian order, disguised in Rustic. Little wonder either, that in wending homewards on the same occasion through the strand, the Peasant and Elia, *Sylvanus et Urban*, linked comfortably together; there arose the frequent cry 'Look at Tom and Jerry – there goes Tom and Jerry!'[1] For truly, Clare in his square-cut green coat, and Lamb in his black, were not a little suggestive of Hawthorn and Logic in the plates to 'Life in London.'

But to return to the table. Elia – much more of House Lamb than of Grass Lamb – avowedly caring little or nothing for Pastoral cottons nevertheless, very kindly to the Northamptonshire Poet, and still more to his ale, pledging him again and again as 'Clarissimus', and 'Princely Clare', and sometimes so lustily, as to make the latter cast an anxious glance into his tankard. By his bright happy looks the Helpstone Visitor is inwardly contrasting the unlettered country company of Clod, and Hodge and Podge, with the delights of 'London' society, Elia, and Barry, and Herbert, and Mr. 'Table Talk,' *cum multis aliis* – i.e. a multiplicity of all.

But besides the tankard, the two 'drouthie neebors' discuss Poetry in general and Montgomery's 'Common Lot' in particular, Lamb insisting on the beauty of the tangental sharp turn at 'O! She was fair!' thinking, mayhap, of his own Alice W——, and Clare swearing 'Dal!' (A clarified damn) 'Dal! if it isn't like a Dead Man preaching out of his coffin!' Anon the Humourist begins to banter the Peasant on certain 'Clare-obscurities' in his own verses, originating in a contempt for the rules of Priscian,[2] whereupon the accused, thinking with Burns,

[1] Riotous characters from *Life in London* (1821) by Pierce Egan (1772–1849).
[2] The Roman grammarian (*fl.* A.D. 450) honoured in the Middle Ages. *Prisciani Grammatici* was much reprinted.

What ser'es their grammars?
They'd better ta'en up spades and shools,
Or knappin hammers,

vehemently denounces all Philology as nothing but a sort of man-trap for authors, and heartily 'dals' Lindley Murray[1] for 'inventing it.'

Hood continues:

It must have been at such a time when Hilton conceived his clever portrait of C——, when he was 'C in alt.' He was hardy, rough, and clumsy enough to look rustic—like an Ingram's rustic chair. There was a slightness about his frame, with a delicacy of features and complexion, that associated him more with the Garden than the Field, and made him look the Peasant of a Ferme Ornée. In this respect he was as much beneath the genuine stalwart bronzed Plough-poet, Burns, as above the Farmer's Boy, whom I remember to have seen in my childhood ... There was much about Clare for a Quaker to like; he was tender-hearted and averse to violence. How he recoiled once, bodily taking his chair with him—from a young surgeon, or surgeon's friend, who let drop, somewhat abruptly, that he was just come 'From seeing a child skinned!'—Clare, from his look of horror, evidently thought that the poor infant, like Marsyas, had been flayed *alive*! He was both gentle and simple ...

Lamb's interest in Clare's poetry went beyond dinner-table bantering; Clare sent him copies of his two books, which Lamb acknowledged in the following letter:

India House, 31 Aug. 1822

Dear Clare,—I thank you heartily for your present. I am an inveterate old Londoner, but while I am among your choice collections, I seem to be native to them, and free of the country. The quantity of your observation has astonished

[1] (1745–1826), author of an *English Grammar* (1795) and a *Spelling Book* (1804); sometimes called the "father of English grammar".

me. What have most pleased me have been Recollections after a Ramble, and those Grongar Hill[1] kind of pieces in eight syllable lines, my favourite measure, such as Cowper Hill and Solitude. In some of your story telling Ballads the provincial phrases sometimes startle me. I think you are too profuse with them. In poetry *slang* of every kind is to be avoided. Theirs is a rustick Cockneyism, as little pleasing as ours of London. Transplant Arcadia to Helpstone. The true rustic style, the Arcadian English, I think is to be found in Shenstone. Would his Schoolmistress, the prettiest of poems, have been better, if he had used quite the Goody's own language? Now and then a home rusticism is fresh & startling, but where nothing is gained in expression, it is out of tenor. It may make folks smile and stare, but the ungenial coalition of barbarous with refined phrases will prevent you in the end from being so generally tasted as you deserve to be. Excuse my freedom, and take the same liberty with my *puns*.

I send you two little volumes of my spare hours. They are of all sorts, there is a methodist hymn for Sundays, and a farce for Saturday night. Pray give them a place on your shelf. Pray accept a little volume, of which I have duplicate, that I may return in equal number to your welcome presents—

I think I am indebted to you for a sonnet in the London for August.

Since I saw you I have been in France, and have eaten frogs. The nicest little rabbity things you ever tasted. Do look about for them. Make Mrs. Clare pick off the hind quarters, boil them plain, with parsly and butter, The fore quarters are not so good. She may let them hop off by themselves. Yours sincerely, Chas. Lamb.[2]

Already Clare harboured a wider aim than the transplanting of a fake Arcadia to Helpston, but the advice to use native words only when they added force to the line was essentially sound, and he took it. His later books need no glossary, and his use of

[1] John Dyer's poem about the river Towy was published in 1726.
[2] Northampton MSS.

dialect became sparing, forceful, in the end, utterly individual.

The two little volumes mentioned by Lamb were those of the 1818 edition of his *Works*, and bore the inscription, "For Mr. Clare, with C. Lamb's kindest remembrances." The third volume was *Tracts by Sir Thomas Browne, Knight, M.D.*, an edition of 1822 containing "Hydriotaphia", "that obscure but gorgeous prose composition." *The Essays*, published in 1823 by Taylor and Hessey, Clare received "with Elia's regards" probably on his third visit, but he was already familiar with them in the pages of the *London*. "Lamb's best poetry is in Elia," he wrote in his Journal; the sonnet mentioned in Lamb's letter expands this thought and gives a measure of Clare's appreciation. It is a tribute to the author of "New Year's Eve", "Witches and Other Night Fears", "Mackery End" and "Dream Children" from one who wrote so often in verse and prose of the poetry of childhood.

Elia thy reveries & visiond themes
To Care's lorn heart a luscious cordial proves
Wild as the mystery of delightful dreams
Soft as the anguish of rememberd loves
Like visions of past days their memory dances
Mid the cool feelings manhoods reason brings
As the unearthly spirits of romances
Peopled with sweet & uncreated things
Such magic themes thy gentle worth enhances
Then wake agen thy wild harps tenderest strings
Sing on sweet bard let fairy [Alice?] love[s] agen
Smile in thy dreams with Childhood extasys
Bright oer our souls will gleam the heavenly strain
Thro the dull gloom of earths realitys[1]

"Dream Children" had appeared in the January *London Magazine*, and Clare's Mary Joyce was as surely lost to him as Lamb's Alice W——n. In the "records of past days" and

[1] From Clare's draft, Peterborough MSS. Clare's second sonnet to Lamb began:

Friend Lamb thou chusest well to love the lore
Of our old bygone bards whose racy page
Rich mellowing time made sweeter then before ...

Peterborough MSS., published 1835, 1908, and 1935.

"anguish of remembered loves" the inner lives of these two men touched in sympathy. But there was another point of contact which was also the subject of a sonnet by Clare. First printed in *Hone's Year Book*, November 18th, 1831, and revised for *The Rural Muse*, it praises Lamb for his devotion to "our old by-gone bards with their warm homely phrase". Lamb's devotion to the "Elizabethan poets of glorious memory" needs no comment from us; Clare's and the form it took, will claim attention later.

Next to Lamb in Clare's portrait gallery appears H. F. Cary, whose life, like Clare's, was to be overshadowed, as Lamb's had already been, by the clouds of mental illness. Renewing former acquaintance, Clare saw a good deal of the shy clergyman during this 1822 visit. Lamb's "model of a country Parson, lean (as a curate ought to be), modest, sensible", Proctor's "mildest and most amiable of men", Hood's "mild and modest Cary", was yet as ready as the rest for the riotous jesting of the *London* dinners. Besides meeting at their publishers', Clare and Cary were both present at Wainewright's dinner on May 27th, and Clare spent two days with Cary at Chiswick. On one of these occasions occurred an incident referred to by Thomas Bennion, Taylor's porter, in a letter to Clare after his return home. Bennion had met Mrs Emmerson:

> she commenced her conversation in the usall Theatrical Manner respecting you, first by enquiring if you had not disgraced yourself very much the night you dine with the contributors of the London Mag and if you had not given great offence to the Revd. Mr. C—— by saying you wished the churches were all in ashes and the parson's sent to beg their bread, i told her i did not hear you say it, and if you did some excuse was to be made for you as you might be a little fresh, i told her that Mr. C——was on very good terms with you so i was sure that he was not offended she said she heard you was very D—— i told her it was not so you was very merry. She said she had heard all this from a friend that you had told, and that she was very sorry to think you was so strong a deist i told her you was but a little way inclined to deism I found out who this friend was before I left her its Mr. R—— you'll know who i mean so

you'll be on your guard if you write to him of what you say as it's sure to go to her ...

Rippingille, "Mr. R.", might have inbibed lessons in discretion from the diplomatic Bennion. But Cary was not the man to take offence at an outspoken opinion, whether it was inspired by ale or not. According to the *Memoir of H. F. Cary*, by his son, a contributors' dinner was held at Chiswick. Clare, Lamb, and James Kenney the farce-writer, were among those present, and the writer comments on the strange mixture of "learning, wit, and puns, bad and good".

According to R. W. King, Cary's biographer, Clare's description "is the best verbal likeness extant, and is fully confirmed by the existing portraits".

& there sits Carey [sic] the translator of Dante one of the most quiet amiable & unasuming of men he will look round the table in a peacful silence on all the merry faces in all the vacant unconsernment imaganable & then he will brighten up & look smilingly on you & me & our next hand neighbour as if he knew not which to address first & then perhaps he drops a few words like a chorus that serve all together his eyes are not long on a face he looks you into a sort of expectation of discoursing & starts your tongue on tiptoe to be ready in answering what he may have to start upon when suddenly he turns from you to thro the same good naturd cheat of a look on others he is a tallish spare man with a longish face & a good forhead his eyes are the heavylidded sort whose earnest look seems to meet you half closd his authorship & his priest hood sit upon him very meekly he is one of those men which have my best opinions & of whom I feel happy with every opportunity to praise on my second visit to London I spent 2 very happy days with him at Chiswick (I was then in good health) his wife is a good sort of person and of so young a look in his company that I mistook her a long while for his daughter he lives [in] the house once occupied by Thornhill the painter & he showd me the window thro which Miss Thornhill elopd with Hogarth & over the chimney piece were some heads sketchd on the wall by Hogarth but the servants

> being left to themselves to whitewash the room in Mr Carys absence from home utterly defacd this precious relic & he greatly regretted the loss when he told me ...[1]

They went to Richmond to visit the grave of James Thomson of *The Seasons*. After Clare's return home, they began a correspondence which was kept up for some ten years. In his first letter Clare wrote, "The two days spent at Chiswick have left pleasant remembrances behind them of friendship and hospitality." Cary also recalled the visit in a later letter: "I often think of you in that walk we took here together, and which I take almost every day, generally alone, sometimes musing of absent friends and at others putting into English Prose old French verses ... "

Allan Cunningham, who had written most of the supposed old Scottish ballads in the *Remains of Nithsdale and Galloway Song* which Rippingille had sent Clare, and whose *Traditional Tales of the English and Scottish Peasantry* was published in 1822 by Taylor and Hessey, had transferred his allegiance from *Blackwood's* to the *London*. Hood calls him "the grenadier of our corps", De Quincey speaks of his "dark flashing guerilla eye", Procter notes that he is "very Scotch in aspect, but ready to do a good turn to any one". Clare's sketch hints at some imperfect sympathies between Cunningham and the rest, for a hater of puns must often have had occasion to keep his head down at the *London Magazine* dinners.

> Then there is Allan Cunningham (Reynolds calls him the Dwarf) comes stalking in like one of [his own] black knights but his countenance is open & his look is hearty he hates puns & is fond of scotch ballads Scotch Poets & everything Scottish down no doubt as far as Scotch snuff—well he is a good fellow & a good poet & when the companys talk is of poetry he is ready to talk 2 ways at once but when puns are up his head is down over his glass musing & silent & nothing but poetry is the game to start him into hillarity again[2]

[1] *The Prose of John Clare, op. cit.* Peterborough MSS.
[2] *Ibid.*

On May 24th, T. G. Wainewright wrote to H. F. Cary, inviting him to dinner on the 27th. "On this next Monday several friends have agreed to eat their dinner with me, at half-past six *precisely*. Their names are Chas. Lamb, Taylor and Hessey, Cunningham, Clare and the Ode to Dr. Kitchener [Thomas Hood]."

The last-named writer has already given us a glimpse of this dinner-party; here is Clare's account of his host:

> Wainewright is a very comical sort of chap he is about 27 & wears a quizzing glass & makes an excuse for the ornament by complaining of bad eyes he is the Van Vinkbooms Janus Weathercock[1] &c of the Magazine He had a picture in the exebition of "Paris in the Chamber of Helen" & the last time I was in London he had one there of "The Milkmaid" from Waltons angler both in my opinion very middling performances but my opinion is but of itself a middling one in such matters so I may be mistaken—he is a clever writer & some of his papers in the Magazine are very entertaining & some very good particularly the beginning of one a description of a Churchyard[2]

Wainewright was later accused of forgery and poisoning, convicted, and died a convict in Tasmania in 1852. But we can recall with Clare the friend of Lamb and Cary, writer of the lively and often discerning, if extravagant, articles in the *London*, one of the few who recognized Blake's genius and bought his books, Lamb's "light and warm-as-light hearted, Janus". He and Clare were more familiar with Cary than were the other *Londoners* in 1822. Writing in the *London Magazine* for June 1820, Wainewright thanks him who "introduced us to the Sylvan Muse of John Clare". In December 1821, he praised Hilton's "natural and characteristic" portrait. In January 1823, appeared "Janus Weatherbound, or the Weathercock Steadfast for Lack of Oil", an article in which he took his leave of the *London* with enter-

[1] *London Magazine*, September 1821: "C. Van Vinkbooms, his Dogmas for Dilettanti. No. 1: Recollections in a Country Churchyard." The pictures mentioned by Clare were exhibited at the Royal Academy in 1822 and 1824 respectively.

[2] *The Prose of John Clare*, *op. cit.* Peterborough MSS.

taining addresses to the contributors, particularly Clare, Cary and Lamb.

> And first, then, for John Clare; for *first* doth he stand in the sixth volume. 'Princely Clare,' as Elia would call thee, some three hours after the cloth was drawn—Alas! good Clare, never again shall thou and he engage in those high combats, those wit-fights! Never shall his companionable draught cause thee an afterlook of anxiety into the tankard! —no more shall he, pleasantly-malicious, make thy ears tingle, and thy cheeks glow, with the sound of that perplexing constrainment! that conventional gagging-bill!—that Grammar!! till in the bitterness of thy heart thou cursedst Lindley Murray by all the stars.— Not once again shall thy sweetly-simple Doric phrase and accent beget the odious *pun*. Thou mayest imbibe thy ale in peace, and defy Priscian unchecked,—Elia is gone!—Little didst thou think that evening would be the last, when thou and I, and two or three more, Messer Brunetto, Dugdale Redivivus, T—— that anthery Cicero, parted with the humanity-loving-Elia beneath the chaste beams of the watery moon, warmed with his hearty cheer—the fragrant steam of his '*great plant*,'—his savoury conversation, and the genuine good nature of his cousin Bridget gilding all. There was something solemn in the manner of our clasping palms,—it was first 'hands round,' then 'hands across.'—That same party shall never meet again! ...
>
> One word at parting, John Clare! and if a strange one, as a stranger give it welcome. I have known jovial nights—felt deeply the virtues of the grape and the barley-corn—I have co-operated in 'the sweet wicked catches,' 'bout the chimes at twelve, yet I say to thee— visit London seldom—shutting close thy ears in the abounding company of empty scoffers,—ever holding it in thy inmost soul, that love and perfect trust, not doubt, is the germ of *true* poetry. Thy hand, friend Clare! others may speak thee fairer, but none wish thee solider welfare than Janus.

Clare undoubtedly wrote down his impressions of Thomas Hood, assistant editor of the *London* from 1821, in which capacity, Hessey says, [Hood] first amused himself by concocting humorous notices and answers to correspondents in the "Lion's Head". The success of these quips led to his collaboration with the other jester, Reynolds, whose sister, Jane, Hood married in 1824. Procter describes him as "almost silent" at the dinners, "except when he shot out some irresistible pun, and disturbed the gravity of the company." As the pen-pictures in his *Literary Reminiscences* bear witness, he made good use of his silences. Clare also has his niche in Hood's "Ode to W. Kitchener, M.D." author of the Cook's Oracle:

> Then came John Clare, the poet, nor forbore
> Thy *Patties*

Unfortunately, all that survives of Clare's sketch of Hood is a line or two on a torn page. Clare, like posterity, seems to have appreciated the irresistible punster better than his graver companion, author of "Lycus the Centaur". "Song of the Shirt" and "The Plea of the Midsummer Fairies"; in a letter to Hood he candidly confessed that he could not understand a word of "Lycus", a confession which, Hessey reveals, caused Hood much amusement.

In his memoir of Charles Lamb, B. W. Procter makes mention of Clare in connection with the *London* dinners:

> John Clare, a peasant from Northamptonshire, and a better poet than Bloomfield, was one of the visitors. He was thoroughly rustic; dressed in conspicuously country fashion, and was as simple as a daisy. His delight at the wonders of London formed the staple of his talk. This was often stimulated into extravagance by the facetious fictions of Reynolds.

He seems to be recalling a definite occasion, and it would be strange if Clare overlooked Barry Cornwall, "candid and affectionate as his own poetry", who, with *Marcian Colonna* in 1820 and *A Sicilian Story* in 1821, had become one of the popular poets of the day. However, no description of him has come to light, nor is there any of his books in Clare's library.

It is probable that Clare did not meet De Quincey in 1822. His account of him gives no clue as to the date, but De Quincey's recollection of Clare in *London Reminiscences* clearly refers to 1824; as he did not contribute to the *London Magazine* during the spring and summer of 1822, it is unlikely that he attended the dinners in May and June. We know that he was not very popular with his fellow-guests, and his re-appearance as a contributor helped to sever the connection of some of them with the *London*.

References to the editor by the *Londoners* are few and scanty; many of them merely express disapproval of his policy. De Quincey, in his *London Reminiscences*, remembered the publishers as "both hospitable and friendly men", and noted that Taylor professed himself a religious dissenter and a blind admirer of Locke. Clare's sketch of Taylor was written some years after 1822, when events of those years revealed traits in Taylor's character not in earlier years apparent.

> Taylor is a man of very pleasant address & works himself into the good opinions of people in a moment but it is not lasting for he grows into a studied carlessness & neglect that he carries into a system till the purpose for so doing becomes transparent & reflects its own picture while it woud hide it he is a very pleasant talker & is excessive fluent on Paper currency & such politics he can talk on matters with a superficial knowledge of them very dexterously & is very fond of arguing about the latin & Greek poets with the Reverends and the cambridge [wits] that drop in to his waterloo house he assumes a feeling & fondness for poetry & reads it well—not in the fashionable growl of mouthing spouters but a sort of whine—he professed a great friendship for me at my first starting & offerd to correct my future poems if he did not publish them & wrote to Lord Radstock (in answer to one from his Lordship) so I sent all my things up as I wrote them & neither got his opinion or the poems back again his only opinion being that he had not time to spare from other pursuits to revise & correct them for the press & when I sent for the poems agen he was silent—he wrote the Introductions to both of my Vols of Poems—his manner is

that of a cautious fellow who shows his sunny side to strangers ...

He never asks a direct question or gives a direct reply but continualy saps your information by a secret passage coming at it as it were by working a mine—like a lawyer examining a witness & he uses this sort of caution even in his common discourse till it becomes tedious to listen or reply he sifts a theory of truth either true or false with much ingenuity and subtelty of argument & his whole table talk is a sort of Junius Identified but his patience carrys it to such lengths in seeming consistency till the first end of the ravelled skein which he winds up at the beginning is lost again & unwound in looking for the other—to sum up his character he is a clever fellow & a man of Genius & his Junius Identified is the best argument on circumstantial Evidence that ever was written[1]

In taking leave of the *London Magazine* in the brief heyday of its fame, a letter written by Taylor to his father on June 19th may be quoted. This glimpse of Clare among the *Londoners* is a corrective to the frequent picture of him as the simple country visitor, overawed by high company. The casual observer noted his rustic dress and manners, his naive delight and wonder at the strange new world about him; but those who knew him better recognized, as Taylor did, that his intellectual, original qualities were no less remarkable than the keen observation and nervous sensibility which made him a poet.

... I have only just lost my visitor Clare ... He was excellent Company while he staid, but a little too much elated with a Glass of Ale if you indulged him in it—He saw all our literary Acquaintance, and kept his Ground with all of them. He could not pun, but then he had such a Fund of Good Sense & so many shrewd Remarks to make on what anyone said,—besides his Judgement of Books was so very sound,—that let what would be the Subject of Conversation he was always well worth listening to.—Gilchrist came to Town & carried him to Gifford's and to

[1] *The Prose of John Clare, op. cit.* Peterborough MSS.

> Murray's—he much liked Gifford, who was particularly friendly in his Conduct, & gave him the strongest Encouragement, and much excellent advice—but Murray he set down as 'a mere Craftsman.' I was not much afraid of his being spirited away from us,—if it could have been done Lord Radstock would have accomplished it ...
>
> I entertain no Resentment, because I have no need to feel anything but Pity for this weak-headed old Gentleman—[1]

Events at Helpston led Clare to cut short his visit and return home hurriedly. Bennion and he drowned their regrets at parting in a last drink together on Sunday night, June 16th, just before Clare left town. On his arrival at Helpston, he found that his third daughter had been born on the 16th. She was called Eliza Louisa, after her godmother, Mrs Emmerson, who sent a silver cup and other gifts and later paid for the child's schooling. Lord Radstock sent a gown for Patty, with regrets that he had not had Clare under his roof during the visit.

Charles Lamb's letter of August 31st, 1822, has already been quoted. On the 23rd Clare wrote to Cary, recalling the pleasant days spent at Chiswick. He sent a poem which he had written the day before, on going out again after an attack of fever which had been "raging from house to house in our fenny villages like a plague". He looked forward to Cary's "Lives of the Poets" in the *London*, but thought that some of the other contributors were writing themselves out. In his reply of September 1st, Cary promised to give his opinion of Clare's poems, and recommended him to read Bacon's *Essays* rather than Knox's—Lord Radstock had sent Clare *Essays Moral and Literary*. "I was very glad to hear that your appetite for reading has come again, as I think you said, when I had the pleasure of your company here, that you had in great measure lost it. I have found a fondness for books one of the chief comforts through life."

Hessey wrote on August 30th about Clare's sonnets which they were inserting in the *London*. In the September and October numbers six sonnets appeared, of which only one was signed, the publishers thinking, oddly, it best not to let Clare's name appear too often. At home he was frequenting his old "secret

[1] Quoted from *Keats's Publisher* by Edmund Blunden (Jonathan Cape, 1936).

nooks", musing there on distant friends, reading in his favourite books, recalling his childhood and early loves, finding new joys in contemplation of simple weeds:

> Star pointed thistle with its ruddy flowers
> Wind waving rush left to bewildered ways
> Shunning the scene which cultures toil devours

These were the "native endearments", "keepsakes and pledges" whose passing Clare deplored each year as Enclosure and fen-drainage progressed.

In the same letter Hessey sent news that Woodhouse had been very seriously ill and had gone to the sea. He suffered from the same weakness as his friend Keats, and succumbed to tuberculosis in 1834, at the age of forty-six. There was also news of Hood and Cunningham, and a note about Reynolds's long-delayed marriage to Miss Drewe.

Mrs Emmerson wrote in September with news of a "new and delightful correspondent": Derwent Coleridge, younger brother of Hartley, then studying at St John's College, Cambridge, was contributing to *Knight's Quarterly Magazine* above the pen-name "Davenant Cecil". Mrs Emmerson became acquainted with him through his aunts, Martha and Eliza Fricker, whom she had met in Bath. She found Derwent an "amiable and kind creature—poet in all his doings and sayings". He visited her several times in the years before the young poet of promise was lost in the brilliant schoolmaster, linguist and divine; later he became the first Principal of St Mark's College, Chelsea.

Clare also heard from friends nearer home. Drury, now at Lincoln, invited Clare to visit him. Gilchrist wrote in October; he was very ill, but cheerful as ever. December brought a letter from Frank Simpson of Stamford; he had been endeavouring to get something inserted in the *London*, but with no success; he was busy making sketches of Gothic crosses. Clare evidently tried to help friends at home by introducing them to friends in London.

During this autumn of 1822 it became more apparent than ever that his publishers had many irons in their fire, a policy which was to have serious consequences for Clare. Taylor's preoccupation with the *London* had already led to the delay in the appearance of *The Village Minstrel.* Clare was now given other causes for dissatisfaction with his publishers' conduct of his affairs. The first is trivial enough in itself, but of interest in view of the oft-repeated charge that Clare had no aptitude for business affairs. From 1820 onwards he kept a careful account of all money sent by Taylor and Hessey; but they did not always state the source of the money sent. He also noted once more that he had received nothing for his *London Magazine* poems. With the new year he had a more irksome negligence to complain of—the delay in sending him his dividend, which was due on January 1st. Mrs Emmerson thought it unpardonable, since they knew his limited means. On February 5th Hessey wrote: "The enclosed £10 note has been lying on my desk for you for some time."

On January 13th came a letter from Thomas Bennion, in which mention is made of a visit to Milton to see Henderson and Artis. "Was it a trial of strength between your old friend John Barleycorn and you?" asked Bennion. "i am sorry to hear you are so troubled with the blue devils i have only to say i wish it was in my power to relieve you of them and to send them to oblivion for ever as for myself i no nothing of this infernal tribe." Clare had dedicated to him a sonnet intended for the *London*; Bennion, whom Hood classed among the contributors because of his valiant struggles with the English language, records sadly of his own literary offspring: "i can never satisfy myself with what I doo, so that I commit them to the fire in their young days."

Clare had sent poems for his next book, but Taylor had been too busy to deal with them, and he was now ill through overwork. "I am anxious to hear," Clare wrote to Hessey, "but you take no notice in the world about it men of Business and poets are the worst correspondents that can come together—I am sorry Taylor is ill but I am very poorly myself & have had a regular sickness every morning as soon as I got up for this 3 weeks."[1] A second issue of *The Village Minstrel* was being prepared, and Clare wanted some copies to present to London friends, Cunningham, Reynolds, Hood, and Hilton. He asked

[1] *The Letters of John Clare, op. cit.*

for Cunningham's *Sir Marmaduke Maxwell* and a copy of *The Opium Eater*. "If you will give an opinion of my poetry you shall have 'The Parish,' but if you will not I am determined I will send no more for your criticism at present."

He was no doubt acting on Mrs Emmerson's advice to withhold his manuscript until he obtained satisfaction. She condoled with him on his "mental depression", due to the apathy of Taylor and Hessey, and mentioned the possibility of new publishers. Her counsels were usually for moderation and peace; evidently something was afoot to make her take this line. Clare's depression must have been so apparent in his letters that she felt something must be done. On March 14th, Lord Radstock came into action again with a flourish of trumpets.

> We have formed plans in our minds concerning you, but these, unless manfully and steadily pursued by yourself, can avail nothing ... You have long known my opinion of T——. The more I hear of him, the more am I convinced that that opinion was well founded—in a word that it is his determined resolution to keep you in *Bondage* and *obscurity* so long as he has the power of so doing—Now if these vile and ignominious chains be not speedily broken the fault will not be mine ... therefore he shall learn, I trust, to his *cost* that I clearly see through all his ... duplicity.[1]

On March 31st, 1823, Hessey wrote that copies of the "second edition" of *The Village Minstrel* would follow in a few days. This "second edition" consisted of the second thousand copies of the first edition, which had been bound; so there were no changes in the text, but a sketch of Clare's cottage by Cowen was engraved to prefix the second volume. Hessey eventually sent the promised books on May 16th, with apologies for delay. "I know how tantalising it is to wait beyond the time when one has reason to expect a pleasant thing ... but I have been pestered to death almost with such variety of matters that I have not been able to write before." Taylor was too busy with his editing to attend to anything else. Clare did not hear from him until August.

[1] Letters, British Museum.

Lord Radstock and Mrs Emmerson had another score against Taylor. The Rev. W. Allen had written a critique of Clare's poetry in the form of four letters to Lord Radstock, dated February 1823. They wanted Taylor to publish them in the *London*; he declined; when they decided to have them published in book form, he would not even mention the book in his list of new publications. *The Four Letters* contain detailed comments on the poems in Clare's two books, with frequent reference to the earlier poets, sound criticism, and discerning praise. Allen had a wide acquaintance with the highways and byways of English poetry, and his comparisons and contrasts are illuminating; but he also had a keen eye for what was new in tone or treatment, and his critique is the fullest contemporary account of Clare's poetry.

On April 12th, Cary wrote in answer to a letter in which Clare had voiced his discontent with Helpston society. "Do not wish for a residence near London," Cary wrote: "you would ere long have cause to wish yourself away again. Be contented with seeing the 'freckled fair one,' as I think Cowper calls it, now and then." Clare had also mentioned his intention of visiting Cowper's haunts. Cary had just met Wordsworth, and found in him

> much frankness and fervour. The first impression his countenance gave me was one which I did not receive from Chantrey's bust of him, that of his being a very benevolent man. Have you seen Barry Cornwall's new volume? He is one of the best writers of blank verse we have; but I think blank verse is not much in favour with you. The rhyme that is now in fashion runs rather too wild to please me. It seems to want pruning & nailing up. A sonnet like a rosetree may be allow'd to grow straggling. But a long poem should be train'd into some order.[1]

A sonnet of Clare's which appeared in the 1823 *London* in July under the pen-name "Percy Green" was admired by Cary before he discovered its authorship. "Percy Green" was a joke of Clare's. He had written a letter to Taylor in October 1822, signed by that name, offering to send a small collection of poems

[1] *Ibid.*

for perusal. He enclosed a ballad as a specimen, and his postscript ran thus: "I have heard it affirmed that your predilection for the Northamptonshire Peasant's poetry has made you blind to the more high and refined style. Be as it will, I have made the attempt, whether it be attended with success or not." Clare was never enamoured of the rôle of "peasant poet", and his anxiety to know whether his poems were appreciated for their own sake showed itself again and again from now on. Cary's notice of the poem pleased him. Three of the *London* sonnets in 1823 were signed "Percy Green".

Through the *London Magazine* poems we can trace some of Clare's moods during this year. He is preoccupied with the contrast of present and past, with change and decay. He muses upon "a venerable tree, pining away to nothingness and dust"; or in the sonnet which Cary liked, greets an old friend, in "Round-Oak Spring", which also change has not spared:

> Sweet brook lifes glorys then were thine & mine
>   Shades clothed thy spring that now doth naked ly
> Oer thy white boiling sand the sweet woodbine
>   Darkend & dipt its flowers—[1]

or, as in "Antiquity", he plunges into a remoter past and marks the grassy mound, the grave of one of those Roman camps which he sometimes helped his friend Artis of Milton to explore.

There are also three poems to Mary. These mark the third stage in the pilgrimage of Clare's love for her. He had loved her in youth's happy day. Fate parted them, and he bade farewell. Now, when life is threatening to reveal that it may hold no happiness like that which is past—now he must make, as T. S. Eliot might have said, "the best of a bad job". Because Clare was the realist he was yet would not give up the vision of ideal love—his thoughts kept returning to Mary as the epitome of earliest authentic joy. He addresses to her the Valentine which was printed in the May *London*, "from one who loves thee still." Yet he asks himself: what kind of love is this? For the past is for ever dead, and "With me thy love's a withered joy". He concludes that it is a shadow love, haunting the memory.

[1] Peterborough MSS.

In two sonnets published in the August *London*, we find that this idea has found fertile soil and begun to germinate. Since change and decay are rules of life, and "The flower that's gathered beauty soon forsakes", perchance this remembered love is better than the reality, being beyond time and change.

I met thee like the morning though more fair
And hopes gan travel for a glorious day
& though night met them ere they were aware
Leading the joyous pilgrims all astray
Yet know I not though they did miss their way
That joyd so much to meet thee if they are
To blame or bless the fate that bade such be
Thou seemdst an angel when I met thee first
Nor has aught made thee otherwise with me
Possession has not cloyed my love nor curst
Fancys wild visions with reality
Thou art an angel still & Hope awoke
From the fond spell that early raptures nurst
Still feels a joy to think that spell neer broke

In July, Octavius Gilchrist died, after a long illness, at the age of forty-four. Clare felt deeply the loss of this good friend and jovial companion. With Gilchrist dead and Drury at Lincoln there was little incentive for Clare to visit Stamford, although he was always welcomed by Mrs Gilchrist and the Simpsons.

On August 1st, 1823, Taylor wrote at last with the news:

I shall be very agreeable to the Publication of another Volume this ensuing Winter & what with the Magazine Poems & some long & good ones you have besides I doubt not a very creditable Volume may be completed without any great Difficulty. Talking the other day with Hessey it occurred to me that a good title for another book would be —'The Shepherd's Calendar.'

Once more Taylor effectively countered Lord Radstock's challenge: so long as Taylor was willing to go on publishing his poems, Clare had no desire to part company with a man who had done much for him. Had he known that *The Shepherd's Calendar* promised for the next winter was destined to remain on the publishers' stocks for nearly four years, he might have taken other counsel.

During September, Sir Michael Benignus Clare, M.D., a rich West Indian, sent him five guineas for the name's sake. Hessey thought optimistically that he was "in all probability a Relation (who knows but you may be his heir!)".

In the letter which contained this news, Hessey spoke of the death of Bloomfield and of the unhappiness of his later days. Bloomfield's and Clare's circumstances were similar in that Bloomfield's *The Farmer's Boy* sold 26,000 copies in the three years after its publication in 1800. Yet Bloomfield died in poverty. Bloomfield and Clare did not meet, but they corresponded and exchanged books, and Clare had intended to visit Shefford on his way back from London. On May 3rd, 1822, Bloomfield had sent his *May-day with the Muses*, with a note to "Neighbour John".

When, in March 1825, Joseph Weston, then engaged on a life of Bloomfield, wrote to Clare for permission to publish his letters to the Farmer's Boy, in his reply Clare said:

> I sincerely loved the man and admired his Genius and had a strong anxiety to make a journey to spend a day with him on my second visit to London ... He died ripe for immortality and had he written nothing else but 'Richard and Kate' that fine picture of Rural life were sufficient to establish his name as the English Theocritus and the first of Rural Bards in this country.

Clare also sent three sonnets which form a sequence he had written in 1823 "in a melancholy feeling" after Bloomfield's death; the best of them was included in *The Rural Muse*. In a "pretty, inaffected letter", added to Weston's reply, Bloomfield's daughter Hannah spoke of her father's regard for Clare, and his regret that they never met. Many years later Hannah Bloomfield visited Clare in St Andrew's, and he wrote some verses to commemorate the visit.

At harvest-time Clare found work in the fields again, but he continued to send up poems for his next book. Hessey complained because they were too much like what he had written before, and he could find none suitable for the *London*. After the two sonnets to Mary in August 1823, no poem from Clare's pen was published in the *London Magazine* until July 1824, and the sonnet in that number was the last.

Toward the end of 1823 appeared the first symptoms of an illness more severe than any Clare had yet experienced; he had had little rest or respite for two years. Not surprisingly, symptoms took the form of acute mental distress. Mrs Emmerson wrote in November asking the reason for his two months' silence; in her next letter she had heard from him and wrote sympathetically of his "abiding shadow of misery", his "fiery torments", wondering what could be the cause. In her Christmas letter she asked him to send particulars of his present means of support, since Lord Radstock meant to discover what Taylor held on Clare's behalf in his accounts. Radstock had also written again to Lord Milton soliciting a cottage and a piece of ground, a small-holding, for Clare.

On January 5th, 1824, Clare's first son was born; he was christened Frederick. Cary wrote on the 3rd, dating his letter 1823:

> I am glad to see a New Shepherd's Calendar advertised with your name. You will no doubt bring before us many objects in nature that we have often seen in her but never before in books; & that in verse of a very musical construction. These are the two things, I mean description of natural objects taken from the life, & a sweet melodious versification that particularly please me in poetry; and these two you can command if you chuse. Of sentiment I do not reck so much. Your admiration of poets I felt most strongly, earlier in life, & have still a good deal of it left, but time deadens that as well as many of our other pleasantest feelings.

In January we hear again of W. Sharpe, who in 1821 sent writing paper. Sharpe paid a visit to Helpston; Clare and he met at Lolham Bridges, where they both had a fit of the "blue devils". Sharpe, who worked in the Dead-letter Office, did Clare good service later by acting as his representative in certain business matters.

The correspondence during the first quarter of the year has many references to Clare's illness. Hessey sent him pills from Dr Darling, who had a wide practice among literary men and artists. He had doctored Keats, Hazlitt, J. Scott, Wilkie, and Haydon. Clare met him in 1822 at the *London* dinners. Taylor suggested a visit to town to consult him. Meanwhile Lady Milton had sent her own physician, Dr Walker of Peterborough, and he had assured Clare that he would soon recover. Taylor also wrote to Dr Arnold of Stamford asking him to attend Clare. From Mrs Emmerson's letters we gather something of his symptoms, nervous and mental; his "mind was dead", he had spoken of "loss of memory", of "being nearly blind", of "wandering pains" and "cold chills". She thought—accurately—he was suffering from "high nervous debility, which is of all diseases the most painful to the poor patient"; she sympathized the more because she had suffered from it herself: "It is the mind's disease, and the body only suffers in sympathy." She assured him that his mind was as sound as ever. Clare needed the assurance: he was certain he was dying. In this belief he determined to make his will. He wrote to Hessey, who handed his letter to Richard Woodhouse, who was a solicitor. Woodhouse sent him a long and sympathetic letter, with a will form to fill up. Clare left £10 to his sister, Sophy, now married, four shillings a week to his parents out of the copyright of his works, and the interest from the Fund-money to his wife and family. Taylor was to publish his books and edit his Remains: "he was one of the first friends I met & I wish to leave him one of my last."

Casting about for the cause of his illness, Clare further troubled his mind with regrets for past follies; he decided to turn his back on John Barleycorn. He also sought solace in religion, and contemplated joining the Ranters. "I do not wonder at the feelings you describe," Hessey wrote, "nor am I sorry that you experience them—a broken heart and a contrite spirit are much more welcome in the sight of God than undue presumption."

By the end of April, his health not improved, Clare decided to take Taylor's advice and consult Dr Darling in London.

CHAPTER ELEVEN

Crowds and Cities Pass Away: 1824–1825

Clare arrived in London toward the end of May. It was only after his return from this visit that he began to record his impressions of his three visits:

> A journey for pleasure is a precarious sympathy soon robd of its enjoyments by unforseen disasters but a journey for the improvement of ill health undertaken by that smiling encourager hope hath little to make it palatable tho the joys of the one are as much to be relied on as the other
>
> Upon this last matter my journey to London was made I went for the benefit of advice to a celebrated scotch phisician Dr Darling the complaint lay in my head & chest I was very ill when I first went but I gradualy recievd benefit some reccolections of this visit shall be the subject of this chapter they are observations of men & things thrown together in a myscellaneous manner this was the third time I had been up so the vast magnitude of that human ant hill that strikes every stranger with wonder had lost its novelty ...
>
> On this my last[1] visit I amused my illness by catching the most beautiful women faces in the crowd as I passed on in it till I was satiated as it were with the variety & the multitude & my mind lost its memory in the eternity of beautys successions & was glad to glide on in vacancy with the living stream[2]

After resting for some days at Fleet Street, he visited the

[1] He went a fourth time in 1828: "last" here means at the time of writing.
[2] *The Prose of John Clare, op. cit.* Peterborough MSS. Two fragments.

Emmersons; Mrs Emmerson wrote to Patty on May 31st, 1824, that she had seen Clare that morning for the first time, and that his health had improved since his arrival in London. After that he divided his time between Stratford Place and Fleet Street, as on his second visit. Under Dr Darling's treatment, or else merely from the holiday, his bodily health improved considerably; his mental distresses were more stubborn. Demons were as much at home in London as at Helpston.

> When I used to go any w[h]ere by myself especially Mrs Es I used to sit at night till very late because I was loath to start not for the sake of leaving the company but for fear of meeting with supernatural [agents] even in the busy paths of London & tho I was a stubborn disbeliever of such things in the day time yet at night their terrors came upon me tenfold & my head was as full of the terribles as a gossips – thin deathlike shadows & goblings with saucer eyes were continually shaping on the darkness from my haunted imagination & when I saw any one of a spare figure in the dark passing or going on by my side my blood has curdled cold at the foolish apprehension of his being a supernatural agent whose errand might be to carry me away at the first dark alley we came too ... I coud not bear to go down the dark narrow street of Chancery Lane I[t] was as bad as a haunted place to pass & one dark night I resolved to venture the risk of being lost rather then go down tho I tryd all my courage to go down to no purpose for I coud not get it out of my head but that I shoud be sure to meet death or the devil if I did so I passed it & tryd to find fleet street by another road but I soon got lost & the more I tryd to find the way the more I got wrong so I offerd a watchman a shilling to show me the way thither but he said he woud not go for that & asked a half a crown which I readily gave him when he led me down many narrow alleys & I found myself in Chancery Lane at last[1]

Clare attributed these night fears to an incident in his youth, when he was terribly frightened by a wandering cade-foal in a

[1] *The Prose of John Clare, op, cit.* Peterborough MSS.

The cottage at Helpston

The cottage at Northborough

John Clare in 1844, from the portrait by Thomas Grimshawe (By kind permission of the Northampton Central Library Committee)

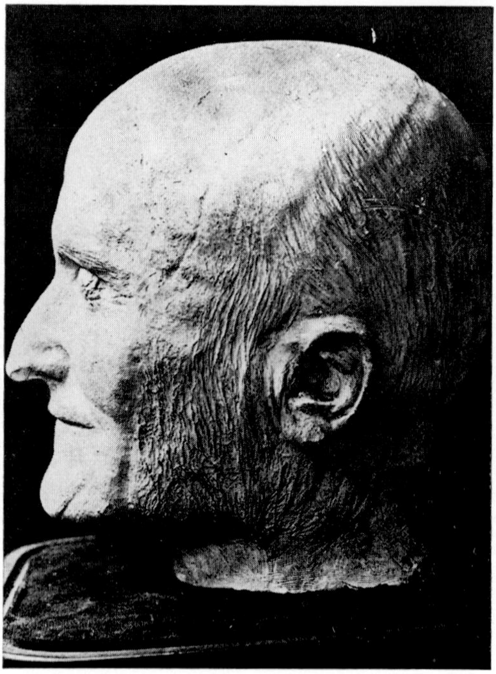

Death-mask of John Clare (By kind permission of the Northampton Central Library Committee

lonely lane one summer evening. He did not venture far in London unless he could find a companion.

I used to go with Thomas Bennion Taylor's clerk or head porter about the city when he went out on errands & very often went into each curiosity that came our way & each & often had names or claptraps to ease the pocket of its burthen I remember going into the Bullocks Mexico[1] with the Editors Ticket that Taylor gave me & the fellows at their several posts of money catching fancying I daresay that I was the criticising editor looked with much supprise at my odd clownish appearance and asked me so many pumping questions that I was glad to get out agen without paying much attention to the wonders of the show—Tom was very fond of introducing me to the booksellers w[h]ere he had business who were too busily occupied in their own concerns to take much heed of mine[2]

On another occasion,

I went with Hessey to visit a very odd sort of character at the corner of St Pauls Churchyard he was a very simple good sort of man with a troublesome sort of fondness for poetry which was continually uppermost he wrote ryhmes himself which he thrust into anyones notice as readily as if they were anothers he had two daughters who seemed to be very amiable girls one of which kept an album in which her fathers productions were very prominent he seemed to be very fond of translating Davids Psalms into ryhme he was a friend & acquaintance to Miss Williams[3] to whom he had sent a copy of my poems at his house I met with Etty the painter he was a man of reserved appearance & felt as awkwardly situated I daresay as myself when Mr Viney[4] proposed healths and expected fine speeches in reply for tho Etty replyed he did it very shortly & when mine was

[1] An exhibition of Mexican curiosities held by W. Bullock, at the Egyptian Hall
[2] Peterborough MSS.
[3] Helen Maria Williams, whose work Wordsworth admired.
[4] Evidence from a letter of Hessey's (May 10th) suggests that Clare meant Vowler, whom they met at Etty's.

drunk I said nothing & tho the companys eyes were expecting for some minutes I coud not say a word tho I thought of some several times & they were wishes that I was out of the house Mr Viney appeared to be a sort of patron to Etty[1]

William Etty,[2] fellow-student of Hilton and Haydon, was recognized as a "historic" painter. His works in the nude, now seen as among his best, were in the 1820s thought indecent. He became an A.R.A. in this same year and an R.A. in 1828, competing for that honour with Constable, whom he was one of the few to appreciate at that time.

At Taylor's Fleet Street shop Clare renewed his acquaintance with several of the contributors to the *London*, besides making some new friends. Since his last visit, the *London* had passed from high summer to the verge of winter. Dissatisfied with the editor's conduct of affairs, many of the contributors had fallen away, among them Hazlitt, Wainewright, Hood, and Procter. Lamb felt like the last rat lingering among the creaking rafters, and only his sense of loyalty kept him contributing. Taylor was overworked, and the business suffered with his health. He favoured some of his team unduly—De Quincey certainly had more than his share of the space at this time—and he affronted others by withholding or curtailing their contributions. There were complaints about delay in payment. However, Cary, Cunningham and Elton still appeared regularly, and there were newcomers since 1822 whom Clare now met for the first time.

The falling off of the contributors had been noted by Thomas Bennion when he wrote to Clare in March:

The Dinner, that was given to the Contributors of the L. Mag. this last time was attended by only two of the old Contributors, that you know, the one was Reynolds and the other Mr. C. Phillips those two where the chief sport of the party indeed i may say the verry life and soul of it after dinner, and you was mentioned twice or thrice during the night. Your old friend Elia was prevented from being

[1] Peterborough MSS.

[2] For a documented life of the painter see Dennis Farr's *William Etty* in Herbert Read's *English Master Painters Series* (Routledge and Kegan Paul, 1958).

one of the party thro being ill but he is better, but there wanted him and you and then there would have been more mirth among them.[1]

The contributors present on that occasion were "Van Dyk, H. Taylor, G. Darley, C. Phillips, Dr. Darling, Revd. Mr. Percival, Reynolds, Taylor, and Hessey".

Charles Phillips, barrister and miscellaneous writer, Clare had evidently met in 1822. Van Dyk and Darley he now met for the first time and formed friendships with them which lasted for several years.

George Darley, that "sometimes glorious poet", had come from Dublin to London in 1821 "to conquer the literary world with a volume of poems in his pocket". Beddoes saw him in 1824 as "a tallish, slender, pale, light-eyebrowed, gentle-looking baldpate, in a brown surtout with a duo-decimo under his arm—stammering to a most provoking degree ... " Darley did not become intimate with Cary and Lamb till 1827, but the friendship he made with John Taylor, his publisher, long outlasted the *London* days.

Yet not *Errors of Ecstasie* in 1822, or *Labours of Idleness* in 1826, or *Sylvia* in 1827, conquered the literary world for Darley. *Letters to the Dramatists of the Day*, begun in the *London* of July 1823, where he could never help—as he wrote to Clare—"cutting, slashing, pinking, and carbonadoing" the rest of the brotherhood, only earned for Darley the appellation of "the bloody John Lacey". In 1861 Palgrave knew so little of him that he placed his "Ryghte Pythie Songe", "It is not beautie I demande", between poems by Milton and Carew. Yet that was its spiritual home. It is significant that immediately after this visit Clare began writing his "imitations" of those same poets from whom Darley drew inspiration. Darley certainly recognized in Clare's poetry that "musical singing note" which he held was the mark of the poet. Clare, also interested in Darley the mathematician, praised those popular text-books in geometry, trigonometry, algebra, and astronomy, by writing which Darley soothed a sensitive conscience on the subject of his life's devotion to literature.

[1] Letters, British Museum.

In 1824, Harry Stoe Van Dyk was a young man of leisure to whom literature was a hobby rather than a profession. On the failure of his estate in the West Indies he was driven to depend on his pen for a livelihood, and after that his story is one of declining hopes, poverty, and ill health, closed by his death in 1828 at an early age. Clare found in him a congenial companion, and left this brief account of him among his reminiscences:

> I got acquainted this time with Van Dyk a young man whose literary manners sat very quietly about him he was of a very timid & retreating disposition before strangers but to a friend he was very warm hearted he published a little volume of Poems called *Theatrical Portraits*[1] he was very ready at writing an impromptu which he would often do very happily he went back with me to Mrs Es where we met with Lord R. who was very friendly with him

Soon after Clare's return home Van Dyk offered to prepare poems for *The Shepherd's Calendar*. Busied with his other affairs Taylor was glad to accept the offer, and Van Dyk acted as editor for about a year.

Mrs Emmerson wrote to Patty on June 14th with news that Clare's health was still improving, though slowly. He was getting about town much more, visited the Emmersons frequently and picnicked with them on Hampstead Heath. Rippingille came up from Bristol, and Clare had a round of sight-seeing with his old friend. They were accompanied on some of these jaunts by Charles Abraham Elton, who had come with Rippingille from Bristol. Elton, Greek scholar and translator of Hesiod and Propertius, supplied the *London* with poems, translations, and articles, under the pen-name "Olen". Clare and Elton met frequently during this visit, and enjoyed each other's company. After their return home, Elton sent Clare a letter in verse, with a copy of *The Brothers*, 1820. "The Idler's Epistle to J. Clare", which was printed in the *London* for August, is a record of their

[1] *Sketches of Actors and Actresses*, published in 1822. Van Dyk collaborated with John Bowring in *A Batavian Anthology, or Specimens of the Dutch Poets* (1824); and a novel, *The Gondola*, appeared in 1827.

friendship and common tastes, and a perceptive word-sketch of Clare mentally and physically.[1]

So loth, friend John, to quit the town?
'Twas in the dales thou won'st renown:
I would not, John for half-a-crown
    Have left thee there;
Taking my lonely journey down
    To rural air.

What thou hast been the world may see,
But guess not what thou still may'st be;
Some in thy lines a Goldsmith see,
    Or Dyer's tone:
They praise thy worst; the best of thee
    Is still unknown.

Some grievously suspect thee, Clare!
They want to know thy form of prayer;
Thou dost not cant, and so they stare
    And smell free-thinking;
They bid thee of the devil beware,
    And vote thee sinking.

. . . . .

I would not have a mind like thine
Thy artless childhood tastes resign,
Jostle in mobs, or sup and dine
    Its powers away,
And after noisy pleasures pine
    Some distant day.

And, John! though you may mildly scoff,
That curst confounded churchyard cough
Gives pretty plain advice, be off!
    While yet you can;
It is not time yet, John! to doff
    Your outward man.

. . . . .

[1] Twelve verses have been omitted here. The poem was reprinted in Elton's *Boyhood.*

Does Agnus[1] fling his crotchets wild,
"In wit a man," in heart a child?
Has Lepus'[2] sense thine ear beguiled
With easy strain?
Or hast thou nodded blithe and smiled
At Herbert's[3] vein?

Does Nalla,[4] that mild giant, bow
His dark and melancholy brow;
Or are his lips distending now
With roaring glee,
That tells the heart is in a glow,
The spirit free?

Or does the Opium-eater quell
Thy wondering sprite with placid spell?
Read'st thou the dreams of murkiest hell
In that mild mien?
Or dost thou doubt, (yet fear to tell,)
Such e'er have been?

And while around the board the wine
Lights up the glancing eye-ball's shine,
Seest thou in elbow'd thought recline
The poet true[5]
Who in Colonna seems divine
To me and you?

But, Clare the birds will soon be flown;
Our Cambridge wit resumes his gown:
Our English Petrarch[6] trundles down
To Devon's valley:
Why, when the Mag is out of town,
Stand shilly-shally?

. . . . .

[1] Charles Lamb.
[2] Julius Hare (1795–1855).
[3] J. H. Reynolds. The *Boyhood* version has "Janus" (Wainewright).
[4] Allan Cunningham.
[5] From here to the close of the next verse is omitted in the *London*.
[6] Taylor's partiality to De Quincey at this time was at the expense, some thought, of the "poet true", Barry Cornwall, and others.

And Rip Van Winkle[1] shall awake
From his loved idlesse for thy sake;
In earnest stretch himself, and take
Pallet on thumb;
Nor now his brains for subjects rake;
John Clare is come.

His touch will, hue by hue, combine
The thoughtful eyes that steady shine
The temples of Shakespearian line,
The quiet smile,
The sense and shrewdness which are thine,
Withouten guile.

To return to Clare's sight-seeing:

After I had been in London a while Rippingille came down from Bristol with Mr Elton & as I was much improved in health under Dr Darling I indulged in some of the town amusements with my old comrade for he was fond of seeking after curiosity & traversing about the town he was always for thinking that last exercise taking all weathers rough & smooth as they came was the best phisic for a sick man & a glass of Scotch Ale only served to strengthen his notions the first jaunt we took together was to see 'The art of Self defence' practised at the fives court it was for the Benefit of Oliver & I caught the mania so much from Rip for such things that I soon became far more eager for the fancy than himself I watch'd the appearance of every new hero on the stage with as eager curiosity to see what sort of fellow he was as I had before done the poets & I left the place with one wish strongly uppermost and that was that I was but a Lord to patronise Jones the Sailor Boy who took my fancy as being the finest fellow in the Ring[2]

Tom Oliver was one of the "old ones" in 1824, and as such entitled to an annual benefit. Jones the Sailor Boy provided some

[1] Rippingille.
[2] *The Prose of John Clare, op. cit.* Peterborough MSS.

of the "prime Sparring" at several such benefits. Clare's memories of these scenes sank deep into his mind, to reappear in strange forms later, when many rounds had been added in his long struggle with adversity. It was Jack Randall he remembered, and in whose name he issued his "Challange To All The World": the Prime Irish Lad was the Nonpareil of Reynolds's sonnet, "Good with both hands and only ten stone four", whose fight with Ned Turner Keats had witnessed in 1818, the "Out and Outer" whose deeds and fame Clare marked since they were celebrated in many verses and in the pages of *Boxiana*. In 1824 Randall kept the Hole in the Wall at 45 Chancery Lane, which Clare visited.

Clare next tells how, in the company of Rippingille and Elton, he went to see Deville, a phrenologist from Paris, who had a shop in the Strand where he entertained the many visitors who came to have their "phrenological developments" explained and to see his collection of plaster casts of the heads of noted people. Clare allowed a cast of his head to be made and found the operation very stifling. He has left a full account of the methods of this high-priest of phrenology who pronounced Coventry Patmore's adolescent "bumps" to be those of a poet, and whom Thomas Hood mentions in his poem "Craneology", where he pokes fun at the fashionable craze. Deville's plaster cast of Blake's head may be seen in the National Portrait Gallery:

> ... he is a kind simple hearted good humoured man Phrenology is with him somthing more than a System it seems the life & soul of his speculations he is never weary of talking about it or giving Lectures on heads Strangers of all descriptions—Poets Philosophers Mathematicians & humble unknown beings that with the world have no name are all welcomd up his stairs & led to his matchless head gallery while he with smiling politeness satisfys every eager enquiry as readily as it is askd for they have only to pull off their hats & drop half hints & then the lecture on heads commences he mostly begins with 'Why Sir I shoud say heres order very strong—or vice versa the want of it heres plenty of constructiveness I shoud say youre fond of mathematics & heres ideality I should say that you had a

tallent for poetry I dont say that you are a poet but that you have a tallent for it if applied heres the organ of color very strong I shoud say you are fond of fine colors & vice versa where theres the organ of form without color nothing showy is liked here is benevolence very prominent I shoud say you seldom pass a beggar or street sweeper without dropping a copper heres veneration very high I shoud say you are religious the head perhaps is worldly minded and remains silent I dont say youre a Christian mind but you have a veneration for the deity thats sufficient for our system heres combativeness very large I shoud say you are not slow at avenging an insult particularly if it be offerd to a female for the amorous propensitys are large also I shoud say you have a love for the fair sex but not so as to make it troublesome aye aye sir now I look again heres order very strong sure enough I shoud say that things being put out of order displeases you very much & that you are often tempted while at table to put a spoon or knife & fork in its place I shoud say its the most likely thing to create disturbances in your family heres form very strong I shoud say you are a painter or that you have talents for painting if applied ... are you a poet sir (yes) aye aye the systems right but I shoud not venture so far to decide upon that as many heads develop poetry very strongly where it has never been applied Well sir you see the system is correct he then in smiling silence waits your decision of his remarkable prophecy & hard & earthlike is that soul who can return an harsh & unbelieving opinion on the system but I believe he is seldom paid so unkindly for his good naturd trouble His predictions are so cautiously utterd with so many causes for the likelihood of failures in nice points that even failings themselves in his lectures strike as convictions ... Deville then leads your eye to his collection points out on particular heads the most convincing proofs of his system in the characteristics of Murderers Poets Painters Mathematicians & little actors of all work where his vice versas become very frequent he then takes you below where the apparatus is always ready to bury you in plaster if you chuse & of Literary men & Artists he politely hints that he shoud like a cast they cannot do less than comply & the satisfaction of adding fresh materials to his gallery doubly repays him for all his trouble[1]

We hear how:

Rippingille also introduced me to Sir T. L.[2] who was a very polite courteous & kind man which made the other matters sit very agreeable about him—just as we got up to the door Prince Leopold was going in to sit for his picture—& we took a turn up the Square for a while & did not offer to venture till we saw him depart Rip sent in his Card & we were instantly sent up into his painting gallery w[h]ere we amused ourselves till he came & kindly shook me bye the hand & made several enquirys about me he paid Rip several fine compliments about his picture of the Breakfast at an Inn & told him of his faults in a free undisguised manner but with the greatest kindness after he had shown us about his painting room & chatted a considerable time we proffered to start when he followed us & said he coud not let me go without showing me a brother poet & took us into another room w[h]ere a fine head of Walter Scott stood before us—I left his house with the satisfied impression that I had never met with a kinder & better man then Sir T. L. & I daresay Rip was highly gratified with the praise he had recieved for Sir T. told him that the Royal family at a private view of the Exebition before it opened to the public took more notice of his picture then all the rest but Rip woud not own it for he affects a false appearance in such matters

Other acquaintances made in Rippingille's company, besides Lawrence and Etty of the "reserved appearance", were Frank Howard, remembered for his series of clever outline plates, "The Spirit and the Plays of Shakespeare", and the genial and witty T. K. Hervey, critic of art and literature, who edited the *Athenaeum* from 1846 to 1853.

It was one of Rippingille's foibles to affect an interest in

[1] *The Prose of John Clare, op. cit.* Peterborough MSS.

[2] Sir Thomas Lawrence, president of the Royal Academy, and painter of more crowned heads in Europe than any other British artist before or since.

things of which he understood little. "With this feeling," Clare continues,

> we went 2 or 3 times to the french Playhouse somew[h]ere in tottenham court road none of us understood a word of french & yet we fancyd ourselves delighted for there was a very beautiful actress that took our fancys & Rip drew a Sketch of her in pencilling for me which was something like her tho he stole none of her beauty to grace it
>
> We also went to Astleys Theatre[1] w[h]ere we saw morts of tumbling

Clare's account of Charles Lamb was written when the memory of his visit to Islington in 1824 was fresh in his mind. We are indebted to Crabb Robinson for another record of one of these occasions. He wrote in his diary for July 6th: "Took tea with Lamb—There were Hessey and Taylor, Clare the shepherd poet, Bowering, and Elton the translator from the classicks. Clare looks like a weak man but he was ill—Elton a sturdy fellow more like a huntsman than a scholar."

"Bowering" was John Bowring, master of some fifteen languages and an authority on their literatures; his translations frequently enriched the pages of the *London* at this time. He prepared numerous anthologies, was a friend of Jeremy Bentham and Cobden, and eventually won fame and a knighthood for his political services at home and abroad. He had lately published his successful *Specimens of the Russian Poets, Ancient Poetry and Romances of Spain*, and a volume of devotional verse called *Matins and Vespers*.

Clare met Lamb again at Taylor's, along with other old acquaintances and some new ones. Elton referred to one of these gatherings in a letter to Clare on September 8th: "I went down to Islington & dined & smoked a pipe in the evening with Lamb he got a little into the romps as he did at Taylors but was very entertaining the capital paper on the old country house was written at my instance though he chose the subject himself."

"Blakesmoor in H——shire" appeared in the September

[1] Philip Astley was the founder of the modern circus. His amphitheatre stood near the south end of Westminster Bridge.

London, the first contribution from Lamb's pen for that year; he had been in indifferent health and low spirits during the first half of 1824.

It was at Taylor's also that Clare met De Quincey, whose *Confessions of an English Opium Eater* was a favourite book of his:

> A little artless simple seeming body somthing of a child overgrown in a blue coat & black neckerchief for his dress is singular with his hat in his hand steals gently among the company with a smile turning timidly round the room—it is De Quincey the Opium Eater & that abstruse thinker in logic & metaphisics X.Y.Z.[1]

De Quincey's comments on Clare and his poetry were included in his *London Reminiscences*:

> ... I very much doubt if there could be found in his poems a single commonplace image, or a description made up of hackneyed elements ... in 1824, perhaps upon some literary scheme, he came up to London, where, by a few noble families and by his liberal publishers, he was welcomed in a way that, I fear, from all I heard, would but too much embitter the contrast with his own humble opportunities of enjoyment in the country ... One thing, meantime, was very honourable to him,—that even in this season of dejection he would uniformly become animated when anybody spoke to him of Wordsworth—animated with the most hearty and almost rapturous spirit of admiration. As regarded his own poems, this admiration seemed to have an unhappy effect of depressing his confidence in himself. It is unfortunate, indeed, to gaze too closely upon models of colossal excellence. Compared with those of his own class, I feel satisfied that Clare will always maintain an honourable place.

There is other evidence that Clare's appreciation of Wordsworth had grown steadily since 1820. In a journal entry for

[1] *The Prose of John Clare, op. cit.* Peterborough MSS.

October 29th, 1824, he gave a list of his favourite poems and told of his first discovery of Wordsworth's greatness. "Wordsworth bids fair to be as great in one way as Byron was in another," he wrote, also in 1824. "His having little share of living popularity is no proof to the contrary." But Clare was not so depressed by gazing upon "models of colossal excellence" as De Quincey imagined. His natural modesty could be misleading, and his admiration was never blind. In 1820, after praising Wordsworth's truth to nature, he wrote: "But after all I dont think I favour his affected Godliness in some of his longer pieces theres some past all bearing still with his faults & abilities he is a poet with whom for originality of description the present day has few if any equals."

Clare fought shy of all men and all poetry that seemed to have, in Keats's phrase, "a palpable design". Godliness, unless unobtrusive, was suspect; nor was he happy with what he called Wordsworth's "mysteries": not because he was unable to see nature as Wordsworth saw it, but because his own vision was so natural, obvious and spontaneous:

> Wordsworth's vision came to him by flashes, therefore it seemed to him an abnormal and extraordinary visitation which needed to be related by thought and meditation to ordinary experience. If Wordsworth had seen a primrose as Clare saw it—and he did occasionally see things thus—he would have felt that he was seeing 'into the heart of things,' whereas Clare—who seems always to have seen in this way—felt that he was merely seeing things[1]

We know less of Clare's opinion of Coleridge, though he coupled him with Wordsworth in 1820 as among his favourite poets. Coleridge was present at one of the gatherings during this third visit to London: unfortunately, Clare's sketch of him is fragmentary:[2]

> There was Coleridge at one of these Partys he was a man with a venerable white head fluent of speech not a "silver

[1] "Clare and Wordsworth", *The Times Literary Supplement*, August 21st, 1924.
[2] *The Prose of John Clare, op. cit.* Peterborough MSS.

tongued hamilton"[1] his words hung in their places at a quiet pace from a drawl in good set marching order so that you woud suppose he had learnt what he intended to say before he came it was a lecture parts of which ...[2]

At Mrs Emmerson's Clare met Coleridge's and Southey's sisters-in-law, Martha and Eliza Fricker. With them he talked of Southey and Wordsworth:

I never saw him [Southey] but I heard somthing about him by meeting in company two of his wifes sisters at Mrs Emmersons those 'Pretty milliners of Bath' as Byron calls them but I cannot say much for his judgment if these sisters are to be taken as a sample for the rest they are sharp ready witted girls but rather plain I learned from them that Southey was a livly sort of man always in gay spirits who wrote both in prose & verse with a great deal of ease but the Number of his publications woud almost tell us that this is the fact he writes amid the noise of his children & joins in their sport at intervals Wordsworth on the contrary cannot bear a noise & composes with great difficulty I shoud imagine he prefers a mossy seat on the mountains to the closet for study at least his poems woud lead one to think so Southey presents a copy of every work he publishes to his wife & he wrote a copy of *Roderic* on french green paper on purpose to present to her[3]

On Monday, July 14th, Byron's funeral cortège crossed London. It was at the bottom of Oxford Street that George Borrow, arrested by the gathering crowds, watched the passing of the hearse with the long train of empty carriages, and mused upon the dead poet and his fame. A similar chance found Clare in Oxford Street at the same time:

While I was in London the melancholly death of Lord Byron was announced in the public papers & I saw his

[1] A politician who acquired a reputation for eloquence—though he was sometimes called "single-speech Hamilton".

[2] Peterborough MSS.

[3] *The Prose of John Clare, op. cit.* Peterborough MSS.

remains born away out of the city on its last journey to that place w[h]ere fame never comes tho it lives like a shadow & lingers like a sunbea[m] on his grave it cannot enter therefore it is a victory that has won nothing to the victor—his funeral was blazed forth in the papers with the usual parade that accompany[s] the death of great men I happend to see it by chance as I was wandering up Oxford Street on my way to Mrs Emmersons when my eye was suddenly arested by straggling gropes of the common people collected together & talking about a funeral I did as the rest did tho I coud not get hold of what funeral it coud be but I knew it was not a common one by the curiosity that kept watch on every countenance bye & bye the grope collected into about a hundred or more when the train of a funeral suddenly appeard on which a young girl that stood beside me gave a deep sigh & utterd poor Lord Byron ... I lookd up in the young girls face it was dark & beautiful & I coud almost feel in love with her for the sigh she had utterd for the poet it was worth all the Newspaper puffs & Magazines Mournings that ever was paraded after the death of a poet ... the common people felt his merits & his power & the common people of a country are the best feelings of a prophecy of futurity they are the veins & arterys that feed & quicken the heart of living fame the breathings of eternity & the soul of time are indicated in that prophecy ... they felt by a natural impulse that the mighty was fallen & they movd in saddend silence the streets were lind as the procession passd on each side on but they were all the commonest of the lower orders ... the young girl that stood by me had counted the carriages in her mind as they passd & she told me there was 63 or 4 in all they were of all sorts & sizes & made up a motly show the gilt ones that led the procession were empty—the hearse lookd small & rather mean & the coach that followd carried his em[bers] in a[n] urn over which a pawl was thrown tho one might distinguish the form of the [blank left in MS.] underneath & the window seemd to be left open for that purpose—I believe that his liberal principals in religion & politics did a great deal towards gaining the notice & affections of the lower orders be as it will it is better to be beloved by those

low & humble for undisguised honesty then flatterd by the
great for purchasd & pensiond hypocrisy —[1]

The essay on "Popularity", begun soon after his return home, contains a further estimate of Byron. In September Clare first read *Don Juan*, lent him by Henderson of Milton; he had already written a sonnet in memory of Byron, "A splendid sun hath set!" He returned to the same theme in prose; in a passage headed "Necessity for mercy in criticism rather than fault-finding", he concluded that Byron "had great faults" but "won the applause of popularity less by his sterling merits as a poet than by his oddities as a man," that his exploits in Greece were those of an actor playing the part of hero; yet his infirmities were but as spots in the sun: "He is enrolled among the immortals & shines as the jewel in the crown of modern literature." Clare criticized alike the friends who surrounded him "with every virtue under heaven" and "every meddling hypocrite who professes to be a saint" and "utters his condemnation". Clearly the fame and moral courage of Byron had begun its inroads into Clare's mind by 1824. He puzzled until he reached a conclusion on the superiority of "true fame" over "present fame". He finished the essay on "Popularity" in the autumn of 1824.

Whilst he was still in London on July 13th, Mrs Emmerson wrote again to Patty, telling her not to worry because she had not heard from Clare; he was not sufficiently recovered to enable him to give a satisfactory account of himself. It is not surprising that two months' treatment had failed to remove all traces of an illness due at least in part to years of emotional sense of Enclosure's outrage, to isolation and to physical and mental strain; when the tonic results of the change had worn off, the symptoms of nervous, imaginative hypertension reappeared. Dr Darling desired to continue his treatment with the patient under his eye. Hessey wrote to Patty on July 31st that Clare had been anxious to return home for some weeks, and nothing but the positive orders of his doctor kept him in London. These did not keep him much longer. His mind was set on home. On Friday, August 8th, he left Fleet Street for Helpston. He says that he hastened home to get ready some lectures on

[1] Peterborough MSS.

painting which Rippingille intended to give at the Bristol Institution.

A letter to Thomas Inskip, friend of Bloomfield, written soon after his return, reveals that the chief object of his visit to London had not been achieved.

> I have been in London 3 months for the benefit of better advice & I am sorry to acknowledge that I feel very little better I have been in a terrible state of ill health six months gradually declining & I verily believe that it will upset me at last I was taken in a sort of appoplectic fit & have never had the right use of my faculties since a numbing pain lies constantly about my head & an acking void at the pit of my stomach keeps sinking me away deeper and deeper ... I shall only be at home for a few weeks to try the air to be sure if it improves my spirits I shall remain if not the next thing for me to try is salt water ...[1]

During August and September he continued to receive from Dr Darling pills and prescriptions. According to Hessey, the situation of Clare's cottage was unhealthy; there was talk of obtaining another from the Marquis of Exeter. Hessey also suggested that pies and puddings, which had been forbidden by Darling, had disordered Clare's stomach. "I can do nothing with Sir John Barleycorn now," Clare wrote to Inskip. There was an impression abroad in 1824, as a hundred and fifty years later, that civilized people ate and drank too much; Clare's friends frequently suggested with unconscious irony, that his ills must be due to over-drinking or over-eating, if not to irresponsible sexual indulgence. Strict dieting was the fashionable treatment of the day, though it had not ousted bleeding from its old pride of place, and we find both prescribed even for diseases like consumption. Clare was as little likely to benefit from such treatment as Keats, since he suffered from chronic under- rather than over-nourishment. This, with the continual worry of trying to make ends meet and the suspense and disappointment that attended his literary work, seems to have been at the root of much of Clare's trouble. An examination of

[1] *The Letters of John Clare, op. cit.*

the symptoms of his illnesses suggests that the physical derangements were results, not causes, of nervous distress.

September 1824 brought letters from several friends. Rippingille wrote twice, asking if Clare had forgotten "the Delia fun" at the French Playhouse, and the "atmosphere of smoke, smocks, smirks, smells and smutty doings". He sent his "Echo" verses for the *London*, and urged Clare to come to Bristol where Elton and he would be delighted to see him. Elton repeated the invitation and inveighed against Catholics and Calvinists and "the superstitions and bigotry of this pretended liberal age". Cunningham wrote on the 23rd, thanking Clare for a letter of Bloomfield's which he had given him. "I am glad to hear that you are a little better—Keep up your heart and sing only when you feel the internal impulse and you will add something to our Poetry more lasting than any of the Peasant Bards of Old England have done yet." On the 18th, Clare had written to Cary, whom he had met again in London and visited at Chiswick:

> I am ill able to write or do anything else I thought I was getting well but Ive not a hope left me now I have employed myself when able since I came home at writing my own life which if I live to finish it I shoud like to trouble you to read it & give your opinion of it for my own judgment in such matters is very often faulty ... [1]

Cary replied on the 22nd, sympathizing with Clare, discussing his own *Life of Chatterton* which Clare had commended, and assuring him that he would read Clare's autobiography with interest. On December 30th, Clare reported progress:

> I feel anxious to finish it & I feel also anxious that you shoud see it & I shall be greatly obliged for your opinion of it as I mean if I live to publish it I have gotten 8 chapters done & have carried it up to the "Poems on Rural Life" &c—I feel it rather awkard to mention names as there are some that I cannot speak well of that is w[h]ere I feel an objection I cannot flatter over it & I woud not willingly

[1] *The Letters of John Clare, op. cit.*

offend any one I have made free with myself & exposed my faults & failings without a wish to hide them neither do I care what is said about me but if you shoud see anything that might be against me in speaking of others I shall be thankful of your advice & also your remarks on the thing altogether for it is written in a confusd stile & there will doubtless be found a deal of trifling in it for I am far from a close reasoner in prose ... [1]

Cary renewed his promise in a letter of February 19th, 1825. The correspondence then lapsed until the end of 1827, so that the history of Clare's later autobiographical fragments (two manuscripts surely), is uncertain. There is no record that a fair-copied version was sent to Cary. The exercise book entitled "Sketches in the life of John Clare Written by himself & addressed to his Friend John Taylor Esqr March 1821" re-emerged from among John Taylor's possessions a century and ten years later. This is the version edited by Edmund Blunden in 1931. It ends at 1820. The fate of any fair copy of Clare's 1821–4 autobiography is unknown.

During the months following his return home he read widely —Shakespeare, Chatterton, Pope,[2] Coleridge, Byron, Wordsworth—and Blake: "whose fame stirs onward like the mighty sea." He wrote many poems, some to be copied up by Van Dyk for the new book. His fair copies of between 1824 and 1832, "The Midsummer Cushion" and another of poems written for his children, must be among the most beautiful of poets' manuscripts. Whilst the energy of hope was in him, his punctuation still consisting of a few well-placed dashes, his spelling was almost normal. "The Parish—a Satiric Poem", which he thought the best thing he had done so far, was finished by January 1823. New poems were for the *London Magazine*, other magazines and Annuals; some were not published until 1835; others not until 1908; still others not until 1920, 1924, or 1935. In prose, besides autobiography, he wrote sections or chapters of one, two, or three novels—"The Two Soldiers or the

[1] *Ibid.*

[2] Clare wrote of Pope whose reputation was then under cloud: "some doubt wether they shoud call him a poet or no poet at all if he is no poet where are we to look for one".

Protection of Providence" and "The Adventures of Uncle Barnaby" and "The Bone & Cleaver Club". His mind seethed with ideas. He seems to have begun "Village Characters" but the form is not clear. Whether the five letters from a grocer's wife to her son at school and other letters in quaint spelling belong to "Village Characters" or to "The Bone & Cleaver Club", is also in question:

> Der bye
>
> This cums with oure kynd luv to you hopping it will finde yu in gud helth as it leeves us at this praisent thank Godd for it ... [1]

and

> Der Mrs Huggergubbel
>
> This cums with thee kind herted luv of us all ... we hev all hed the steriks at the counts of the colleflour Morpus in our newspeper & as we hev hed a meny cowshuns about it the fizikel men out to go to the seeside & stap it from cummin over but our gud Mr Snip seeing wir cristeon fright on the subject gave me a preceal [?] out of his bewtiful Herberybuk that is a stonishing cure for the plage ... [2]

In the form of letters to Hessey, who suggested the idea, he began a "Natural History of Helpstone" though he himself meant to call it "Biographys of Birds & Flowers". He contemplated "The Moris Danse—a Popular Village Drama", thought of a long Tale in Verse, "The Robber's Tragedy", to have been carried out in Spenserian stanzas. Angry as he had been over the cuts Taylor had allowed Radstock to dictate for the fourth edition of *Poems Descriptive*, with Taylor a "button hole lower" in his opinion, "cursd affectation worse than hell I hate", he wrote. Perhaps with Hazlitt's Round Table essay "On Posthumous Fame" in mind, he began essays on subjects such as "Praise", "Self-consciet", "Resolution", "Landscape", "On Nothing", and "Common Honesty": "Truth is the integrity of

[1] Peterborough MSS.
[2] *Ibid.*

action not the correctness of speech"; one on "Money-Catching" recalled John Billings's old book *The Pleasant Art of Money Catching*. Another he returned to again and again – "Pretention" or "False Appearances" or "Affectation": "... I read history & am astonished at the lesson it gives of the vanitys of pride pomp & power – mind alone is the sun of the earth – it lives on when the clouds & paraphenalia of pretention are forgotten – "

Again he was writing at what he called "a cursed risky rate", his intense mind and powerful feelings often under "black melancholly", "blue devils", or unnerving symptoms of "numbness" and "sinkings". When he returned from London, his physical health not really restored, that "fickle hussey" his Muse was so extraordinarily active as to be a burden. The 220 sonnets he wrote between 1824 and 1836 Dylan Thomas thought among his best work; though now and then Clare protested against the "short-winded peevishness that hovers round this 14 line article", he continued to write sonnets until his last days. He collected over a score of old songs from his father's and mother's singing – the "Old Ballad of John Randall", the "Origin of Burns's Red Red Rose", the "Maid of Ocram", "The Banks of Ivory", "Nelson and the Nile", "Benbow". Nelson and the Battle of the Nile, Randall (echoing both John Randall and Jack Randall the boxer) – as well as Jones the Sailor Boy – all will crop up disguised, with the human mind's chronic adeptness at displacement of image later in his mental pilgrimage. Behind pseudonyms – Percy Green, Frederic Roberts of Milton and James Gilderoy – thinking he might succeed *that* way, he continued to "father" poems on the older poets, Marvell, Sir John Harington, Wotton, D'Avenant.

From September 6th, 1824, to September 12th, 1825, he kept a Journal "to give my opinion of things I may read or see & set down any thoughts that may arise either in my reading at home or my musings in the Fields".[1]

Supplementing his Journal and the letters to Hessey he made a long and full list of the birds of his neighbourhood as well as one of north Northamptonshire's wild orchises. He has left accounts of birds he is familiar with – nuthatch, kingfisher, fern owl, firecrest, firetail, grasshopper lark, pettichaps (chiffchaff)

[1] *The Prose of John Clare, op. cit.*

"bumbarrel" or long-tailed tit, many more. With mention of others now rare—corncrake, crossbill, grosbeak, bittern, he tells of the superstitious awe in which the then common "butter-bump" was held during his boyhood; he gives descriptions of the nightingale, plentiful still in the Clare country, and he has left a long descriptive poem—with what looks like involuntarily inwoven rhyme—"The Nightingale's Nest". Beside Clare's bird, on one at least of the two mentioned by Coleridge in his "The Nightingale; a Conversation Poem", "Perched giddily/On blossomy twig still swinging from the breeze" must rest strong suspicion that Coleridge's nightingale was a blackcap warbler.[1] In a sonnet to "The Wren" Clare compared the vociferous stave of that very small bird with the cuckoo's and the nightingale's chants:

> Why is the cuckoos melody preferred
> & nightingales rich[2] song so madly praised
> in poets ryhmes ...

He tells of the birds which, besides boyhood's pets, he had lately managed to tame—a jackdaw, a raven, four pigeons, and two hawks which he thought were hobbies. His jackdaw, thief and mimicker, through vanity "got drowned in a well". His hawks, whose flight gave him pleasure to watch so that he could not cage them:

> grew very tame & woud come at a call or whistle when they were hungry they made a strange noise that piercd the ear with its shrillness they was very fond of washing themselves often doing it twice a day in winter after being fed they woud play in the garden running after each other & seizing bits of clods or fallen apples in their claws or catching at flies ... one was much larger then the other & the large one was much the tamest when I went awalking in the fields it woud attempt to flye after me & as I was fearful of

[1] Clare's "March nightingale", "mock nightingale", could have been the great tit, the marsh or willow tit or the blackcap warbler. His list of birds shows the confusion of his day among these.

[2] Not *sick* as given by Eric Robinson and Geoffrey Summerfield in their selection of Clare in the *New Oxford English Series* (1966).

losing it I usd to drive it back but one day it took advantage of watching & following me & when I got into the fields I was astonishd & startld to see a hawk settle on my shoulder it was mine who had watchd me out of the town & took a short cut to flye after me I thought it woud flye away for good so I attempted to catch it but it woud not be made a prisoner & flew to the trees by the roadside I gave it up for lost but as soon as I got out of sight it set up a noise & flew after me agen—when I got upon the heath w[h]ere there were no trees it woud settle upon the ground before me & if I attempted to catch it it woud run & hide in the rabbits burrows & when I left it it took wing & flew after me & so it kept on to the other end of my journey when it found home as soon as I did after this I took no more heed of losing them tho they woud be missing for days together a boy caught one by surprise & hurt it so that it dyd & the tamest dyd while I was absent from home 4 days it refusd food & hunted for me every morning & came to sit in my empty chair as it woud do till I got up they thought it fretted itself to death in my absence but I think the meat I gave was too strong for it & I believd it was not well a good while before I left it I felt heartily sorry for my poor faithful affectionate hawk[1]

Poems on the nests of birds were intended for a volume to be called *Bird Nesting*. In it were to be pictures of the "small bird of saddened green", marsh tit, or, sometimes for him, blackcap; of the reed-bird or sedge-warbler, into whose covert the boys throw stones to make him start his song again; of the mysterious and seldom-seen landrail, that

sort of living doubt
We know tis something but it neer
Will blab the secret out

of the wryneck; of the "teasing melody" from the ventriloquist firetail or redstart, of the willow-biters (willow-warblers); of

[1] Though hobby hawks are birds of passage, James Fisher thought these two, because of the shrillness of their voices, must have been, as Clare says, hobbies.

the painted red-cap (goldfinch); of a blackbird's nest with "a snake lapt up within"; of a magpie, whose reputation, against the fury of gamekeeper and game-rearer, Charles Waterton also defended, "on account of its having nobody to stand up for it". For Clare snipe among the solitudes of Whittlesey Mere was:

> Mystic indeed
> For isles that ocean make
> Are scarcely more secure for birds to build
> Then this flag-hidden lake
>
> Thy solitudes
> The unbounded heaven esteems
> & here my heart warms into higher moods
> & dignifying dreams
>
> I see the sky
> Smile on the meanest spot,
> Giving to all that creep or walk or fly
> A calm & cordial lot.

The Mere's lonely reaches were then strongholds for birds and bog-plants which are now far scarcer than they were then. In 1850 it was laid dry and the sanctuaries lost. Peter De Wint sketched its "Dutchlike scene", as did E. W. Cooke, R.A., and other nineteenth-century landscape-painters. In 1825, when the land was rapidly being divided into private properties of "No entry", "keep out" or "Trespassers will be prosecuted", the Mere remained for Clare a place in which to wander freely and botanize. He made expeditions to it with Artis and Henderson, or his children, or his old friend John Billings. Or, during that excessively hot summer of 1825, there was Helpston Heath—that part of the original common which remained heath—belonging to Lord Fitzwilliam, to which he had access. There green grass-snakes were so plentiful, he says, that often at every step he took by a dyke-side they "dropped into the water by scores". In the Fens they crept up milk-pails set to cool of an evening at the doors. Clare has accounts of adder, scarcer viper and slow-worm; of how some people still believed that a snake-skin worn round the hat was a charm against headache; of how the French prisoners at Norman Cross Camp during the

Napoleonic War used to buy adders or grass-snakes strung on poles from the country people, to eat; of how he had seen snakes "creeping half-erect by the sides of the fallen oaks that were pilled putting their darting horse-hair-like tongues every now & then to the tree": they were catching the flies attracted to the newly peeled trunks. His entry concerning these "wild wormes" might have interested Waterton, sedulous to correct the errors of the zoologist and the post-mortem naturalist. Clare's outlook unites W. H. Hudson with him across the century which divides them, in appraisal of the living creature rather than scientific docketing of the dead specimen.

It is this, not any comprehensive or classified knowledge in his nature musings, which gives them value. The nineteenth century, with its taste for game in covert or on table, a rage for further Enclosure and gainful intensive cultivation, predilection for dissecting and museums, has, more than all preceding ages, lessened abundance, variety and intricate balance of life among wild birds and plants. Clare saw this devastation and felt with anger the deadness that can lie at the heart of some scientific knowledge.

1824 was for him a crucial year. After his return from his third London visit he seems to have determined, with the rigid refusal of genius to be deflected from its purpose, but also with the strange capacity he knew from childhood to find solace from all ills in the everyday life of the most insignificant creature and plant, to continue as poet and writer. Slowly jubilance fades out of his letters to John Taylor as confidence in Taylor's approval and trust in Taylor's intentions die. Though the decision to continue writing was perhaps the only one possible for Clare, his frequently reiterated fears about his mind suggest that he cannot have been wholly unwitting of the price he might be asked to pay for his decision not to cease, not to turn aside, whatever the cost.

CHAPTER TWELVE

The Shepherd's Calendar: 1825–1827

Meanwhile, preparation of *The Shepherd's Calendar* had been proceeding under Van Dyk's supervision. The book had been announced in the magazines; in the event, this advertisement harmed rather than helped its chances, for delay disappointed those whose interest had been aroused. As early as October 1824, Van Dyk was regretting for Clare's sake that he had taken the work on, since he was too busy to make quick progress. In November, Hessey wrote that Taylor and he were reading the manuscripts with difficulty, and they were by no means fit for the public eye yet; he also criticised the poems because they abounded in description and lacked sentiment and human interest; the world would expect something new from Clare this time. Hessey had seen Dr Skrimshire of Peterborough, whom Clare called "a curious man who collected the eggs of English birds". He was attending Clare again and gave a better account of his health. In December the question of a settlement of accounts was again mooted, Mrs Emmerson and Van Dyk agreeing with Clare that it was high time he had one. On January 28th, Hessey promised that in his next letter he would give an account of the sales of the poems and the profit that might be due to Clare. Taylor was too busy to do anything in the matter and had been unable to continue reading the manuscripts. He was, in fact, engaged in a last attempt to revive the *London Magazine*, which had declined rapidly of late. He had handed over the editorial duties to Henry Southern, the size of the magazine was increased and the price raised; the first number of the new series did not justify the change. "It is whip syllabub, 'thin sown with aught of profit or delight,'" Lamb commented. Taylor had other troubles, among them a fierce dispute with W. S. Landor over the publication of

Imaginary Conversations. It is not surprising that he had no time left for editing *The Shepherd's Calendar*.

In January, Clare's friend Sharpe called upon the publishers and did not know what to think of the situation. He hoped they were Clare's friends, since he was certainly in their power and kept a strange account with them. On February 10th, 1825, came news from Van Dyk that all the poems were copied except the first one, "January", which had been overlooked; as soon as it was done, Clare should have the first proof sheet and all would go "swimmingly"; the book would be out in six weeks. Tired of waiting, Clare wrote in his diary that he would edit his next book himself. A month later the first proof arrived and was sent back corrected; no more followed. Van Dyk's next letter of March 15th, was not forwarded by the publishers until May. On March 29th he wrote again with the news that he now found Taylor had omitted to give him some of the poems in his possession, and the printing was held up while they were being copied. Clare's Journal entries for March 30th and April 17th disclose this.

Artis, in London in March, had called on Taylor and Hessey three times and sent oftener for some manuscripts Clare wanted back; he had written for them himself several times, and Hessey had promised to send them. On April 15th he heard from Radstock that Van Dyk was going out of town. "This is the man," Clare confides to his Journal, "that was to get my new book thro the press in 6 weeks & with the assistance of Taylor & Hessey has been a month about one proof of it."

A rough draft of a letter to Hessey has survived. Clare says in his Journal he was very loath to write but he set forth his grounds for complaint soberly, mentioning the retention of manuscripts, the failure of Taylor either to edit the poems himself or give them into Van Dyk's hands, and the continual, exasperating delay.

"If this is to be the plan of proceeding I woud really from my heart that my MSS were returned altogether & I left to do them myself." In a letter of April 17th he concluded: "I do not wish to hurt the feelings of anyone nor do I wish they shoud hurt mine—but when a delay is carried into a system its cause must grow a substitute for a worse name—I will go no further but I will just ask you to give a moments reflection to my situation &

see how you woud like it yourself." How a comment presumably added later gets into the letter is not clear: "These [the poems he had wanted] never were returned nor accounted for."

Taylor replied immediately, saying that Clare's letter had had its intended effect of turning his attention to the manuscript once more. He confessed that his heart was not in the business, because he did not think he could make of the poems a volume equal to the previous books. But he would do his best, for he had never intended to delegate all control to Van Dyk. As to the hints and cautions which Clare had received from his friends, it would be better to terminate their connection at once rather than continue it in distrust. He dwelt on the difficulties of the work; he had pondered for hours over the first poem.

As was his custom, Taylor answered charges by ignoring them and advancing counter-charges. It had taken him eighteen months to discover that the first poem was full of difficulties. Nervously Clare wrote at least two drafts of a letter to Taylor on May 5th, 1825. One he sent. Another, among the Peterborough manuscripts, accepted Taylor's "hard words" for himself but defended others concerned: " ... the opinions of those friends I aluded to are not utterly despisable they may be under a mistake as well as others but they can have no interest in wishing to do me wrong ... " In the sent letter he wrote:

> ... whatever harm may come from complaining of matters that appear to claim no commendation I am sure no good can come from speaking in their praise – when I feel anything I must speak it I know that my temper is hasty & with that knowledge of myself I always strive to choke it & soften hard opinion with reasonable interpretations – but put yourself in my place for a minute & see how you woud have felt & written yourself & if you feel that you shoud have acted otherwise then I will take it as an example & strive to correct my failings & be as perfect in an imperfect world as I can.
>
> I have no desire to seek another publisher neither do I believe any other woud do as well for me as you may do ... if you want to get out of the job of publishing my poems you may tell me so & I will seek another & trust to providence but if you have no desire to turn me adrift

> [nothing but, *crossed out*] the speedy publication of my poems will gladly convince me that I was mistaken & I shall be happy to prove that you are my friend as usual ...[1]

Taylor accepted the olive-branch, admitting that he had been slow. "Perhaps I have no just cause ... Had I been in your place I should probably have complained as much as you." At midsummer, Hessey and he were to dissolve partnership, Hessey retaining the retail business and Taylor the publishing. In July came the news that they had resolved upon selling the *London Magazine* also: they were worn out with the labour it imposed on them and they had found a purchaser. This was the acting editor, Henry Southern, in whose hands the *London* lingered on for a while, a mere shadow of its former self.

Since his return from London, besides reading widely among the "modern" poets, Clare had turned with renewed interest to the poetry of the sixteenth and seventeenth centuries as represented in Ritson's *English Songs* and Ellis's *Specimens*. Perhaps some talk with Lamb or Darley had inspired him, although his interest in the Elizabethans was firmly established years before through his friendship with Gilchrist. However, the winter of 1824–25 saw a curious and more active development of his veneration for these poets "of glorious memory". On January 13th, 1824, he had drafted a letter to James Montgomery, who edited the *Sheffield Iris* for thirty-one years:

> I copied the following verses from a MS on the flye leaves of an old book entitled "The Worlds best Wealth, a Collection of choise Counsils in Verse & Prose printed for A. Bettesworth at the red Lion in Paternoster row 1720" they seem to have been written after the perusal of the book & are in the manner of the company in which I found [them] I think they are as good as a many old poems that have been preserved with more care & under that feeling I was tempted to send them thinking they might find a corner from Oblivion in your entertaining literary paper the *Iris* but if my judgment has misled me to overrate their merit you will excuse the freedom I have taken & the

[1] *The Letters of John Clare, op. cit.*

> trouble I have given you in the perusal—for after all it is but an erring opinion that may have little else then the love of poesy to reccomend it[1]

There followed nineteen stanzas headed "The Vanitys of Life".[2] There are at least five drafts of this poem or part of it. A letter dated January 7th, 1825, contained the draft sent. The Journal for February 19th, five weeks later, confirms the poem's publication in a "newspaper". As "The Vanities of Life" it reached the *Rural Muse* in 1835. From a Peterborough draft:

> What are lifes joys & gains
> What pleasures crowd its ways
> That man shoud take such pains
> To seek them all his days
> Sift this untoward strife
> On which thy mind is bent
> See if this chaff of life
> Is worth the trouble spent
>
> Is pride the hearts desire
> Is power thy climbing aim
> Is love thy follys fire
> Is wealth thy restless game
> Pride power love wealth & all
> Time's touchstone shall destroy
> & like base coin prove all
> Vain substitutes for joy ...

Flattering comment in the *Iris*, Montgomery cautiously repeating the story of its origin as on Clare's authority, and adding praise of its "condensed and admirable thought" and "felicity of language", encouraged Clare to keep up the fiction. He wrote to Mrs Emmerson assuring her that he was not the author, and he proceeded to "father" some more poems on older writers. Perhaps, as Cherry suggested, he had Chatterton in mind; he had been reading Chatterton again in September 1824,

[1] Peterborough MSS. Two drafts.
[2] In Clare's first (?) draft, "vanitys".

and the Journal entry for the 14th of that month gives some point to the suggestion.

Among his papers is a draft of a letter to William Hone of the *Every-day Book*, enclosing some verses, "On Death". It is signed "James Gilderoy" and says the verses, ascribed to Andrew Marvell, were printed in a volume of *Miscellanies* published by the Spalding Society of Literature. On July 27th, Clare received the twenty-eighth number of the *Every-day Book* with the poem in it. "I shall venture again under another name after awhile," he commented. He ventured again on August 2nd, this time taking the name of Frederic Roberts of Milton and sending to Hone "A Farewell and Defiance to Love", fathered on Sir John Harington,[1] and supposed to be taken from a small book called *The Court of the Muses*. In another draft of the same letter he said he had found it on the fly-leaves of an old copy of *Reliquiae Wottonianae*. The letters were copied out in a disguised hand. This poem was not accepted by Hone, but it appeared later in the *European Magazine*, as did "Thoughts in a Churchyard", written in imitation of Sir Henry Wotton, "The Gipsy's Song", of Tom [sic] Davies,[2] and "Go with your tauntings, go", of Suckling. "To John Milton, From his honoured Friend, William Davenant"[3] was printed in the *Sheffield Iris*, on May 16th, 1826. By this time, Clare had made confession to Montgomery, who had written on May 5th, 1826, asking for definite proof of the authenticity of "The Vanitys of Life", which he had thought all along to be Clare's work: "I thought that the glorious offence carried its own redemption in itself, and I would not only forgive but rejoice to see such faults committed every day for the sake of such merits." He wished to include the verses in a collection of *Christian Poetry* if they were indeed the work of an old writer, and he asked to see the volume in which they were written. Clare replied on the 8th, saying how much Montgomery's kind notice had heartened him.

> ... But your question almost makes me feel ashamed to own to the extent of the falsehood I committed; and yet I will

[1] 1561–1612, godson of Queen Elizabeth.
[2] This could be either John Davies (1565–1618) or Sir John Davies (1569–1626).
[3] Sir William D'Avenant (1606–68), who was said to have been Shakespeare's godson?

> not double it by adding a repetition of the offence. I must confess to you that the poem is mine, and that the book from whence it was pretended to have been transcribed has no existence (that I know of) but in my invention of the title. And now that I have confessed to the crime, I will give you the reasons for committing it. I have long had a fondness for the poetry of the time of Elizabeth, though I have never had any means of meeting with it, farther than in the confined channels of Ritson's 'English Songs,' Ellis's 'Specimens,' and Walton's 'Angler'; and the winter before last, though amidst a severe illness, I set about writing a series of verses, in their manner, as well as I could, which I intended to pass off under their names, though some whom I professed to imitate I had never seen ... [1]

"The Vanities of Life", title corrected, poem punctuated and reprinted in *The Rural Muse*, did not prevent its appearing in *Ancient Ballads and Songs of the Peasantry of England*, 1857, with a note by the editor, R. Bell, retelling the story of its discovery, with additions, and making some deductions about the character of the unknown author. In *Notes and Queries*, 1873, J. H. Dixon, LL.D., wrote that he had included the poem in his *Ancient Poems, Ballads, and Songs of the Peasantry of England*, 1846, that it had found its way into various selections, that he did not believe Montgomery ever had any doubts about it as a genuine old poem, and that because of its elegance and lack of any "little slip that detects the forger", he was convinced that Clare's claim to it betrayed mental aberration. "Could it be proved that Clare was really the author," he added, "it would place him beside Burns." In that same year, 1873, J. L. Cherry closed the discussion by giving proof of Clare's authorship of the poems.

Clare's recapturing of the spirit of these old writers took the form of a fanciful essay which seems to have been the outcome of that day described in his Journal, September 8th, 1824, when he read *The Compleat Angler*. He imagined a day spent "with some delightful company the latchets of whose shoes I am not worthy to unloose & yet they were very civil to me & seemed

[1] This letter is quoted from J. L. Cherry's *Life and Remains of John Clare*.

quite at home with my rudeness." They were Izaak Walton, Sir Henry Wotton, Sir Walter Raleigh, Dr Donne, Charles Cotton, George Herbert, and Richard Hooker. Some of the company repeated fragments of their own verses; a nest of gipsies sang Frank Davison's[1] "Song of the Beggars", "till a sudden sprinkling shower made us leave our angles & seek shelter under a sycamore tree" there the haymaking damsel sang again "that sweetest of Melodies made by Kit Marlowe", after which the company betook them to a tavern and spent the night in mirth and memories.

Clare continued to write imitations of older poets for some years; there are a score of them among his manuscripts. "I am still going on with my verses after the manner of the old poets but not with the success I began with," he wrote to Montgomery in 1827. Nor did he put aside the idea of publishing them as originals; but in 1829 he was dissuaded by Taylor and Cary.

The publication of *The Shepherd's Calendar* still hanging fire, Clare was glad enough to find any market for the poems which he continued to produce with amazing fertility. In 1825 the outlook for poetry gave every sign that the boom of the first quarter of the century was drawing to an end. "The literary world is dulness itself—scarcely a book of any value published," Hessey wrote in May, and Beddoes had exclaimed in 1824, "If I were the literary weather-guesser for 1825 I would safely prognosticate fog, rain, blight in due succession for its dullard months ... " The more prudent editors, who knew their public as Taylor undoubtedly did, restricted their activities in time; the more reckless or unwary went on to suffer in the crash of 1826. In September, Taylor fell seriously ill with brain-fever; his recovery marked a new period in his life. Literary interests took second place, and scientific and theological became predominant. He was no longer proud of his reputation as a free-thinker, and he began to look about for some means of linking his new interests with his business. Overwork and disappointment, culminating in a breakdown, had entirely changed his outlook; but he also discerned a change in the taste of the reading public which fitted in with his own inclinations. As the general interest in poetry declined for a decade or more,

[1] Francis Davison (1575?–1619).

the demand for works of useful knowledge, for text-books and novels, continued to increase steadily. While the best work of poets such as Darley, Beddoes, Wade, R. H. Horne, H. Coleridge, and Clare, went almost unregarded, in the magazines and annuals glow-worm lights of verse still caught the public eye until the rising star of Tennyson outshone them.

It was through Van Dyk that Clare had a few poems in the *European Magazine*, for which Van Dyk himself was writing at this time. Here was published the only one of Clare's essays to see the light of print—the essay on "Popularity in Authorship". Clare was grappling with an unfamiliar medium: "far from a close reasoner in prose," he had difficulty in achieving the orderly exposition of a theme. His mind was like Coleridge's for profusion; thought crowded on thought. The essay on "Popularity" touched on the neglected theme of what ordinary people will read if given half a chance. It ends with an eloquent comparison between the fierce blaze of "fashionable popularity" and the "quiet progress of a name gaining ground by gentle degrees in the world's esteem".

Clare had 12*s.* 6*d.* a page for his writing in the *European Magazine*; Van Dyk scolded him for giving away poems to Montgomery, Hone, and others. "Do nothing without being paid for it ... If I had £10,000 a year I would be paid rather than encourage so dangerous a precedent." He spoke as the professional journalist who saw his market being flooded by the productions of amateurs who desired only to see their writings in print. The spectacular genius of Byron and Scott had modified the taste of the public. In 1820 there was still a fair demand for poetry; the tide of enthusiasm ebbed rapidly in the following years. Yet it left behind it a host of readers and writers who dabbled in pools on the margin. The curious may study the tastes of purveyors and public alike in the Annuals which came into being in 1823 and 1824, flourished and multiplied in the late eighteen-twenties, and declined in the eighteen-thirties.

Although the names of most of the talented writers of the day may be found among the contributors, even Lamb, Scott, and Wordsworth yielding occasionally to the urgings of friendship, the Annuals will attract or repel the modern reader chiefly as literary museums, with a few gems shining here and there. As their primary aim was decorative rather than literary, literature became in them the handmaid of the steel engraving, and the editors, saddled with the heavy expenses of their "sumptuous embellishments", and dependent for success upon large sales, could afford neither to risk transcending what they believed were the tastes of the general reading public nor to pay highly for much literary work of quality. Scott might obtain his £5 a page for the sake of advertisement; but if Clare could be persuaded to accept a copy of the book in lieu of payment, most of the editors had no scruples about offering it.

Clare began contributing to the Annuals in the summer of 1825. The *Literary Souvenir* for 1826, edited by Alaric Watts, published two poems, one of them being "First Love's Recollections", a tribute to Mary Joyce, whom he had last seen nine years before. Clare was also represented in the 1827 and 1828 volumes. With Thomas Pringle, editor of *Friendship's Offering*, the son of a Scottish farmer and friend of Hogg and Cunningham, Clare's relationship was entirely good. Pringle found Clare, he said, a man after his own heart; they corresponded on very friendly terms between 1828 and 1834, in which year Pringle set the seal on his labours as secretary to the Anti-Slavery Society by signing the document which proclaimed the abolition of slavery. Ten of Clare's poems, some of considerable length, appeared in *Friendship's Offering*, and Pringle saw that Clare was paid for them. Clare also had ten poems in the *Amulet*, but had the greatest difficulty in extracting payment from S. C. Hall, the editor, despite many promises and professions of friendship on Hall's part. Others appeared in Ackerman's *Forget Me Not* and *Juvenile Forget Me Not*. Marshall, publisher of *A Pledge of Friendship*, was another of those against whom Clare's London friends had to undertake dunning expeditions.

In 1829, two of the *Londoners*, both regular contributors to the Annuals, turned editors, and applied to all their friends for support. Allan Cunningham prepared the *Anniversary* for John Sharpe, in an effort to outshine the popular *Keepsake*. Clare's contribution was that mature and vital poem "Autumn", of which a later and better version was printed in the *Rural Muse*. The other new venture of 1829 was Thomas Hood's *Gem*, an annual which did not entirely belie its name; there were several gems among the usual tales and verses of domestic affections and Oriental disaffections. Clare's contribution "Thou art gone the dark journey" was one. He sent it after Hood had refused "To the Rural Muse", which became the first poem in his fourth book.

Beside contributions to the Annuals, we find poems by Clare in several newspapers and magazines of this period: the *New Monthly* in 1824; the *Literary Magnet*, 1827 and 1828; the *Spirit and Manners of the Age*; the *Morning Post*; and Moxon's *Englishman's Magazine.* He found a place in the *Living Poets of Great Britain*, Paris, 1827, and his considerable share in the *Naturalist's Poetical Companion*, 1832, shows that he had admirers here and there to replace the many who had forgotten him. He also supplied a number of songs to the composers Power, Barnett, and Hodgson. All these activities added a little to his income at a time when he badly needed money, though the difficulty of obtaining payment from some of the publishers added not a little to his worries.

Mrs Emmerson's letters to Clare toward the end of 1825 contain references to incidents in his domestic life which he evidently discussed with Regency frankness in his letters to her. He was still receiving advice from Dr Darling, who wrote in December telling him to make his conscience easy about his children, who had been ill, "for however much they may suffer, it is through no voluntary fault of your own." He was not to give way to low spirits or abstain from exercise. When Mrs Emmerson wrote before Christmas she was waiting for Clare's "unreserved and free explanation of what may have taken place since I was in Deeping ... your poor heart is alas! too yielding for your general good." The explanation must have arrived and she replied on January 10th, 1826. He had been wandering from home, himself, and happiness; she deeply regretted the cause of his late "outbreaking from propriety"; "but why my dear Clare, will you allow the temper or injudicious conduct of others, to harry you away from your own reason." She averred she was neither prude nor moralist, but would prevail on him "by every gentle kind and reasonable entreaty" to give up his acquaintance with —— [sic]. "It is an *unworthy* connection and can only bring you a train of miseries." She besought him to return to home and family and hoped —— would do all in her power to make his mind more contented and enable him to pursue his literary labours. In March she again pleaded with him to rid himself of domestic discontents and rouse himself from his "infatuated, tortured, besotted, and inactive" state.

The letters throw no further light on this domestic disharmony, until the end of 1827, the occasion of his next illness. Meanwhile, his relationship with John Taylor survived yet another crisis. It was six months since Taylor had taken over the editing again, yet little progress had been made. Mrs Emmerson had had a long talk with him about Clare's affairs in December 1825, and had mentioned the possibility of another publisher being found. Taylor hoped Clare would not risk his reputation by letting his manuscripts pass into other hands. He again promised that a statement of accounts would be sent at once, and said that if Clare needed money he had only to ask for it. He thought there was about £40 profit on *The Village Minstrel*. In January, Clare evidently wrote to remind Taylor of his promise to bring out *The Shepherd's Calendar* without delay. The publisher replied on the 28th expressing no little indignation at Clare's "frank censure", which had, however, relieved him from the irksome situation of submission and apology and self-blame to which he had lately submitted. Now he could speak out. Clare, and Clare alone, was responsible for the delay and present total stoppage in the work. The manuscript of "July", on which he was engaged, was almost unreadable, and his copyists could do nothing with it. It was "slovenly written and slovenly composed". He sent it back for Clare to judge for himself.

The first "July" is one of Clare's more difficult scripts but why, unless with his usual self-justification Taylor snarled so is hard to see. In the poem activities are crowded: the nightingale doesn't sing after the third week in June and threshers wouldn't surely by then have started to thresh. Promptly Clare supplied a second, shorter version, more orderly, though much less rich. This became the 1827 printed version. In Clare's reply to Taylor's strictures, he did not point out, as he might with justice have pointed out, that the delay since Taylor began on this poem was brief compared with the delay before he set about it; nor did he mention that Taylor had definitely asked him to send up his manuscripts as he wrote them and leave copying and correction to him. He simply agreed that the matter now rested with him and, though he "never was fond of copying", that he would do his utmost. He enclosed the new draft of the poem, and was willing to try again if it was still unsatisfactory. Taylor was highly delighted with the second "July" and sent back the remaining manuscripts for transcription. Obviously Clare could have done his own copying and correcting long before if he had been allowed to do so—or perhaps if he had been less filially acquiescent with Taylor.

The publication of the essay on "Popularity" had encouraged him to continue prose-writing. He had finished a character-sketch, "The Farmer and Vicar", which he proposed to remodel as "The Harvest Supper, or a Sketch of Old Customs". He had some idea of making a book of essays, and Taylor encouraged him, suggesting a criticism of the poets of the past and present ages as a suitable subject, a suggestion which Clare took up. He also began a tragedy in the Elizabethan manner, and planned to publish locally a long satiric poem: "The Parish", for which no place could be found in *The Shepherd's Calendar*, waited until 1935 for publication.

During 1825–26 Clare corresponded with Elizabeth Kent, Leigh Hunt's sister-in-law, to whom Hessey had shown the letters on natural history. Her *Flora Domestica*, published in 1823 by Taylor and Hessey, had contained pleasant mention of Clare. On April 8th, Taylor remarked that Darley was gratified by Clare's opinion of his book; this, presumably, was *Labours of Idleness*: or *Seven Nights' Entertainments, by Guy Penseval*, which Taylor published in 1826. Taylor wrote in pessimistic vein; business was flat; he was weary of it, and contemplated retiring to live on his means and amuse himself with his own vagaries as Clare did. He saw none of the *Londoners* now except Lamb, Darley and Cunningham, and had found that what was called friendship was merely self-interest. In May there came a rumour that Taylor had gone bankrupt, and Clare was worried by it until he heard that it was unfounded. He had been visiting at Stamford and Milton and had found the change of company beneficial.

June brought a bombshell in the form of a brusque letter from Edward Drury, demanding settlement of a bill for over £40. Taylor, evidently still engaged in winding up the affairs of the firm of Taylor and Hessey, had sent Drury a claim for £100 which had been advanced by the firm years before in the form of books sent to booksellers to whom Drury owed money. Drury countered this with a claim for money and goods supplied to Clare during the writing of *The Village Minstrel*, for procuring medical advice for his mother, and for binding books. Taylor refused to admit this to the firm's accounts, and advised Drury to settle it with Clare. Drury's demand for immediate settlement perturbed Clare greatly. Taylor assured him that Drury had no right to charge anything, because his account had been received and allowed by the firm long before. But Drury wrote again, threatening legal proceedings, so Clare asked Taylor to get the matter settled for him. This was eventually done by Hessey, who discovered that some of the money claimed had in fact been paid already. A balance of some £30 was placed on the debit side of Clare's account with the firm. With that his relationship with Drury again lapsed, until the arrival of the long-delayed statement of accounts in 1829 convinced Clare that he had been not only unkindly but unfairly treated by his old friend.

During the summer and autumn of 1826, Clare worked again in the fields and felt happier, although Hessey's envy of his happy lot as a peasant was scarcely justified. He had renewed his confidence in Taylor, who was now pressing forward with *The Shepherd's Calendar* and showed interest in Clare's prose writings. The scheme for the publication locally of "The Parish" also showed signs of reaching fruition; details of printing and costs were being discussed. In his spare time Clare was busy making in his garden a shrubbery of hedge-plants and wild flowers, a plan which he followed later at Northborough. In June a second son had been born, and was baptized on the 18th—"John, son of John Clare, Poet."

> Two little girls and two little boys
> Are quite enough for wedded joys

Mrs Emmerson, who had no children, wrote.

In September the title-page and dedication of the new book were under discussion; there was talk of a frontispiece by Hilton or De Wint, and Hessey suggested that Clare should write a preface himself, as there was little to say except to account for the long delay—on the score of ill-health. Thus Clare was to bear the onus of his publishers' shortcomings and provide an excuse which was only partially true. The only illness which had delayed the book was Taylor's own; and that for no more than six months of the four years. At last, toward the end of November, Clare received six copies of the book; but it was not yet ready for the public, for De Wint's first drawing had proved unsuitable, and a second was made and engraved. Thus five more months were added to the long struggle of *The Shepherd's Calendar* toward the light.

During those five months Clare spent some time with his friend Artis, and helped him in his excavation of a Roman villa on the side of the North Road, near Water Newton. Artis had left Milton in August 1826, through trouble arising out of a love-affair; but he continued his work on the Roman remains in the district, and was preparing for publication his book on the fine mosaic pavements and remains of Roman baths, villas, and potteries which he had unearthed around Castor since 1822. A brief account of these remains, "by far the most curious and extensive that have been explored in Britain," appeared in the *New Monthly Magazine*, in October 1826. The *Durobrivae of Antoninus*, which Artis published in 1828, consists of a series of plates illustrating these finds, but without any letterpress.

Early in the new year, Clare wrote to George Darley, who had just published a text-book on geometry and was busy with others on algebra and trigonometry. Taylor sent a copy to Clare, remarking that it was a subject for which the two poets had a common taste. Darley replied on March 2nd. Discussing his mathematical work, he agreed with Clare that the writers of scientific text-books treated the public as babies, designing to titillate their fancy rather than improve their reason. Clare had been unwell again in January, and Darley referred to this:

> I was sorry to hear from Taylor yesterday that you were not in good health. What *can* be the matter with you, so healthfully situated and employed? Methinks you should live the life of an oak-tree, or a sturdy elm, that groans in a storm, but only for pleasure. Do you meditate too much?—or sit too immovably? ... Poetry, I mean the composition of it, does not always sweeten the mind as much as the reading of it—There is an anxiety, a fervour, an impatience, a vain-gloriousness attending it which untranquillizes even in the

sweetest-seeming moods of the poet. Like the bee, he is restive and uneasy, even in collecting his sweets.

Writing on March 30th to inform Clare that De Wint had finished the frontispiece drawing, which he did *gratis*, but that the engraver was delaying with it, Taylor remarked that Darley and he had been reading Clare's poems together, and Darley liked "The Dream" best. "Darley is the only good that ever came from the London Magazine—He is a staunch Friend, & one of the gentlest & kindest of Human Beings—It is very odd that I have never seen Reynolds for nearly 2 years. He has lately lost an Infant Child."

By the end of April, the last of the many delays had come to an end and *The Shepherd's Calender* was ready for the public. Clare's brief preface expressed his long-felt desire to appear before the public simply as a poet.

But *The Shepherd's Calendar* had waited too long. The public, whose memory had lasted just long enough to redeem *The Village Minstrel* from complete failure in 1821, could not be expected to remember without informative aid for six years more. By 1829 only 400 copies had been sold. Clare's dream in which he saw the proofs of the book crumble into dust had foreshadowed reality. The reviews were few and most of them poor. The *Eclectic Review* again gave him a kindly reception and just praise. The *Literary Gazette* thought there was fine poetry in the book, but held out few hopes of its success with the public, since its poetry was not romantic enough; the reviewer added with unconscious irony that there was too much regular routine of comfort in the life of the English peasantry for it to be very picturesque. It was certainly not a surfeit of comfort that produced the rick burnings of the 1820s and the Swing riots of 1831. The *Literary Chronicle* published a favourable review by a friend of Van Dyk's, but it was too hastily written to be impressive; *Blackwood's* mentioned *The Shepherd's Calendar* as the work of the Ettrick Shepherd. Another writer thought it would be manifest injustice to take Clare at his word and view his work apart from a consideration of his rustic character; it would be unfair to judge the poems by too high a standard. Similar notices appeared in the *Monthly Magazine* and the *Magnet*.

Yet even if the public's memory had been jogged more by the reviews, a miracle would have been needed for public response to have been in 1827 what it had been in 1820. From all sides came complaints that there was no demand for poetry. The age was changed, Taylor said. "All the old Poetry Buyers seem to be dead and the New Race have no taste for it." He thought men's circumstances were not so prosperous as formerly and they had no money for luxuries. He intended in future to publish only works of utility; he was busy with Darley's new book, *Sylvia,* which appeared in November, but he had no great hope that it would sell. In August he asked Clare to keep his expenses within bounds, as he had had to pay the late firm of Taylor and Hessey £80 for advances made to Clare and he saw no prospect of getting it back from the new book.

Writing to Montgomery in September, Clare suggested that the rage for novels was perhaps the cause of the decline of interest in poetry. Montgomery replied, "Poetry has had its day in the present age and two more generations must go by before there is such another revival in its favour, as was excited by the agitation of human minds of every degree and order, by the events of the French Revolution."

Van Dyk, too, now struggling hard to avert direst poverty, voiced his complaints; his publisher had failed, and he had lost all his profit on *The Gondola*; he was writing for periodicals and music-setters, but had difficulty in getting payment; he cursed editors for dolts who preferred the commonplace to the original.

All this meant that Clare's attempt to earn a livelihood by his pen was foredoomed to failure; and because his finest work was disregarded—much of it, indeed, never published—succeeding generations have remembered him as the "peasant-poet" of 1820 who failed to stay the course. The poets who are anathematized in their day, as were Keats and Shelley, may with confidence expect redress from oncoming generations; those who are simply neglected or forgotten, as were Blake, Clare, Darley and others, may languish in obscurity for a century.

We may understand why the reviewer in the *Literary Gazette* fell into the old 'pastoral' fallacy from ignorance about social conditions in Britain and the poverty of the peasantry. His ear had heard joy audible all through *The Shepherd's Calendar*: therefore Clare and his like spent the year in comfortable if unpicturesque routine. Others have made the same pathetic mistake since then, and Clare's verse aids and abets this age-old nostalgic error. In 1827, with troubles and poverty behind him and with little else visible ahead, comes his third volume; and not a month of the twelve which the title-poem celebrates but has its chronicle of delights: January, with winter stories told by the dame round the fire; February, with one of those glorious spring days and then a sullen throw-back into winter; March, when the ploughmen were as busy as the birds, and, like them, members of a naturally unified universe, not vain masters of it; April, a "fairey month" with "sunny hours" yet "north cutting gales", and with childhood's "treasures"—violets, primroses, horse blobs[1], cuckoo, martins, swallows; May, with its flowers made glorious; June, with the furmety-feast after sheep-shearing; July, with its heavy noon-pause while white feathers lie still on the still water and the heat shimmers up over the fields; and so on round to December. This was no pastoral or "romantic" looking back. He was describing what he saw every day.

The other poems in the book, such as "The Approach of Spring" and "The Last of Autumn", continue the story; autumn was a season whose triumphant, wild, or peaceful witness gave Clare deeply religious content no less than June's dappled sky. Hard to credit that "Each year with brighter blooms returned", how he saw every new season more clearly than the last. The eternal spring was "one that weeps Life's faded majesty". These two poems were among the collection of "Village Scenes" which Clare had prepared for the press in 1820.

The Shepherd's Calendar as a whole offers a surer vision to its readers than can be found in the earlier books. It was not only the happiness of his childhood he was reliving—he *did* relive that at times all through his life; but present things, "grey veined ivy", or the colt knapping his furry hide in winter, gave him a joy which did not depend on youth or belief or personal circumstances for its being. He found it in spite of all the difficulties of manhood.

"Philosophy" is a high-sounding term with which to burden

[1] The excellent 1964 edition of *The Shepherd's Calendar* gives *blebs*. Clare used *bleb*—verb; a horse blob, water blob, is a marsh marigold, *Caltha palustris*.

the memory of a man like Clare. Better to speak of a realization which he had of his own life and his own time and the relationship of both these with all life.

The core of this realization lies in that joy of which *The Shepherd's Calendar* is so full. We shall not expect to find the careful, self-conscious expression of it in intellectual terms, a metaphysic chained beneath the Etna of the mind. We shall not find him discussing man's attitude to the whole of nature or the whole of life. But the attitude is none the less implicit in every poem. It is instinctive, not self-conscious, united with his art, and almost united, as we shall see, with his whole life. Yet because we are used to deliberate, extraneous expression of the personal philosophy of poets, Clare's has been thought non-existent.

Every sound, colour and shape in nature moved him; he submitted himself and sang of them endlessly: formlessly too, sometimes, with the redundant persistence of *bard*, *scop*, *filidh*, or *skald* chanting or singing in the days before poetry was written down. To examine, philosophize, or explain would have been to dessicate and in the end come no nearer to discovering the reality of what he described or to evoking response in readers. So Clare became a voice crying, almost prophetically, perhaps vainly, from the further side of the age of machines, for a recognized and acknowledged kinship with every living thing in the natural universe. As the outlook of a happy man, comfortably circumstanced, the odds against him not too great, this might carry weight. As the lifelong faith of a man circumstanced as Clare was, it becomes an impressive gospel.

Since Clare was living, however desperately, by his faith, and plying his art accordingly, his art was almost as spontaneous as his faith and life. Yet his art could not and did not escape the rigours of the intellect. He had always fretted after knowledge, knowing it, not wisdom but, a necessary part of wisdom. In *The Shepherd's Calendar* his melodies become his own, his words and phrases more memorable, shapes, colours and details clearer. The sense of life in bird, squirrel, stones and flints is more surely translated. All this implies deliberate, exhaustive selection of word, idiom, phrase. Clare was not, after his apprenticeship, led away by the sentimental, the literary, or the sonorous. The ostentation of mere sound he definitely avoided: accuracy was all, a word's power as a verbal substitute for the thing it was to represent. Living near the native ground of Dryden and Shakespeare, he had inherited a dialect singularly pure, rich in Danish influence as well as Anglo-Saxon. His publisher, who did not tamper with Keats's manuscripts and wrote that he did not want to "misinterpret" Clare, but who knew his public, was against dialect words; the few dialect words in *The Shepherd's Calendar* need no gloss. They are traditional country words, Anglo-Saxon–Danish. They belong to the sub-song of English poetry, poetry less deflected by Norman-French and Renaissance–classical influence than English literary poetry has been. In the "bright, glib ice" of January (not forgetting Hunt's predilection for the word in "The Nymphs") "glib" is as inevitable a northern word as any that can be found to describe ice. To feel the re-creation of a July midday no more is needed than the passage which remains both in the "July" Taylor rejected and the second "July" Clare supplied, and which Taylor (with emendations) printed in 1827:

The tottergrass upon the hill
& spiders threads is hanging still
The feathers dropt from moorhens wings
Upon the waters surface clings
As stedfast & as heavy seem
As stones beneath them in the stream
Hawkweed & groundsels fairey downs
Unruffled keep their seeding crowns
& in the oven heated air
Not one light thing is floating there
Save that to the earnest eye
The restless heat swims twittering bye ...

As an expression both of his singularly traditional poetic faith and as an example of his mature artistry, *The Shepherd's Calendar* of 1827 is a milestone in Clare's story. Read in the Oxford edition of 1964, with Clare's original text finely restored, and not forgetting *The Village Minstrel* or "The Parish", it is, as the Oxford editors say, the "truest" poem of country life. Certainly it is one of the most accurate, so close and faithful is it to its subject.

Autumn

CHAPTER THIRTEEN

Skies O'ercast: 1827-1830

In June 1827, another child was born, but died before it was baptized. Clare was still not well, but able to go out with Henderson in search of bee-, fly- and spider-orchis. Early in July, Henry Behnes the sculptor, a friend of the Emmersons, paid him a visit, to which Mrs Emmerson referred in a letter of July 8th: "Harry B. told me of your welcome, of the pleasant hour he spent with you, of your harvest, or rather Botanical pursuits, of your delightfully rustic attire, your 'unshaven' chin and all the etcetera that are so peculiarly the attributes and habits of the genius of solitude." She also mentioned a dinner at the Bishop's, and hoped Clare had been at his ease there. Behnes had actually been greatly disturbed at the situation in which he found Clare and his family; writing after his return to London, he urged Clare, for the sake of Patty and the children, to make his want known to the people who were too ready to think that poets live on their imagination; when he had gained independence he could become a recluse again. Frank Simpson had also seen Clare and was equally concerned; he wrote from London offering to do anything in his power to help. Clare confessed to having fled to an old friend for comfort; Mrs Emmerson could joke about his recent attachment to John Barleycorn; she probably realized it was not sufficiently grave to mount the high moral horse about: "yet inasmuch as it made you happy I must be glad."

In October the Bishop of Peterborough visited Clare, and we learn from another letter of Mrs Emmerson's that he could not invite the Bishop into his cottage because the door was locked against him—whether by accident or design is not clear. The same letter mentions his reading at this time—Dryden,

Bell's *Life in London*, Sturm's *Reflections*,[1] and *Boxiana*—a mixed bag. Both Pierce Egan's *Boxiana*[2] and the Sporting journal Bell's *Life in London* will have effect on the compromise Clare's emotional strength will be seen to make with his mental integrity later, after years of poetic activity under strain. Meanwhile, despite, or because of, the poor reception of *The Shepherd's Calendar*, Clare's ambition, undiminished, had shifted from desire for present popularity, even acknowledgement, to preoccupation with "after-fame". He was planning a new volume for 1828, which was to beat all his other performances hollow.

Taylor proposed that Darley and he should come to Helpston at Christmas, but the visit had to be postponed because Darley was too busy. He was anxious about the reception of his *Sylvia*, and he had just proposed himself as candidate for the Professorship of English Literature at the new University of London. Lamb and Cary had given him handsome letters of recommendation, but Taylor thought that he was too little known as an author, although he had written so much. Whatever the reason, Darley did not get the post. Clare received a characteristic letter from him in December, together with a copy of *Sylvia*, "as a mark of my regard and *brotherly* feeling." Darley spoke with pleasurable anticipation of "the threatened invasion of the Cottage at Helpstone, next Spring". He thought it would please him more than Clare; "For I have no faculty at conversation—dull as a sign post." In this same month, Taylor was appointed publisher and bookseller to the University of London. Despairing of further success with poetry, having for some time specialized in the publication of text-books of useful knowledge, he was well fitted for his new post, which assured him freedom from business worries and some leisure to pursue his own curious researches. Although the affairs of the defunct firm of Taylor and Hessey were not finally disentangled until 1829, Clare realized that this new appointment meant that he must look for another publisher; and he pressed repeatedly for the long-promised statement of accounts.

[1] *On the Evidence of God and His Providence Throughout All Nature for Every Day of the Year.*

[2] Or "Sketches of Ancient and Modern Pugilism", founded on an earlier work by George Smeeton, first printed in parts in 1812–13, reprinted and added to up to 1829

On November 4th, he renewed his correspondence with Cary after a long silence, due, he said, first to his illness, then to shame at having neglected for so long to reply to Cary's last letter. Unless some correspondence has been lost, this was the letter of February 1825, in which Cary promised to read Clare's memoirs. There is no reference to them in the renewed correspondence. Clare asked Cary's opinion of *The Shepherd's Calendar*, and spoke of his present "attempts after the manner of the olden Bards in the reign of Elizabeth", mentioning the compliment paid him by Montgomery. He looked forward to the appearance of Cary's *Lives of the Poets*: he had always turned first to them in the *London Magazine*. He thought Johnson, beginning only with Cowley, missed out the best.

Clare renewed correspondence with Taylor in November, after a silence on both sides. He spoke of his indifferent health, and asked for some engravings of De Wint's frontispiece and a copy of the *Eclectic* with the review of *The Shepherd's Calendar*. This review was by Josiah Conder whose poems[1] Clare admired; he wished to write to him: praise from a fellow-poet always heartened. Taylor sent the plates and the magazine, and in his reply Clare spoke of the pleasure with which he looked forward to the proposed visit by Taylor and Darley. He had enjoyed reading *Sylvia*; the characters of the peasantry in it reminded him of those in *As You Like It*.

Toward the end of the year, indisposition, so often a delayed action after sustained mental effort and severe disappointment, took a not entirely unexpected turn. Frank Simpson had talked with Patty about her husband's health, and was much concerned. Mrs Emmerson's letters referred frequently to his distress of mind and pains in the head; Dr Darling's letters mention eruptions on the body which he thought were due to Clare's eating more and working less and generating bad humours in his corporeal frame. He thought there was no cause for alarm, but in January he wrote that in the doubtful character of the complaint it was unsafe to trust to prescription at a distance, and advised Clare to consult his local doctor.

There are three entries in Clare's journal—for February 6th, 7th and 9th, 1828, which he must have added at this time but

[1] *The Star in the East* (1824).

which he placed among entries for February, 1825.[1] Those for the 7th and 9th run:

> Greatly disturbed today & uncommonly ill O what a blessing is health we know not how to prize it till we loose it Dr Darling restored me to health but my foolish follys has compelled her to leave me again & I fear for ever
>
> Went to Stamford today with Patty in great distress to Dr Cooper I have set it down here to see if I shall live till 1829 to see it again I fear not but so be it I am not my own maker

Clare was tormenting himself. Whether about drinking or sexual disease is not clear. Later February found him still depressed, unable to accept a second invitation of kindly Mrs Marsh's to the Palace at Peterborough. Mrs Emmerson urged him to London to see Dr Darling and to discuss his affairs with Taylor, and he decided to accept her invitation. The good poem, "Autumn", was written during this period of fresh forms of illness. He sent it to Mrs Emmerson, who recognized it as "by far the best and choicest thing" he had written. Clare had told her to shut out Collins's "Evening" when she read it, but she thought no such effort necessary, since the poem itself obliterated the memory of Collins's ode, "with all due respect to the harmony of his flowing lines."

Clare's fourth visit to London began in the latter part of February and lasted about five weeks; he stayed with the Emmersons in Stratford Place, where his "sky-chamber" at the top of the house had been prepared for him. What we know of this visit is gleaned from letters. On February 25th, to Patty, he wrote:

> Mr Emmersons Doctor a Mr Ward told me last night that there was little or nothing the matter with me & yet I got no sleep the whole of last night but I hope for better success tonight I have as yet taken no medicine & perhaps I shall not but I shall most likely see Dr Darling before long for satisfaction[2]

[1] Given in *The Prose of John Clare* (*op. cit.*) as belonging to 1825.
[2] *The Letters of John Clare, op. cit.*

There were no dinners for contributors of the brilliant, but short-lived *London* now, and of that company only Darley, with whom Clare talked poetry again, had kept in close touch with Taylor. Even if the company had been there, ill-health would have made a round of visits a painful pleasure. For this reason, perhaps, Clare hesitated to call even upon his old friend Cary, now installed at the British Museum Library. Taylor prevailed on him to go, and Cary showed him over the library, where he was at once delighted and awed at the sight of so many books. With Taylor Clare found occasion to discuss his affairs and the immediate result was a plan for Clare to take copies of his poems at a reduced rate to sell locally.

Another old *Londoner* whom Clare met again was Allan Cunningham; he paid a visit to Cunningham's home and gave him the poem "Autumn" for *The Anniversary*. Cunningham praised it, and advised Clare to try his hand at prose tales. Clare replied by letter just before he left for home, sending a "shake of the hand on paper" by way of good-bye.

Clare *had* tried his hand at prose tales. In "The Stage Coach", the hero, a courteous gentleman, rescues three ladies, who are travelling by coach, from the attentions of two fops, and then holds a long discussion with the ladies upon the follies of the day, the arrogance of riches, and the prevalence of bad novels. In "The Two Soldiers, or The Protection of Providence", intended as a novel, two soldiers returned from service abroad get lost at night in the country, and, seeking lodging at a large house, are turned away as suspicious characters. As in many of the essays these drafts of stories show a recurrent theme of the exposure of arrogance, suspicion and discourtesy, especially of rich towards poor not surprising for the 1820s.

Rippingille wrote while Clare was in London, hoping to see him if he stayed for a month or two. Rippingille had met nothing but disappointments of late, and intended going to Italy "to be among people guided by passions instead of self-interest". He was able to achieve this ambition in later years, and became "one of the best delineators of Italian groups" for a time. De Wint was in Normandy. Hilton wrote soon after Clare's return home, reproaching him for failing to visit him while in London. Van Dyk was confined to his bed with the illness to which he was soon to succumb. His last letters in 1827 reveal a story of struggle against misfortune and poverty. He had ceased to call on the Emmersons, being sensitive about his situation.

> Had circumstances permitted, you would have seen me long before this, but I have found, Clare, that poverty, which divides us from the rich, makes us even aliens to the poor. Having to cater from day to day, we are like shipwrecked men who speedily lose all thoughts of humanity except those that immediately concern themselves.

Despite this preoccupation with his own troubles, he was ready to do what he could on Clare's behalf. He managed to get some money which was owed by the editor of the *European Magazine*, and he offered to try to get a publisher for some "National and Provincial Melodies" of Clare's. Later in the year he overcame his illness and visited the Emmersons again. They had him moved to better lodgings, where he could receive proper attention, but he declined rapidly and died in June 1828.

Clare spent some time in the company of Harry Behnes, who, in 1828, was setting out to make his name as a sculptor; to avoid confusion with his more gifted but degenerate brother William, he became Behnes Burlowe. For some years to come he worked zealously on Clare's behalf, taking his poems round and extracting money from editors for them. Another result of the friendship was the bust for which Clare sat during this 1828 visit. Of bronze, it is now in the Northampton Public Library.

Clare also met some of the editors of the Annuals to which he was contributing, and visited Marshall and other publishers to arrange for future contributions and try to obtain payment for past: with little success, however; he was a poor debt-collector. He met Alaric and Mrs Watts at the house of Mrs Emmerson, who suspected lion-hunters and was not impressed by them. But Watts, Clare says, was kind to him, offering to help in procuring a publisher for a new volume of poems. He also made the acquaintance of S. C. Hall, whose letters had been full of friendly professions, but who was unwilling, or unable, to pay for the many poems he accepted. His *Book of Gems of Modern Poets*, 1838 and 1844, giving selections of Wordsworth,

Shelley, Coleridge, Crabbe, Scott, Keats and others, included Clare's "June", "The Quiet Mind" and "Mary Lee" and contained this sketch of Clare as Hall saw him in 1828:

> ... His appearance, when some years ago it was our lot to know him, was that of a simple rustic; and his manners were remarkably gentle and unassuming. He was short and thick, yet not ungraceful, in person. His countenacce was plain but agreeable; he had a look and manner so dreamy, as to have appeared sullen—but for a peculiarly winning smile; and his forehead was so broad and high, as to have bordered on deformity ...

Another and less vivid picture was given in *A Book of Memories*, 1871, where Hall explained, a little tardily, that he was ignorant, when he had dealings with Clare, of Clare's circumstances. Unhappily for Hall we know that Clare's friend Sharpe visited him again and again in 1828 and 1829 to represent Clare's need of the considerable sum then owing to him. April 1829 found Sharpe still unsuccessful, and his quarry "as hard to catch as a little eel. I hunted him from place to place." There is no record that the eel was ever caught.

Clare seems to have spent most of the five weeks of his 1828 London visit at Stratford Place; as he explained to Allan Cunningham, he was too ignorant of the "great Babel" to venture far without a guide, and a guide was not always procurable. If he went out by himself, he would turn his steps toward Fleet Street and St Paul's, for that was the only part of London with which he was familiar and familiarity was important to him.

By the end of a month, he had grown homesick, as usual, and on March 21st he wrote to Patty to announce his return the following week:

> ... I am anxious to see you & the childern & I sincerely hope you are all well I have bought the dear little creatures four Books & Henry Behnes has promisd to send Frederic a wagon & horses as a box of music is not to be had—the books I have bought them are *Puss in Boots*, *Cinderella*, *Little Rhymes*, & *The Old Woman & Pig* tell them that the

pictures are all colored & they must make up their minds to chuse which they like best ere I come home—Mrs. Emmerson desires to be kindly remembered to you & intends sending the childern some Toys I hope next Wednesday night at furthest will see me in my old corner once again amongst you ... I have been poorly having caught cold & have been to Dr Darling I woud have sent you some money which I know you want but as I am coming home so soon I thought it much safer to bring it home myself then send it ... Kiss the dear Childern for me all round give my remembrances to all & believe me my dear Patty yours most affectionatly[1]

Evidently he departed from London hurriedly; he left behind his greatcoat and a number of books, which Mrs Emmerson, who had been ill for the greater part of his visit, had to forward. Soon after his return, a third son was born, and was baptized William Parker, on May 4th. Another mouth to feed; but Clare's affection for his children was strong and sustained, if emotional rather than practical. Apart from that, his visit to London had heartened him considerably. At this time it did appear, as Mr Emmerson remarked in a letter, that the Annuals might be one means of ameliorating the struggle with poverty. The unsound scheme by which Clare was to become his own bookseller at first held promise of some success. He wrote to Taylor on April 12th, asking a second time for the books to be sent; he had advertised them, had three orders already, and hoped to sell sets to visitors. Then the Emmersons sent news of a plan which they thought would bring comfort and security to Clare and realize an ambition which he had nourished for some years. A Mr and Mrs Henry Ryde of Burghley had dined with them, and had offered to get Clare a cottage and a few acres of land at Barnack. The plan was mentioned frequently in the letters of the summer of 1828, but nothing came of it.

Meanwhile Clare was still tormenting his mind over physical symptoms. Any aftermath of the infatuation which he had confessed to Mrs Emmerson in 1826, was surely behind him, whether or not it was connected with earlier "follys" or the

[1] *The Letters of John Clare, op. cit.*

February 1828 ones. This time his confidant was Hessey. Hessey in reply was glad to find that Clare's alarm had not so serious a foundation as he then supposed.

> But as there is reason for the suspicion you entertain, from the character of the person concerned with you, I think you should not be content without taking the opinion of a Medical man on the case, unless you actually find that all the symptoms have entirely disappeared. On your wife's Account, (whose name I am ashamed to couple with yours in speaking on such a subject), this is proper and your duty, and I trust you will think with me & act accordingly.

Answering Clare's question as to how he should make his peace with God, he advised him to humble himself before the God of Purity, as King David did when he had been led to commit the double crime of adultery and murder. "You have sinned like him in the first instance, and in intention have been guilty of the second, but it pleased God to frustrate your rash design upon your own life, and to afford you time for Repentance." Whatever the extent of Clare's sins or symptoms, whether he had actually attempted suicide or thought he had contracted venereal disease, or both, he paid as usual in mental stress.

In July 1828, the question of the long-promised accounts cropped up again. Writing to Taylor on the 2nd, Clare had no good news to communicate; he had sold only two sets of his poems and "got paid for one". He had to request an extra £5 to cover expenses. With many apologies, he pressed for a settlement of the accounts, so that he might know his exact position. Hessey sent the money. Taylor did not reply. Nor could Mr Emmerson obtain anything more substantial than promises. Even a letter from Lord Milton, whose influence Henderson enlisted on Clare's behalf, brought no answer from the publisher.

In September, Clare paid a visit to Boston, after repeated invitations from Henry Brooke of the *Boston Gazette*, to meet the bookworms of the old Lincolnshire town, once the commercial capital of England; its chief pride in Clare's day, as now, its tall church tower, Boston "stump", can be seen for forty miles across the wide levels of the fen and the shallow basin of the Wash. Clare's reception by his admirers at Boston warmed his heart; he was introduced to the literary circle of the town, met all the local versifiers, and was received by the Mayor, who gave a supper in his honour, at which Clare resolutely refused to make a speech, so that, as Mrs Emmerson remarked, the Bostonians hardly knew whether to treat him as a lion or a lamb. The Mayor's liberality was a bit of a test. He confessed to Taylor:

> ... one night took a little more liquor than I was in the habit of doing ... A lady at the table talked so ladily of the Poets that I drank off my glass very often without knowing it and he [the Mayor] as quickly filled it with no other intention than that of hospitality and I felt rather queer and got off almost directly after finding myself so but I was nothing like disordered yet it was wine and I was not used to the drink & tho it made me ill for two days or at least helpd to do so for I had a sort of cold at the same time it was nothing of that kind that caused my illness after my return,[1]

His stay lasted several days, and he sent home to Patty for sets of his poems which the Mayor and others had ordered.

He returned home cheered in mind, but for the next month or more he and his whole family suffered from "a very bad Fen fever", presumably brought back from Boston by Clare. He had told Taylor how he refused to make a speech: "realy this speechifying is a sore humbug & the sooner its out of fashion the better—" Characteristically Taylor went on assuming that the family's fever or at least Clare's post-Boston sickness must have been due to an overdose of hospitality. Glad that he had recovered without "one dose of phisic", Clare continued—moral exhortations from Taylor about drink extending to January 1829—again to reassure him:

> ... I dont think I have drank a pint of ale altogether

[1] *The Letters of John Clare, op. cit.*

> this two years in fact I can drink nothing strong now in any quantity & as to spirits I never touch & yet without them I feel hearty & hale & have quite recovered from my last ailments & hope to prolong the lease of life for a good season tho I dont think I am much qualified for an old man—[1]

His return to health, apparently sudden as so often with him, is reflected in renewed energy over a new volume of poems. He asked Taylor but the publisher, immersed in work for the University, saw little prospect of making a book of poems pay, and advised Clare to stick to the Annuals. Hessey also had begun a new venture in December 1828, as a publisher of books of religious knowledge. These fresh interests loosened further the ties between Clare and his publishers; neither of them was now in a position to entertain plans for a book of verse. "Time", Clare wrote to De Wint thanking him for the frontispiece to *The Shepherd's Calendar*, "has made sad havoc with my little catalogue of friends."

He had mentioned to Taylor in December that he was contemplating a long poem on the "Pleasures of Spring". "I had some desire to try one on 'The Last Judgment' but expecting I shall be on the wrong side in this world as well as the next by so doing I dare not." "Pleasures of Spring" was not published until 1947—by Kenneth Richmond in *Poetry and the People*. It is a poem of 500 lines on the level of *The Shepherd's Calendar*, redundant, loitering, of a "soodling" pace, as Clare called it—but a poem belonging to the indigenous English canon he spent so much of his life striving to revitalize. He did write the poem on Judgment. He was still turning over the idea of a volume of poems in the manner of the older poets, and on January 3rd he sought Cary's advice on this matter.

> ... I write to beg your opinion of the inclosed Poem ["Death"] as one of those I intended to pass off as the writings of others—this I sent to the *Everyday book* as the production of Andrew Marvell & the Editor took it for granted that it was so & paid me a compliment in praising

[1] *Ibid.*

it which he woud not have done perhaps had it passed under my own name & as I still have thoughts of going on with the deception I have sent it to request your opinion of it ... the old manner is all that I attempt with sprinkling a few old words [h]ere & there – but Taylor wished me not to disguise them under the names of others but publish them under the Title of "Visits of the Earlier Muses" but I thought if I coud succeed well I shoud like to have published them as old things found in imaginary Books and MSS. There woud be no harm in it I think woud there?[1]

In his reply, dated for January 18th, Cary agreed with Taylor that "it will be better not to attempt any deception":

In truth I must own I like you better in your own natural guise of John Clare than in the borrow'd trim of Sir Walter Raleigh, Sir Henry Wotton or any other Sir of Elizabeth's or James's days. What you most excel in is the description of such natural objects as you have yourself had the opportunity of observing, and which none before you have noticed, though every one instantly recognises their truth. Now nothing of this sort can be introduced into such imitations as you meditate. They must consist of mere moralizing. Forcible you may indeed make them, but still they will want the livelier touches of your pencil.

It may have been sound advice. Clare took it; no more is heard of the projected volume. But the problem which it was an attempt to solve remained. Clare was ready enough to write poems in his own style; his manuscripts already contained enough to make several new volumes. But where was the publisher who would undertake to print them? And was there a public who would read them? He had been busy for some months with the long "Pleasures of Spring". Taylor judged from the title that it would be too much like poems which had already been published; Clare asked Darley's advice. Replying in a letter dated March 14th, 1829, Darley criticized the idea. But:

[1] *The Letters of John Clare, op. cit.*

I cannot see why you might not infuse a dramatic spirit into your poem on Spring, which is itself only the development of the living principle in Nature. See how full of life those descriptive scenes in the Midsummer Night's Dream and the Winter's Tale are! ... Thomson has a little of this, but not enough. Imagine his 'Lavinia' spread out into a longer story, incidents and descriptions perpetually relieving each other: imagine this, and you have a model for your Poem. Allan Ramsay's 'Gentle Shepherd' would be still better; only that his poem *is* cut into actual dramatic characters. Besides, though with plenty of feeling, and a good deal of homestead poetry, he wants imagination, elegance, and a certain scorn of mere earth, which is essential to the constitution of a true poet. You want none of these; but you want his vivacity, character, and action: I mean to say you have not *as yet* exhibited these qualities. The books with which you have hitherto fished for praise in the ocean of literature, have not been garnished with *live-bait*; and none of us can get a bite without it.

By "live-bait" Darley meant human character; but even Clare's shortest lyrics did not lack people and characteristic movement.

Clare defended his method in a letter to Taylor.

I think many of the productions of the day that introduce action do it at the expense of nature for they are often like puppets pulled into motion by strings & there are so many plots semiplots & demiplots to make up a bookable matter for modern taste that its often a wonder how they can find readers to please at all

In this letter he returned to the difficulties of writing for the Annuals: "what one often thinks good the Editors return back as good for nothing while another gives them the preference & what one thinks nothing of they often condescend to praise."[1]

In February 1829, he paid a visit to Northampton on the invitation of George Baker, author of a monumental but

[1] *Ibid.*

unfinished history of Northamptonshire, and brother of Anne Elizabeth Baker, whose *Glossary of Northamptonshire Words and Phrases* was to be published in 1854. Clare had much in common with these two retiring and indefatigable students.

In summer he was well and busy in the hay and harvest fields again, with little time for writing; in August he received the long-delayed statement of accounts. The firm of Taylor and Hessey, dissolved in 1825, had just succeeded in winding up its business affairs. If all its accounts were kept in the same way as those pertaining to Clare, the length of the proceedings need cause no surprise. These accounts have been more than once held up as models of accuracy and Clare's criticisms of them dismissed as the flounderings of the unbusinesslike mind supposed to be the natural temperament of poets. In fact the evidence is all the other way; the accounts were very inaccurate, and Clare, consulting the records which he had himself carefully kept in a memorandum book, was able to point out many of these inaccuracies and omissions. In every instance the letters prove that he was right.

To his regular income of £40 a year, occasional gifts and the money earned by harvesting and writing for periodicals may have added £10. Account A, the general account, showed that the money paid out to Clare from 1820 to 1829, together with Drury's bill of 1826 and a book account of £24, exceeded the money received from the dividends, annuities, and profits by £140. Thus Clare and Patty had actually made ends meet on about £60 a year. By way of comparison it may be mentioned that Taylor had been paying Darley £120 a year, a sum which the publisher considered just "enough for his bare subsistence". The £140 adverse balance, however, favoured the firm somewhat; an examination of Account A exposes numerous omissions, which, since they occur on both sides, must be due to careless book-keeping rather than to intention to defraud. On the debit side, several sums of money sent to Clare and noted in his memorandum book do not appear; others are placed under wrong dates. But there are graver omissions on the credit side, totalling some £50 and including the money due for the poems inserted in the *London Magazine*.

Clare also criticized the book account of £24, chiefly for copies of his own books sent him to sell. He had been charged at a higher rate than that promised by Taylor; he was also charged for the paper on which his poems were copied, and as the originals had never been returned to him, he considered this unfair.

Account B, containing the list of subscribers and details of the Fund-money, needs no further notice, but Account C, which deals with the four editions of *Poems Descriptive*, is an interesting document. On the first three editions, Drury and the publishers shared profits of £88, and Drury was repaid the £20 for the copyright. No profits were shown to Clare; instead, the £100, which still stood in the subscription list as the *gift* of Taylor and Hessey, was repaid to the firm. Of the fourth edition, 600 copies had been sold at a loss of £5, advertising costs having risen to £30. Taylor also received commission for his work as editor—£30 in all. The credit side of the account looks straightforward enough; but the appearance is deceptive. One thousand copies at 3*s.* 7*d.* are made to yield some £7 less than the true figure. This was evidently due to a system by which the firm counted 25 sold copies as 24 to cover bad debts, for a proportionate discrepancy occurs in all accounts. It may have been a customary device among publishers, but why should it be thus disguised? And whether 5,000 copies, as Clare says Drury told him were printed, or 4,000 as the Account says, is not clear.

The Village Minstrel account, D, showed a profit of £56 on the 1,250 copies sold. The firm and Drury took half, and half was entered on the credit side of the general account for Clare, the only profit actually shown to him on all three books. Commission and advertising ran away with £80, and 15 guineas was put down for the portrait of Clare by Hilton. As Clare pointed out, this portrait was painted for Taylor at his own request; he could not see why it should be charged to *The Village Minstrel* account in addition to the £26 for the engraving of it by Scriven.

Of *The Shepherd's Calendar*, only 425 copies had been sold, and Account E had an adverse balance of £60. In these last two accounts the discrepancy of 4 per cent. on the credit side amounted to £22 on the copies sold.

Having examined the accounts, Clare felt that something must be done to rectify the errors he found in them. He decided to write to Taylor as soon as the harvest was over and he had leisure. It is clear, from the many drafts of this letter, that he disliked intensely the idea of haggling about money, and began with many far too humble apologies on this score. Having pointed out the errors and omissions in the accounts, he went on to speak of his plans for the future; faced with the failure of his hopes to earn a living by his pen, yet he was glad to know the worst: "for in losing hope I have cleared the prospect to see a little further as to how I must proceed for the future & my intentions are to get a small farm or cottage as soon as possible & I have written to Lord Milton for the purpose but have recieved no answer as yet ..."[1] He hoped to use his Fund-money for the purpose, but of course that was as impossible now as it had been years before. It had already been suggested by Clare in August, and approved by Henderson, that he should again approach Lord Milton for a cottage and land, which would enable him, as Henderson wrote,

> to lift a more independent head than the muses, I fear, will enable you to do; at least you would free your mind of much of the present harassing uncertainty ... Labouring work is now out of the question and indeed any kind of employment requiring confinement would not suit while you continue to write. A cottage with land could be managed partly by yourself, and partly by your wife.

But Clare had to wait three more years for his cottage and land. Three critical years of anxiety, struggle, and deferred hope do not leave many men unscathed.

Clare's letter to Taylor was written at the end of harvest-time; Taylor replied on January 6th, 1830, sending the dividend, with the cheerless news that if the Government carried out their intention of lowering the interest rate, Clare's little income would be still further reduced. He had consulted Hessey —who had failed in his publishing business and set up as a book and print auctioneer—about the points raised by Clare, and there were some that ought to be and should be corrected: "I am much pleased with the manner in which you have stated them."

When these corrections had been made, Clare still owed his late publishers, according to them, a considerable sum, with

[1] *The Letters of John Clare, op. cit.*

little prospect of being able to pay it back. Yet he can hardly be held responsible for a debt about which he was kept in the dark for so long. He had done his best years before to get a statement of his position; but, as he wrote to Taylor, "when I expressed a desire to have a settlement years back Hessey urged me to patience & told me to wait & that I should be in the end 'rich & happy' I am not amiss off for happiness but the other part of his prophecy is badly fulfilled."[1] One decision he now made which he might well have made to his advantage earlier if he had been given the information he had asked for; he would have nothing more to do with the system of half-profits. As he wrote to Sharpe when S. C. Hall had promised to find a publisher for a new book, he would "rather take a small sum for the volume altogether than a large promise in half-profits". He kept to that resolve and was able in 1835, to get £40 for *The Rural Muse*—a small enough sum, but better than the £28 which his previous two volumes had yielded.

Meanwhile correspondence with Drury wiped out the last traces of their friendship. Clare's chief cause of complaint was the £20 for copyright repaid to Drury in addition to the £30 allowed in 1826. Clare said he had not received a farthing beyond that £30, and hoped Drury would admit the mistake and have it corrected. He mentioned that he had not had anything in the way of remuneration for writing songs; he knew that Drury had received payment for some of them. Finally, Drury still had a number of manuscripts which he would like back. Drury replied in November, insisting that the claim was correct and begging to be excused from any further interest in bygone causes, since Clare had long ago transferred all his confidence to Taylor. There are three drafts of a reply to this letter—and none of the one sent—in which Clare discussed the strange business of that first agreement in detail. As he saw it, instead of receiving £20 for *Poems Descriptive*, as asserted, he had been charged £20 for his own property—"a damnable luxury". "You never gave me an item of accounts in your life what had I of you in 'money and goods' to amount to £51 let me ask you."[2]

[1] *Ibid.*
[2] Northampton MSS.

A few more details come to light in an unsent letter to Drury of December 1829:

> ... the reccolection I have of the matter is this that you wished me to say you had bought the copyright for £20 & you wished me to write that down in your account book one evening which I did remarking at the same time that you should cross out £20 of the accounts & not trick me into an additional debt by my agreeing to your desire
>
> I now find I acted foolish in the matter but thats no use all I know is that your explanation of the matter is as utterly void of foundation as the instrument you talk of was of honesty ... [1]

In the letter to Taylor of November Clare had explained:

> ... '*Paid Mr Clare for Copyright pr Drury £20*' now you will be astonished to hear that this is a lye—for mind I never recieved a farthing extra beyond the debt which he claimed of me & which you settled—the selling the copy right was all fudge & pretence he persuaded me to agree that it ought to be so merely as he said to prevent you from hurting him in the end yet whatever tricks he may have played with my ignorance in my acquaintance with him in those hours of hilarity with which I frequently indulged at his house I cannot now remember but this I can say that the selling of the copy right is all fudge ... [2]

There is the manuscript note already referred to: "I once signed an agreement of Drury's which alowd me a quarters profit I was fresh at the time ..."[3]

Whatever the whole of this transaction, all the facts were not likely to be disclosed after ten years. Clare was partly to blame; but if, after a glass of ale, he took too readily as a bond the word of those who controlled his affairs, Drury undoubtedly took advantage of that trust. He intended at first to serve Clare's interests as well as his own; but he took good care to be well

[1] Northampton MSS.
[2] *The Letters of John Clare, op. cit.*
[3] Peterborough MSS.

prepared against the day when those interests should clash, and he knew his cousin Taylor well enough to realize that they must clash. He was able to make good terms for himself, and when there were signs that the business was declining, he hastened to seize what he could from the sinking ship.

The part played by John Taylor cannot be so easily defined. As a young publisher, helped pecuniarily by his brother George, he displayed almost a genius for perspicacity in regard to both Clare and Keats. A man, also, of "close designs", who often shrouded his intentions and motives, however generous or innocent, in a veil of secrecy, he remains something of an enigma. The honesty of his motives in his dealings with Clare is not in question. Their friendship had survived storms and difficulties; nor did it end in 1829. Taylor helped to edit *The Rural Muse*; he contributed towards the cost of Clare's upkeep at High Beech. We do not know how the balance ultimately stood between them in 1864; but up to 1829 the firm had certainly not lost money through their connection with Clare, if we take into account their profits and commissions as publishers, book-sellers, and editors. Taylor also took the copyright of poems and all the unsold copies of the books, which he eventually remaindered, and he hung on to many manuscripts.

Taylor deserves posterity's gratitude for his introduction of Clare to the public, even for his conscientious if mistaken editing, and for his appreciation, not far from visioned, of the poet; but there is an imposing list on the other side. When careful allowance has been made for illness and overwork, those unfulfilled promises, those chronic delays in the preparation of poems, in the payment of money, in the answering of letters, remain inexplicable except on some such assumption as Clare himself made, that by a defect of character Taylor "erected delays into a system". There is evidence that he had such a system; he expressed in writing at least twice that he felt justified in holding over an author's profit on one volume to meet possible losses on the next. We know that he considered manuscripts he published as his own property. This inability to distinguish clearly between the firm's property and rights and the author's seems to have been the cause of the amazing lack of tact which Taylor sometimes evinced in his dealings with other men, a failure to apprehend their point of view. It was a policy of penury and delayed payment which ruined the *London Magazine* and alienated nearly all its contributors. It was Taylor's exposition of his system of delayed payment which provoked Landor's extravagant outburst. Hood also fell foul of the firm: "Is Taylor or Hessey dead?" he asked in 1825, telling how he had met a viper in his path and had cut him in two with a stone, a token that he was to overcome an enemy: "I thought of Hessey's long backbone when I did it." Lamb also, faithful *Londoner* as he was, had little admiration for his editor, and criticized his methods in characteristic style. It was Taylor's illegal claim to the copyright of *Elia*, leading to a lawsuit with Moxon in 1833, which brought from Lamb the comment: "The more I think of him, the less I think of him. His meanness is invisible with aid of solar microscope; my moral eye smarts at him. The less flea that bites little fleas! The great *beast*! the beggarly nit!" And this was the publisher whose generosity to Keats was beyond an author's dreams, who in his younger days had earned a reputation for fair and honest dealing. That was in the firm's prosperous days, before Taylor's brain fever. Even in the lean late 'twenties George Darley was given no cause for complaint.

"Firm in counsel but weak in purpose and doing," was Edward Drury's shrewd comment on his cousin's character. In this Hamlet quality, this gap between his intentions and his actions into which the many difficulties of his life as publisher and editor slipped like a wedge, may lie the solution of those puzzling inconsistencies. The editing of the *London Magazine* tried him sorely at his weakest point. That highly individualistic team of writers needed generous, even inspired, treatment occasionally. Taylor was capable of both; but, when difficulties arose, he was betrayed into procrastination and evasion, became secretive, refused to share his work and responsibility with others, and resented criticism as a personal affront. He did much for Clare; yet his way of doing it often increased the poet's difficulties not a little. In the name of independence he sought to rescue Clare from the attentions of patronage; but the relationship bordering on another kind of patronage he substituted for it aggravated the very dependence from which the poet was struggling to escape. We do not know how much Taylor may have given Clare in, for instance, "an extra £5" such as Clare asked for in July 1828. But for ten years he kept him in ignorance of his financial position, assuming full responsibility for the conduct of his affairs and resenting any interference by others. At the end of the ten years he withdrew his support and left Clare without a publisher, without a public, without experience in editing his own texts, and without the means of using his own money to better his prospects. He allowed the considerable popularity which Clare had gained by his first two books to be lost in six years' unrelenting silence and procrastination between 1821 and 1827. And the anxieties, the disappointments, the unceasing struggle for independence during those years, contained the severest aggravation of what shadowed Clare's later days.

CHAPTER FOURTEEN

A Thinker from a Boy: 1830–1831

In 1927 J. L. and Barbara Hammond in *The Village Labourer, 1760–1832*, wrote:

> ... Those who recall the discussions of the time, and the assumption of the upper classes that the only question that concerned the poor was the question whether Enclosure increased employment, will be struck by the genuine emotion with which Clare dwells on the natural beauties of the village of his childhood, and his attachment to his home and its memories. But Clare's day was brief and he has few readers.

1830 for him dawned in uncertainty. He *was* looking back to the Helpston of his youth and to that January ten years before when his "hopes 'gan travel for a glorious day". Such a mood of retrospect pervades his letter to Cary on January 25th, in which he recalls some of the old familiar faces of his earlier London visits:

> ... Do you ever see or hear anything of Wainwright that facetious good hearted fellow I long to hear something of him agen & where is Charles Lamb? I have never seen him since the year 1824 what a season—do you ever see or hear anything of him now or do you know where he is to be found ... [1]

Cary replied to these enquiries in April:

[1] *The Letters of John Clare, op. cit.*

> I have not seen either Lamb or Wainewright since last summer, when the former spent one day with me here & another day we all three met at the house of the latter, who now resides in a place he has inherited from a relation at Turnham Green. Lamb is settled at Endfield [*sic*], about seven miles from London, with his sister, who I fear is in a very indifferent state of health, so that his friends see very little of him. When I meet either one or other of your old companions, whom I regard as much as you do, I will not fail to acquaint him with your anxious enquiries.

Cary went on to express his disappointment at the settlement of Clare's affairs with Taylor, whom he had not seen lately. He had much to say of "this grand Age of Utility", which had little respect for poets and painters. He remarked on the rate of increase of both of their families, which was greater than Mr Malthus would approve; but at least Clare and he had obeyed the earlier command to multiply and replenish the earth.

It was natural enough Clare should feel that the world had passed on and left him stranded in the backwater of Helpston. But there was in him also a lighter side, a capacity for amusement as well as joy. There is a manuscript draft of a very long letter to "Friend Allan"—Cunningham[1]—headed, "On the Wonders of inventions and curiosities, strange sights and other remarkables of the last forty days in the Metropolis, in a Letter to a Friend." Clare, as the amazed country bumpkin, a role he had often assumed to amuse his London friends in the old days, jested about new wonders, with many a fanciful excursion and digression among old wonders outfaced. After reading of Gurney's steam-engine, balloon ascents, schemes for a tunnel under the sea to France and the building of a "pyramidal sepulchre", of Siamese twins and learned pigs, Clare, "left among the primitives", was inspired to predict:

> ... You are getting on so rapidly in wonders that if I heard it announced that you was going to [editorialize?] some Encyclopedia or quarterly review for the man in the moon I shoud not wonder at all how you was for getting there

[1] Peterborough MSS.

... You will have communications with all nations bye & bye & steam will be boiling from one end of the world to the other yours will be the worlds market & sellers will muster like locusts from all quarters on the wings of all the winds ... methinks with a long pole youll be shaking hands with Affrica & with some patent ear trumpet be bidding goodnight & goodmorning to all the world[1]

One wonder he could not swallow, in spite of his faith: "It is said that the next meeting of the assembly of St. Stephens is to be for the good of the country." Clare enquired after old friends:

Where is Friend Lamb the keenest & the wittiest Lampoon in the world & the heartiest fellow upon earth where is Charles Lamb is he grown into a gentleman & got above us in parading with country esquires be as it may he is not a publisher & though he had no further interest in our friendship then good wishes he has no interest to forget us[2]

Forgotten as he thought himself by those who had "mistaken Collinss Ready Reckoner for a treatise on friendship", little prospect as there seemed for that new volume of poems, Clare went on planning and hoping. His London friends were looking out for a publisher there. He himself was exploring the publication of a volume locally, making a selection from all his unpublished poems, and copying those he considered worthy of preservation into a large manuscript book. He had not grown too dependent on Taylor for the correction of his texts; he now set about that task himself, and wooed the minor muses of grammar and punctuation, as may be judged from Mrs Emmerson's patient answers to his queries. He must have been comforted by her remark that punctuation, at least, was arbitrary: it was then the fashion not to "point" at all. Clare had no desire to be unfashionable in that respect. His imprecations on the pedantic Lindley Murray had amused the *Londoners*; like Linnaeus, Clare would undoubtedly rather "have his ears

[1] Peterborough MSS.
[2] *Ibid.*

boxed thrice by Priscian than once by Nature". Some of his manuscripts show clearly his progress in the task. Part of his trouble was that he hadn't one woman, let alone three as Wordsworth had, to copy a single poem for him.

The spring of 1830 found him botanizing again, alone or with Henderson, searching for rare plants, among whose ancient habitations the changes of Enclosure had made great inroads. The good health which he had enjoyed for some time gave way in July to an illness which lasted in its acute form for two months, and prevented him from harvesting. It was preceded by an incident which increased the mental distress that, for him, accompanied any bodily ailment. In June, Mrs Marsh had invited him to dine at the Palace at Peterborough and accompany a party to the theatre, where a touring company performed for three months every summer. The Bishop and his wife were keen playgoers, and Clare made one of their party on several occasions; he was on friendly terms with the manager of the company, Robertson. On July 14th, Clare was invited to dinner and the play. On the 18th, Frank Simpson wrote mentioning that "unfortunate affair at the Theatre". He advised Clare to write at once to his "offended patroness" and apologize. He felt sure it was Clare's frailty and the warm yet unwise conduct of his companions and not his "viciousness" which had led him into error. According to the traditional story, Clare had risen and cursed Shylock vigorously in the middle of *The Merchant of Venice*,[1] not a "vicious" or even an "unwise" proceeding R. D. Laing today might say.

Letters in August 1830 from Behnes Burlowe, Mrs Emmerson, Hessey, and the Simpsons are full of references to Clare's serious illness. Physical symptoms were similar to those of his last attack—inflammation and discharges, indigestion. Medical knowledge will say that these could all have been results of years of mental and emotional strain with insufficient nourishment. Violent pains in the head could be a symptom of a physical brain condition, but they could also be psychosomatic. Acute misery could be symptom or cause of any of the other conditions. Treated by local physicians he found the remedies

[1] Frederick Martin placed this incident in 1836, thus taking it for a sign of sudden mental breakdown in Clare. But the evidence for 1830 is conclusive.

as painful as the unknown disease. He told Taylor in late September:

> ... I have been bled blistered & cupped & have now a seaton[1] in my neck & tho much better I have many fears as to recovery but I keep my mind as quiet as I can—& am able to read a Newspaper—all I regret is that I cannot describe my feelings sufficiently to benefit from our friend Dr Darlings kind advice in whom I always had the greatest confidence—my fancys & feelings vary very often but I now feel a great numbness in my right shoulder—& the seaton tho I cannot bear it to be dressed for 3 or 4 mornings together discharges so much that I fear I shall fall into a Decline at last—but thank god my head is more relieved tho it stings now & then as if nettled I cannot describe what I have suffered but all I now dwell on is that I am getting better—[2]

Yet a prescription from Darling, whom he trusted, included leeches applied to the temples, a seton to the neck, cold cloths constantly to the head, and poultices to the body. He was to eat little and drink only water. Clare felt that these remedies were increasing his weakness. He was assured that they were necessary to carry off "the inflamed humours". There is further record of his mental sufferings in a letter from Taylor, in which he compared Clare's illness with his own in 1825. Taylor had the same "suspicion of those around", but not the "imagination of unreal sights and sounds", being able to form a "tolerably correct judgement of what was going on around", wherein Clare's illness surpassed his in the violence of its effects. But he had the same "convictions of the indestructible nature of my own soul", which had turned his mind, previously sceptical, toward religion on his recovery.

Clare's overall attitude, in accord with his general mental outlook, was a reverence for true Christianity but a scepticism of easy orthodoxy. Upon those matters of which he had direct personal knowledge, he held decided views; on all others he

[1] A seton was a much-used, general remedy—a thread or piece of tape drawn through a fold of skin to maintain an opening for discharges.

[2] The manuscript of this letter is in the collection of Geoffrey Harmsworth.

tried to keep an open mind. Where he saw hypocrisy and insincerity in religion, as elsewhere, he condemned it in good set terms; he was as ready with praise of sincerity and simple integrity. His scathing criticism of the corrupt churchgoers and officials in "The Parish", is balanced by his warm appreciation of the old vicar in his prose sketch, whose religion lay rather in his everyday honesty and common sense than in his sermons. Clare's "antidote to my deepest distresses", the Bible, which "contains the best Poetry and the best morality in the world", had been the subject of more than one entry in his journal; and "Shakespeare", he wrote in a letter, "is the only poet worthy of being placed by the side of the Bible"; in them both simplicity and truth to nature combined with sublimity. He had clear views about the function of sermons and biblical expositions, of which he had a great many sent him by Lord Radstock.

> Such things are entertaining but I do not like to see opinions insisted upon as facts for where exposition is the foundation we must not take it for granted that truth is the fabric we know that the world was made & we know its architect from no other book then the bible—but being a part of the architecture ourselves we cannot go to comprehend the whole we know but little about the matter of which we ourselves are but a portion & altho new theories may entertain us by their novelty they seldom lead us to truth[1]

The same down-to-earth sensibility marked his attitude toward the different religions and creeds. Like Keats, Shelley and Hunt he inclined to scepticism. He admired Montesquieu because "he did not stop at the bounds of creeds as the bounds of right and wrong" but "boldly declared that the basis of all religions ought to be humanity". Of his own early struggles towards faith he wrote:

> My mind was always hung with doubts I usd to fancy at times that religion was nothing & woud say to myself if there is a god let him dry up this pond of water or remove this stone & then I will believe & then on seeing things

[1] Peterborough MSS.

remain as they were I concluded that my doubts were true but after reflection upbraided my foolish presumption & my consience woud struggle to cancel [*correct*] my errors[1]

Later, and more maturely:

My creed may be different to other creeds but the difference is nothing when the end is the same if I did not expect & hope for eternal happiness I should be ever miserable & as every religion is a rule leading to good by its professor the religions of all nations & creeds where that end is the aim ought rather to be respected than scoffed at[2]

His impatience with what he considered humbug, "cursd affectation worse than hell I hate", sometimes disclosed a chink in his armour of tolerance. Although, like his friend Henderson, he sympathized with the movement for Catholic Emancipation on grounds of fairness, he noted on one occasion that the Catholics deserved to lose because of the "sacred humbugs which their religion hoards up and sanctifies"; there follows a list of relics preserved in a Catholic church. The Established Church, with its ritual and prayers, satisfied Clare's feeling for tradition and poetry, but, convinced as he was that truth could not be found with the narrow bounds of any one creed, he committed himself wholly to none. At one time he thought of joining the Ranters, whose chapels he had frequented in 1820; at another time, after reading Richard Wright,[3] the Unitarian missionary—he talked of becoming a Unitarian. Because they were content to go their own way in meekness and humility, interfering with no man, he considered the Quakers the prince of sects, the "Israel", that "seems pitched nearer the Jordan of Christianity and higher up the hill of Calvary than any". They have suffered persecutions and have hardly murmured about them & certainly made no boast, but "let it pass as a matter of course & were thankful".

[1] Peterborough MSS.
[2] Northampton MSS.
[3] (1764–1836). Wright wrote at least forty books, mostly on religious questions.

Questionings and doubts distressed him most, as they did Keats, in illness; he felt the need then for the comforts of steadfast belief, and, as some of the poems written at these times reveal, he did not always search in vain. The advice of Mrs Emmerson and Hessey, that he should simply believe and question nothing, was not what his temperament could accept or wished to accept, save when his mind was distraught with lonely brooding and he was assailed with visions of eternal punishment for past errors.

His advice to his children was to avoid controversy, and, until they could arrive at a creed of their own, to attend church and hear those prayers, "the best ever written or uttered," in which he had found much comfort. But for Clare's own positive creed we must search rather among his thoughts about poetry and nature. He was more at home in the fields than in a church: "solitude and God are one to me." There emotions and intelligence not astonishingly harmonized, and he could accept with less question a Creator, or at any rate a sense of purpose in Creation. In a poem which combines philosophic insight with the exact observation of a naturalist, he developed an idea, glimpsed as early as 1821, that ignorance, the result of being ourselves a portion of creation, is a secret of the scheme of things; and that frailty as well as crude force, has enduring strength, so that suffering and weakness are not useless.

This blessed ignorance is half the sum
Of providence thus all are blessed indeed—
The weak the strong the timid & the bold
Thus will the hare feel safe in its retreat
Where lay the murdering fox an hour before
& upon boughs warm with the falcons feet
The wren will perch & dream of harm no more
Kind providence amid contending strife
Bids weakness feel the liberty of life

In September 1830, Sophia, the sixth child to survive, was born. Parson Mossop sent the news, with an account of Clare's health, to London. Hessey's reply, dated September 15th, contained news that he had seen Elton and Rippingille at Clifton. Darley had gone to France. Lamb was the same kind-hearted creature as ever, but Mary was again suffering from her distressing complaint. "Poor Hazlitt is very ill indeed – I fear on his death-bed. I saw him twice on Monday, but yesterday he was too ill to see me. I fear his Mind is quite as ill at ease as his body." Hazlitt died three days later, and both Hessey and Lamb were at his bedside. Woodhouse was still abroad, in Madeira, seriously ill with consumption. Hessey had not seen Reynolds or Hood lately, and Cunningham only by chance. Taylor was preparing a new edition of Cary's Dante and was interested in Cabinet Cyclopedias, which, with Albums and Family Libraries, made up the sum of the public's demands on him at the moment. Hessey ended with a tribute to John Taylor, "that most kind and generous and friendly and disinterested of men," who had been a true friend to him for thirty years.

In his reply, Clare thanked Hessey for his news. "I am glad to hear the names of my old friends repeated, for I still believe them as such, though I have a heavy catalogue of sins against most of them." He was sorry that Darley had not written before he left; "of that exquisite oddity of friendship Charles Lamb I have heard by the excellent sample of patient sincerity and goodness Mr Cary who still writes to me in the kindest manner possible."

By October Clare had renewed his correspondence; he was better in body and spirits. Yet he feared that what had happened in July was a loss of his identity or self-control. He recovered to face the old anxieties again; but he reported to Hessey that he and his family were "well and hearty":

> & as to Patty she is never or so seldom ill that she forgets time to time what illness is & I have heard her declare that she never knew what the head ache was in her life untill within these last few years – she has been of much comfort to me both in illness & in health & I always feel happy that I met with such a fortunate accident that brought us together[1]

He wrote to Mrs Marsh, evidently apologizing for the scene at the theatre; her reply of October 9th bade him not distress

[1] *The Letters of John Clare, op. cit.*

himself; they had been so soon informed of his illness that whatever alarm they felt had long vanished; he was to obliterate the incident from his memory. She sent books, grapes, gingerbread. Clare's letters to Mrs Emmerson marked the improvement of his spirits toward the end of 1830. He had sent in December a charming picture of real comfort, "of chimney-corner enjoyment, of winter delight, of social and sweet cottage love," with "an excellent account of the feud and turmoil of party feeling at Stamford". One result of this political agitation was the publication in November of a new local paper, *The Bee or Stamford Herald and County Chronicle*, a Constitutional newspaper, issued as a counter-blast to the Radicals. Both Frank Simpson and Henry Ryde were interested in the venture, and thought Clare should contribute; he was glad enough to find a new market for his poems now that the Annuals were failing. The editor, Clark, paid him a visit, and during the next two years he contributed a considerable number of songs, sonnets, and longer poems to *The Bee*. But the old story was repeated; promises made by Clark and the proprietors, but in 1831 we find Frank Simpson writing that Clare had done right to discontinue feeding *The Bee*, since he had received none of its sweets. Clare was not altogether sorry to dissociate himself from the "violent and high" politics of the paper. Mrs Emmerson pointed out that he had friends on both sides and should not concern himself with such matters. True enough; he was contributing as freely to Drakard's *Champion* in 1830 as to *The Bee*. Clare made his position clear in a letter to Simpson: "I hate party feuds and can never become a party man but where I have friends on both sides there I am on both sides as far as my opinions can find it right but no further not an inch."

The comments on social and political affairs among Clare's manuscripts were all results of this attitude. In politics, as in religion, he desired to stand apart from the strife of parties, to work out his own conclusions from personal experience and direct observation. "I never meddle with politics," he wrote in another letter:

> in fact you would laugh at my idea of that branch of art for I consider it nothing more or less than a game at hide & seek for self interest & the terms Whig & Tory are nothing

> more in my mind than the left & right hand of that monster the only difference being that the latter lies nearer the windfalls of success than the other but that there are some and many who have the good of the people at heart is not to be doubted[1]

He expressed the same conclusion in an essay fragment in another form: "Politics may be said to be an art of money-catching the terms Whig and Tory are only distinctions between the actors in the play their discourse is of their country but when their parts are done we see they only meant themselves". Native shrewdness made him distrustful of "mouthing sprouters", whether politicians or parsons, who sought to impose their beliefs on others, with threats of ruin in this world or damnation in the next.

> I think it is very perceivable to common sense that such men only want power to be equal to the greatest tyrants that ever existed & that the basest deeds would not be blushed over to attain their ends though burnings & bloodshed were the price of its attainment[2]

Beneath the banner of politicians, emblazoned with the devices of patriotism or liberty, justice or progress, he saw arrayed the forces of self-interest, hypocrisy, and tyranny. Yet there were two forms of violence and excess, the blind violence of the mob no less than the disguised and legalized violence of the rich oppressor. He regarded Cobbett as one of the most powerful prose-writers of the day; but he regretted that men could not regard these vital questions except through the distorting glasses of party politics.

> I am no politician but I think a reform is wanted not the reform of mobs where the bettering of the many is only an apology for the injuring of the few nor the reform of parties where the benefit of one is the destruction of the other but a reform that would do good & hurt none I

[1] Peterborough MSS.
[2] *Ibid.*

> am sorry to see that the wild notions of public spouters always keep this reform out of sight & as extremes must be met by extremes the good is always lost like a plentiful harvest in bad weather

This was written in a letter to Mrs Marsh towards the end of 1830, when the southern counties were ablaze with the fires of the revolt of the English peasantry and there were fears that the Midlands also would be involved. There had been rick-burnings in Northamptonshire and risings of labourers around Peterborough and Oundle. The Archbishop of Canterbury, by command of the Privy Council, had prepared a special form of prayer to the Almighty to "defeat and frustrate the malice of wicked and turbulent men". But earthly justice did not wait for divine intervention. The prisons in the south, Winchester, Salisbury and Dorchester, in 1830, overflowed with men whom *The Times* on December 6th described as "industrious, kind-hearted, but broken-hearted beings, exasperated into madness by insufficient food and clothing, by utter want of necessaries for themselves and their unfortunate families".

The only asylum provided by the state was death, the galleys, or the penal settlements.

Few understood better than Clare the hardships and degradations which had driven the peasantry of his day to this desperate means of calling attention to their lot. He was one of them; he had shared their misfortunes during his youth and early manhood and he still spent some weeks of the year in their company as a day labourer. This placed him in a good position for accurate observation and faithful recording. He had smarted under the lash of village gossip; but he was grateful for the education his parents had contrived for him; as he in turn managed education for his children at *6d.* a week in those difficult 1830s.

> I should like to see the effect of schools established by government in every village I should think they would put human life & common sense into the dull & obstinate class from whence I struggled into light like one struggling from the nightmare in his sleep[1]

[1] *Ibid.*

The details of Clare's life should be read with that struggle for its background and with constant reference to the odds against him. When he was born, the English peasantry had entered the darkest period of their history since their emergence from feudal serfdom around the fourteenth century. Enclosure was sweeping the country, backed by the powerful interests of a ruling class, justified in the name of enlightenment and progress, and supported by the moral, aesthetic and economic standards of the eighteenth century. To landlords and tithe-owners it brought increased rents, to the farmer larger profits, but for the smallholder and the labourer ancient rights of commonage were swept away, and they had to buy commodities which they had previously produced themselves; the rise in the cost of living far outstripped increase in wages. The family budgets compiled by Eden and Davies show that even on starvation diet the peasant could not make ends meet. His choice was between starvation and pauperdom; when the Speenhamland system of making up the labourer's wage to subsistence level by a parish allowance was generally adopted, he found himself enclosed by a rigid organization of pauperism; the parish which had been the home of a prized human independence came near to being a prison.

Undermined by these changes, the very foundations of village social structure crumbled. The old system, however wasteful and clumsy, had provided a place for each individual in the community, a means of livelihood, and a chance, however small, of bettering his condition. The new order removed incentives and independence. It disrupted communities which had been six centuries in the making. By 1830 men were ready to risk their necks to assist in the breaking of a machine or the burning of a rick.

Clare had witnessed Enclosure at close quarters, and had suffered with his fellows from the consequences of it. He spent the impressionable years of his boyhood under the old system, the difficult years of early manhood, when ambition was most ardent, under the new. The fortunes of the Clare family reached their lowest ebb, as other peasants' fortunes did, in the post-Napoleonic-war years of meagre harvests, rising prices, and unemployment; how John went from place to place in search of work, joining the "catch-work" gangs, that "foul and revolting species of agricultural slave-driving"; how at length unemployment reduced the slender resources of the family, and the parish brand was set upon their goods—these events made a deep impression, and affected the course of Clare's life and thought. They quickened his ambition to publish his verses in an effort to escape from the state of hopeless dependence and apathy into which his fellows were slipping. Against this background, too, must be set his need for independence as a writer and as a smallholder, his desire to manage his own affairs, his touchiness about patronage and begging-lists, his tirades against pride, pretension, hypocrisy, and self-interest. He turned back to his childhood as to a golden age now vanished. He found a never-failing inspiration for his poetry in Eden-compared recollections of what had been. Here, as elsewhere, he was a country realist, as well as a romantic. The world of his youth had vanished, and Clio, as well as Euterpe, owes a debt to the man who sighed over its "pleasant names of places" and left so accurate a record of the characters and customs, the holiday games and everyday occupations, of its inhabitants.

> Glimpses of the days before
> Enclosure came & trampled on the grave
> Of labour's rights & left the poor a slave

crowd the poems of this date and the autobiographical prose. The fullest picture of the new order which had succeeded the old is to be found in "The Parish" which he had finished by early 1823: this poem:

> was begun & finished under the pressure of heavy distress with embittered feelings under a state of anxiety & oppression almost amounting to slavery—when the prosperity of one class was founded on the adversity & distress of the other—The haughty demand by the master to his labourer was work for the little I chuse to alow you & go to the parish for the rest—or starve—to decline working under such advantages was next to offending a magistrate & no oppertunity was lost in marking the insult by some unquallified oppression—but better times & better prospects have opened a peace establishment of more

sociable feeling & kindness – & to no one upon earth do I owe ill will

"The Parish" begins:

The Parish hind oppressions humble slave
Whose only hopes of freedom is the grave
The cant miscalled religion in the saint
& Justice mockd while listening wants complaint
The parish laws & parish queens & kings
Prides lowest classes of pretending things
The meanest dregs of tyrany & crime
I fearless sing let truth attend the rhyme[1]

Clare describes the old-time farmhouse, where "master, son, and serving-man and clown" lived as one large family. Now all was changed, the old hospitality vanished. The farmer apes the squire. His daughter, no longer the rosy-cheeked girl who sang folk ballads or old songs as she milked her cows or shared in the household tasks, now scorns toil, and, "pale & bedrid", spends her days before a glass, paints "unnatural daubs", "screams a tune", affects learning, dresses fashionably and ogles for the favours of young Squire Dandy. The farmer's son is "just returnd from France". But, husband mad, she runs off with young farmer Bigg,

of this same flimsey class
Wise among fools & with the wise an ass

Bigg struts like a squire, "braced up in stays as slim as sickly miss," turns the heads of the village girls, and is an easy prey for all flatterers. His relative, young Headlong Racket, "deals more openly in sin"; he brags of his conquests, all his talk of horses, dogs, and women; and he

Prepares by turns to hunt a wh——e & shoot
Less then a man & little more then brute

[1] Peterborough MSS. See also Elaine Feinstein, *John Clare: Selected Poems* (University of London, Tutorial Press, 1968).

Dandy Flint, Esquire, whose dirty name has grown into a "proverb for bad deeds" is

> A sot who spouts short morals oer his gin
> & when most drunk rails most against the sin
> A dirty hog that on the puddles brink
> Stirs up the mud & quarrels with the stink[1]

"Proud Farmer Cheetam turnd a rogue by stealth." Saveall has grown rich by meanness yet professes piety, praises neighbourly goodwill, and locks up his very wells in dry weather. Dr Urine has replaced the old village doctress, a herbalist of skill. Urine is a "Quack" who almost, but not quite, cures a broken limb with pills. Like Jack Randall, and like Nelson of the Nile, Dr Urine will reappear in Clare's 1841 Byronically-titled "Don Juan", an errant poem full of coarseness straight out of a sub-conscious released from strain. With a candidness akin to some of Swinburne's still-suppressed poems, "Don Juan" is as outspoken as some twentieth-century writing.

Religion, Clare goes on in "The Parish", has fallen on evil days in the village. It is "little more than cant" of "Ranter priests"; for many, but a cloak of outward piety which they slip on when the bells ring for service and cast off when they leave the church; the fixing of fresh rates upon the needy poor was regularly discussed in the church porch. Others joined the new church and became "pious maniacs, regularly mad", accounting themselves a chosen race. The drunken cobbler left his wickedness and his shoes to save men's souls and unravel mysteries which had puzzled the wise. Old Ralph, "the veriest rake the town possessed," converted, turned preacher, and was well on the way to sainthood; but a simpering Eve crept into his garden; he fell, and, after leading a double life for some time, was found out by his flock, and the new-born saint became the old sinner again.

Behind the clamour for reform raised by squire-aping farmers Clare saw lurking the wolf of self-interest; power might change hands, but the poor would not benefit; as in France, the cause of

[1] Peterborough MSS. See also Elaine Feinstein, *John Clare: Selected Poems*, *op. cit.*

freedom would become a tyrant's tool. The village politician, as Clare in his lonely days saw him, was often a tyrant on a small scale:

> Who votes equality that all men share
> & stints the pauper of his parish fare
> Who damns all taxes both of church & state
> & on the parish lays a double rate

Churchwardens, constables, and overseers made up a hierarchy of village government, with the parish clerk to carry out their decisions and do "whatever dirty jobs they choose". He clapped the parish brand on the goods of the pauper labourer, "On parish bounty rather pined than fed"; he claimed fresh taxes from the needy.

Justice Terror, "a blunt, opinionated odd rude man", whose capricious judgments made him feared by all, leaned to the stronger side; yet over him Clare's critical denunciations grew more balanced: the poor had worse governors than Terror; his Christmas gifts were regularly given, he reprimanded farmers as well as paupers, and spoke against luxury and pride on all occasions. His young kinsman, the curate, was more the tradesman than the priest; his chief study was the extortion of higher fees from the parishioners; he would have his half-crown before he signed the register.

The old vicar of the days before hunting parsons and trading curates, was a good, plain man with little wealth, but what he had was at the service of his flock. The old vicar was almost forgotten, and the parish clerk lived in his house, scarcely more pretentious than the surrounding cottages; docks and nettles had usurped the place of the vicar's pinks and roses; the hive bees, his only stock, perished with their owner; the very churchyard which he tended so carefully wore a different face. "Who'll feed and clothe us if the Vicar don't?" the children asked when he died.

In a cold corner with a northerly aspect stood the new parish workhouse, "a makeshift shed for misery."

> Here dwell the wretched lost to hopeless strife
> Reduced by want to skelletons in life

Over them reigned a tyrant king, "y-cleped an overseer," Farmer Thrifty, who cloaked his roguery in an outward show of honesty and piety, "an outside Christian but at heart a Jew." He tyrannized, gave them curses when they asked for bread, and pleaded bad times when justice criticized his methods.

The workhouse-keeper was a subject too low even for satire; the bailiff, Bumtagg, a fawning puppy to his master and a wolf to the unfortunate; the gamekeeper, king of the forest, delighted in his task of preventing the poor from gathering the fruits, nuts and fallen wood of the woods, their ancient inalienable right. Knowing that he had revealed the very dregs of tyranny and oppression towards country people, Clare concluded his raw, yet not wholly unsuccessful poem. Satire was one voice of his feeling but it was not his genre, though he returned to it in 1841.

Mrs Emmerson saw the manuscript of "The Parish" but as most of her letters to Clare have not survived, what she thought of it cannot be known. Not surprisingly, no suggestions for publication of "The Parish" came in its author's lifetime.

Had the process of Enclosure been carried out with more regard for the rights of the peasantry, it still would not have found an enthusiastic supporter in Clare. It was his conviction that earth had its justice, *that* beauty and *that* justice were as important for happiness as was Benthamite utility. He saw the ploughing up of heaths and pastures and their enclosure within the fences of private ownership with deep dismay; heath and pasture were made parish slaves with the rest. Yet Clare arrays his indignation with some pity not only for the spoiled but for the spoiler; for the "poor greedy souls" who, though already blessed with plenty, still hanker after more, who miss peace and beauty in a mad lust for worldly possessions. And despite his losses, material and otherwise, though there is bitterness in Clare's letters to his friends, there is also desire to pierce the clouds of hypocritical self-deception and see plainly about men and events. No one knew better than he that dangerously patient endurance of his class which those who favour "progress" are so often willing to exploit. He gave Taylor his view of the situation in 1830:

> the Farmer is on the look out for 'high prices & better markets' as he stiles them tho these markets are always

curses to the cottager & the poor man the Parson is now rather stirring into radicalism for a partial reduction of individual taxes merely because he sees somthing must be done & as he wishes to keep his tythes & his livings untouched he throws the burden on government The Speculator—is he looking up to a paper currency which places a false value on his bargains & therefore enables the cunning to cheat the honest ... I think a paper currency upon just principles a very commodious way of traffic much better than gold ... & I think that a universal reduction of tythes clerical livings placemens pensions & taxes & all renovated & placed upon a reasonable income suitable to the present decreased value of money & property is the only way to bring salvation to the country ... I am no leveller for I want not a farthing of any ones property all I want is to keep the little that fortune alowed me to call mine but if government goes on taking a little from those who have little & leaving the wealthy untouched—I shall quickly be what I have been but no matter times must change & if for the better I am willing to suffer my little with the rest[1]

Times did change, but with the characteristic slowness of historical time. It would be true to say that by 1870 more people in Britain were better off materially than they ever had been. But any precision in such a statement dare not minimize the aggregate of poverty endured in the 1830s in Britain. "Our present laws defend the properties of the great but they often leave the properties of the poor man to the care of providence alone."

A note of Clare's of the 1830s deals with misconceptions of the peasant's lot perennially prevalent among other classes. How often had friends envied his supposedly idyllic pastoral content: "Every discontented tradesman declares the poor peasants lot to be the happiest in the world & the hardest labour the best exercise yet he would sooner choose any lot than that of a poor man & any labour but that of hard work."

On one occasion at least indignation at injustice provoked

[1] *The Letters of John Clare, op. cit.*

Clare to depart from his policy of not meddling with political matters. There is a rough draft of a letter written about this time to the editor of a newspaper. It is headed "An Apology for the Poor". Clare wanted to know whether, amidst all the present stir about taxation, tithes, agricultural distress, and reform, the poor were to benefit with the rest; they had had fine promises made to them before. Fulfilment had not followed. They were to benefit when the tax was taken off leather, yet shoes were dearer than before. Had the removal of the duty on spirituous liquors reduced the price of gin? Would the reduction of the tax on malt and beer benefit anyone except the farmer and brewer? The poor man was forced to go to the petty village retailer for all necessities, and was sold the worst articles at the highest price. Clare feared that even the repeal of the corn laws would be of little service to those who were so low in the thermometer of distress that benefits to others never reached them; they remained just a little above freezing-point.

> Some years back when grain sold at 5 & 6 guineas the quarter poor men in hundreds of parishes worked for 10 shillings a week ... I myself was one of them I can point out a many villages where the farmers under a combination for each others interests would give no more in winter than 10 shillings per week I will not say that all did so for in many places & at that very time Farmers whose good intentions was 'to live & let live' gave from 12 to 15 shillings per week & these men would again do the same thing but they could not compel others & there it is w[h]ere the poor man looses the benefit that ought to fall to him from the farmers "better markets" & "high prices" for corn[1]

This letter must have been published in a Stamford paper. A draft following it replies to an attack made by a correspondent, a clergyman, upon the first letter. The clergyman wrote, Clare said, as if he had ' "all the blood of all the Howards" in his veins —who is he—clear the stage let me listen to this mountebank'. Hatred of tyranny and pretension roused, he went on:

[1] Peterborough MSS.

> There was a time when the prosperity of others was universally popular yet at that time the poor man was as an alien in a strange land he was not suffered even to open his mouth about his distresses for if he had he would have been instantly thrust into jail as a raiser of mobs and seditions & who were the lords and tyrants of every village that treated the rights of the poor with such contempt as not even to let the murmurs of sorrow to go unpunished Why these very farmers who are now raising up mobs themselves they were metamorphosed into special constables & paraded the dirty streets with shouldered muskets in all the swaggering awkwardness of the raw lobsters that now infest the metropolis & if a poor man only smiled upon the ridiculous groups of armed animals when it was almost impossible to resist laughter he was instantly guarded to prison by these files of ridiculous assumptions these treasons upon honour and libels on courage who would have retreated from the bray of a jackass as the cannon of the enemy & turned their backs on a scarecrow if it had been invested with a red jacket[1]

That the peasantry had been almost pauperized by conditions which brought prosperity to all above them seemed to Clare, as to other keen observers, the most distressing aspect. The poor, Crabbe wrote of the Agricultural-Industrial revolution:

> Are as the slaves that dig the golden ore
> The wealth around them makes them doubly poor

"When farmers become *gentlemen* their labourers become *slaves,*" was a text Cobbett expounded.

Clare has left an account on the effect of Enclosure injustice on the minds of villagers, of those who had not sunk into an apathy of mental servitude. This manuscript fragment, perhaps an attempt at an ironic novel, was "The Bone and Cleaver Club". A village society met at the Butcher's Arms. Members, though unnamed, make speeches:

> Now to please everybody Mr President we must act justly

[1] Peterborough MSS.

to nobody—thats truth we must praise the church to the parson Mr President & abuse it to the parishioners we must speak well of justice & belie it in our actions Mr P thats fact we must miscall magistrates wise men to their faces Mr P & knaves to our neighbours Mr P thats truth we must go to church with farmer Folly to be good & get an hours sleep in the pew only contriving to waken to sing Amen with the clerk in the prayer for the royal family Only go to church Mr P thats all go to church wait in the porch to make a bow to the priest & praise his dull sermon Mr P thats truth Then go home & drink to the abolition of English slavery (applause) tithes parsons & taxes in the company of radicals & then we stand in the praise of all Mr P as good men good subjects & good everything thats truth Mr P Cant humbug & hypocrisy are the three-in-one grand principles of this age Mr P thats truth If you would be upright you must suffer buffets from one party or the other Mr P thats truth & whats the use? if we decline opinions we are insinuators if we give opinions we are enemies to our country or infidels to religion if we decline to praise ministers we are traitors Mr P thats truth & whats the use of it If we fancy patriots bribe-fishers the mob worries us for Government men Mr P thats fact & whats the use of it If we say parsons have great sallaries Mr P we are deists & devils & worse & whats the use Mr P But if we say these things as opportunity offers we are saints Mr P aye—everything Mr P very Caesars Mr P fit for one of the oracles of family devotion & public worship Mr P a very saint a downright saint & only inferior to a red letter saint in the almanack & a stone & mortar saint in the church thats fact Mr P Cant and hypocrisy are the grand necessitys of the world & theres no help for it Mr P thats fact—And now for a song[1]

[1] *The Prose of John Clare, op. cit.* Peterborough MSS.

CHAPTER FIFTEEN

Pilgrim of Love: 1831–1832

By January 1831, as we know from Mrs Emmerson's letters, Clare had written many new poems since being ill in the previous late summer and autumn. He was tired of giving poems away to the Annuals, the *Bee* and the *Champion*. He sent some to John Taylor, reported to be thriving in his business and greatly increasing his connections. Taylor replied that Clare's poems were always interesting to him, but he could not publish any more of them.

In January 1831, Clare's half-yearly dividend from the Fund fell from £9 *7s. 6d.* to £6 *17s. 9d.* Even this he did not receive till late in the month; Taylor, with one of his lapses, tried to pay it in the form of a bill which Drakard and Wilson of Stamford owed him and which Clare was to present. To Taylor's surprise, Clare refused to accept his dividend in this form; he himself had a small account with Drakard and Wilson which he was unable to pay. Of this debt Wilson wrote some months later:

> You need not be under any apprehension that I could, as one of the agents for the spreading of literature, attempt to lay the iron hand of oppression on a son of the Genius of poetry. I am, in common with most other booksellers, devilish poor, and that was my only reason for making application for payment. You will, I am persuaded, not let me be forgotten in the throng.

Debts were accumulating. Few of the creditors were prepared to treat Clare as Wilson treated him—though Dr Skrimshire of Peterborough at least twice reduced his bill.

By the end of 1831 two years' rent was owing, and the landlord had been talking of it in the village; there were unpaid doctors' bills too. "I am at the world's end, Harry," Clare wrote to Behnes Burlowe, "& if you could get Mr. Hall to pay me ever so little of what he promised me, I shall be set up & satisfied." This letter tells of another commission which Burlowe had undertaken. He had seen George Cruikshank and discussed the possibility of his illustrating some of Clare's poems. Cruikshank, whom Clare may have met in London, wished to see some poems, to decide whether they would be suitable for his pencil. Clare sent "The Summons", which had been printed in the *Champion*, and "The Hue and Cry"—satirical ballads on his obsessive theme of callousness and hypocrisy in high places. The scheme fell through. Cruikshank wished to have nothing to do with "political" poems.

By early March Clare was beseeching Taylor—some letters in his debt—to reply, and not to delay asking Dr Darling for prescriptions:

> I was taken 3 weeks back or more with a pain at the stomach which would not go off & as it affected my head very much I felt alarmed & took a part of Dr Ds last prescription which checked it & subdued the humour in some measure but whenever I attempted to walk friction brought it on as bad as ever & the pain at my stomach started again as bad as ever & I then finished the packet of powder & on last saturday night by the reccomendation of Mr Mossop (having nothing left of my last prescription) I took a blue pill & on sunday morning I waked with a dreadful burning humour in my lisks & a contraction such as almost prevented me from making water on monday I commenced a second course of Dr Darlings medicine & the humour tho abated is not subdued—for I awoke this morning with a burning heat in my fundament where the humour again made its appearance with prickly pains in my head arms & shoulders & they are as bad just now—I fear I shall be in the same state I was in last summer for untill last night I got tollerable rest but the pain at my stomach was more frequent in its attacks & I awoke in dreadful irritation thinking that the Italian liberators were kicking my head about as a football—my future prospects seem to be no

sleep—a general debility—a stupid & stunning apathy or lingering madness & death—my dreads are very apprehensive & uneasy I dislike this prickly feel about the face & temples worse than anything & a sobbing or beating when I lay my head down on the pillow was first felt last night for a long time[1]

As over the 1826 confession to Mrs Emmerson about some temporary unfaith to Patty, over the February 1828 "foolish follys", over Hessey's advice after Clare's 1828 return from London about "the suspicion you entertain" and "the character of the person concerned with you", the mind may jump to thoughts of gonorrhoea or syphilis. It has been suggested that in 1820 or 1828 or both Clare contracted one of the forms of venereal disease and that he was accidentally cured by the malarial "Fen fever" virus he caught at Boston in 1828. But his physical and psychological symptoms of March 1831, though more severe, are similar to what he had experienced for years: there were the early epileptiform attacks of unconsciousness; there were the "sort of appoplectic fit" and "numbing pain" he mentions in his letter to Inskip of August 1824; pains in head and stomach, numbness after being "bled blistered & cupped", "humours", "discharges", "sinkings", fears of a "Decline" through weakness, and inability to "keep my mind quiet", presumably both to stop its activity and its sadness: those "vain imaginings", that "eternal ditty" burning the mind "To leave some fragment of itself behind".

Dr James Harper, Medical Director of St Andrew's in 1972, wrote:

> ... Clare's ... description of his symptoms in his letter of 1831 are compatible with an attack of gonorrhoea, but it is not uncommon for people who are severely depressed to have various aches and pains and suffer from general hypochondriasis ... Years later, a person who has contracted syphilis, may develop General Paralysis of the Insane, which is due to syphilitic brain infection ... As far as I am aware there is not the slightest suggestion that John Clare

[1] *The Letters of John Clare, op. cit.*

ever had G.P.I. and, in fact, his symptoms are quite incompatible with this diagnosis ...

Dr Darling's advice in his letter of December 1825, telling Clare to make his "conscience easy", for his children's sufferings arose through no "voluntary fault" on his part, and Dr Ward's words in 1828 that there was "little or nothing wrong", indicate no contemporary medical suspicion of sexual disease. Clearly Patty and Clare were not in continuous disharmony. In 1828 she went with him to Dr Cooper of Stamford. In 1831 his parents' chief concerns were for him to get another book out.

Late spring of that year found him preparing poems for a new volume and arranging his prose. He had begun an essay on "The Sublime & Beautiful in Poetry", with selections to accompany it. Taylor approved the plan when he wrote in July. He was staying with Hessey who had turned schoolmaster and had an establishment in the country three miles from London. Clare thought anthology selection was often "haphazard". He wanted to try his skill. "... respecting the poems," Clare added, "yet again I cannot say anything in the matter further than that you may act with them just as you would do if they were your own property for I know you are my friend ... "[1]

His library contained some three hundred books, the poets well represented. He commented to Taylor on two notable omissions among modern poets: he had never read a poem by Leigh Hunt, and he knew little of Shelley except that he was "a fine writer". Fragments of the essay on "The Sublime & Beautiful" have survived, but the work of selection was interrupted by his preoccupation with a venture which promised the independence which he had sought so long.

Ryde, agent of Burghley, was still assuring the Emmersons that he would get a cottage and some land for Clare. In July, Henderson wrote about a cottage which was being built at Northborough on the Fitzwilliam estate; there would be land for two cows, and Clare was to apply – to rent, of course. There was no question of a gift. The application was successful, and the cottage was to be made ready by January 1832. From July

[1] *Ibid.*

to October Clare was too ill to read or write, so that Parson Mossop had to inform the Emmersons of the promised domain, magnified considerably into five acres of garden, orchard, and meadows. By October, Clare was sufficiently recovered to take stock of his affairs; the Promised Land was in sight. But beset by debts, he had little or no means of stocking his small farm; he wrote to Taylor in October:

> ... All I want to go on is a stimulus an encouraging aspiration that refreshes the heart like a shower in summer —instead of that I have nothing but drawbacks & disappointments I live in a land overflowing with obscurity & vulgarity far away from taste & books & friends Poor Gilchrist was the only man of letters in this neighbourhood & now he has left it a desert ... [1]

An unsent letter of January 1832, also to Taylor, declares how Northborough would mean parting from

> ...the woods & heaths & favourite spots that have known me so long for the very molehills on the heath & the old trees in the hedges seem bidding me farewell—other associations of friendship I have few or none to regret for my father & mother will be often with me & altho my flitting is not above three miles off there is neither wood nor heath furze bush molehill or oak tree about it & a Nightingale never reaches as far in her summer excursions[2] ...

He was exaggerating. Northborough's flat, unwooded, heathless fen did, as he found later, harbour a nightingale or two. Yet, in the same letter:

> do you know I feel as happy at this moment as ever I did in my life for I am looking at a sunny prospect ... & I think I shall yet live to see myself independent of all but old friends & good health & as the best way to end well is to begin well my desire is to start upon a new leaf—to get out of

[1] *The Letters of John Clare, op. cit.*
[2] *Ibid.*

> debt before I leave here & to keep out when I commence a cottage farmer—

He was reluctant to meddle with the Fund-money, but could see no other way out of his difficulties. He needed £20. But he could not bring himself (as we know from unsent and unfinished letters) to ask Taylor point blank for that sum. He was beginning to write letters and not send them. He sought Taylor's advice.

Taylor did not reply, and Clare's next letter, also unsent, also for January 1832, runs:

> In the paralysing suspence your silence completely stultifyes my intentions—I was in hopes that I was at the end of my pilgrimage & that the shadow of independence if not the substance was won as all I wanted was to use my own means to sink or swim as good luck or bad luck might hereafter alow me & to free myself from talking & writing kindnesses that hang like a millstone about my feelings — I thought that one word to you would procure this & that I should launch into the broad ocean of liberty in my own boat—but no such thing the conclusion of your letter to my neighbour came like a broad big wave overpowering every struggle & throwing me back upon the shore among all the cold apathy of killing kindness that has numbed me for years I am ready to start & not able for I wish to stand out of debt & if twopence would do it I could get no such bond here ... [1]

The neighbour was Parson Mossop, who frequently wrote letters on Clare's behalf at this time. When Taylor sent the dividend on January 13th, he said he could do nothing until Richard Woodhouse returned from Italy in May; but he thought that the trustees had no power to use the principal in the way suggested. Clare replied that if the money was thus tied up it had been done against his intention, and he hoped for better news soon and better advice than that which had been given him by his neighbours, who all thought that he would prosper in any kind of farming—except that in which they were themselves engaged.

[1] *Ibid.*

> Some tell me that cows are excellent profits and some tell me that pigs are excellent profits, others that ploughed land would be far better than either, and others who have land under the plough say that I am far better off with green-sward. Nothing disheartened, I hear this confliction of opinions and strife of tongues with the determination to try, and if God gives me health I have a strong hope in the end that I shall succeed. My whole ambition is to arrive at that climax when I can say I owe no man a shilling and feel that I can pay my way. To me this is independence, nothing else; of money I know no other value than its paying its way and further than that to me it is a worthless matter.[1]

Clare's hope that he might be able to use some of his capital was further dashed when Taylor forwarded him a letter from George Woodhouse, Richard's brother. George had found a draft of the Declaration of Trust made by Taylor and Richard, from which it was clear that the principal could only be used to provide income during Clare's lifetime.

A faint hope remained that something might yet be done when Richard Woodhouse returned, but Clare's inability to pay his debts troubled him. Patty, he wrote in one of his many unsent letters, "very unreasonably", considered them as "of my own making". Some of his creditors, hearing of his projected removal, were pressing for settlement. Another unsent letter to Taylor says that he was feeling the truth of Solomon's remark, "My son it is better to die than to be poor." "I have hopes & they are strong ones that I shall see the expected haven but I am so cast down by turns [times] that I don't know that I shall wether the storm"[2]

The winter brought minor ills in the form of rheumatism and colds; the Bishop's wife, Marianne Marsh, supplied him with medicine and provisions as well as books – Cobbett's tracts, and *Robinson Crusoe* for the children. She saw Clare and the family frequently and understood their needy situation; she gave her

[1] I have not found the original of this quotation: it is given as in the 1932 edition of *John Clare: A Life*.

[2] *The Letters of John Clare, op. cit.*

alms with tact and delicacy: "To show you how much I wish to cheer you, I am trying to make you laugh at sending you Cakes as one does to children."

Other glimpses of Clare's mind during the months of 1832 are provided by his letters to Thomas Pringle. Pringle, editor of *Friendship's Offering*, also remembered for his South African poems, had been making enquiries with a view to finding a new publisher for Clare. He wrote on February 8th to report no success: poetry was unsaleable. The days when Scott, Byron and Rogers achieved popularity and made money from poetry were past. Clare's reply to Pringle is some testimony that on certain points his sense of values remained unimpaired by poverty and neglect as by brief prosperity—whatever tricks his subconscious mind might be preparing to play on him:

> I became a scribbler for downright pleasure in giving vent to my feelings, and long and pleasing-painful was my struggle to acquire a sufficient knowledge of the written language of England before I could put down my ideas on paper, even so far as to understand them myself. But I mastered it in time sufficiently to be understood by others. Then I became an author by accident and felt astonished that the critics should notice me at all and that one should imagine I had read the old Poets and that others should imagine I had coined words which were as common around me as the grass under my feet. I shrank from myself with ecstasy and have never been myself since. As to profit, the greatest profits, most congenial to my feelings, were the friends it brought me and the names it rendered familiar to my fireside, scraps of whose melodies I had heard and read in my corner. But had I only imagined for a moment that I should hold communion with such hereafter, that would have then been to me "as music in mourning." But I wrote because it pleased me in sorrow, and when happy it makes me happier; and so I go on, and when they please others whose taste is better than mine the pinnacle of my ambition is attained. I am so astonished that I can hardly believe I am myself, for nobody believed I could do anything here and I never believed that I could myself. I pursued pleasure in many paths and never found her so

happily as when I sang imaginary songs to the woodland solitudes and winds of autumn.[1]

Meanwhile Thomas Emmerson had been consulting with Taylor about the Fund-money. There appeared to be no way out of the difficulty; he advised Clare to proceed with his plans and make the best of it. Clare had to consent to take this advice. Henderson and he went to view the cottage in March, and Clare wrote gaily to the Emmersons of his new abode. In April, Henderson sent careful instructions about the laying out of the garden, and told Clare to take no notice of certain Northborough wiseacres who had been indulging in gloomy prophecies. In May, Clare left his native village, the old cottage, the heaths and woods, to settle in the fen village of Northborough. He did not exaggerate the difference in scenery between Helpston's pastures and woodlands and Northborough's flats. But "May it be the paradise of health and peace to my friend; may he gather into his garner the fruits of extended years," Mrs Emmerson wrote to "Farmer John". John's own feelings in those early days were mixed. He found that the nightingale *did* sing at Northborough, and in his very orchard; but that he must let his pasture for less money than he paid for it, since he had no means of stocking it himself.

Through the kindly zeal of the Emmersons that situation was relieved. Mr Emmerson, having again visited Taylor, had realized that the Fund-money was beyond reach, and he asked Clare on June 27th for an exact account of his circumstances, his debts, and the stock he would require. In July came news that the Emmersons had decided to raise a private subscription to provide necessary stock. They themselves would give £10, which was to be laid out in a cow "to be named Rose or Blossom or May"; Taylor promised £5 for two pigs, and they hoped to raise another £5 for tools. Cary may have helped, for he mentioned the subscription in his next letter.

Grateful as Clare was for this, he could not hide his traditional countryman's regret that his difficulties could only be solved by means of another "begging-list" and more "killing kindnesses".

[1] The present whereabouts of this letter to Pringle is doubtful; it is therefore printed as in the 1932 edition of *John Clare: A Life*.

He had unbosomed himself freely to the Emmersons about the other "begging money", the way it had been put "into prison for life" without Lord Radstock, the Emmersons, or himself being consulted, about his poor recompense for the poems published by Taylor and Hessey and the depreciation of the interest: until "what would make a great coat & full suit & to spare in one ministry will not make out for a spencer in another".

These letters were seen by Taylor. In his July letter he reminded Clare that he did not carry on business to have the opportunity of giving away what he did not get. As for the Fund, when Woodhouse returned, he would divest himself of a trust which exposed him to calumny and had become "an odious duty". Mossop could take his place and lend the money on mortgage, as he had proposed. He thought a new subscription would not easily be raised in these hard times. This little storm might have ended as usual in mutual explanations, but events were to occur in the summer of 1832 which kept Taylor's resentment alight for some time.

Northborough is a straggling village between Glinton and Market Deeping. It contains two notable buildings—the ancient church of St Andrew's and the Manor House, where once lived Elizabeth, Cromwell's favourite daughter, wife of Sir John Claypole. The village, which had a population of 227 in 1831, is pleasant compared with the bare levels of the surrounding fen; it has trees, and most of the earlier cottages stand, in the way of Anglian settlements,[1] apart from their neighbours, private in gardens and orchards. Clare's thatched cottage, of silvery-grey Barnack Rag, built upon what was known among the villagers as a two-acre piece, was no exception. It contained six rooms, a sitting-room used by Clare as a study, a spacious kitchen, a large back-kitchen, cool on the hottest summer day, and three bedrooms. It stands well back from the road, and, at Clare's request—the builder was a friend of Henderson's — it was made to face away from the road; from his front and only door Clare stepped into his secluded garden. Later, in fits of deep melancholy when he could not bear to meet visitors, he could see them approaching from his study window and slip out unobserved

[1] As in many Northamptonshire stone villages, additions in housing since the 1950s have spoilt its homogeneity.

through the garden and orchard into the fields beyond. Local tradition still recalls these visitors driving up to see the poet Clare. Patty, a moment after her husband had made his escape, would reply truthfully that he had just gone out; while sometimes, even as she was denying knowledge of the way he had taken, Clare would be not two yards away behind one of the three thick yew-trees which he taught his sons, John and William, to cut into circles and cones. In a district where the cottage gardens are fine and, even in those days of poverty, were proudly kept, Clare's garden with its communion of wild and cultivated plants, honesty, Bedlam cowslip, horehound, herb-paris, hellebore, marjoram, pasque-flower, makes him locally remembered as "a wonderful man with flowers". Beyond the flower-garden and long kitchen-garden lay the orchard. Beyond the orchard and bounded by pollard willows was pasture for his cow. Yews, apple and pear trees he planted, gooseberry and other bushes so that he could

> Walk round the orchard on sweet summer eves
> & rub the perfume from the black currant leaves

are gone now and the cottage is much modernized.

A visitor who accompanied Clark of the Stamford *Bee* to Northborough soon after Clare's removal gave an account in a sympathetic review of *The Rural Muse* in the *Druid's Magazine*. After commenting on the commodious cottage and fine flower-garden, the writer continued:

> The first glance at Clare would convince you that he was no common man; he has a forehead of a highly intellectual character; the reflective faculties being exceedingly well developed; but the most striking feature is his eye, light-blue, and flashing with the fire of genius: the peculiar character of his eyes are always remarked by persons when first they see him: his height is rather below the common. His conversation is animated, striking, and full of imagination, yet his dialect is purely provincial; his ideas being expressed in the most simple manner, you can compare his conversation to nothing but the line of Goldsmith—
>
> Like a fair female, unadorned and plain.

Clare took his visitors round the garden and orchard, pointing out in the hedge a nightingale's nest which had been despoiled, expressing his indignation.

Clare went to Northborough with the hope that he would achieve a most necessary human independence. The rent was higher than that of the Helpston cottage, yet the small farm provided something to eke out his income. Patty was an excellent manager, the house was palatial compared with that he had left, and Clare shook off depression to plunge into a scheme for publishing a new volume by subscription.

Yet when we read between the lines of the letters and poems written at this time, we find evidence that the disappointments and cares of years had been sapping the foundations of an originally strong and vital enough mentality.

His later friend and physician, Dr Allen, recorded that in cases of nervous derangement where the victim is a person of marked individuality the first symptoms often make their appearance, not as discrepancies in the character, but as slight exaggerations of already existing traits. The condition may lurk for years, evading discovery until it reaches a stage when cure becomes most difficult. The crisis of the removal to Northborough marked a danger-point in Clare's story. His spontaneous power of recovery from severe disappointment has been recorded again and again. That power was still with him; nor did he lose it; but its normality and elasticity were gone; Clare had to summon his will to his aid. Letters sent and unsent reveal how the mood of hope, of determination to make a success of his new life, was literally imposed upon a melancholy sense of crippling odds. He had to scold himself continually, assure himself that it was absurd and unmanly to feel such misery and regret, to "dwell in trifles like a child", because he was moving a few miles to a new home where he could not be worse off and might well be better. He succeeded in calming the surface of his mind. The struggle went on beneath. The feeling that he was uprooted and would not survive transplantation found expression in "The Flitting"; this had as its occasion not an enforced banishment to some "remote Bermudas", but a voluntary removal to a village three miles away:

Alone & in a stranger scene
Far from spots my heart esteems
The closen[1] with their ancient green
Heath woods & pastures sunny streams
The hawthorns here were hung with may
But still they seem in deader green
The sun een seems to lose its way
Not knows the quarter it is in

. . . . .

Here every tree is strange to me
All foreign things where ere I go
Theres none where boyhood made a swee
Or clambered up to rob a crow ...

Again he turns from new scenes that seem strangely shadowy to recall old haunts. In "Remembrances", a companion piece to "The Flitting" (but neither published until 1908) Clare compiled yet another gazetteer of the country of his boyhood, before the havoc Enclosure had done to Langley Bush, Eastwell Spring, Lea Close Oak, Round Oak, Sneap Green, Puddock's Nook, Crossberry Way, Swordy Well and Hilly Snow. The "pleasant names" of all those places rang in his memory. The poem is in a measure similar to that of Reynolds's "Shrewsbury":

By Langley bush I roam but the bush hath left its hill
On cowper green I stray tis a desert strange & chill
& spreading lea close oak ere decay had penned its will
To the axe of the spoiler & self interest fell a prey
& crossberry way & old round oaks narrow lane
With its hollow trees like pulpits I shall never see again
Inclosure like a buonaparte let not a thing remain
It levelled every bush & tree & levelled every hill
& hung the moles for traitors—though the brook is running still
It runs a naked stream cold & chill[2]

[1] A close is a very small field or paddock near a house. Clare has used the Anglo-Saxon plural, sometimes still used as singular today.
[2] Peterborough MSS.

In *The Primitive World and its Transformations* of 1953, Robert Redfield has described two types of generic personality which separated out after Neolithic urban specialization set in and towns began to grow up: one Redfield calls a traditional country personality and the other a town personality. His country personality sets small store by power and money, prefers stability to change, habit to adventure, and stays in one spot often for life; has little use for aggression or war or overt quarrels, values what is commonly called honesty or loyalty sexual and social, sees pleasure or happiness not separate from toil and emphasizes "freedom", pristine independence, "liberty". Whatever the validity of Redfield's general thesis Clare's personality, acquired character and patterns of thought are all very much those of Redfield's country man. He lacked the talent of acquisitive cunning almost completely and change of scene threatened his balance as it did Emily Brontë's.

There is further evidence that the removal to Northborough marked a crisis in Clare's inner life, and that his surmounting of it had effects both good and bad on his mind in his later years. The flitting was another stage in a process of the separation of the lover from the objects of love:

> Their memory lingers round the heart
> Like life whose essence is its friends

It was ten years since he first expressed the conflict between self and being in the belief that in losing Mary Joyce in the flesh he had won her in the spirit. Since then he had addressed poem after poem to her, and in all, the idea of her nearness to him was dwelt upon, sometimes as an intolerable pain, sometimes as a blessing:

> When lovers part the longest mile
> Leaves hope of some returning
> Tho mines close by no hope the while
> Within my heart is burning
> One hour would bring me to her door
> Yet sad and lonely hearted
> If seas between us both should roar
> We were not further parted

"Last night, Oct. 13, 1832," he wrote in one of his notebooks,[1]

> I had a remarkable dream that Guardian spirit in the shape of a soul stirring beauty again appeared to me with the very same countenance in which she appeared many years ago & in which she has since appeared at intervals & moved my ideas into extasy—I cannot doubt her existance

Clare dreamed that he was in a strange room among a fine company receiving much kindness and attention. Yet he was in low spirits until the lovely creature came to him in a familiar way and with "witching" voice and cherishing smiles spoke words which he could not recollect on waking. He then tells of the first dream in which she appeared to him. It was many years before, when he had not published a line. She had led him from his home to an open field called Maple Hill, near Hilly Snow and Swordy Well. An immense crowd surrounded them—mounted soldiers performing evolutions, ladies in splendid dresses, crowds as at a fair.

> I felt shamed into insignificance at the sight & seemed to ask her from my own thoughts why I had been so suddenly brought into such immense company when my only life and care was being alone & to myself—you are only one of the crowd now she said & hurried me back

The scene changed to a bookseller's shop in a city, and there, on a shelf, among a vast crowd of books, he saw three volumes lettered with his name. "I see them now I was astonished & turning to look in her face I was awake in a moment but the impression never left me & I see her still she is my good genius & I believe in her ideally almost as fresh as reality."

He then describes yet another dream of a later date, which he embodied also in a poem, "The Nightmare". He dreamed he was in Long Close, and all the villagers were hurrying past him northward; it was morning, but the sky had a dull, unnatural hue and the sun shone with a pale, "moonstruck" light. He felt the

[1] Peterborough MSS.

sudden conviction that all were called to Judgment, and he followed the crowd into the church, feeling depressed and uneasy. Then his guardian appeared, "in white garments beautifully disordered but sorrowful in her countenance". A light streamed in a corner of the chancel, and thence appeared to come "the final decision of man's actions in life". He heard his own name called: "my conductress smiled in exstacy & uttered somthing as prophetic of happiness I knew all was right & she led me again into the open air"

He awoke to the sound of soft music:

> —& I felt delighted & sorrowful & talked to her awake for a moment as if she were still bending over me—These dreams of a beautiful presence a woman deity gave the sublimest conceptions of beauty to my imagination & being last night with the same presence the lady divinity left such a vivid picture of her visits in my sleep dreaming of dreams that I could no longer doubt her existence so I wrote them down to prolong the happiness of my faith in believing her my guardian genius the cause I cannot tell the fact is truth if so it may be said of dreams[1]

Most of us know dreams from which we wake apprehensive or depressed and other dreams from which we wake unaccountably happy. Such dreams may be part of a humanly inscrutable makeup beyond the everyday industrial-practical. Clare's ability to identify delight with sorrow or sorrow with delight may also be part of what the recent translator of *Beowulf*, Kevin Crossley-Holland, has called a traditional "relish" for sadness in many Celtic–Anglo–Saxon poets and their poems.

Clare was frequently aware, as he records in "A Shadow of Life, Death and Eternity", of a shadow moving by one's side

> A shadow moving by one's side
> That would a substance seem
> That is & is not …

[1] *Ibid.*

Occasionally he was aware, too, of the "nightmare misery of a coming doom". But in the dreams recorded above may be part of the secret of his 1832 recovery from a depth of despair which seems so out of proportion to the circumstances of removal to Northborough. The breaking of links with the past led him to take stock of the years since 1820, to weigh things up—achievements against mere hopes. He saw himself threatened with pretty total failure, with a shipwreck of his "life's esteems", the three essentials for him of independence, love, poetry. Twelve years after he had received recognition he was still begging and in debt. As a poet he had lost his public. The old, old contradiction between "love" and the often dreary ache of everyday relationships stared at him. He had lost Mary Joyce in the flesh but he could not forget her. He had seen a still earlier love, the Helpston of his boyhood, ravaged by change. He had lost that changed Helpston too.

The waning of present popularity troubled him less once he had thought it out. But the chance that his poems might be forgotten by posterity, that he might miss "true" fame, the poetic immortality he had come to value—that, too, had to be faced:

> I woud not that my being all shoud dye
> & pass away with many a common lot
> I woud not that my humble dust shoud lye
> In quite a strange & unfrequented spot
> By all unheeded & by all forgot

To this theme which was also his struggle he returned again and again, sometimes the mood one of fatalistic resignation:

> Alas to me no home belongs
> But what my dreams create
> Vain cuckoo like I sing my songs
> & leave the rest to fate

But when "Fame's hopes with me are faint to look upon" and he wished he could reject the struggle, be realistic—

> Yet do I follow with unwearied eyes
> The shadowy recompense for real toils

Ah would the heart cease aching & be wise
& think life vainly spent staked for a doubtful prize

He could not give up. He could not even tolerate any of the reactionary complacencies that creep often stealthily unawares on a man as middle age approaches. The realization which came to him in the doubts of 1832 was of Mary Joyce as spirit of natural beauty, spirit of first, ideal love, and guardian pledge of deserved recognition after death: a trinity, if you like, saving him from paranoia; in other terms, symbols of hope acceptable to an extremely impressionable mentality and a nervous system burdened from childhood with long odds, beleaguered confidence and imposed guilt:

I heard of parnass hill castalias stream
& in my dreams had worshiped beauty long
I heard alas but never did I dream
That aught of birthright could to me belong
In that rich paradise of dainty song
Yet have I loved & worshiped & the spring
Of hope—tho not an eagle in the sun
Did like a bird to its rude dittys cling
& of[t] oer visions with a weary wing
Did brood & linger in the day begun[1]

Clare's surmounting of his crisis in 1832 foreshadows the story of the remainder of his life. In support of this interpretation there is evidence in a poem which, though not published until 1920 by Edmund Blunden and Alan Porter, was written in 1832 soon after "Decay" and "The Flitting". It arose from the mood Clare reached at the end of the earlier poem, when he could feel again

a love & joy
For every weed & everything

In "Song's Eternity" he catches in onomatopoeia—a tricky enough technical achievement in poetry — the bluecap's song.

[1] Peterborough MSS. Clare's draft; cf. the printed version, with Mrs Emmerson's emendations, in *The Rural Muse*.

This takes on the "tone" of the poet's poem. Song and poem are as old as civilization's "6,000 years"—an accurate enough date for poetry's beginnings. The eternity which these three celebrate some geo-physicists posit today:

What is songs eternity
Come & see
—Can it noise & bustle be
Come & see
Praises sung or praises said
Come and see
Wait awhile & these are dead—
Sigh sigh
Be they high or lowly bred
They die

What is songs eternity
Come & see
Melodys of earth & sky
Here they be—
—Ballads of six thousand years
Thrive thrive
Songs awakened with the spheres
Alive

Mighty songs that miss decay
What are they
Crowds & cities pass away
Like a day
Books are writ & books are read
What are they
Years will lay them with the dead
Sigh sigh
Trifles unto nothing wed
They die

Dreamers list the honey bee
Mark the tree
Where the bluecap tootle tee
Sings a glee
Sung to Adam & to eve—

Here they be
When floods covered every tree
Noahs ark
Heard that ballad singing now
Hark hark

Tootle tootle tootle tee
Can it be
Pride & fame must shadows be
Come & see
Every season own her own
Bird & bee
Sing creations music on
Natures glee
Is in every mood & love
Eternity[1]

Someone has remarked that Clare was more interested in the bird than in the eternity. Not true: the bird is there because Clare hears in its song, untroubled by thoughts of yesterday or tomorrow, a symbol of that eternity which man, by inventing Time, forswears and then allows himself to be driven to re-invent. Again, he was not turning back. But like all victories this of Clare's was won at a cost. He was exalting so-called ideals and dreams over present actualities. As the years to come would bring him no whole relief or "freedom", fatally dreams became more and more real to him. It was a sacrifice—how deliberate we cannot know — of man to poet. His doctors and friends would rightly soon agree to call some of his dreams delusions, and Clare insane.

[1] Peterborough MSS.

CHAPTER SIXTEEN

The Midsummer Cushion: 1832-1835

On September 1st, 1832, Clare received from Clifton, a Peterborough printer, a hundred copies of his own proposals for the publication of a volume of cottage poems, with *his* title "The Midsummer Cushion". He explained this title: "It is a very old custom among villagers in summer time to take a piece of green sward full of field flowers & place it as an ornament in their cottages which ornaments are called Midsummer Cushions." Here is part of his letter duly punctuated by the printer for subscribers:

> The proposals for publishing these Fugitives being addressed to friends, no further apology is necessary than the statement of facts ... the truth is that difficulty has grown up like a tree of the forests, and being no longer able to conceal it, I meet it in the best way possible, by attempting to publish these for my own benefit, and that of a large family.
>
> It were false delicacy, to make an idle parade of independence in my situation; and it would be unmanly to make a troublesome appeal to persons public or private, like a public petitioner.
>
> Friends neither expect this from me, or wish me to do it to others, though it is partly owing to such advice, that has induced me to come forward with these proposals, and if they are successful they will render me a benefit; and if not, they will not cancel any obligations that I may have received from Friends public and private, to whom my best wishes are due; and having said thus much in furtherance of my intentions, I will conclude by explaining them.[1]

[1] Peterborough MSS.

The book was to be printed on fine paper and the price would not exceed 7*s.* 6*d.* Prospectuses were distributed among Clare's friends and acquaintances, and by the end of October a list of two hundred subscribers had been collected. In this work the Emmersons, the Simpsons, the Mossops, Mrs Marsh, and Henderson were prominent. Early in November, Clare changed his plans on the advice of the Emmersons. They had been negotiating with J. How, who was connected with the publishing firm of Whittaker (or Whitaker), and suggested that on the security of his two hundred subscribers Clare should sell the volume outright to How and thus relieve himself of the risk and anxiety of its publication.

The manuscript of "The Midsummer Cushion" contains the fruits of Clare's labours during the ten years before 1832. Since he had realized that he could no longer rely on Taylor as editor and publisher, he had been constantly revising and re-copying his poems. He had taken the best of them and transcribed them carefully into a finely-bound manuscript book. By the autumn of 1832 he had collected more than three hundred poems from thirty-five earlier manuscripts. With its neat and vigorous unpunctuated script, this book offers convincing proof of Clare's ability to edit his own poems. Could it be printed as it stands with its own title, it would represent adequately the work, untampered with, of Clare's maturity.

Meanwhile, the zeal of some of Clare's friends in giving publicity to his new scheme outran discretion. A paragraph in the *Athenaeum* for August 25th, 1832, stated that Clare's cottage had been bestowed on him by Lord Milton rent *free for life*; the Stamford *Bee* repeated the story. Clare was annoyed. Commenting on the gossip, he wrote to Mossop: "It troubles me and injures my feelings of a propriety of independence." He added that he had already told Clark, the editor of the *Bee*, that he was to pay rent as his neighbours did. He also wrote to his London friends to have the matter corrected there; but the correction gave birth to such a crop of further errors that Clare noted that he felt he had as much to fear from friends than from enemies. A notice appeared in the *Alfred* giving the correct facts about the cottage, but suggesting that he had been cheated out of all profits by his publishers and that he had only £15 a year on which to maintain his wife and six children. The Stamford *Bee* repeated this story on October 5th, and on the 13th the *Athenaeum*, correcting its previous statement about the cottage, quoted the *Alfred* story, and reprinted Clare's proposals as evidence of its truth. The fountain-head of both these misstatements appears to have been Charles Jacob, a Peterborough printer. He sent them to his relative, How, who supplied them to the *Athenaeum* and the *Alfred*. The second *Athenaeum* notice was from the pen of Allan Cunningham.

Clare's indignation was tempered by the realization that his friends had erred in trying to serve him, but he was angry that Taylor's honesty had been publicly questioned. He wrote at once to How, stating that he did not want publicity of that kind, that he "felt a stubborn belief that Taylor was a sincere friend", that the trouble had been caused by the double-dealing of Drury, for Taylor was "utterly above such things and like myself a man of business only by necessity". He felt that Clark was less blameless in repeating statements which he must have known were false. "Had I been aware of his intentions to meddle in my affairs I should most assuredly have treated him as a foe in disguise," he wrote to Simpson; "I am no beggar for my income is £36"; and to the editor himself, "I wish not to have my difficulties trumpeted by everyone who chooses to pen his spleen in my favour ... Officious interferences as to my adversity add nothing to my prosperity ... I never solicited praise or profit from any individual in my life ... I am not seeking charity but independence." Again and again in his letters to his friends Clare repeated this last definition of his material ambitions. To find his latest attempt to achieve independence turned into an appeal for charity was almost the last straw, especially where he suspected, as he did with regard to the *Bee*, that he was being used as a political catspaw.

Yet larger hopes and fears remained untouched by what he called the stings of summer insects. He wrote to Allan Cunningham in the autumn of 1832, thanking him for his help in advertising the "Midsummer Cushion" prospectuses and setting forth his aims:

> I have those around me that make me turn to the practical matters of pounds shillings & pence ... I have a strong opinion of Taylor & shall always respect him & I think if

> the matter had been entirely left to business & I had sold them out & out even for a trifle I should have been better off & much better satisfied ... I cannot but say God protect all hopes in difficulties from the patronage of trade

There is a draft of what appears to be a letter to Cary, which illustrates Clare's efforts to regard such bothers as but minor details in life. Cary had written: "Had you been as expert an agriculturist or mechanic as you are a Poet, you also might by this time have acquired competence or even wealth. But would you be satisfied to exchange conditions on those terms?"

"Your philosophy of quietness was better than medicine to my mind," Clare replied in August and went on to tell of his latest schemes:

> ... your commendation given early and continued long gave me a pride that the ephemeral opinions of unknown interferences cannot take away ... I wished to be judged of by the book itself without any appeals to want of education lowness of origin or any other foil that officion [officiousness] chuses to encumber my path with but it seems I must be encumbered never mind I must write on for ambition to be happy in sadness as verses make me urges me onward[1]

He enclosed a prospectus of his "little cockleshell".

> ... If you laugh at my ambitions I am ready to laugh with you at my own vanity for I sit sometimes & wonder [ ] over the little noise I have made in the world untill I think I have written nothing as yet to deserve any praise at all so the spirit of fame of living a little after life like a name on a conspicuous place urges my blood upward into unconscious mel[o]dys & striding down my orchard & homestead I hum & sing inwardly those little madrigals & then go in & pen them down thinking them much better things than they are untill I look over them again & then the charm vanishes into the vanity that I shall do somthing better ere I die so in

[1] *The Letters of John Clare*, *op. cit.*

> spite of myself I ryhme on & write nothing but little things at last ...[1]

He thought all his old friends had "gone away with the world", but was glad to find there was still one, "almost the last of the flock," who still remembered him. Yet he hoped to see them all again, "as earnest in their affections ... & then I shall shake hands with old time & be more happy than when old time was new to me God bless you my dear Sir."

The year 1833 opened with reverberations of the distasteful newspaper worry of the previous autumn. Taylor's grievances over the business of the Fund-money had been aggravated by those public aspersions of his character for which he held Clare partly responsible. He had not written since July 1832; on January 9th, 1833, he announced that he was instituting an action for libel against the proprietors of the papers. The news found Clare in no fit condition to cope. He was troubled by an hallucination that he was bewitched by evil spirits. Both Mrs Emmerson and Taylor wrote assuring him that there was no such thing as witchcraft. Meanwhile, the plans for the new volume were at a standstill, and debts began to accumulate again as months passed. Clare was driven to ask whether How would advance money on the manuscripts already completed; Mrs Emmerson wrote in June urging him to exert himself, since no publisher would countenance such a proposal. "Good heavens Johnny, how can you sink down to such apathy?" Evidently she did not know that he had been ordered by his doctor to abstain from reading and writing. He was hurt by her failure to understand. She rarely failed him.

Not the least of his anxieties at this time was for his family, which had been increased by the birth of a son, Charles, in the previous December. It is a fact that the births of his children often found him ill. The education of the elder children was a constant theme of his letters to Mrs Emmerson. He sent such a formidable list of books for her to procure that she asked if he was about to turn schoolmaster. Another list he sent to Taylor, requesting him to deduct the cost from the next dividend. "For do you know I wish to make all my children scholars & the

[1] *The Letters of John Clare, op. cit.*

expenses for school books make the charges so high that I am troubled often in which way to pay them." He wanted blank summing books, arithmetic text-books and selections in prose and verse. He had ideas about the kind of book he wanted, having talked of such matters years before with Cary and Darley. He did not like Murray's textbooks; they taught set tasks which were not entertaining to children. He wanted books that would please them to read and profit them to remember. We find elsewhere a list of "Christmas Boxes promised to my children"; they were all books, from *Valentine and Orson* for Anna down to *The House that Jack Built* for Sophy. In 1830 the Emmersons had tried to get Fred into Christ's Hospital, but they were unsuccessful.

Clare's interest in his children's education went beyond provision of schooling and books. In one of his manuscripts is a letter of advice to his sons, written under the impression that he could not live to advise them in person. He warned them against bad company and false friends; they were to consider their master's interests as their own, and value common honesty above all things. Better not meddle with political contentions: "for there are many whose superior abilities force them into that storm & strife of opinion who would give all the wealth they possess for that quiet which you may enjoy for nothing." This need not prevent them from taking an intelligent interest in politics. "If you can be impartial read the speeches & they will improve you & if style or composition or purity of diction delight you there you will find it in perfection in the orations of both parties for to me they have been of great benefit."

Clare's affection for his children was deep and sensitive. There is a family tradition that he could not bear to see them punished. Patty, in flashes of anger, sometimes gave them hearty thrashings. Clare would plead for them it is said, offering to bear the stripes himself.

In July 1833, he was able at last to write to Taylor, who was "gratified with your expression of friendly Regard and kind recollection of our early and long-continued acquaintance". He had now overcome his feeling of annoyance at the newspaper gossip and had decided to drop the libel action. As soon as his health allowed, Clare completed the copying up of his poems, and by August the beautiful manuscript of "The Midsummer

Cushion" was in Mrs Emmerson's hands. She was delighted with it, but suggested changing the title—to *The Rural Muse*. Nothing more was effected in 1833, owing to changes in the firm of Whittaker. Among the scanty records of these months is a letter from Cary, sending his translation of Pindar. "It is all about chariot & horse-racing, boxing, running, heathen gods and goddesses, &c., &c.; so I don't expect it will be much to your taste; & therefore don't insist on your reading it. Only it serves to show that you are not forgotten."

In January 1834, Thomas Emmerson obtained How's solemn promise to bring out *The Rural Muse* in the spring. Clare received the news with gratitude. His debts had crept up to £35, including £20 owing when he left Helpston. The rent of the Northborough cottage—so Ryde of Burghley told Mrs Emmerson—was £15 a year. Some of the children were ill; even the milch cow, May, whose arrival Mrs Emmerson had celebrated with a sonnet, had failed to perform well. The pressure of these anxieties brought a return of illness early in 1834; fears of witchcraft and other nervous and morbid fancies troubled him. Dr Darling could do no more than urge him not to aggravate his ills by these "figments of the imagination". He prescribed verses from the Psalms. Taylor at first declined to help with the editing of *The Rural Muse* but he offered to look over the proofs.

In March a letter from Thomas Emmerson brought much-needed financial relief. At once this effected a temporary improvement in Clare's spirits. The copyright had yielded £40, with which Clare was able to settle nearly all accumulated debts. But the clouds of depression dispersed by this timely wind soon collected again; although Clare's ambition burned no less fiercely, though his determination to struggle through to better days was hardly less dogged, they could not now demand the same ready obedience from the mind and body which served them. Recovery was slower, strewn with relapses. There is evidence of this in a series of letter drafts in one of his manuscripts, all dated 1834 and all unfinished. Several of these cries for help are fragments, the superscription and one or two lines: then the writing trails off as Clare found the completion of a brief note too great a burden. All the fragments tell the same story; he is scarcely able to write, cannot even express his gratitude, wants to see Dr Darling. In July he made an attempt to realize this wish, feeling that a visit to London might benefit his health as it had done in the past. Unfortunately, Mrs Emmerson was going out of town on a visit to Smallcombe Grove, near Bath, "a spot of exquisite beauty" where they had just purchased a country retreat; and Taylor had no room for him just then.

Clare had managed to write the preface for *The Rural Muse* by August, and the poems were in the printer's hands. A month later Taylor was busy editing the proofs with his over-meticulous care; most of his alterations were made in the interest of grammar or clarity, but he spoiled lines which did not jump with the personal opinions of his middle age as when he changed "Death's long, happy sleep is won" to "Heaven's eternal Peace is won"; he preferred, he explained, bad divinity to good atheism.

How had left Whittaker's. On December 6th he wrote suggesting that Clare should apply to the Literary Fund for help; he was acquainted with some of the committee, and thought Clare might ask for £50, which would keep him in comfort over the winter. The application was successful, the money arrived in January. Thanks to this gift from the Literary Fund, which had accomplished much good relief-work since its establishment by David Williams in 1780, Clare was able to pay off his remaining debts and face the new year with less anxiety. Again there was an immediate improvement in his spirits and health.

Taylor's letter of January 9th, 1835, contained news of the death of Charles Lamb in the previous December; Woodhouse also was dead, and had left Taylor all his papers, with many poems by Keats. Taylor said he would like to publish a complete edition of Keats, but he feared that the world did not care enough to buy it. He also pointed out a reference to Clare in Ebenezer Elliott's poem "Love":

> Mother of Men, be proud without a tear!
> While round your hearth the woe-nursed virtues move,
> And all that manliness can ask of love;
> Remember Hogarth, and abjure despair,
> Remember Arkwright and peasant Clare.
> Burns, o'er the plough, sung sweet his woodnotes wild,
> And richest Shakespeare was a poor man's child.

Cary had commented on Elliott's "words that scald": Clare was acquainted with the work of the prolific Sheffield Corn-law rhymer and master-founder, though none of his books are in Clare's library.

Towards the end of 1834 Earl Spencer died, and Clare feared that the annuity of £10 would be discontinued. Taylor advised him to ask the earl's successor to continue the kindness, and drafted a letter for him; Clare was grateful and in January 1835 wrote: "though I could scarcely do without the money I had not the resolution to write for it & I think I should never have done so." The new earl responded. The annuity went on as before.

The publication of *The Rural Muse*, which fulfilled the promise of 1820 and should have raised his star of recognition at least to second magnitude, produced a very mild and brief Indian summer of interest. For a few months the book sold fairly well, and Whittaker had hopes of disposing of the first edition. A number of old acquaintances looked up from their affairs to applaud. Derwent Coleridge, now a schoolmaster in Cornwall, visited the Emmersons in July and expressed appreciation. Mrs Emmerson hoped—vainly, it appears—that Henry Nelson Coleridge, Sara's husband, would write a review of it for the *Quarterly*. Alaric Watts praised it, and James Montgomery. Rippingille, just returned from a lecturing tour in the north, sent congratulations; there came news of Charles Elton, who was about to publish his *Boyhood*, which included "The Idler's Epistle". Mrs Emmerson had given a copy of *The Rural Muse* to Harry Phillips, the popular singer and disciple of Izaak Walton. Captain Sherwill, visiting London after years of European travel, revived the memory of old days, and promised books. Dr Bowring wrote, and from an American bookseller came a letter proposing an arrangement (which did not materialize) for selling the book there. A new correspondent was George Reid of Glasgow, who showed his appreciation in practical form by sending books for Clare's library.

In *Blackwood's Magazine* for August, Professor Wilson welcomed the poems with a long and, in the main, sympathetic review; yet, after exhorting the public to buy a book so full of beauties, and commenting, ironically enough, on Clare's comfort beside Bloomfield's and Burns's deaths in poverty, North incurred Taylor's contempt by inviting Clare to imitate

Bloomfield. There was a warmly appreciative article in the *Literary Gazette*; the *Athenaeum* recommended the book briefly but sincerely, as did the *New Monthly*. The reviewer in the *Druid's Magazine* described his visit to Northborough, and was enthusiastic in praise of the book. But he agreed with North that Clare's popularity might be increased if he confined himself to describing the manners and feelings of the "lower orders".

Could these critics have seen the manuscript of "The Midsummer Cushion" and the many poems which Mrs Emmerson omitted in her selection, they might have revised their statements. Mrs Emmerson was an enthusiast who knew a good poem when she saw it, but she did not always recognize a poor one. Occasionally her omissions were justified. Sometimes nothing but a personal bias or a strict eye on the dimensions desired for the book could have helped to decide between one poem and another. She missed excellent ones like "The Firetail's Nest", "The Progress of Rhyme", and of course "The Toper's Rant" – all of which waited until Arthur Symons printed them in 1908:

Come come my old crones & gay fellows
That loves to drink ale in a horn
We'll sing racey songs now we're mellow
Which topers sung ere we were born
For our bottle kind fate shall be thanked
& line but our pockets with brass
We'll sooner suck ale through a blanket
Then thimbles of wine from a glass

Away with your proud thimble glasses
Of wine foreign nations supply
We topers neer drink to the lassies
Over draughts scarce enough for a flye
Club us with the hedger & ditcher
Or beggar that makes his own horn
To join us oer bottle or pitcher
Foaming oer with the essence of corn ...

Eliza Emmerson missed too the interestingly modern "Country Letter". A place for these poems could have been found without lengthening the book, by the omission of a number of album verses—"Adventures of a Grasshopper", "Nature's Hymn to the Deity", "Woman's Love", which had been written to meet stated requirements of editors of Annuals.

The Rural Muse was dedicated to Earl Fitzwilliam. Clare's preface was short. He did not want indulgence. He would be satisfied with the good opinion of readers.

In the book he imprisoned the living moment in nature, conveyed the image of "pranking bat", expressed wood-silences with that "easy thoughtlessness of thought" he claimed for the highest poetry. From "Summer Images":

I love at early morn from new mown swath
To see the startled frog his rout pursue
& mark while leaping oer the dripping path
his bright sides scatter dew
& early lark that from its bustle flyes—
To hail his mattin new
& watch him to the skyes ... [1]

Clare was still attached to the Elizabethans. His struggle to transcend the undiminishing difficulties of his circumstances let loose a lyricism not present in his work hitherto. A Lear-like note has crept in while his subject is still "natural" happiness—as if he had taken on himself a little of the "mystery of things". The Elizabethans certainly helped him find his own lyric note; a new authority, as when he returns to the theme of the eternity of nature, is there:

Man Earths poor shadow talks of earths decay
But hath it nothing of eternal kin
No majesty that shall not pass away
No soul of greatness springing up within
Thought marks without hoar shadows of sublime
Pictures of power which if not doomed to win
Eternity—stand laughing at old time
For ages in the grand ancestral line
Of things eternal wearing to divine

[1] Peterborough MSS., "Midsummer Cushion" draft.

I read magnificence where ages pay
Worship like conquered foes to appenine
Because they could not conquer—there sits day
Too high for night to come at—mountains shine
Outpeering time too high for his decay[1]

There are lines and phrases in these poems which are harbingers of poems to come. He had longed for the "wizard" voice of the November storm that he might "breathe a living song". It almost seems as if he is acquiring a sibylline melody of that "eternal ditty". Trying again and again to capture some of the very notes of robin song and so prolong its "happy prime" he appears almost to have achieved identification:

Giving to stocks & stones in rapture's strife
A soul of utterance & a tongue of life

He heard and saw all around him as vividly as if he used *peyotl* every day of his life. If we remember "Song's Eternity", "The lark he rises early", as well as poems in *The Rural Muse* such as "The Nightingale's Nest", "The Shepherd's Tree"[2] and those quoted, we may at least say that Clare has become by this period of his life the foremost representative among English poets from the perennial world of nature.

[1] Peterborough MSS.

[2] Given by the editors Eric Robinson and Geoffrey Summerfield in the New Oxford Selection as "Salter's Tree". There are at least three manuscript drafts of this sonnet. In "The Midsummer Cushion" fair copy Clare titled it as above.

CHAPTER SEVENTEEN

Shipwreck: 1835–1837

The few tributes he received from old and new acquaintances after the publication of *The Rural Muse* relieved, but could not remove, the prolonged sense of frustration which clung about Clare's mind. He might transmute conscious resignation into poetry. Dealing with unconscious frustration was much less easy. Complete control of such frustration with its protean, mental manifestations was by then probably impossible. Soon he was ill again. One of the many unsent letters of this period and belonging to autumn 1835, to Dr Darling, reveals:

> I write to tell you I am very unwell & though I cannot describe my feelings well I will tell you as well as I can—sounds affect me very much & things evil as well [as] good thoughts are continually rising in my mind I cannot sleep for I am asleep as it were with my eyes open & I feel chills come over me & a sort of nightmare awake I got no rest last night I feel a great desire to come up but perhaps I shall not be able & I hope you [will] write down directly for I feel you can do me good & if I was in town I should soon be well so I fancy for I do assure you I am very unwell & I cannot keep my mind right as it were for I wish to read & cannot—there is a sort of numbing through my private parts which I cannot describe & when I was so indisposed last winter I felt as if I had inflamation [?] in the blood & at times as if it went round me & at other times such a sinking as if I was going to sink through the bed—& though not so bad now I am realy very uneasy in fact I have never been right as it were since then here is all I can say just now

> but I hope you can send somthing to benefit me give my respects to Taylor ... [1]

He added a postscript: "I fear I shall be worse & worse ere you write to me for I have been out for a walk & can scarcely bear up against my fancys or feelings."

For such a condition of what sounds akin to nervous collapse there could have been but one cure in days before drugs and electric therapy for the many forms of insanity—a complete change of environment, with protracted relief from the anxieties aggravating such a situation. The removal to Northborough and the family's venture into cottage farming were crippled from the start by inadequate backing. He could expect no more windfalls from the Literary Fund. Most Annuals failed to pay more than a copy in which his poems appeared. The first edition of *The Rural Muse* sold reasonably well but there was no hope of more profit.

Could Clare have given up even then as poet and accepted failure to achieve independence as a peasant, he might still have spared himself torment to come: like so many of the peasants of England in those days, a slave mentality engendered by long odds might have made the lot of near-serfdom temporarily endurable. But there was determination in him amounting to rigid refusal to submit. Hope still glowed. With "self-creating joy", an inward flame of the "haunted mind" was still

> Burning the soul to leave behind
> The memory of a name.

In early days of anonymous village poets he might not have known what Kenneth Richmond has called in *Poetry and the People* this "anxious lust for a private immortality". As it was he made plans for yet another volume, though he saw faint chance of print for it. The poems written between 1835 and 1837 have little of the direct personal reference which inspired many of the preceding period. Yet the crisis of 1832 and the uprooting from Helpston had ended in a renewal of faith in life's joy. After that, to find serenity when he walked in the fields or took up his pen,

[1] *The Letters of John Clare, op. cit.*

he turned his back on the world of men. The transition from discord and "the very noise of troublous man" to such lonely harmony was neither easy nor safe, and it was prolonged:

> To be & not to be & still to know it
> Like toad life-buried in the solid rock

shows the darker side of the struggle to persuade himself that love and solitude could prevail over "scorn and noise".

He had often raised his voice against the cruelty of man towards his fellows as well as towards fellow creatures. The poems he wrote—copied into a manuscript book by means of a terrible homemade ink[1] which ate into the paper as the desire to be recognized and remembered was eating into the poet's mind—of Northborough fen scenes and occupations are more starkly objective than any he had so far written. He described badger-baiting, harrying of marten, polecat, vixen with young, hedgehog, despoiling of wild ducks' and wild bees' nests. To this series belong such poems as "Braggart", "Lout", "Clown", "Outcast", "Tramp", "Molecatcher", "Gipsies". In "The Badger" he obtained dramatic objectivity through the contrast between the shouting, excited mob of men and boys and the hunted animal, "demure and small", beating off a dozen yelping dogs:

> Till kicked and torn and beaten out he lies
> And leaves his hold and cackles groans and dies

In "Braggart", "Outcast", "Tramp" and the rest, a capacity to see into, and acutely to feel, the point of view and the mental situation of what or whom he is depicting, distinguishes Clare from many more immediately successful contemporaries.

Among this group of stark poems there are glimpses of a capacity for happiness—undoubtedly connected with his sense of community with natural life—which cannot be overlooked. From "Break of Day":

[1] "Take three ounces of bruised Nuttgalls put them into a pint & a half of rain water let it stand for three days then put in One ounce & a half of Green Coppurs & a piece of Stone blue & shake it up every day & it is fit for use." Peterborough MSS.

The lark he rises early
    And the ploughman goes away
Before its morning fairly
    At the guessing break of day
The fields lie in the dawning
    And the valleys hid in gold
At the pleasant time of morning
    When the shepherd goes to fold

The maiden laughs and hollos
    When she sees the feeding cows
They switch their tails and follows
    When she cant get over sloughs
I love the gentle dawning
    And the valleys hid in gold
At the pleasant time of morning
    When the shepherd goes to fold[1]

On December 18th, 1835, Clare's mother died at the age of seventy-eight. His parents had not accompanied him to Northborough: they had left the Helpston cottage a few years before Clare's removal, presumably to make room for the growing family. A visitor to Helpston some time between 1832 and 1835 found Ann Clare gleaning in the fields. Parker Clare, who went to Northborough after his wife's death, lived until 1846, reaching his eighty-second year. Clare seems to have inherited from his parents a physical tenacity and, if not a burly or robust frame, the wiry and resilient constitution of the agricultural poor.

Yet the year 1836 shows that he is "no better" than when he had written to Darling in 1835. His letters to Eliza Emmerson become mere notes. One dated March 23rd, 1826, must be in fact for 1836—unsent:

My dear Eliza

Did you get the vol of poems I sent a long time ago I wished you to write directly & as you did not write we think you did not get them I still keep ill & am no better[2]

[1] Peterborough MSS.
[2] *Ibid.*

She sent him a waistcoat in that month, chequered—as flowers were out of fashion—and Allan Cunningham's early *Songs*, given her by Henry Phillips the writer on angling. Clare was as greedy as ever for books and wrote to Sherwill to remind him of his promise to send some. In June Rippingille wrote from London—much more serious than the Rippingille of Clare's memory, sobered by family troubles and years of waiting on fortune to little purpose. Whittaker—though Mr Emmerson reported him to have said he thought they would "get off the first edition" of *The Rural Muse* – wrote to Clare that no new one would be required as the first was unsold.

On November 29th Taylor sent word from Retford that he hoped to visit Northborough on his way back to town. He left an account of that visit, which occurred early in December:

> The following morning at seven I set off to see Clare in a chaise accompanied by a medical gentleman of Stamford who was to give me his opinion respecting poor Clare's health. We found him sitting in a chimney corner looking much as usual. He talked properly to me in reply to all my questions, knew all the people of whom I spoke, and smiled at my reminding him of the events of past days. But his mind is sadly enfeebled. He is constantly speaking to himself and when I listened I heard such words as these pronounced a great many times over and with great rapidity—'God bless them all,' 'Keep them from evil,' 'Doctors.' But who it was of whom he spoke I could not tell—whether his children, or doctors, or everybody. But I think the latter. His children, seven in number, are a very fine family, strongly resembling him; the youngest, a boy of three or four years old; the eldest, a girl, sixteen. There are three boys and four girls. The medical man's opinion was that Clare should go to some asylum. His wife is a very clever, active woman, and keeps them all very respectable and comfortable, but she cannot manage to control her husband at times; he is very violent, I dare say, occasionally. His old father is still living with them. We went thence to see a clergyman who had been always kind to Clare for twenty years, and he has promised to see Earl Fitzwilliam about an asylum.

Taylor remarked in a letter after his return to London that, as other visitors noted, Clare's outward appearance and most of his behaviour showed few signs of illness. Occasionally the thread of his words might be broken by some irrelevance, and at times melancholy plunged into apathy or rose into fierce anger. But by this time Clare had certainly developed his first permanent delusion. This was that Mary Joyce was his first wife and Patty his second—the theme of Dante, Beatrice and Gemma rewritten with variation. Projection from fantasy, dream or imagination was in process: the visionary "guardian spirit" and the real Mary Joyce, for many years united in thought, were being transferred to everyday existence. The girl he had lost twenty years before became his wife. He seems to have had no wish to discard Patty. Despite her quick tongue, inadequate sympathies, and incapacity to understand his writing, his appreciation of her quality remained singularly unchanged and his memory of their attachment stayed unsoured to the end. We know this from "Maid of Walkherd" written at High Beech in 1840 or 1841, from the St Andrew's poem dated October 20th, 1848, "O once I had a true love/ As blest as I could be," as well as from High Beech and St Andrew's letters to her who couldn't read. Clare would not comprehend why Mary, whom he said he had seen, kept or was kept from him. It was not, in fact, impossible for him to have seen Mary Joyce: she lived no more than three miles away at Glinton, unmarried, until 1838. Clare's grandson told how, when Patty could do nothing with her husband, one of the elder boys would take him aside and calm him by talking quietly of country things.

A memory of him which has come down in the family tradition is that he was in general moody, of a strong temper, not averse to female company, occasionally but not habitually given to strong drink and strong language. And there is a manuscript note of the 1820s revealing a capacity for self-analysis which has its place in his struggle against the intellectual domination and condescension, however well meant, of his affluent friends. This was part of his need to hold on to what he was beginning to call by the oddly modern term, self-identity:

> I have been accused of being a drunkard & of being ungrateful toward my friends & patrons ... I wished to thank them

& tell them that I felt their kindness & remained silent neither did I trumpet the praises of patrons eternally wherever I went ... I was never utterly cast down in adversity I struggled on Neither was I at any time lifted up above my prosperity I never attempted to alter my old ways & manners I harboured no proud notions nor felt a pride above my station ...

Every friendship I made grew into a warm attachment I was in earnest or I was nothing, & I believed everything that was uttered came from the heart as mine did when I made a familiar friend I gave him my confidence and unbosomed my faults and failings to him without hesitation and reserve putting my all into his hands and thereby making myself bare to his temper without caring to enquire into his own as a holdfast or earnest to keep secrets

On the other hand I have a fault that often hurts me though I cannot master it I am apt to mistake some foibles that all men are subject to as breaches of friendship and thereby grow dissatisfied and lose my sincerity for them and when I feel disappointed in my opinions of them I never can recover my former attachment, though I often try I always wear the silent enmity of an enemy when I can no longer feel the sincerity of a friend I know I am full of faults though I have improved and tempered myself as well as I was able but these that stick to me were born with me and will die with me[1]

Clare did not suffer from any overplus of self-confidence. A religious upbringing, though not severe, and the moralistic persuasions of his friends left his impressionable mind with a heavy load of guilt to deal with. Both lack of the thrust of self-confidence as well as a quick sense of shame played their part in his determined struggle for the essential self-in-freedom which was also the poet.

Letters give events as far as we know them for the first half of 1837. No letter has survived from Mrs Emmerson since the previous August. In March she thanked Clare for his letters, which she thought gave proof of improvement in health. Her

[1] Peterborough MSS.

next letter mentioned the "afflicting malady" in his head. She had got back from How the manuscript book used for *The Rural Muse*: Clare wanted to use some of the many unpublished poems in the new volume he was preparing; he had given Mrs Emmerson an account of poems recently written.

George Reid of Glasgow[1] continued his correspondence during these months. He sent books and some small donations from friends whom he had interested in Clare. Mrs Emmerson wrote that Clare should not trouble his mind about Unitarianism: Richard Wright, though a clever writer, might be in the wrong. Clare should believe without questioning. But Clare could achieve that comfortable orthodoxy at this point no more easily than he had ever been able to.

During his visit Taylor had mentioned that the Rev. Charles Mossop might approach Earl Fitzwilliam about medical aid. But before anything came of this, Taylor met Dr Matthew Allen, whose *Essay on the Classification of the Insane* he published that year. Privately Taylor concluded that here was a man to help Clare. Plans were made with his habitual secrecy. Mrs Emmerson knew nothing until months later, and then her information was incorrect.

In June 1837, a man presented himself at the Northborough cottage. A note, dated the 13th, from Taylor to Clare said: "The bearer will bring you up to town and take all care of you on the way ... the medical aid provided near this place will cure you effectually."

Clare's last letter to Mrs Emmerson, written just before he knew of the plan for his departure, had been gloomy. She replied on July 13th: "Up, up brave Spirit." But the "brave Spirit" was by then in Dr Matthew Allen's private asylum at High Beech, near Epping Forest in Essex.

[1] Whether George Reid was a son or grandson of Thomas Reid (1710–96) of Glasgow, leader of the Common Sense school of philosophy, in opposition to the ideal philosophy of Locke, Berkeley and Hume, I have not been able to find out.

Winter

CHAPTER EIGHTEEN

With Shadows Tost: 1837-1841

Matthew Allen, M.D., asylum physician, lecturer, writer, a man of wide interests and personal charm, was in the forefront of those reformers of the early nineteenth century who lifted treatment of the insane in Britain out of medieval ignorance towards more humane care. Clare was in Allen's care for four years. Allen tended and is said to have cured of derangement the only son of Thomas Campbell.

From 1819 to 1824 Allen was with Dr Lang at York Asylum and earned the thanks of the governors for his "constant and successful efforts in establishing and perfecting the mild system of treatment there". The York Asylum, after thirty years of the harsh treatment all too common in institutions of the kind, had adopted a more enlightened system in 1814. On leaving York, Allen decided to embody his clement theories in an institute of his own, and in 1825 he fixed on High Beech, near Epping, as the most suitable situation for his purpose: "here, together with domestic comfort, diversity of occupations and amusements suited to their various states, the retirement, pure air and sweet scenery around, afford ample scope for walks without annoyance, and apparently without restraint, which, with judicious moral and medical management combine many acknowledged requisites to assist the disturbed and diseased mind to regain its tranquillity."

In *Cases of Insanity*, 1831, and *Essay on the Classification of the Insane*, 1837, Allen described—in days when whip and chains were accepted treatment for the mentally sick—his method. The patient was to be encouraged in every kind of healthy amusement and occupation for mind and body, and moral restraint was to take the place of physical. In the application of this aim, Allen made his most original contribution to the cause. The first essential for the encouragement of self-control in the patient was a relationship of confidence and friendship between patient and attendant; the truth must never be violated or deceit resorted to, not even to get the sufferers from their homes. Many, Allen held, had been cured by candour and honesty alone. The moral effect of this personal relationship was to be strengthened by social amenities; but careful organization was necessary here. To plunge a patient among a crowd of fellow-sufferers, each with his own derangement and at a different stage of control, might be as harmful as solitary confinement. Allen emphasized the need for an elastic organization which would enable patients to be divided into suitable small groups according to their needs.

High Beech lies in a wooded valley on the south-west borders of Epping Forest, north of London. In 1837 the asylum consisted of three separate buildings, with cottages and grounds; Fair Mead House was demolished some sixty years ago; Leopard's Hill Lodge, four hundred yards distant but connected by the grounds, still stands; across the road was Springfield, now a farmhouse. One of the buildings was reserved for women, tended by Mrs Allen, while the doctor took charge of those cases which required the most careful attention—chiefly incipients, convalescents, and the partially deranged. But organization of all three houses was similar. Each was divided into two parts; the back consisted of small rooms and galleries, inhabited by those not sufficiently recovered to share social privileges; the front or family part was planned to look exactly like an ordinary home, where the convalescent patients could share the family life of the doctor and his assistants. The removal from back to front was an important stage in recovery; the patient was cut off from his old associations, solaced and encouraged; he appreciated his privileges and realized that failure to control himself meant social disgrace. Family parties exchanged visits, played games together, edited newspapers and shamed in conduct and pursuits many sane families. Many convalescents were placed on parole and allowed in the grounds and forest unattended, using a passkey to go in and out as they pleased. Allen recorded that scarcely any took advantage of this freedom to escape; fortunately for his plans, few of his patients had the acute nostalgia of John Clare.

Clare could not have fallen into better hands than Matthew Allen's. The doctor had made a special study of those forms of affliction which resembled Clare's. Such cases, where the sufferer had been able to exert control and retain his individuality for long after the trouble arose, required the most delicate attention. He emphasized the need for early diagnosis and expert treatment; when it was delayed, recovery was a long and difficult process. To recall those descriptions of symptoms which year after year Clare sent to his London friends is to deplore the chance that kept Dr Allen from the scene until 1837.

The common practice in those days was to discourage mental exertion in the insane; Allen felt that the judicious exercise of the mind, as well as of the body, was conducive to improvement. Clare at High Beech was encouraged to wander in the forest and to write; and these, the stolen delights of his youth, the happy occupations of his maturity, became a solace of his years of purgatory.

Under Allen's guidance Clare was led from labyrinths of despair to avail himself of the occupations and diversions which High Beech afforded: "I write to tell you I am getting better ... the place here is beautiful," he wrote to Patty in November 1837; "I meet with great kindness ... the country is the finest I have seen."[1]

A letter from Mrs Emmerson to Patty in April 1838, mentioned his improved health of which Frederick had written to her. She had just paid £5 to Taylor as her portion of the subscription for Clare's maintenance at High Beech. With this token of her solicitude, and she was by then almost a permanent invalid, leave may be taken of Mrs Emmerson. Clare did not see her again. For seventeen years she had advised and encouraged him; if there was more enthusiasm than critical judgment in her counsels, Clare needed it in his years of neglect and disappointment.

A letter from Allen to Taylor in December 1839, reported Clare stout and rosy in appearance, in good spirits, all life and fun; he was now working. A similar letter is extant for July 1840. "He is looking very well and his mind is not worse," and Allen mentioned the publicity being given to Clare's cause in

[1] *The Letters of John Clare, op. cit.*

some newspapers. S. C. Hall's 1838 *Book of Gems* had appealed for some Good Samaritan to rescue Clare from the "Cave of Despair" into which penury had led him. In 1840, a report was inserted in the *Halifax Express*, presumably by Clare's friend Crossley, of the poet's death in York Asylum. This report strayed into *The Times* for June 17th, 1840. On the 23rd, that newspaper published a letter from Allen, contradicting the report, giving an account of Clare and appealing for subscriptions. The *London Saturday Journal* for July 25th printed this letter, and added a poem which Clare had given Dr Badely, one of the visiting physicians at High Beech. The *Athenaeum* for June 27th called attention to this belated scheme to improve the poet's fortunes.

Dr Allen wrote: "He is at present in excellent health, and looks very well, and is in mind, though full of many strange delusions, in a much more comfortable and happy state than he was when he first came."

Allen continued:

> It is most singular, that ever since he came, and even now at almost all times, the moment he gets pen or pencil in hand he begins to write most beautiful poetic effusions. Yet he has never been able to maintain in conversation, nor even in writing prose, the appearance of sanity for two minutes or two lines together, and yet there is no indication whatever of insanity in any of his poetry.

Despite reported improvement in Clare's physical well-being, vigour, and hence spirits, with Matthew Allen at High Beech, two or three more delusions were adding themselves to the first one of Mary and Martha, his two wives. That he continued to write poems without hint of insanity does not medically prove that in any as-yet-not-understood way he was other than what is called mentally sick even when relieved of care and swept out of anxiety. Four years couldn't cure what had been forty and more in developing. But penury, and prolonged frustration of attempts to communicate what he had to say, had at least helped to plant the *kind* of delusion, if not the delusions themselves. We all have illusions, often delusions. Absence from home, with relief from care, supplied every condition for sanity for Clare—except one.

Cyrus Redding, who ran the *English Journal*, paid him a visit, or perhaps two visits, in the spring of 1841. Redding expected a clownish countryman. Of his various accounts the best is that printed in *Sketches in the Life of John Clare by Himself*.

I found Clare in a field cutting up thistles, a small man and slender rather than stout. He was pleased to see me. We entered at once upon the subject of poetry. He was in his conversation as simple as in his verse. He had nothing of the clown about him but his dress. He leaned upon the tool he was using, and spoke of Byron and his poetry in perfect good taste. He said he wanted to be at home with his family (Dr. Allen had told me he might be so for anything connected with his complaint). In the midst of some observations on Byron's poetry, he broke off at once into remarks upon boxing. This confusion or interruption of the chain of his discourse was all that characterized his insanity, so mild was it. I found the man agreeable and attaching—one fit for the Shepherd's cast of Virgil or Theocritus. I never before saw so characterized personally the *Poeta Nascitur*, &c. I mean that indescribable something which lifts men of genius above the herd. I promised to send him some of Byron's works for he complained of a want of books, he wanted works of imagination.

The books Redding gave, or sent, a memorandum in one of Clare's 1841 notebooks[1] discloses:

Received from C. Redding while in prison on Leopards Hill Eleven books two given & the rest returnable—viz—Child Harold—Reddings Poems—& following lent viz Don Juan 1 vol 5 Cantoes—2nd Part lent to 6, 7, 8 Part 3rd Cants 9, 10, 11 Part 4th 12, 13, 14—Part 5 Cants 15, 16

Much of that spring Clare must have read Byron. In another of Redding's accounts, that in the *English Journal* for May 15th, 1841:

[1] Northampton MSS.

The principal token of his mental eccentricity was the introduction of prize fighting, in which he seemed to imagine he was to engage; but the allusion to it was made in the way of interpolation in the middle of the subject on which he was discoursing, brought in abruptly, and abandoned with equal suddenness, and an utter want of connection with any association of ideas which it could be thought might lead to the subject at the time; as if the machinery of thought were dislocated, so that one part of it got off its pivot, and protruded into the regular workings; or as if a note had got into a piece of music which had no business there. This was the only symptom of aberration of mind we observed about Clare; though, being strangers to him, there might be something else in his manner which those who knew him well could have pointed out. To our seeming, his affection was slight; and it is not at all improbable that a relief from mental anxiety might completely restore him.

Redding speaks of 'we' and it is possible that William Henry Hunt the painter was his companion on one visit. If so, Hunt's *A Self-taught Genius* of 1841 is a welcome portrait of Clare as Hunt and Redding saw him.[1]

Allen repeated that if Clare could be with his family but without the corroding conditions of former years, there was every hope of complete recovery; at least, Allen said, he would be happier at home, so slightly was his mind affected. An appeal for £500 was proposed, sufficient to raise Clare's income to £60 a year and place the family beyond need. In earlier years Patty and Clare had made ends meet on far less than that. The Appeal was commended to the public by Cyrus Redding in two articles in his *English Journal* for May 15th and 29th, 1841, by James Devlin in the same, and by an unknown in a collection of verse entitled *Poetry*, 1841. Matthew Allen, in support, wrote plainly to P. S. Ackerman:

My dear Sir,

I enclose at your request some of Clare's writing. Why

[1] See *John Clare: his Life and Poetry*, by J. W. and Anne Tibble (Heinemann, 1956).

show respect to the mere hand writing, and no humanity to the man nor his family.

I pledge myself, that if a small annuity could be secured for him, he will very soon recover and remain so—and yet people desire the autograph of a man who but for me would have been a hopeless case permanently confined and lost in the mass of paupers in some public Establishment or perhaps what is worse exposed to the idle gaze of fools.

You have never fulfilled your promise.

According to a notice printed later in the *English Journal* the Queen Dowager sent 20 guineas, Lord Fitzwilliam a handsome subscription. The Marquis of Northampton promised £5 a year. Whatever the final sum subscribed it fell far short of the £500 appealed for. Presumably the sum received was used to help pay for Clare at High Beech—for which Taylor and the Emmersons had been responsible.

Redding printed a number of poems of Clare's in the *English Journal*. As Geoffrey Grigson has observed in his Introduction to *Poems of John Clare's Madness* Clare's stimulus for these poems is chiefly Epping, not memories of Northamptonshire. There is, however, among them, "Maid of Walkherd" with its ballad lilt:

By thy hand of slender make,
By thy love I'll ne'er forsake,
By thy heart I'll ne'er betray,
Let me kiss thy fears away!
I will live and love thee ever,
Leave thee and forsake thee never!
Though far in other lands to be,
Yet never far from love and thee.

There is also:

In Love's delight my steps were led,
I sang in Beauty's choice;
I saw her in the books I read,—
All then was Mary Joyce.[1]

[1] The punctuation in both these poems is Redding's.

In this chronicling there is no more than an echo from that logical-unconscious underworld where Mary Joyce was firmly established as Clare's first, more important, wife. Among Redding's printing is a poem to Wordsworth:

> Wordsworth I love: his books are like the fields,
> Not filled with flowers, but works of human kind.

But as the fourth year at High Beech went by and hope of a return home looked like disappearing under the inadequacy of the response to Allen's and Redding's Appeal, Clare, who knew of the Appeal, was coming to regard continued stay as captivity. In a letter to Patty a new eccentricity appears: he begins every word with a capital:

> Leppits [Leopard's] Hill March 17 1841
>
> My Dear Wife Patty
>
> It Makes Me More Than Happy To Hear That You & My Dear Family Are All Well—And You Will Be As Well Pleased To Hear That I Have Been So Long In Good Health & Spirits As To Have Forgotten That I Ever Was Any Otherways—My Situation Here Has Been Even From The Beginning More Then Irksome But I Shake Hands With Misfortune & Wear Through The Storm—The Spring Smiles & So Shall I—But Not While I Am Here—I Am Very Happy To Hear My Dear Boy Mention His Brother's & Sister's So Kindly As I Feel Assured That They Love One Another As They Ever Have Done—It Was My Lot To Seem As Living Without Friends Untill I Met With You & Though We Are Now Parted My Affection Is Unaltered—& We Shall Meet Again I Would Sooner Wear The Troubles Of Life Away Single Handed Then Share Them With Others—As Soon As I Get Relieved On Duty Here I Shall Be In Northamptonshire—Though Essex Is A Very Pleasant County—Yet To Me "There Is No Place Like Home"—As My Childern Are All Well—To Keep Them So Be Sure & Keep Them In Good Company & Then They Will Not Only Be Well But Happy—For What Reason They Keep Me Here I Cannot Tell For I Have Been No Other-

ways Than Well A Couple Of Year's At The Least & Never Was Very Ill Only Harrassed By Perpetual Bother —It Would Seem By Keeping Me Here One Year After Another That I Was Destined For The Same Fate Agen & I Would Sooner Be Packed In A Slave Ship For Affrica Then Belong To The Destiny Of Mock Friends & Real Enemies—Honest Men & Modest Women Are My Friends

Give My Best Love To My Dear Childern & Kiss The Little One's For Me Good Bye & God Be With You All Forever

I Had Three Seperate Dream's About Three Of My Boys & Your Boys Frederick John & William—Not Any Ways Remarkable Only I Was In A Wreck With The Latter—Such Things Never Trouble Me Now In Fact Nothing Troubles Me & Thank God It Is So—I Hope The Time Is Not Long Ere I Shall See You All By Your Own Fireside Though Every Day In Abscence Seem's To Me Longer Then Year's

—I Am My Dear Wife Your Affectionate Husband
John Clare

P.S. Give My Love To The Dear Boy Who Wrote To Me & To Her Who Is Never Forgotten
God Bless You All

Clare recorded in his notebook[1]

Easter Sunday—1841 Went In The Morning To Buckhurst Hill Church & Stood In The Church Yard—When A Very Interesting Boy Came Out While Organ Was Playing Dressed In A Slop Frock Like A Ploughboy & Seemingly About Nine Years Of Age He Was Just Like My Son Bill He Was About The Same Age And As Stout Made—He Had A Serious Interesting Face & Looked As Weary With The Working Days As A Hard Working Man I Was Sorry I Did Not Give Him The Last Halfpenny

[1] Northampton MSS. The contents of this notebook are too disjointed for us to be sure that these two prose notes have anything to do with the poems he was at this time writing though he has written "Note for Child Harold" immediately before.

I Had & Ask Him A Few Questions As To His Age & Name & Parents But Perhaps I May See Him Agen

Easter Monday—At The Easter Hunt I Saw A Stout Tall Young Woman Dressed In A Darkish Flowered Cotton Gown As A Milkmaid Or Farm Servant & Stood Agen Her For Some Minutes Near A Small Clump Of Furze—I Did Not Speak To Her But I Now Wish I Had & Cannot Forget Her—Then I Saw Another Get Out Of A Gig With A Large Sctoch [sic] Shawl On & A Pretty Face

Between these two entries, though with *Byron* only in Clare's handwriting,

Boxer Byron
Made of Iron alias
Boxiron
At Springfield

Springfield was the women patients' house at High Beech. "Boxiron" is a private pun about how difficult the women were to get at, but "Boxer Byron" might have managed.

Clare enlarged on the delusion that he was a prize-fighter, a bruiser or a wrestler, mention of which had cropped up in the conversation with Cyrus Redding, in another High Beech notebook:

Jack Randalls[1] Challange To All The World

Jack Randall The Champion Of The Prize Ring Begs Leave To Inform The Sporting World That He Is Ready To Meet Any Customer In The Ring Or On The Stage To Fight For The Sum Of £500 Or £1000 Aside A Fair Stand Up Fight Half Minute Time Or Loose He Is Not Particular As To Weight Colour Or Country All He

[1] Randall was "The Nonpareil" of the Ring when in 1824 Clare had visited with Rippingille the "Hole in the Wall". One of Clare's father's favourite ballads was "Lord Randall". Recall also the Stamford pub to which Clare was taken whilst he was a gardener-boy at Burghley, and the "Hole in the Wall" as a medieval means of detecting unchastity in women.

Wishes Is To Meet With A Customer Who Has Pluck Enough To Come To The Scratch

Jack Randall

Four pages later in the same notebook are notes concerning what Clare seems to have regarded as inadequate agricultural payment for his work at Allen's:

1 Weeks Labour—2/6 ...
. . . .
Matthew Gammons over *5d* a day—
6d—due or left *2s* ...

Two draft letters, one from his High Beech notebook which is clearly inscribed "John Clare's Poems Feby 1841", give clues on his mental state between February and July of that year. The first, to some girl or woman he had known at Helpston or Northborough, or knew of at High Beech:

My dear Eliza Phillips

Having been cooped up in this Hell of a Madhouse till I seem to be disowned by my friends & even forgot by my enemies for there is none to accept my challanges which I have from time to time given to the public I am almost mad in waiting for a better place & better company & all to no purpose It is well known that I am a prize fighter by profession & a man that never feared anybody in my life either in the ring or out of it—I do not much like to write love letters but this which I am now writing to you is a true one—you know that we have met before & the first oppertunity that offers we will meet again—I am now writing a New Canto of Don Juan which I have taken the liberty to dedicate to you in remembrance of Days gone bye & when I have finished it I would send you the vol if I knew how in which there is a new Canto of Child Harold also—I am my dear Eliza

Yours sincerely
John Clare

The second letter has a beginning, with initial capitals for each word, which continues for four lines only. The full draft, probably written not long before the poem "Written in a Thunderstorm July 15th 1841", since it immediately precedes that poem, runs:

My dear Wife Mary

I might have said my first wife & first love & first everything—but I shall never forget my second wife & second love for I loved her once as dearly as yourself—& almost do so now so I determined to keep you both forever—& when I write to you I am writing to her at the same time & in the same letter God bless you both & forever & both your familys also—I still keep writing though you do not write to me for if a man has a wife & I have two—but I tell it in a couplet with variations as my poetry has been the world's Hornbook for many years—so here 'tis

For if a husband will not let us know
That he's alive—he's dead—or *may*be so

No one knows how sick I am of this confinement possessing two wives that ought to be my own & cannot see either one or the other if I was in prison for felony I could not be served worse then I am—wives used to be alowed to see their husbands anywhere—religion forbids their being parted but I have not even religion on my side & more's the pity I have been rather poorly I might say ill for 8 or 9 days before haymakeing & to get myself better I went a few evenings on Fern Hill & wrote a new Canto of "Child Harold" & now I am better I sat under the Elm trees in old Matthews Homestead Leppits Hill where I now am—2 or 3 evenings & wrote a new canto of Don Juan—merely to pass the time away but nothing seems to shorten it in the least & I fear I shall not be able to wear it away—nature to me seems dead & her very pulse seems frozen to an iceicle in the summer sun—What is the use of shutting me up from women in a petty paltry place as this merely because I am a married man & I dare say though I have two wives if I got away I should soon have a third & I think I should serve you both right in the bargain by doing so for I dont care a damn about coming home now—so you need not flatter yourselves with many expect[at]ions of seeing nor do I expect you want to see me or you would have contrived to have done it before now—My dear Mary take all the good wishes from me as your heart can feel for your own husband & kiss all your dear family for their abscent father & Pattys childern also & tell Patty that her husband is the same man as he was when she married him 20 years ago in heart & good intentions—God bless you both & your familys also I wish you both to keep in good health & be happy as I shall soon be when I have the good luck to be with you all at home once again—the love I have for you my dear Mary was never altered by time but always increased by abscence

I am my dear Mary
Your affectionate husband
John Clare[1]

Within a few days of writing both poem and letter Clare evaded Allen's "jailers called keepers" and, with notebook and a little tobacco in his pocket, set out to tramp eighty miles to Northborough. The first three days after his arrival at home he employed writing the following account.

[1] Northampton MSS.

CHAPTER NINETEEN

The Journey from Essex: July 1841

July 18–1841–Felt very melancholly–went a walk on the forest in the afternoon–fell in with some gipseys one of whom offered to assist in my escape from the madhouse by hiding me in his camp to which I almost agreed but told him I had no money to start with but if he would do so I would promise him fifty pounds & he agreed to do so before saturday on friday I went again but he did not seem so willing so I said little about it–On Sunday I went & they were all gone–I found an old wide-awake hat & an old straw bonnet of the plumb pudding sort was left behind–& I put the hat in my pocket thinking it might be usefull for another oppertunity & as good luck would have it, it turned out to be so

July 19 Monday–Did nothing

July 20 Reconnitered the rout the Gipsey pointed out & found it a legible one to make a movement & having only honest courage & myself in my army I Led the way & my troops soon followed but being careless in mapping down the rout as the Gipsey told me I missed the lane to Enfield Town & was going down Enfield Highway till I passed the "Labour in vain" Public house where a person I knew comeing out of the door told me the way

I walked down the lane gently & was soon in Enfield Town & bye & bye on the great York Road where it was all plain sailing & stearing ahead meeting no enemy & fearing none I reached Stevenage where being Night I got over a gate crossed over the corner of a green paddock where seeing a pond or hollow in the corner I [was] forced to stay off a respectable distance to keep from falling into it for my legs were nearly knocked up & began to stagger I scaled some old rotten paleings into the yard & then had higher pailings to clamber over to get into the shed or hovel which I did with difficulty being rather weak & to my good luck I found some trusses of clover piled up about 6 or more feet square which I gladly mounted & slept on there was some trays[1] in the hovel on which I could have reposed had I not found a better bed I slept soundly but had a very uneasy dream I thought my first wife lay on my left side & somebody took her away from my side—which made me wake up rather unhappy I thought as I woke somebody said "Mary" but nobody was near—I lay down with my head towards the North to show myself the steering point in the morning

July 21 Daylight was looking in on every side & fearing my garrison might be taken by storm & myself be made prisoner I left my lodging by the way I got in & thanked God for his kindness in procureing it (for anything in a famine is better than nothing & any place that giveth the weary rest is a blessing) I gained the north road again & steered due north—on the left hand side the road under the bank like a cave—I saw a Man & boy coiled up asleep which I hailed & they woke up to tell me the name of the next village[2]

Somewhere on the London side the "Plough" public house a Man passed me on horseback in a slop frock & said "here's another of the broken down haymakers" & threw me a penny to get a half pint of beer which I picked up & thanked him for & when I got to the plough I called for a half pint & drank it & got a rest & escaped a very heavy shower in the bargain by having a shelter till it was over—afterwards I would have begged a penny of two drovers who were very saucey so I begged no more of anybody meet who I would[3]

[1] Closely woven hurdles used for penning sheep. A. E. Baker, *Glossary of Northamptonshire Words and Phrases.*

[2] Baldeck [Baldock]. (Clare's note.)

[3] "On searching my pockets after the above was written I found part of a newspaper vide 'Morning Chronicle' on which the following fragments were pencilled soon after I got the information from labourers going to work or travellers journeying along to better their condition as I was hopeing to do mine in fact I believed I saw home in every ones countenance which seemed so cheerfull in my own—'There is no place like home' the following was written by the Roadside

Ist Day—Tuesday started from Enfield & slept at Stevenage on some clover trusses—cold lodging

Wednesday—Jacks Hill is passed already consisting of a beer shop & some houses on the hill appearing newly built—the last Mile stone 35 Miles from London got through Baldeck & sat under a dry hedge & had a rest in lieu of breakfast." (Clare's note.)

I passed 3 or 4 good built houses on a hill & a public house on the road side in the hollow below them I seemed to pass the Milestones very quick in the morning but towards night they seemed to be stretched further asunder I got to a village further on & forgot the name the road on the left hand was quite over shaded by some trees & quite dry so I sat down half an hour & made a good many wishes for breakfast but wishes was no hearty meal so I got up as hungry as I sat down – I forget here the names of the villages I passed through but recollect at late evening going through Potton in Bedfordshire where I called in a house to light my pipe in which was a civil old woman & a young country wench making lace on a cushion as round as a globe & a young fellow all civil people – I asked them a few questions as to the way & where the clergyman & overseer lived but they scarcely heard me or gave me no answer

I then went through Potton & happened with a kind talking country man who told me the Parson lived a good way from where I was or overseer I don't know which so I went on hopping with a crippled foot for the gravel had got into my old shoes one of which had now nearly lost the sole Had I found the overseers house at hand or the Parsons I should have gave my name & begged for a shilling to carry me home but I was forced to brush on penniless & be thankful I had a leg to move on – I then asked him wether he could tell me of a farm yard any where on the road where I could find a shed & some dry straw & he said yes & if you will go with me I will show you the place – its a public house on the left hand side the road at the sign of the "Ram" but seeing a stone or flint heap I longed to rest as one of my feet was very painfull so I thanked him for his kindness & bid him go on – but the good natured fellow lingered awhile as if wishing to conduct me & then suddenly reccolecting that he had a hamper on his shoulder & a lock up bag in his hand cramfull to meet the coach which he feared missing – he started hastily & was soon out of sight – I followed looking in vain for the countrymans straw bed & not able to meet it I lay down by a shed side under some Elm trees between the wall & the trees being a thick row planted some 5 or 6 feet from the buildings I lay there & tried to sleep but the wind came in between them so cold that I lay till I quaked like the ague &

quitted the lodging for a better at the Ram which I could hardly hope to find—it now began to grow dark apace & the old houses on the road began to light up & show the inside tennants lots very comfortable & my outside lot very uncomfortable & wretched—still I hobbled forward as well as I could & at last came to the Ram the shutters were not closed & the lighted window looked very cheering but I had no money & did not like to go in there was a short of shed or gighouse at the end but I did not like to lie there as the people were up—so I still travelled on the road was very lonely & dark in places being overshaded with trees at length I came to a place where the road branched off into two turnpikes one to the right about & the other straight forward & on going bye my eye glanced on a milestone standing under the hedge so I heedlessly turned back to read it to see where the other road led too & on doing so I found it led to London I then suddenly forgot which was North or South & though I narrowly examined both ways I could see no tree or bush or stone heap that I could reccolect I had passed so I went on mile after mile almost convinced I was going the same way as I came & these thoughts were so strong upon me that doubt & hopelessness made me turn so feeble that I was scarcely able to walk Yet I could not sit down or give up but shuffled along till I saw a lamp shining as bright as the moon which on nearing I found was suspended over a Tollgate before I got through the man came out with a candle & eyed me narrowly but having no fear I stopt to ask him wether I was going northward & he said when you get through the gate you are; so I thanked him kindly & went through on the other side & gathered my old strength as my doubts vanished I soon cheered up & hummed the air of highland Mary as I went on I at length fell in with an odd house all alone near a wood but I could not see what the sign was though the sign seemed to stand oddly enough in a sort of trough or spout there was a large porch over the door & being weary I crept in & glad enough I was to find I could lye with my legs straight the inmates were all gone to roost for I could hear them turn over in bed as I lay at full length on the stones in the porch—I slept here till daylight & felt very much refreshed as I got up—I blest my two wives & both their familys when I lay down & when I got up & when I thought of some former difficultys on a like occasion I could not help blessing the Queen[1]

Having passed a Lodge on the left hand within a mile & half or less of a town I think it might be St Ives[2] but I forget the name I sat down to rest on a flint heap where I might rest half an hour or more & while sitting here I saw a tall Gipsey come out of the Lodge gate & make down the road towards where I was sitting when she got up to me on seeing she was a young woman with an honest looking countenance rather handsome I spoke to her & asked her a few questions which she answered readily & with evident good humour so I got up & went on to the next town with her—she cautioned me on the way to put somthing in my hat to keep the crown up & said in a lower tone "You'll be noticed" but not knowing what she hinted—I took no notice & made no reply at length she pointed to a small tower church which she called Shefford Church[3] & advised me to go on a footway which would take me direct to it & I should shorten my journey fifteen miles by doing so I would gladly have taken the young womans advice feeling that it was honest & a nigh guess towards the truth but fearing I might loose my way & not be able to find the north road again I thanked her & told her I should keep to the road when she bade me "good day" & went into a house or shop on the left hand side the road

I have but a slight reccolection of my journey between here and Stilton for I was knocked up & noticed little or nothing—one night I lay in a dyke bottom from the wind & went sleep half an hour when I suddenly awoke & found one side wet through from the sock in the dyke bottom so I got out & went on—I remember going down a very dark road hung over with trees on both sides very thick which seemed to extend a mile or two I

[1] In the small memorandum book which Clare evidently forgot to use when fair-copying the full account is:

> The man whose daughter is the Queen of England is now sitting on a stone heap on the high way to bugden [Buckden] without a farthing in his pocket & without eating a bit of food ever since yesterday morning—when he was offered a bit of Bread and cheese at Enfield—he has not had any since but if I put a little fresh speed on hope too may speed tomorrow—O Mary mary If you knew how anxious I am to see you & dear Patty with the childern I think you would come & meet me

[2] It was St Neots. (Clare's note.)

[3] Shefford is south of Buckden, St Neots and Potton: Clare's account of the order of villages he passed through is not very clear.

then entered a town & some of the chamber windows had candle lights shineing in them—I felt so weary here that I forced to sit down on the ground to rest myself a while & while I sat here a Coach that seemed to be heavy laden came rattling up & stopt in the hollow below me & I cannot reccolect its ever passing by me[1] I then got up & pushed onward seeing little to notice for the road very often looked as stupid as myself & I was very often half asleep as I went on the third day I satisfied my hunger by eating the grass by the road side which seemed to taste something like bread I was hungry & eat heartily till I was satisfied & in fact the meal seemed to do me good the next and last day I reccolected that I had some tobacco & my box of lucifers being exausted I could not light my pipe so I took to chewing Tobacco all day & eat the quids when I had done & I was never hungry afterwards—I remember passing through Buckden & going a length of road afterwards but I don't reccolect the name of any place untill I came to Stilton where I was compleatly foot foundered & broken down when I had got about half way through the town a gravel causeway invited me to rest myself so I lay down & nearly went sleep a young woman (so I guessed by the voice) came out of a house & said "poor creature" & another more elderly said "O he shams" but when I got up the latter said "o no he don't" as I hobbled along very lame I heard the voices but never looked back to see where they came from—when I got near the Inn at the end of the gravel walk I meet two young women & I asked one of them wether the road branching to the right by the end of the Inn did not lead to Peterborough & she said "yes" it did so as soon as ever I was on it I felt myself in homes way & went on rather more cheerfull though I forced to rest oftener than usual before I got to Peterborough a man & woman passed me in a cart & on hailing me as they passed I found they were neighbours from Helpstone where I used to live—I told them I was knocked up which they could easily see & that I had neither eat or drank anything since I left Essax when I told my story they clubbed together & threw me fivepence out of the

[1] "The Coach did pass me as I sat under some trees by a high wall & the lamps flashed in my face [*not* "chips flew hard" as given by Robinson and Summerfield in the *New Oxford Selection of Clare*] & wakened me up from a doze when I knocked the gravel out of my shoes & started." (Clare's note.)

cart I picked it up & called at a small public house near the bridge where I had two half pints of ale & two penn'o'th of bread & cheese when I had done I started quite refreshed only my feet was more crippled then ever & I could scarcely make a walk of it over the stones & being half ashamed to sit down in the street I forced to keep on the move & got through Peterborough better then I expected when I got on the high road I rested on the stone heaps as I passed till I was able to go on afresh & bye & bye I passed Walton & soon reached Werrington & was making for the Beehive as fast as I could when a cart met me with a man & woman & a boy in it when nearing me the woman jumped out & caught fast hold of my hands & wished me to get into the cart but I refused & thought her either drunk or mad but when I was told it was my second wife Patty I got in & was soon at Northborough but Mary was not there neither could I get any information about her further then the old story of her being dead six years ago which might be taken from a bran new old Newspaper printed a dozen years ago but I took no notice of the blarney having seen her myself about a twelvemonth ago alive & well & as young as ever—so here I am homeless at home & half gratified to feel that I can be happy anywhere

May none those marks of my sad fate efface
For they appeal from tyranny to God
Byron

July 24th 1841 Returned home out of Essex & found no Mary —her & her family are nothing to me now though she herself was once the dearest of all—& how can I forget[1]

[1] This final entry begins the account. Northampton MSS.

CHAPTER TWENTY

Don Juan and Child Harold: 1841

He had been three nights and almost four days on the road. When the story of his journey was finished, at home on the 27th Clare added a draft letter "To Mary Clare—Glinton" in his High Beech notebook:

My dear Wife

I have written an account of my journey or rather escape from Essex for your amusement & hope it may divert your leisure hours—I would have told you before now that I got here to Northborough last Friday night but not being able to see you or to hear where you was I soon began to feel homeless at home & shall bye & bye feel nearly hopeless but not so lonely as I did in Essex—for here I can see Glinton Church & feeling that Mary is safe if not happy I am gratified... though my home is no home to me my hopes are not entirely hopeless while even the memory of Mary lives so near me God bless you my dear Mary Give my love to your dear beautifull family & to your Mother—& believe me as I ever have been & ever shall be

My dearest Mary,
Your affectionate Husband
John Clare

At the end of August he wrote to Dr Allen; a draft of this letter,[1] written round the edges of a local newspaper, throws light both on his cumulative thought and feelings during the High Beech four years and on the impact of his return to Northborough.

[1] Bodleian MSS.

Having left the Forest in a hurry I had not time to take my leave of you & your family but intended to write & that before now but dullness and dissapointment prevented me for I found your words true on my return here having neither friends or home left but as it is called the "Poets cottage" I claimed a lodging in it where I now am – one of my fancys I found here with her family & all well – they mett me on this side Werrington with a horse & cart & found me all but knocked up ... for I had travelled from Essex to Northamptonshire without ever eating or drinking all the way save one pennyworth of beer which was given me by a farm servant near an old [*odd*] house called the plough I eat grass to keep me going – but on the last day I chewed tobacco & never felt hungry afterwards – where my poetical fancy is I cannot say for the people in the neighbourhood tells me that the one called "Mary" has been dead these 8 years but I can be miserably happy in any situation & any place & could have staid in yours on the forest if any of my friends had noticed me or come to see me – but the greatest annoyance in such places as yours are those servants & stupid keepers who often assumed as much authority over me as if I had been their prisoner & not liking to quarrel I put up with it till I was weary of the place altogether so I heard the voice of freedom & started ...
I care nothing about the women now for they are faithless & deceitfull & the first woman where there was no man but her husband found out means to cucold him by the aid & assistance of the Devil. but women being more righteous now & men more plentiful they have found out a more godly way to do it without the devil's assistance. & a man who possesses a woman possesses losses without gain the worst is the road to ruin & the best is nothing like a good Cow – man I never did like much & woman has long sickened me ...

Told by neighbours who had seen him, Patty *had* met him four miles from Northborough. He did not know her. At first he had refused to get into her cart. It is often the case that relationships with those most familiar become difficult to the mentally sick. Clare was probably told about Mary Joyce's death but he had already confused the time. Ambivalent attitudes towards the opposite sex are common enough even among the normal. Clare's were growing more complexly contradictory. Strongly sexed, needing physical contact with women, and finding in them, as Edward Thomas pointed out, as well as in nature, much of his inspiration towards poetry, his banishment to High Beech obviously brought confusion out. All this was intensification of attitudes which, as Allen had said, often lie undetected for years.

Allen replied on November 18th with friendly advice. He invited Clare back. He said the Queen had given a donation to the Appeal fund, not an income as Clare supposed. Nothing more had been contributed since Clare left the Forest.

If Clare had been able to avail himself of this offer and return to High Beech, he would have witnessed the misfortunes which led within a few years to the ruin and untimely death of his friend Dr Allen. The story has been preserved in the poem "Sea Dreams" of that poet who, in 1842, took literary England by storm and restored to poetry a popularity which it had not known since the days of Byron. Soon after Clare's departure from Epping, Allen took up a scheme for carving wood by machinery. He sought to enlist his acquaintances and neighbours in the venture, among them the Tennyson family, then at Beech Hill. The Patent Decorative Carving and Sculpture Company was formed, and Alfred Tennyson was persuaded to invest in it all available family funds. To judge by his letters his enthusiasm equalled Allen's. The enterprise collapsed; Allen became a bankrupt in 1843, and for the Tennysons a period of hardship ensued, during which Alfred suffered from such severe hypochondria that his life was despaired of. Dr Allen did not long survive his misfortune; he died in 1845, and, as Edward Lushington had insured his life for part of the debt, his death brought relief to the Tennysons.

The only other correspondence during Clare's months at Northborough of which we have any record was with George Reid of Glasgow. Removal to Epping had broken the threads of many friendships as effectually as if Clare *had* been in prison.

But between the spring of 1841 and December 29th of that year he completed two long poems. He mentions both in the letter to Eliza Phillips : a "New Canto of Don Juan" and a "New Canto of Child Harold". In the notebook these appear as

Speedily will be published
The Sale of Old Wigs and Sundries
a Poem By Lord Byron
in Quarto 8vo and twelves

and

In a short time will be published
A New Vol of Poems By Lord Byron
Not yet Collected in his works
Containing Songs New Cantos of Child Harrold [sic]
And additional Hebrew Mel[o]dies
~~Letters &c~~[1] Fragments &c

He began both long poems in the spring and continued them in summer, autumn, and to December 1841. There is at least one problematic stanza which may have been written later.

That the canto of Don Juan had an earlier title, "The Sale of Old Wigs", or "The Sale of Old Wigs & sundries", is fairly certain. There is plenty of evidence in Clare's writing since the later 1820s for his interest in the social justice of political parties, and in his jottings of the 1840s for interest in verbal punning. Since in his draft of stanzas of the poem, "Whig" is frequently spelt "wig"; and since in 1841 Whigs, who were in power, came in for much criticism in the Press concerning Corn Laws, poverty and social unrest; since, also, by that September Melbourne the Whig was at last replaced by Peel the Tory—in view of Clare's interest the title "The Sale of Old Wigs" is not unlikely. From out of the welter of the sub-conscious mind, the underlying meaning of "The Sale of Old Wigs" might be interpreted as, "away with old falsities and repressions." Reading so much Byron, lent him by Cyrus Redding, and impressed, as he had been since at least 1824 by Byron's apparent success as poet and his social defiance, Clare forgot his first idea and entitled his poem as if it were one of the literary, imitative exercises not uncommon in the decade after the publication of Byron's sixteen "Don Juan" Cantos between 1819 and 1824.

[1] Scored through.

Clare's poem is in *ottava rima* as is Byron's. Clare uses audacious rhymes, mockery and cynicism (none of which is difficult to imitate). The poem contains two lyrics or songs breaking its thirty-four eight-line stanzas, as Byron's third Canto contains "The Isles of Greece".

It is not accurate to call these two poems of Clare's "Byronic creations". With titles and stanza-forms the parallel ends. Byron, for his Juan poem form was indebted to J. H. Frere, for content to some extent to Shadwell. Clare was indebted to Byron for his poem's name. Clare's is an anti-woman, politico-social poem of total disillusion, with a safety-valve coarseness in its disclosures about Allen's "Hell" and its criticism of those dark and cruel days in British social-industrial life. We know from Clare's critical essays his earlier detestation of "false delicacy", "taste trimming", "cant and hypocrisy". How often since Radstock's rumpus over the indelicacy of "Dolly's Mistake" in *Poems Descriptive* had he agreed politely with his wealthy patrons, as also over Taylor's cutting of his vivid, traditional words. How often at High Beech must he have as politely agreed with the idealistic Allen—ignoring the patients' subterranean world of sexuality which Allen either shut his eyes to or wasn't aware of. In his "Don Juan" Clare wrote with the acute pleasure, which not only the psychotic know, of getting away with saying what is in the mind: much of the poem comes from that mental under-layer we now call the subconscious which has little to do with the often insincere concurrences of civilized politeness.

"Poets are born"—& so are whores—the trade is
Grown universal—in these canting days
Women of fashion must of course be ladies
& whoreing is the business—that still pays
Playhouses Ballrooms—there the masquerade is
—To do what was of old—& now adays
Their maids—nay wives—so innoscent & blooming
Cuckold their spouses to seem honest women

Milton sung Eden & the fall of man
Not woman for the name implies a wh——e
& they would make a ruin of his plan

Falling so often they can fall no lower
Tell me a worse delusion if you can
For innocence – & I will sing no more
Wherever mischief is tis womans brewing
Created from manself – to be mans ruin

The flower in bud hides from the fading sun
& keeps the hue of beauty on its cheek
But when full blown they into riot run
The hue turns pale & lost each ruddy streak
So 't is with woman who pretends to shun
Immodest actions which they inly seek
Night hides the wh——e – & cupboards tart & pasty
Flora was p–x–d & womans quite as nasty

Marriage is nothing but a driveling hoax
To please old codgers when they're turned of forty
I wed & left my wife like other folks
But not until I found her false & faulty
O woman fair – the man must pay thy jokes
Such makes a husband very often naughty
Who falls in love will seek his own undoing
The road to marriage is – "the road to ruin"

. . . .

I wish – but there is little got bye wishing
I wish that bread & great coats ne'er had risen
I wish that there was some such word as "pishun"
For ryhme sake for my verses must be dizen
With dresses fine – as hooks with baits for fishing
I wish all honest men were out of prison
I wish M.P.s. would spin less yarn – nor doubt
But burn false bills & cross bad taxes out

. . . . .

Childern are fond of sucking sugar candy
& maids of sausages – larger the better
Shopmen are fond of good Sigars & brandy
& I of blunt[1] – & if you change the letter

[1] Slang for money.

To C or K it would be quite as handy
& throw the next away—but I'm your debtor
For modesty—yet wishing nought between us
I'd hawl close to a she as vulcan did to venus

I really cant tell what this poem will be
About—nor yet what trade I am to follow
I thought to buy old wigs—but that will kill me
With cold starvation—as they're beaten hollow
Long speeches in a famine will not fill me
& madhouse traps still take me by the collar
So old wig bargains now must be forgotten
The oil that dressed them fine has made them rotten[1]

. . . . .

"Child Harold" is a much longer poem than "Don Juan". One or two of its stanzas are not pretty, but it is not a coarse poem. Like Clare's "Don Juan" it was not printed as a whole until 1948, when, with a poet's intuition, Geoffrey Grigson[2] saw it as the seasonal poem it unquestionably is; the idea of the four seasons typifying four seasons of a man's life was by no means novel: its spring, summer, autumn and winter stanzas symbolize the seasons of Clare's life. It is in Spenserian, nine-line stanzas, and its title "Child Harold" is indebted to Byron as Byron is indebted to the medieval word "Child" or "Childe" to indicate, sardonically or not, a youth of noble parentage. Some seventy-seven stanzas and twenty-three lyrics are scattered over six of Clare's manuscripts so that the finality Clare intended for his poem can never be more than guessed at. From internal evidence certain stanzas belong to spring, the Thunder storm poem is dated July 15th, 1841, other stanzas and songs are in the note-book which he used on his journey from Essex, still other stanzas in manuscripts used after his return to Northborough; the shortened fair copy he made whilst at home ends with one winter stanza. Its metres vary from sophisticated verse-form to traditional English rhythms and medieval ballad swing.

[1] Northampton MSS., Peterborough MSS. and Bodleian MSS.

[2] *Poems of John Clare's Madness* (Routledge and Kegan Paul, 1949). The introduction contains also Geoffrey Grigson's valuable contribution to the chronology of the St Andrew's poems.

"Child Harold" is a poem of sexual deprivation. The conflict between sexual ethics and a strongly sensuous, intelligent make-up was partly the result of stern pressures on an extreme impressionability. Both Clare and Keats were beaten to their knees by the unending battle, hardest of all for the poet, between ideal love and the demands of physical impulse. Clare's conflict took a different, more terribly prolonged, form from Keats's inability to reconcile what he called "goatish, winnyish, lustful love with the abstract adoration of the deity".

Clare's "Don Juan" and "Child Harold" are quarries for the psychologists. These would say that "Don Juan"s' coarseness is the measure of Clare's so-often unwilling submission to Radstock, Taylor, Mr and Mrs Emmerson, Allen, and, later, Prichard. "Child Harold's" perspective of tragic discernment concerns failure, the extraordinary resilience of human hope, and that loving affirmation which Clare deliberately and to the end preferred above the negative, ungenerous cynicism so often the outcome of life's frustrations. It also concerns the happiness of inner being. Bitterness, resentment and hate reveal themselves as necessary components in a struggle—the struggle of all of us—towards the personal reconciliation of feeling and thought that is life, but which must remain shadowy, never to become wholly triumphant or secure:

Many are poets—though they use no pen
To show their labours to the shuffling age
Real poets must be truly honest men
Tied to no mongrel laws on flatterys page
No zeal have they for wrong or party rage
—The life of labour is a rural song
That hurts no cause — nor warfare tries to wage
Toil like the brook in music wears along—
Great little minds claim right to act the wrong

. . . . .

My mind is dark & fathomless & wears
The hues of hopeless agony & hell
No plummet ever sounds the souls affairs
There death eternal never sounds the knell
There love imprisoned sounds the long farewell

& still may sigh in thoughts no heart hath penned
Alone in loneliness where sorrows dwell
& hopeless hope hopes on & meets no end
Wastes without springs & homes without a friend[1]

. . . . .

The paigles[2] bloom in showers in grassy close
How sweet to be among their blossoms led
& hear sweet Nature to herself discourse
While pale the moon is bering over head
& hear the grazeing cattle softly tred
Cropping the hedgerows newly leafing thorn—
Sounds soft as visions murmured oer in bed
At dusky eve or sober silent morn
For such delights twere happy man was born[3]

. . . . .

There are Northborough jottings in the High Beech notebooks, quotations from Byron; one on "imputed madness" from Dryden—on being forsaken and forsaking all; and nature notes; all revealing the mental struggle of 1841.

4 November, a immense flock of sturnels settled on an ash tree & when they took wing it was like a large roll of thunder

and

12 December. Found a Cowslip in flower

A "Fen description"[4] conveys his delight in being at home. A Northborough piece of 1841 called "Self-identity" reveals the

[1] This stanza is from the High Beech notebook, Northampton. Each word in this and the following stanza begins with a capital letter.

[2] Cowslips.

[3] Clearly a spring stanza. For full, and contradictory, versions of "Child Harold", see *Later Poems of John Clare*, edited by Eric Robinson and Geoffrey Summerfield (Manchester University Press, 1964); and in its seasonally significant form, *Poems of John Clare's Madness*, edited by Geoffrey Grigson, *op. cit*. Also *John Clare: Selected Poems*, edited by J. W. and Anne Tibble, Everyman Edition, (Dent, 1965).

[4] See *The Prose of John Clare*, *op. cit*.

continuing effort to hold on to what we call reason, precarious under pressures physical, mental, personal and social:

> —forget thyself & the world will willingly
> forget thee till thou art nothing but a living–
> dead man dwelling among shadows & falsehood ...

There are verse renderings from the Book of Job and from Revelations, probably written at Matthew Allen's.

Letters for the months of the autumn of 1841 between John Taylor and Matthew Allen show Taylor still taking some responsibility for Clare's practical welfare. He consulted Dr Darling who thought Clare might as well stay at home. Allen replied to Taylor that Patty "thought him so much better that she wished to try him for a while". Allen hoped again that if Clare did not remain well he would return to High Beech.

Perhaps there were renewed difficulties, or a fresh darkening of Clare's mind. We have no evidence of either. In December 1841, though we do not know at whose instigation, Clare was interviewed by two local doctors: Fenwick Skrimshire of the Peterborough Infirmary, who had attended him intermittently since 1824, was one, and William Page the other. Dr Skrimshire testified, without much detail and as was customary in certificates of insanity of that time, that Clare's disease was "hereditary". This vague phrase could mean a number of things, but no evidence of insanity in the family has come to light. The document stated that Clare had had several attacks, the first symptoms having been apparent fourteen years before. The "existing attack" was stated to have begun four years previously. The statement underlined information that the patient had "escaped" from High Beech, but that he had never attempted violence to himself or to others and was not "idiotic, mischievous, or dirty". To the question whether insanity had been preceded by "any severe or long-continued mental emotion or exertion" the author of *The Village Pastor's Surgical and Medical Guide in Letters from an old Physician* made no mention of poverty, loneliness, frustration, or sensitively high intelligence, but gave his now notorious reply: "After years addicted to Poetical prosings".

Arrangements were immediately made for Clare's removal to

the Northampton General Lunatic Asylum. Here he was entered as a farmer, to be paid for by Lord Fitzwilliam at the rate of eight (or eleven) shillings a week, amounts charged for pauper patients. On December 29th, 1841, after five months at home, Clare was removed from the cottage at Northborough. This time he was dragged, hearsay tells, protesting and resisting strongly.

CHAPTER TWENTY-ONE

Beyond the Tomb: 1841–1864

Clare had written years before how time had "had a hand" with him. However Patty might have wished, in 1841, to keep him, there was sure to be a half-sense of relief once the sharp memory of his reluctance to be forced from home a second time faded. His "infirmities were not noxious to society", as Johnson saw Christopher Smart's were not, but not of so devout a character as Smart's, and Clare kept losing his "identity": he could not, as the "chameleon" Keats could when other people's identity pressed *him* to annihilation, find it again at will. Had there been a Charles Lamb to engage his life upon the recapture, even if occasional, of that elusive, fugitive quality, Clare's story might have been different and some of his subsequent misery at least diminished. If he could have received adequate care, bodily comforts and freedom from anxiety over money for his wife and children, at home in his rational periods he might have been as tranquil as Mary Lamb or Cowper were in similar circumstances. But means by which he might secure personal ease deprived him of the scenes necessary to his spiritual content. Partly from the fact of his growing old, but also from his own outlook—during the times when the clouds of delusion lifted—he grew to accept his second alienation at St Andrew's as he had not accepted High Beech.

Northampton General Lunatic Asylum, now St Andrew's Hospital for Mental Diseases, was opened by the third Earl Spencer, in 1838, to accommodate fifty-two paupers and thirty private patients. Not the sumptuous building it is today, it yet had a pleasant situation, about a mile from the town, standing high, with wooded grounds sloping to the valley of the Nene. Its superintendent between 1841 and 1854 was Dr Thomas Prichard, a man, as the editor at that time of the *Northampton*

Mercury testified, "not mad, but just on the other side of that thin partition by which madness is said to be bounded. A tall, athletic, handsome man, impulsive, energetic, daring, he possessed a peculiar faculty of influencing his patients, even when they were far from his presence."[1] Like Matthew Allen, Prichard was among the earliest mind-specialists to improve on our previous harshly primitive methods of treating the insane. Instead of cowing them into docility by inflicting punishment and suffering, Prichard seems to have exerted, however dubiously by today's standards, an almost mesmeric influence, and to have obtained compliance that way.

As at High Beech, those patients of St Andrew's who were classified as "harmless" were allowed a certain freedom. They might go into the town, or wander by themselves, while Dr Prichard remained calmly assured that they would not abuse this liberty. On his arrival Clare was at once found to be one of these "harmless" ones. He was allowed the privilege of coming and going in spite of his record escape six months before. He used to walk to the town a mile away, and his frequent resort was beneath the stone portico of All Saints' Church in the town centre. There in summer he would sit for hours. In the next years his bodily health steadily improved, as it had done at Epping. Had he not been of wiry constitution, if of slight frame, some vital organ must have given out years before from continued under-nourishment. At St Andrew's he grew sturdy.

Dr Prichard wrote to Charles Mossop on November 10th, 1843:

> Poor Clare is in good health but his state of mind has not improved. It rather appears to become more and more impaired, he used at one time to write many and very good pieces tho' he scarcely ever finished them. He now writes but little and in a coarse style very unlike his former compositions. I much fear the disease will gradually terminate in dementia.[2]

The "one time", when Clare wrote "many and very good

[1] From a letter by G. J. De Wilde, printed in *The Times Literary Supplement*, June 30th, 1921.

[2] British Museum MSS.

pieces", is not clear and poems of 1841 to 1843 in a (nineteenth-century) "coarse style" have not come to light either. Clare's mental state did not terminate in the total derangement which is dementia. But his delusions did not lessen. The one about his two wives, Mary and Martha, persisted: he wrote her name, "Mary Joyce Clare", among the many girls' or women's names he began to list in his St Andrew's notebooks. There is no evidence—so far as we know, other than that he called St Andrew's his "prison", "Hell", "Sodom"—to support the statement that he supposed himself jailed for marital unfaithfulness. Because of the development of human morality many sensitive melancholics suppose themselves punished for some wrong they have done. Clare's conviction was rather of innocence. He insisted on identifying with pre-moral nature. Such thinking brings paradox. It contains both wisdom and unwisdom. It accounts both for Clare's loneliness and his capacity for "simple mirth" to the end. His obsession with the natural, impulsive happiness of sexual love, first love particularly but also other loves, often not spoken of, is linked with conflict of guilt concerning mental and physical infidelity and is part of a traditional, largely non-urban, ethic. Guilt imposed by religion concerning the bestial quality of strong physical desire, pushed below the surface in Clare's mind, undoubtedly played its part in driving him over the invisible frontier.

People who visited him testified to other delusions. Earlier in this year, 1843, in May, Spencer T. Hall, "The Sherwood Forester", a self-educated man and a mesmerist, found him

> instead of the spare, sensitive person he appears in the portrait of him from Hilton's painting ... rather burly, florid, with light hair and somewhat shaggy eyebrows, and dressed as a plain but respectable farmer, in drab or stone-coloured coat and smalls, with gaiters, and altogether as clean and neat as if he had just been fresh brushed up for market or fair ...
>
> On my asking him how he was, he said 'Why, I'm very well, and stout, but I'm getting tired of waiting here so long, and want to be off home. They won't let me go, however; for, you see, they're feeding me up for a fight;

but they can get nobody able to strip to me; so they might as well have done with it and let me go.' 'But, Mr. Clare,' said I, 'are you not more proud of your fame as a poet than your prowess as a prize fighter?' When, rather abstractedly, as if considering or trying to recollect something, he answered, 'Oh, poetry, ah, I know, I once had something to do with poetry, a long while ago: but it was no good. I wish, though, they could get a man with courage enough to fight me ...'

Next I asked him if he remembered ever receiving from me at High Beach [sic] a copy of the *Sheffield Iris* and a letter I had sent him. " 'Sheffield Iris?' " he exclaimed: 'Oh, of course, I know all about the "Iris". You know I was editor of it, and lived with the Misses Gales, and was sent to York Castle, where I wrote that "Address to the Robin" '—thus identifying himself with James Montgomery. On my saying that I was going to London, and would have a pleasure in doing anything I could for him there, he seemed for a moment a little uneasy, and then replied, 'Ah, London; I once was there, but don't like it. There is one good fellow there: if you happen to see him you may remember me to him very kindly—and that's Tom Spring!' Such was the talk of a man who would not have hurt a fly or bruised a flower, much less have been one of the fraternity of Tom Spring, the greatest bruiser, of his day, in England![1]

Suppose for a moment that Clare said "he" not "I" in two places, or Hall misheard, what Clare said about Montgomery to whom he had sent poems in the late 1820s, is fact. He himself wrote at least four poems on the Robin but no "Address". James Montgomery, hymn-writer, and editor of the *Sheffield Iris* for thirty-one years, had been imprisoned in York Castle on a flimsy charge, in days of political threat and fear, of having published something detrimental to the progress of the war with France. Montgomery wrote "Verses to a Robin Redbreast" in York among his *Prison Amusements*. There rises a suspicion about Hall's visits, as about the visits and questions of others

[1] Spencer T. Hall, *Biographical Sketches of Remarkable People*, 1873.

to Clare that occasionally Clare suspected he was being "drawn out", resented this, led questioners on, and, as he himself wrote in one of his Mary poems, was moved "to think and speak contrary".[1]

Hall added:

> This was just after he had been writing a beautiful and logical poem for my friend Mr. Joseph Stenson, the iron-master ... Another time on my seeing him, after he had just returned from a long and favourite ramble, he described it all, up to a certain point, with great accuracy and apparent pleasure, in beautiful language, and then broke into talk it would be wrong to repeat.

A pity Hall was squeamish. What impressed Robert Barringer, brother and assistant to a Northampton tobacconist, were Clare's keen blue eyes, the massive forehead, and the country gait. Barringer too records the tales his visitor had to tell of encounters with fists in which he came off victorious. In seeking to trace associations in the intuitive part of the brain we may remember the 1824 visits with Rippingille to watch Randall, Spring and Caunt.[2]

G. J. De Wilde, editor of the *Northampton Mercury*, met Clare about the town. De Wilde remarked on the countryman's tread, the thick eyebrows penthouse-wise over the eager eyes, the expression as of habitual contemplation. Clare's forehead, De Wilde went on:

> was like that of Napoleon as described by Browning—'oppressive with its mind.' So towering a forehead had Shakespeare.
>
> The question answered was followed by another, rational enough and commonplace, but some remark about the scenery led me to think my querist was not an ordinary commonplace man. I did not then know he was Clare.
>
> We walked side by side towards Kingsthorpe, and at

[1] "I sleep with thee and wake with thee."

[2] In *The Monthly Review* for 1821 which Clare saw there is mention of *Jack Randall's Diary of Proceedings at the House of Call for Genius*, edited by Mr Breakwindow (Simpkins and Marshall, 1820).

last he startled me with a quotation from *Childe Harold* and then one from Shakespeare. I do not recall what the passages were, but I was still more startled when he said they were his own. 'Yours!' I exclaimed, 'Who are you? These are Byron's and Shakespeare's verses, not yours!' 'It's all the same' he answered, changing a quid from one cheek to the other. 'I'm John Clare now. I was Byron and Shakespeare formerly. At different times you know I'm different people—that is the same person with different names.'

And then he went on to identify himself with a most miscellaneous and unselect lot of celebrities—great warriors, prize fighters, and some eminent blackguards. I saw him very often after that in the Asylum, and on his favourite seat under the portico of All Saints Church. He was very taciturn, and as a rule unsocial in his manner, which seemed to, and very probably did, arise from embarrassment.

His answers were the briefest possible. You won his heart, however, with a screw of tobacco, of which he never lacked a store. People out of doors were very kind to him, too kind sometimes, and at the Asylum he had, one may say, boundless liberty as long as Dr. Pritchard[1] was its Superintendent ...

Clare believed him to be possessed of some supernatural power which made it as unsafe to disobey him when he was absent as when he was present. There was once a conspiracy among some of his fellow patients the object of which was to abscond. Clare was invited to join in the project, but he steadily refused.

They did not know, he said, the length of that man's arm, nor his far-seeing as to their whereabouts, and the only result of their attempt would be that they would be haled back to their confinement with no more liberty to ramble where they listed. So they went without him and got into Hertfordshire.

There was some reason for what Clare said. Pritchard spared neither money nor pains to recover an absconded

[1] Dr Prichard.

> patient, and he usually succeeded in regaining him. Accordingly the two culprits were discovered and brought ignominiously back. Clare was present when they were brought in. 'I told you how it would be, you fools,' he said.[1]

In a later letter—of February 25th, 1865, to Frederick Martin—De Wilde wrote:

> He would talk rationally enough at times, about poetry especially, but on one occasion in the midst of a conversation in which he had betrayed no signs of insanity, he suddenly quoted passages from Don Juan as his own. I suggested, gently, that they were usually attributed to Byron, upon which he said that was true; but he and Byron were one; so with Shakespeare; Shakespeare's plays were his composition when he was Shakespeare; and turning round upon me suddenly he said: "Perhaps you don't know that I am Jan Burns and Tom Spring?" In fact he was any celebrity whom you might mention. "I'm the same man," he said, "but sometimes they called me Shakespeare and sometimes Byron and sometimes Clare ..."

Over the past two thousand years many in the East and recently some in Western culture have accepted the idea of reincarnation as a credible part of the Mystery of Being which to the end of his life Clare brooded on.

Townspeople would give him tobacco or a glass of ale. He kept paper and pencil in his pocket to pay with a verse when required. A great number of these scraps were said to have been current in the town, but as with the "coarse" verse mentioned by Prichard none has come to light.

S. T. Hall, in 1843, was the first of a line of visitors. These were not the friends of Clare's youth or of his famous days: Lamb was dead, Cunningham was dead, Cary and George Darley were soon to die. Some visitors found him in good humour and lightened the burden of time by an hour or two's

[1] From De Wilde's letter to J. W. Dalby, Hunt's friend, printed in *The Times Literary Supplement*, June 30th, 1921.

talk. Others, perhaps by too personal curiosity or questions, angered him. Some therefore found him cheerful and talkative, others reported him taciturn.

On July 16th, 1844, Mary Howitt, Quaker and miscellaneous writer, devoted a few hours out of a busy life to visit St Andrew's. She gave Clare William Howitt's *Book of the Seasons*,[1] in which Clare is represented. She received from him a copy of "The Sleep of Spring":

O for that sweet untroubled rest,
 That Poets oft have sung,
The babe upon its mother's breast,
 The bird upon its young.
The heart asleep without a pain,—
 When shall I know that sleep again?—

. . . . .

I love the weeds along the fen
 More sweet than garden flowers,
For freedom haunts the humble glen
 That blest my happiest hours:—
Here—prisons injure health and me,
 I love sweet freedom and the free.[2]

. . . . .

William Howitt, "a poet of the people", husband of Mary Howitt, may have been with her on this occasion. What Howitt later related shows Clare's mind in aberration as retaining the astonishing, pre-literate memory of the boy who knew the third chapter of Job by heart, who wrote drafts of his own long poems from memory. Mary Russell Mitford recorded, some years afterwards, in *Recollections of a Literary Life*, 1852, that Howitt was struck, in Clare,

with a narrative of the execution of Charles the First,

[1] Sixth edition, 1840.

[2] In his notes to *Poems of John Clare's Madness*, *op. cit.* (p. 229), Geoffrey Grigson says there is a copy of "The Sleep of Spring", dated 1844, in Clare's hand, in the possession of Mr Samuel Loveman in America. Punctuation here is given from the Knight Transcripts, Northampton MSS.

> recounted ... as a transaction that occurred yesterday, and of which he (Clare) was an eyewitness—a narrative the most graphic and minute, with an accuracy as to costume and manners far exceeding what would probably have been at his command if sane. It is such a lucidity as the disciples of Mesmer claim for clairvoyance. Or he would relate the battle of the Nile, and the death of Lord Nelson with the same perfect keeping, especially as to seamanship, fancying himself one of the sailors who had been in the action, and dealing out nautical phrases with admirable exactness and accuracy, although it is doubtful if he ever saw the sea in his life.

He did not ever see the sea. But his father's ballad of "Nelson and the Nile" other ballads and his own reading could, without Mesmer or clairvoyance, have supplied details. J. F. Nisbet, writing in 1891, repeated the above in his book, *The Insanity of Genius*:

> His memory was astonishing. He seemed to assimilate everything that he read or heard, picturing events so vividly in his mind that he related them afterwards as if he had seen and taken part in them. Of the execution of Charles I he believed himself to have been an eyewitness, and he was accustomed to tell most graphically his pretended experiences of the battle of the Nile and of the death of Nelson.

This doctor does not seem actually to have heard Clare tell these stories.

"J. N." from Worcester, hearing that Clare was "on most subjects, tolerably rational", saw him, learned that the productions of the uncharted mind were often "coarse and vulgar", witnessed as to Clare's "unlimited" supply of books, commented on his objections to the Royal succession, his pugilistic fancies, and pronounced his delusions "protean". Thomas Grimshawe visited him and painted him in 1844. This portrait is in the Northampton Public Library.

On November 12th, 1844, Queen Victoria and Prince Albert made a Royal Progress through Northampton on their way to visit the Marquis of Exeter at Burghley House. Shops were closed and the town garlanded. Clare was given an excellent place from which to view the procession; but "The Raree Show", easy doggerel, was all that the occasion produced from him. Another poet looked on at this Progress: William Wordsworth had been to Cambridge: "I much regret that it did not strike me at the moment to throw off my feelings in verse," he wrote later to Henry Reed.

A letter from Prichard in July 1845, again to the Rev. Charles Mossop at Northborough, discloses:

> John Clare is in excellent health but his mind is becoming more and more obscured by his distressing malady—He enjoys perfect liberty here, and passes all his time out of doors in the fields or the Town, returning only for his meals and bed.[1]

"Perfect liberty" is surely a euphemism of the sane. In a gloomy letter draft to Patty for 1845 or early 1846[2] Clare—not unnaturally (had he not been deceived about his entry into High Beech and hauled forcibly to St Andrew's?)—saw the asylum world as prison. This led him to uphold again, as he had upheld most of his adult life, the imperfect world of the actual against a world, ideal yet not impossible to achieve. State and Church had failed to uphold the possibility, he thought, of sincerity and avoidance of crookedness and untruth. With an obsessive obstinacy that is also humanly admirable, he continued to see such an ideal world as realizable. To Patty in 1845:[3]

> My dear Wife
>
> I have wrote some few times to enquire about yourself & the Family & thought about yourself & them a thousand other things that I use to think of the childern—Freddy when I led him by the hand in his childhood—I see him now in his little pink frock—seal skin cap—and gold band—with his little face as round as an apple and as red

[1] British Museum MSS.
[2] Notebook dated 1845, Northampton MSS.
[3] Northampton MSS.

> as a rose—and now a stout Man both strangers to each other the father a prisoner under a bad government so bad in fact that its no government at all but prison disapline where everybody is forced to act contrary to their own wishes "the mother against the daughter in law and the daughter against the mother in law" "the father against the son and the son against the father"—in fact I am in Prison because I wont leave my family and tell a falshood—this is the English Bastile a government Prison where harmless people are trapped and tortured till they die—English priestcraft and english bondage more severe then the slavery of Egypt and Affrica while the son is tyed up in his manhood from all the best thoughts of his childhood bye lying & falshood—not dareing to show love or remembrance for Home or home affections living in a world as a prison estranged from all his friends still Truth is the best companion for it levels all distinctions in pretentions Truth wether it enters the Ring or the Hall of Justice shows a plain Man that is not to be scared at shadows or big words full of fury and meaning nothing when done and said with them truth is truth and no further & the rights of man—age of reason and common sense are sentences full of meaning and the best comment of its truth is themselves—an honest man makes priestcraft an odious lyar & coward and a filthy disgrace to Christianity—that coward I hate and detest—the Revelations has a placard in capitals about "The Whore of Babylon" and the mother of Harlots does it mean priestcraft I think it must—this rubbish of cant must soon die—like all others—I began a letter and added a sermon—& the paper too

In April 1845 W. F. Knight became steward at St Andrew's. Soon after his arrival this writer of verse became interested in Clare. Knight began to transcribe poems. These were, he wrote at the beginning of what became two volumes, over 800 poems:

> Copied from the Manuscripts as presented to me by Clare—and favoured with others by some Ladies and Gentlemen, that Clare had presented them to—the whole of

> them faithfully transcribed to the best of my knowledge from the pencil originals many of which were so obliterated that without refering to the Author I could not decipher. Some pieces will be found unfinished, for Clare will seldom turn his attention to pieces he has been interrupted in while writing—and in no instance has ever rewritten a single line—whenever I have wished him to correct a single line he has ever shown the greatest disinclination to take in hand what to him seems a great task.[1]

In October 1845, the friend of Bloomfield and Knight, Thomas Inskip, began again to write to Clare, encouraging him, and getting a few poems published for him in the *Bedford Times* of 1847, 1848 and 1849. Under the encouragement of Inskip and Knight, Clare revived a little. Through what Knight transcribed, what Inskip got printed, and what is to be found in Clare's notebooks, a group of poems written between 1844 and 1850 is preserved. These are the poems which, Geoffrey Grigson has written, pushed Clare "over the border between the pathetically interesting and exquisite into the great; however circumscribed that greatness".[2] They give evidence of a tenacity of lyric impulse. Lyric is so often the output of youth. They are contemplative, semi-mystical poems—"A Vision" (dated August 2nd, 1844), "Love Lies Beyond the Tomb",[3] "I am", "Invite to Eternity", "Love is Life's Spring", "The Sleep of Spring", "Love's Pains" (dated July 13th, 1844), "Sorrow is my Joy", "Hesperus", "A Thought", "Love's Story", "The Autumn Wind" (dated July 13th, 1844), "First Love", "Born Upon an Angel's Breast", "Flowers Shall Hang Upon the Pall" and "I Hid my Love":

> I hid my love in field and town
> Till e'en the breeze would knock me down

[1] The Knight Transcripts, Northampton MSS. Vol. 2 is in at least two handwritings other than Knight's.

[2] Introduction to *Poems of John Clare's Madness*, *op. cit.*

[3] Knight has *lives.* The Peterborough copyist of the (Knight) St Andrew's poems has *lies.* A copy in Clare's own hand survives among the Knight–Stenson MSS. This has *lives.*

The Bees seemed singing ballads o'er
The flyes buzz[1] turned a Lions roar

Disarmingly simple, the paradox of "Love's Story" is also humanly perennial:

I do not love thee so I'll not deceive thee
I do not love thee yet I'm lothe to leave thee

I do not love thee yet joys very essence
Comes with thy footstep is complete in thy presence

I do not love thee yet when gone I sigh
And think about thee 'till the stars all die

. . . .

I cannot hate thee yet my love seems debtor
To love thee more So hating love thee better.

There are also metrical innovations, as in "The Invitation", "Now is Past", "'Tis Spring my love 'tis Spring", "Mary Bateman", "Where she Told her Love". Some non-rhyme experiments make a link with the present century—"Pleasant Sounds", "House or Window Flies" ("These little indoor dwellers"), "Dewdrops", and "Spring". The latter is one of the few poems for which we have Clare's own manuscript:[2]

Pale sunbeams gleam
That nurtur a few flowers
Pilewort & daisey & a sprig o' green
On whitethorn bushes
In the leaf strewn hedge

These harbingers
Tell spring is coming fast
& these the schoolboy marks
& wastes an hour from school
Agen the old pasture hedge

[1] Knight has *buss*. Did he confuse Clare's old-fashioned double "s" with his double "z"? There is no evidence for Elizabethan *buss* (*kiss*) anywhere else in Clare.
[2] Northampton MSS.

Cropping the daisey
& the pilewort[1] flowers
Pleased with the Spring & all he looks upon
He opes his spelling book
& hides her blossoms there

Shadows fall dark
Like black in the pale sun
& lye the bleak day long
Like black stock under hedges
& bare wind rocked trees

Tis chill[2] but pleasant
In the hedge bottom lined
With brown seer leaves the last
Year littered there & left
Mopes the hedge Sparrow

With trembling wings & cheeps
Its welcome to pale sunbeams
Creeping through & further on
Made of green loss
The nest & green blue eggs are seen

All token spring & every day
Green & more green hedges & close
& everywhere appears
Still tis but March
But still that March is Spring

There are Cunningham- Burns- and Lallans-echoing, but very English, verses such as "I'll meet thee on the heather", "To Liberty", "I had na' been so busy" and "Oh, haud yer tongues ye sylvan elves", sonnets like "Poets love Nature", ballads such as the Valentine, "Clare to his Wife" (Knight's title?), "How can I forget?", "First Love" and "The Peasant Poet":

He loved the brook's soft sound
The swallow swimming by

[1] Lesser celandine, *ranunculus ficaria.*
[2] Not *dull* as given in *The Later Poems of John Clare, op. cit.*

He loved the daisy covered ground
The cloud bedappled sky
To him the dismal storm appeared
The very voice of God
And where the Evening rack[1] was reared
Stood Moses with his rod
And everything his eyes surveyed
The insects i' the brake
Where Creatures God almighty made
He loved them for his sake
A silent man in life's affairs
A thinker from a Boy
A Peasant in his daily cares—The
Poet in his joy

Among this 1844–1850 group there are children's poems—"Clock-a-Clay" (ladybird), "The Red Robin", "Little Trotty Wagtail". There are poems of an observation as acute as in his early work—"The Round Oak", "The Bean Field". A poem such as "The Dying Child" makes a link between Clare and Coleridge in the latter's "Something Childish but very natural". We recall Clare's seeing Coleridge in 1824. In the pathos, indefinable, intimate yet remote, of "Adieu", as Edmund Blunden has written, "William Blake, and only he, can be said to resemble Clare." All these lyrics have is a finely controlled "madness".

Though many of the poems of this period cannot be dated with precision, they imply creativity as consistent as poetic creativity sometimes is. There are indications of tranquillity in the notebook dated for 1845:

A pleasant Place

Beautiful gravel walks overgrown
with moss & grass little places where
the poet sat to write

[1] *Rock* in Knight, *Poems of John Clare's Madness*, *op. cit.* and *The Later Poems of John Clare*, *op. cit.*: *rack* (see Clare's own version) is thin cloud (Baker's Glossary); it is a word Clare used frequently.

Clare's portrait was painted by George Marne, a Northamptonshire artist, in 1848.

In 1849 Inskip died. In the next year Knight left St Andrew's for Birmingham. Away went Clare's hope of a new volume. Almost immediately his lyric output diminished.

Yet for the succeeding period, between 1850 and 1860, there are the song "My Old Love Left Me", his last long poem "The Rhapsody" ("Sweet solitude what joy to be alone"), the modernly outspoken "O Love is so decieving" and many other "Halfpenny Ballads", as Clare called the jigging verses he tossed off and gave away to townspeople for tobacco or a glass of ale. These often have titles to girls – to many Marys: Lucy Mary, Mary Ogilvie, Mary Featherstone, Mary o' the plough. Sometimes the jingles are to girls with other names – Irish Kitty, Helen, Jean, Caradora, Ann Bodenham, Alice Grey, Lucy o' Northampton. Knight's letters to Clare between 1845 and 1850 show an appreciation of Clare as an often sane, vitally interesting, person, a friend. Few of Clare's to Knight have survived; but one complains of loneliness and lack of books. Knight's well-meant recommendation was to keep his active mind from sadness and loneliness by writing verse. With few instances of irrationality the resulting jingles are of the quality of:

I pilled the straws for want o' words And plucked up bents to plait
And thought while there the loving birds Had ne'er so sweet a mate
A white straw hat o' smallest plait And green striped cotton gown
Her hiloes[1] bright her stockings white She on the grass sat down

There are, too, for this period, fresh poems for spring and autumn:

[1] Not *lilies* as given in *The Later Poems of John Clare, op. cit.*, with note: "Knight has 'Her hilees white bright'. He has been unable to recognize Clare's euphemism for breasts ... " No euphemism; *hiloes* (high-lows) were high shoes covering the ankles. See Baker's *Glossary* and the St Andrew's "Oh Whither Fair Maiden".

The dark days of Autumn grows cloudy and rainy
The sun pales like sulphur the shadows grow long
To me the dull season the sweetest of any
I love to see yellow leaves pale in my song
The rush covered green and thistle capped mountain
The dead leaves a falling and winds singing round
The willow and ash leaves they choak up the fountain
There's health i' the strife o't and joy i' the sound

I love there to loiter wi' winds blowing round me
Till the strong eddies past and the rain gust is over
Wild pigeons fly over the distance looks downy
With [pollard?] willow rows pieces of clover
Brown pieces o' stubble ground o' turnips bright green
The crows flying over the lakes silver light
Scarce a wild blossom left to enliven the scene
Rauk[1] and mist are for ever in sight

This imperfect poem, with others of the late 1840s, "The night wind is born brief" and "Wilt thou think o' me?", are indicative of Clare, not so much as a remembrancer of Burns, Ramsay and Beattie, "killing time", but as a poet with traditional Celtic–Anglo-Saxon rhythms in his blood, as perhaps was the relish of being sad. Forty years later, Gerard Manley Hopkins explored like rhythms, for his own poetic purposes, giving his use of them a technical name and a theory. They were inborn in Clare.

Towards 1850 he began, as he did in "Wilt thou think o' me?", to try out a consonant code in his pencil notebook 10 of Halfpenny Ballads inscribed John Clare Northborough, Dec. 26th, 1849. Notebook 10 contains lists of books—Gisborne's *Walks in a Forest*, Fenning's *Young Man's Book of Knowledge*, Fisher's *Young Man's Companion*, and so on. There are lists of names of the villages round Helpston—Caistor, Ailsworth, Thornawe, Ryhall, Bridge Casterton—what he had once called those "pleasant names of places". Some field names are in the consonant code—all the vowels and "y", the personal

[1] Knight has *rauk*, as have the Peterborough Transcripts, not *rank* as given in *The Later Poems of John Clare, op. cit. Rauk*—white mist—is a word Clare not infrequently used.

pronouns "I", "you", and the article "a" omitted—wd Ln, Cppr Grn, Clrks Wd, Hgh Clss—Wood Lawn, Copper (Cowper) Green, Clark's Wood, High Closes. Lists of girls' or women's names abound—some 180 of them. Twenty-one of these have been traced to real people of Clare's earlier days or real people living whilst he was at St Andrew's.[1] Three letters to girls or women are in a Northampton notebook and in the consonant code. These girls' or women's names and the use of the code itself indicate desperate loneliness as well as a further loss by Clare of everyday communications. No letters of after 1850 from Knight are available. One by Clare to Knight which has survived confirms consciousness of his predicament: "I am in this d——d madhouse & cant get out."

One of the code letters is to Mary Ludgate, a daughter of the landlady of the White Hart Inn in Northampton during the late 1840s. Another is to Hellen Maria Gardiner, who may have been the daughter of the carrier between Helpston and Stamford in 1820. The third is to Mary Collingwood. Clare has written her name in full. There is a poem to her in Knight, "O Mary gentle Mary let us not disagree". Her identity, though she is mentioned at least twice more in the notebooks, does not seem to have come to light:

To Mary Collingwood

M Drst Mr Cllngwd

M nrl wrn t & wnt t hr frm Nbd wll wn M r hy m t n prc & wht hv dn D knw wht r n m Dbt—Kss's fr tn yrs & lngr stll & lngr thn tht whn ppl mk sch mstks s t cll m Gds bstrd & whrs p m b shttng p m b shttng m p frm Gds ppl t f th w cmmn snse & thn tk m hd ff bcs th cnt fnd m t t hrds hrd

Drst Mr r fthfll r d thnk f m knw wht w sd tgthr—dd vst m n hll sm tm bck bt dnt cm ht gn fr t s ntrs bd plc wrs nd wrs nd wr ll trnd Frnchmn ffsh ppl tll m hv gt n hm n ths wrld n'd s dnt believe n thr nrt mk mslf hvn wth m drst Mr nd sbscrb mslf rs fr vr & vr

Jhn Clr

[1] Eric Robinson and Geoffrey Summerfield: "John Clare: an interpretation of certain asylum letters", *The Review of English Literature*, vol. XIII, No. 50, May 1962.

My dearest Mary Collingwood

I am nearly worn out & want to hear from you nobody will own me or have me at any price & what have I done do you know what you are in my Debt—kisses for ten years & longer still & longer than that when people make such mistakes as to call me God's bastard & whores pay me by shutting me up from God's people out of the way of common sense & then take my head off because they can't find me it out herods herod

Dearest Mary are you faithful or do you think of me you know what we said together—you did visit me in hell some time back but don't come here again for 'tis a notorious bad place worse and worse and we are all turned Frenchmen foolish people tell me I have got no home in this world and as I dont believe any other anyrate I make myself heaven with my dearest Mary and subscribe myself yours for ever & ever

John Clare

The word "believe" is the one word written in full. When Clare was writing in code and therefore secretly, he most probably is saying what he most deeply felt and thought. He was still inconsistent in his beliefs. Many times he has set down his longing for certainty. As much evidence can be found to prove a life-time's agnosticism in him as to prove Christian reliance—not on dogma and institutional religion but—on what can only be called eternal verities.

All his life, when he was not politely subordinating his words to others', he questioned. His sense of Eden was not of any myth but simply of childhood's lost happiness: "Surely the Garden of Eden was nothing more than our first parents entry upon life & the loss of it their knowledge of the world." His belief in the "eternity of nature" belongs rather with post-Darwinian knowledge of the astounding length of geological time, not with the prevalent Creation dogma of his youth. His insistence on sincerity against "cursd affectation" remained realist as well as romantic.

There are gaps among the letters preserved of those Clare must have written home between 1844 and 1850. A letter of

Knight's perhaps to Stenson reveals that early in 1846 somebody in Northampton made Clare drunk and he was confined to St Andrew's grounds. This restriction may not have been permanent. Knight wrote, "It seems a crime to keep him from his loved haunts." Knight also mentioned some "Child Harrold" [sic] stanzas – as if Clare were in 1846 still busy with his long poem.

In 1847 Clare sent a coherent letter home: he was "sorry to hear the News about your Grandfather". Parker Clare died in March 1846; but "are the young children at home I understand there are some". William and John were both married. William and his family were at home.

Among the villagers at Northborough it was thought that since Earl Fitzwilliam paid for Clare's maintenance as a pauper at St Andrew's, they lived rent free, but that supposition was as incorrect as it had been when Clare contradicted it in 1832. Patty did not speak of these things even to her nearest neighbour. She was still a comely woman, of medium height, plump rather than stout, with a full, rosy face, well liked in the village and at market because of her pleasant chatter and her kind heart. She did not, to all appearances, make a trouble of her husband's absence; she rarely spoke of it, and the tradition grew that she cared little. She was known to the villagers as "Widow Clare". Anna, Clare's eldest daughter, died in 1844. Eliza Louisa, though married, was confined to her own home many years through indifferent health. Frederick died in 1843. It is possible that the news of Frederick's and Anna's deaths was kept from him. After the gap in preserved letters home there are eleven letters from Clare for the following eighteen years, two to Patty, eight to Charles, and one to Sophia. After an hortatory one to Charles, the first of the two to Patty, July 1848, runs:

> My dear wife,
>
> I have not written to you a long while but here I am in the Land of sodom where all the peoples brains are turned the wrong way I was glad to see John yesterday and should like to have gone back with him for I am very weary of being here – You might come & fetch me away for I think I have been here long enough I write this in a green

meadow the side of the river agen Stokes Mill & I see three of your daughters and a Son now & then The confusion and roar of Mill dams and locks is sounding very pleasant while I write it and its a very beautiful Evening the meadows are greener then usual after the shower & the Rivers are brimful ... I think it is about two years since I was first sent up to this hell and not allowed to go out of the gates there never was a more disgraceful deception than this place It is the purgatorial hell and French Bastile of English Liberty Keep yourselves happy & comfortable and love one another bye and bye I shall be with you perhaps before you expect me There has been a great storm here with Thunder and hail that did much damage to the glass in the neighbourhood—Hailstones the size of Hens Eggs fell in some places Did your brother John come to Northborough or go to Barnack his uncle John Riddle came the next morning but did not stay I thought I was coming home but I got cheated I see many of your little Brothers and Sisters at Northampton weary & dirty with hard work some of them with red hands but all in ruddy good health ... [1]

There would be no scarcity of barefoot children in the "hungry 'Forties" and Clare was reaching a stage when his family was

> ... not more dear than every girl and boy
> Which time matures and nothing can destroy

Your "brother John" is not Patty's brother but her son and Clare's. John had been to see his father. In Clare's next letter, to Charles—dated October 17th, 1848—he mentions that "Your Brother John promised Mr Knight to send him with your Brothers and Sisters consent the loan of a Volume of MS Poems in your possession—You have my free consent to do so as soon as you like". The next April (1849), though "quite lost in reveries & false hums" Clare is still anxious over the book. Evidently replying further about manuscripts, he wrote to Charles:

[1] Knight's Transcripts.

I know of no "Three or Four Volumes of MS Poems that have not been published" as we searched them all over & completed every fragment for the Press but if you think otherwise you may send them when you like & where you like—for I know nothing but of one Vol which I partly filled the last five months I was at home & I think I reccolect something of the others which I brought home with me send them by all means—I know of none which he prefers but cant you send the "Three or Four Volumes" of MSS as they are & let him see what he wanted himself—do just as you please & you will do right enough—[1]

With good reason, the family must have been reluctant to part with manuscripts. It is difficult to see why Knight had not enough and more than enough among what he called "many pieces that are all very choice" in the first volume of his Transcripts.

There are letters home for June 1848, when Clare wished to be remembered to many old friends, of whom his excellent memory gave a long list, for October, and a November letter in which he got the time of his stay at Northampton correct—nearly nine years. He asked "when Johnny is coming to fetch me away from this Bastile"; and

read books of Knowledge: don't forget you[r] Latin and Greek and Hebrew, nor your Mathematics and Astronomy, for in them you have Truth. When I was a day-labourer at Bridge-Casterton and courted your Mother I knew Nine Languages and could talk of them to Parsons and Gentlemen and Foreigners, but never opened my mouth about them to the Vulgar, for I always lived to myself. Don't forget you have Bibles and Prayer Books; and never act Hypocrisy, for Deception is the most odious Knavery in the World. Stick to Truth and 'shame the Devil.' Learning is your only Wealth ... [2]

An 1849 letter to Frederick advised the boy who had been dead

[1] *Ibid.*
[2] Northampton MSS.

six years: "Think Fred—for yourself". By 1852 someone wrote for Clare to his daughter Sophy because "I do not write so fluent and quick as he does". He hopes Charles will soon be better and adds that he himself is "in very good health, and I think that I never felt in better". But a draft letter reveals that, with Inskip dead, Knight leaving, and hope for a book leaving with him, Clare was slipping towards still darker days. He wrote in his notebook:

> My dear Mary Collingwood
> I long to see you & have Loved from the first Night of my Capture here
>
> Betsey Averey
> Mary Ann Averey
>
> ... My dear Mary but there is no faith here so I hold my tongue—& wait the end out without attention or intention—"I am that I am"—& done nothing yet
>
> J. Clare

In the small notebook a few pages further on after lists of flowers—Red Primroses Marsh Violets—he cautions himself:

Gently John gently John

From these letters and from such poems as "I Am", Martin and others have surmised neglect on the part of Clare's family. Up to 1845 the way to go to Northampton from Northborough would have been to hire a gig to Thrapston and there catch the Cambridge coach which ran in connection with the coach at Oxford. The journey might cost, according to a writer on old Peterborough, £4 there and back. In 1845 the railway to Northampton was completed, and the journey might be made for *3s. 6d.* each way. The impression of one living member of the Clare family is that John and William went to see their father as often as they could, and even the invalid Eliza Louisa, who best understood and sympathized with her father's poetry, went once. Patty did not go.

The cottage into which Clare's letters were received had troubles besides an absent husband and father. There are preserved, with date for March 1850, two or three false starts at an evidently difficult letter from Charles to Patty's landlord, to say that the interest from the Fund-money must be stopped to pay her backward rent. She is ill; William is out of work; her home is in danger, and bills for Clare's doctors are not yet paid. Another letter begs Lord Milton—"Rev'd Sir"—to wait a little longer. Patty cannot sell her cow until July. John Taylor, who also visited Clare at St Andrew's at least once and faithfully kept his interest in the family, was applied to, and in his reply commented on William's unemployment as a "Shame". Charles defended William, at the same time disclosing some details of difficulties often overlooked or not understood by society at large. In those days Britain's agricultural poor were still by no means flourishing with full employment: "My Brother ... would not be Idle if he could get any Employ. He has been to Labouring work the last winter when he could get a day's employ for 1*s.* 6*d.*, and perhaps has got one in a fortnight." Another plea to Taylor for help: Charles's draft letter is undated and unaddressed:

> My eldest Brother [John, since Frederick's death] is now in journey work. My Second Brother [William] has no work at all, and has been living at the expense of my Mother ... My salary is but £4 per annum, which scarcely finds us shoes. If you could advance us a few pounds on the money that is in the Funds ...

Whether Taylor, habitually so cautious, responded is not clear. Charles, on whom fell the task of answering the correspondence of the family, offered to discharge, in monthly instalments, his mother's debt, the money presumably to be paid out of his purse, replete with £4 a year. Charles was at the time articled to a solicitor, Sharp of Market Deeping.

Patty got what profit she could with William to help, out of hay, fruit, cow, and marketing. Very, very occasionally she was asked by a visitor for a copy of *Poems Descriptive* or *The Village Minstrel*. In 1852, at the age of nineteen, Charles died. John and William were robust, in spite of possible undernourishment in their early days at Helpston. Eventually John went to Wales and obtained a fairly good position on the railway at Oswestry.

In time William kept a seed-drill, hiring himself and his machine out to neighbouring farmers.

No more was heard of Knight's project for a book of poems. Taylor, about 1854, appears to have contemplated a "complete edition". The ageing publisher purchased from How of Whittakers the copyright of *The Rural Muse* for £10. But that scheme fell to earth and no more was heard of it.

Most likely Clare resumed his walks to Northampton to his favourite seat under the portico of All Saints' Church in the town square. He would "sit for hours" musing, watching children at play, or jotting down passing thoughts in a pocket book. Claridge Druce, author of *Northamptonshire Botanologia: John Clare, The Flora of Northamptonshire*, and other country floras, as a child saw him—"a little, pathetic, distraught figure gazing into the sky."

In this year and the previous one perhaps, he helped Anne Elizabeth Baker with her *Northamptonshire Glossary*, issued by subscription in 1854. One half of the strictly Northamptonshire words were furnished by Clare. He, she wrote in her preface, "beautifully clothes his ideas in his own rustic idiom." Her two volumes, unsuperseded, collected many instances of the nimbleness of unlettered word-making, with instances also from Dryden, Tusser and Chaucer as well as Clare.

By 1854 Dr Prichard could no longer persuade the St Andrew's governors to support wholeheartedly his not entirely orthodox methods with patients. He left to found an institution of his own at Abington Abbey. Dr Edwin Wing and Dr P. R. Nesbitt became joint superintendents and John Godfrey secretary. For some reason Clare was confined to the asylum grounds. Dr Wing, who remained after Dr Nesbitt left in 1858, is said not to have had the influence with Clare which Dr Prichard had.

Clare's notebooks, in which he confided in moods of withdrawal, again and again betray confusion over his chameleon identity with that of bruisers like Randall and Spring and Jan Burns, boxers like Caunt, and with Byron, Shakespeare, Wellington and Nelson. In the 1850 notebook, after the hopeless note to Mary:

The Humbug called the King or the Fancy owes me as

> forfeits £1,800 & I have been 9 years without a Shilling & in this Prison still
>
> Ben Caunt

Here his sense of the passage of time, often erratic as in the letter to Frederick, is again almost accurate.

In the same notebook his mind switched back to the unpublished poems at home, "Don Juan" and "Child Harold" of 1841:

> Lord Byron was 16 years when he began to write "Child Harold" & finished it in 1818 when he was 25 When he wrote the 4th Canto he was courting one Martha Turner the daughter of Mr. Willm. Turner Walk Lodge—he began it one Sunday afternoon & finished it in three or four hours under an Ash Tree in Her Fathers Home Close

Later, amidst the lists of places, books, and girls' or women's names, after the song "How sweet the spring buds are all bursting to leaves":

> Lord Nelson [John Clare] on Board the 'L'Orient' Flag ship recieving the Swords of the Enemy—Blown up by the Spanish Admirals son—Lord Nelson

And under "Jan. 23 1850":

> Saw my Wife Patty in a Dream she looked well—with little Billy and an Infant carried by someone else all looked healthy and happy—John Clare

Connected with the pleasure in words which helps to produce poetry, as well as the code letters and "Boxer Byron—Made of Iron", is:

> I think while I'm shut up of I D
> & then I cannot hear I silent seem & D I

Also

> Eye on weed } weeding pun
> Ironweed }

Ironweed is *centaurea nigra*, an incredibly tough stemmed plant. The symbolic connection with Clare's dedication to toughness, lastingness, fidelity, even eternity, is obvious.

Still, there were saner, lighter periods in those later years and under closer confinement. Of the period between 1850 and 1860, a fellow patient, William Jerom, remarked his "witticisms and crank sayings", his moral courage, an indomitable quality he had, his "fiery" blue eye.[1] He was not, Jerom says "particularly religious", having no "ripeness of Christian character". Imagining himself Nelson, Jerom supposed, and betraying again the survival toughness which was part of his make-up, Clare would sing:

Fight on, my boys, he said
Till I die, till I die.
Fight on, my boys, he said
Till I die.

There is, of course, no question of his later concept of "freedom" or "liberty" approaching the complexities of the "liberty" of which men like Mill were at that time talking. Clare's was more a basic inheritance. To Jerom the refrain had "a degree of emphasis that seemed to be rather elevating and somewhat touching".

In March 1856, the Rev. Thomas James of Theddingworth lectured on Dryden and Clare. He had recently visited Clare, and the year preceding that had seen Patty at Northborough. A letter from his friend De Wilde, which he read out, informs of the indiscretion which had plied Clare with drink. James admired Clare's poetry and left his rather homiletic account of the poet's life to be later drawn on by J. L. Cherry in 1873.

In November 1857, there appeared in the *London Journal* verses by some well-meaning visitor concerning Clare, an "inoffensive lunatic". The next news of him, almost entirely forgotten in the throng of mid-century music-makers, is in 1860. It is to be suspected that Dr Wing's further confinement of him produced a deeper melancholy which had its consequence in thickening the cloud over his mind. Entries in the casebooks for

[1] Peterborough MSS.

the years previous to 1861 were burnt or have been lost. Entries for the final years have little to report other than of his good bodily health and the irrationality of his mind. He was approaching seventy. For "some years" before 1860 he was said not to have written a line of poetry. Yet, very late in the Peterborough Transcripts occur the ballads "Come the Back Way Dear" and "My Minnie Told All", the short poem "Vetches both yellow and blue", and the "Song for Miss B——", "The thrush in the firdeal is singing till e'en". The last has with it a punctuated copy of a note:

Dear Miss

I beg your acceptance of the enclosed ballad as the best I could make. The spring may bring better days, and better opportunitys to write a better song.

Yours truly,
John Clare

On March 7th, 1860, Clare resuscitated the dead Anna, Frederick and Charles, old Parker and Ann, added another daughter (or granddaughter?) to a repetitive list and wrote to Patty:

My dear Wife

This comes with my kind love to you & the Childern & my Father & Mother hoping it will find you all well I would have written sooner but had no oppertunity is Mr Sefton & Mrs Sefton & the two sons Well how is William & his wife & also the neighbours give my love to Wm & Sophy Kettle also to their two Sons & the daughter—How is Champion John Junr & Frederick & Anna Maria Eliza Louisa Sophia & Julia. give my love to Mrs Kettle, Fanny Kemp & to all inquiring friends

Your loving husband till Death
John Clare[1]

Sophy Kettle may have been his sister. The Seftons were the family into which his daughter Eliza Louisa married. The Kemps were Helpston farmers.

[1] *The Letters of John Clare*, *op. cit.*

The next day, in answer to an enquiry from the outside world by Mr Jas Hipkins, Wing noted that his patient was "very feeble in mind and still the object of many mental delusions"; he persuaded him to write a letter to be enclosed with his. In a shaky hand Clare wrote:

March 8, 1860

Dear Sir,

I am in a Madhouse & quite forget your Name or who You are You must excuse me for I have nothing to communicate or tell of & why I am shut up I don't know I have nothing to say so I conclude

Yours respectfully

John Clare[1]

A lawyer, Robert Walton, in *Random Recollections of the Midland Circuit*, described how, having dined with his friend the former governor, or housekeeper, and four harmless ones who were parlour-boarders, he

> was attracted by the appearance of a man who sat on a stone bench, his hands clasped before him, his eyes looking listlessly towards the ground. Inquiring who he might be, I was told it was no other than John Clare, formerly well-known as the "Northamptonshire poet." And this wreck before me was the man who, from the position of a common labourer, had, by his own unaided exertions, raised himself to a position which, but for the mistaken kindness of friends, might have led to great results. Yes, here was the man whose poetry had charmed me in boyhood by its sweetness and simplicity, the talent of which had drawn to this tiller of the soil the notice of Charles Lamb ... and others of that stamp.

Another visitor revealed that:

> Ingenious Della Cruscan rhymes and florid poetry made no impression on Clare. On one occasion he was visited by

[1] *The Letters of John Clare, op. cit.*

two gentlemen, one of whom read him some lines of "fine writing", written by a friend, and evidently expected his approval. The old man sat listless in his chair and his visitors thought he was unconscious of the reading and not in a poetic mood. But Mr. Godfrey, the secretary, knew more truly how to touch his heart.

"John," he said, "do you know these lines—

" '*The curfew tolls the knell of parting day*?' "

"Oh, yes," said Clare, "I know them, they are Gray's." And then ... with that appropriativeness which we have already remarked, "I know Gray. I know him well."

Strange how so many visitors confused a probable figure of speech with the "appropriativeness" of delusion.

On August 28th, Agnes Strickland, documentary historian and joint author with her sister of the *Lives of the Queens of England*, saw and talked with him when she went over St Andrew's with Lord Spencer and General Spencer. Not surprisingly she found him disposed to be silent:

I told Clare I had been much pleased with his lines on the daisy.

"Ugh! It is a tidy little thing," replied he, without raising his eyes or appearing in the slightest degree gratified by my praise.

"I am glad you can amuse yourself by writing."

"I can't do it," replied he, gloomily; "they pick my brains out." I enquired his meaning.

"Why," said he, "they have cut off my head, and picked out all the letters of the alphabet—all the vowels and consonants—and brought them out through my ears; and then they want me to write poetry! I can't do it."

"Tell me which you liked best, literature or your former avocation?"

"I liked hard work best," he replied, with sudden vehemence. "I was happy then. Literature has destroyed my head and brought me here."[1]

[1] Jane Margaret Strickland, *Life of Agnes Strickland*, 1887.

Clare gave Miss Strickland one of two manuscripts of "The Daisy is a happy flower"; and despite his bitter words to his latest two visitors (which could have been provoked by a hint of patronage in them) there was still a certain "method" in his answers to questions: a half-amused, not so crazy logic, as in the private pun of "eye-on-weed – ironweed", as in some of his answers to De Wilde, Miss Strickland and others.

He may have written no poetry at all for years before 1860, but he who listened to the "suthering wind", noted the "evening rack", "rusted chestnut leaves", "the bee asleep upon the thistle", certainly not long before that year watched

a gnat stupid nameless fly
Two hairs for sail all on one end sail by

Rallying yet again, for a last time but one, in spring 1860 – you can almost count the Asylum years by his spring poems, he wrote two sonnets "Well honest John how fare you now at home?" (February 10th, 1860) and "The Green Lane" (May 28th, 1860). One copy of "The Green Lane" is on a scrap of paper in his handwriting. The Northampton manuscript is headed "Sonnet", the Peterborough Manuscript "The Green Lane":

A Little Lane the brook runs close beside
& spangles in the sun shine while the fish glide swiftly by
& hedges leafing with the green Springtide
From out the greenery the old birds flye
& chirp & whistle in the morning sun
The pilewort glitters neath the pale blue sky
The little robin has its nest begun
& grass green linnets round the bushes flye
How mild the spring comes in – the daisey buds
Lift up their golden blossoms to the sky
How lovely are the pingles[1] & the woods
Here a beetle runs & there a flye
Rests on the arum leaf in bottle green
& all the spring in this sweet lane is seen

[1] Spinney or copse or small clump of trees.

Not entirely unworthy to be placed beside his earlier experiments with the form, the sonnets show once more the rhythm of a traditional voice in an urban culture, a voice which, under urban superiority, retains its links with perennial values and an earlier time.

In 1860 or the first half of 1861, John Plummer, a verse-writer from Kettering, found Clare reading a book from the asylum library in the sitting-room "cosy and comfortable, with its mahogany chairs, table, and couch, warm soft carpets, and a cheerful fire. Plummer remarked, in a well-meaning attempt to bring notice to the forgotten poet, on Clare's "very large forehead, and mild, benevolent-looking features".

"We found him taciturn," a later account of this visit says; "in vain we strove to arrest his attention. He merely looked at us, with a vacant gaze for a moment, and then went on reading his book." The attendant informed the visitor that Clare was generally good-humoured and obedient. In a letter to the editor of the *Northampton Mercury* on June 24th, 1861, Plummer goes further: Clare was said to be "very frequently blithe and talkative". There is no reason for his indifference and reticence during Plummer's visit to have been an attitude of either the aged or the insane. He had had enough of the curious.

From other evidence it is clear that the spring of 1861 found him at intervals "sane" and tranquil, as he had been during parts of the preceding year. At least two more visitors called on him—Paxton Hood, the Nonconformist author of *The Peerage of Poverty* and John Askham of Wellingborough. One or two American admirers may also have visited him.

According to John Godfrey, Clare wrote his last poem about six months before he died. That would place it in the winter of 1863. Yet it is a spring poem. He was asked to write something; after some persuasion he gave himself confidence (as Johnson said *he* often sought confidence from reading other poets' lines before he could begin to write his own) with a Burns quotation—from memory, with but slight error:

> The very child might understand
> The De'il had business on his hand

He then wrote seven lines on a subject which had fascinated him all his life. They contain a detailed and exact picture of a chaffinch's green moss nest, and the nut tree where it may be found in the Fen, not in the track of bleak winds straight from the Urals but in a sheltered, sunny, wooded field corner where birds and animals congregate.

Tis Spring warm glows the South
Chaffinch carries the moss in his mouth
To filbert hedges all day long
& charms the poet with his beautifull song
The wind blows blea oer the sedgey fen
But warm the sun shines by the little wood
Where the old Cow at her leisure chews her cud.

As his strength inevitably diminished, he was wheeled about the grounds of St Andrew's in a bathchair. Sometimes, it was recorded, he would say: "I want to go home," or "I have lived too long." Dr Wing, who died a few months after Clare and so was unable to make his intended study of Clare's mind, described his derangement as "a deep melancholy". He added, "Latterly his intellect had become sadly clouded, yet there were periods when the shadow would be temporarily lifted." From 1862 to 1864 the casebooks tell of his "tendency to apoplexy, his delusions about his identity ... his being haunted by phantoms of his own creation, his bad language to these chimeras, his habit of chewing tobacco, his eventual insensibility to the flowers and sunshine into which he was taken."

This "insensibility" was not so pervasive as to prevent his reaching his favourite window-seat, to look out on the garden beyond, which he did, Cherry says, to within three days of his death. On Good Friday of that year he was taken out for the last time. On May 10th—the month was notable for its excessive heat—he had a paralytic seizure, and Patty was notified of his illness. For Friday, May 20th, 1864, the casebooks record again: "This morning on being visited he was found to be completely comatose, and never rallied, but died quietly late in the afternoon."

Forty years before, craving friendship and rightful recognition, Clare had written for *The Rural Muse* a sonnet concerning his end.

I woud not that my being all should dye,
& pass away with every common lot;
I woud not that my humble dust should lye
In quite a strange & unfrequented spot,
By all unheeded & by all forgot
With nothing save the heedless winds to sigh,
& nothing but the dewy morn to weep
About my grave far hid from the worlds eye ...

Ten years before that, thinking of death, he had written:

> I wish to lie ... where the Morning & Evening sun can linger the longest on my Grave. I wish to have a rough unhewn stone, something in the form of a milestone, so that the playing boys may not break it in their heedless pastimes, with nothing more on it than this inscription: "Here rest the hopes & ashes of John Clare". I desire that no date be inserted thereon, as I wish it to live or die with my poems & other writings, which, if they have merit with posterity it will, & if they have not it will not be worth preserving.[1]

Mr Spencer of Woodcroft Castle and the Bellars took steps to ensure that Clare should be buried in the churchyard at Helpston, as he had desired. He took his first and his last train-journey from Northampton to the village of his birth. His coffin was placed at the inn, the Exeter Arms. Godfrey, the St Andrew's secretary, bore the news to Northborough. Tales went round the village because the coffin was not opened for the family to look at the dead. It was not John Clare who lay there, people said.

Patty, Eliza Louisa and her daughter, and William and his wife, attended the funeral, with Charles Mossop, Mr and Mrs Bellars and a few more friends of his youth. Up and down beside the grave Tom Clare, a kinsman, is said to have stalked growling: "Vanity of vanities; all is vanity." Yet perhaps all is not so vain but that a few of Clare's poems and the story of his poetic vitality may find listeners as long as man and poetry survive.

[1] Northampton MSS., "Journal", Appendix 5.

CHAPTER TWENTY-TWO

Song's Eternity: 1864-1972

If this book does not enable the reader to come to his own conclusions about some of the problems of Clare's life, his poetic achievement, his delusions, the descent of his after-fame and his permanent place in Letters, it will have failed in its main purpose. If the character of the man does not show through his early and late poems and his prose, even through his insanity, we may look for it elsewhere in vain.

Clare has suffered from an unconscious over-insistence by posterity on the "peasant-poet" circumstances in his life at the expense of others equally, sometimes far more, important. His "failures" – in not acquiring recognition, not even print, for so much of his work, his strange, so nearly sane madness – have been allowed to obscure his principal gifts to poetry. These are, in his early work, a precise, particular, self-forgetful seeing, hearing, describing; a lifetime's resistance to the falsity of pastoral half-measures; in his late poems a theme of yes-saying, constancy, love. It is unnecessary to suppose him to have acquired this positive attitude from Wordsworth, Coleridge, Blake or Southey. The idea, as Herbert Read said, is archetypal. This and his insistence on the "natural" in poetry have both been outweighed by the estimate of his basic, but not widely informed, intellectual quality. His humility and striving for what he saw as freedom from cant, have been permitted to mask the independence which was too rigid for self-confidence, too rigorous for self-comfort, but which also lay deep down in his innate self. He has been – and still is – written of as "poor Clare" who went mad, the sport of circumstance, whose gifts were a dreamy sweetness of character, a pathetic, child-like simplicity and a redundant flow of often formless verse. He is not yet beside Blake or Coleridge, Keats or Shelley, where he belongs.

There is no detailed study of his mind, or of his poetry. Dr P. R. Nesbitt, writing to Frederick Martin in 1865, confessed: "I was always led to believe that (Clare's) mental affliction had its origin in dissipation."

This vague statement may be an indictment for heavy drinking, or for sexual promiscuity, or for attacks of gonorrhoea. The first has dogged Clare as badly as one of his own phantoms. The third threatens him. Dr Nesbitt adds, "He was essentially a kind-hearted, good-feeling man with an unusually large cerebral development, possessing great breadth and altitude of forehead, such as we are in the habit of associating with men of the highest order of Intellect."[1]

Dr Thomas Tennant, the late medical superintendent of St Andrew's Hospital, writing in the *Journal of Mental Science* for January 1953, described Clare's "epileptiform" attacks or loss of consciousness under stress in his adolescence; the creative fury which drove him to write for days on end, scarcely stopping to eat or sleep; the "blue devils" of depression in the ensuing years following frustration over the publication and non-sale of his poems; his later delusions of identity. "In my opinion," wrote Dr Tennant, "this was a cyclothymic disorder, and not a schizophrenic one as suggested by one of his recent biographers.[2] Apart from the actual symptomatology, the excellence of much of his poetry written in hospital and the slow development of deterioration support this diagnosis." Dr Russell Brain confirmed this in *Some Reflections of Genius* in 1960. Clare endured this form of insanity, Dr Brain wrote, in common with Smart, Cowper, Newton, Goethe and Samuel Johnson. It is a disorder "to which men of broad general views coupled with a sensitive imagination are naturally exposed".

Clare was not unique in that, after the onset of derangement, he wrote poems, simple-seeming yet in the widest sense metaphysical; meaningful on any level beyond the practical commonplace. He was not alone in his continued capacity to talk and to write lucid prose. The letters Thomas Inskip wrote to him provide the clue that Clare's lost letters to Inskip are a loss to our knowledge of him between 1845 and 1850. As Dr James Harper,

[1] Northampton MSS. Printed in *Sketches in the Life of John Clare, by Himself*, *op. cit.*

[2] See the introduction to *Poems of John Clare's Madness*, *op. cit.*

the present medical director of St Andrew's, has said: "Most patients can talk lucidly on a variety of subjects, and John Clare was no exception to this." What is more unusual is that he continued to be acutely, agonizingly, lyrically aware of his predicament. In "A Vision" he permits an irrational statement to make a sane and valid point about poetry's link with "eternity". Recall the self-identity piece, the letter to George Reid for November 17th, 1841: "my mind is as it always has been from a boy— a disappointment"; the draft letter to Eliza Phillips when he is: "cooped up in this Hell of a Madhouse"; the letter to Patty of July 1848: "here I am in the Land of sodom where all the peoples brains are turned the wrong way"; the poems, "I think and speak of other things/To keep my mind at rest"; and "An Invite to Eternity":

> The land of shadows wilt thou trace,
> And look—nor know each other's face;
> The present mixed with reason gone ...

None of this means that his self-awareness would today allow him to be called sane. Much remains to be known about the forms and causes of mental illness, and tantalizingly little has so far been written on Clare's well-documented and fascinating case—a case which shows the pathos and strange beauty of many of the ways of the human mind.

Before, during, even after, his slow break-up, Clare had an extraordinarily intense, impressionable, receptive and retentive mind. This was what enabled him to enter into the life of nature and men about him. The qualities in his poetry are in his relationships with people. He enjoyed the company of all sorts and conditions of men and women. He was received by most of them as one of themselves, by villagers, the wealthy, intellectuals, gipsies, fellow-poets. Wherever pretension and arrogance were absent Clare was at home. His capacity to form judgments at first hand made him a good listener. When he spoke he was listened to. In his prose as in his poetry he wrote only of what his experience illuminated.

His story reveals a tenacity of both lyric power and of character beneath fragilely impressionable perceptions. Themes shaped in his youth reappear in maturity and age, some transposed, some apparently submerged but never unrecognizable, some direct and accurate as before. Youthful joy—a joy having little or nothing to do with Wordsworth's or Coleridge's "joy"—in Clare (as perhaps in them) is a folk-quality. His pervasive, poet's yes-saying or love, modified to the point where

Love shall be nameless and I will be free

is a human imperative of survival.

No circumstances could have conspired more consistently to wrest all these from a human being, and to fling him into apathy or disillusion or cynicism. But the boy who found freedom and poetry in his native fields became the ageing man who wrote in praise of love, liberty and poetry when the walls of an asylum hemmed him in. He wrote of them, not as a past dream only but as an ever-present reality. He was as physically comfortable and cared for at St Andrew's as Coleridge was with Gillman, or Swinburne with Watts-Dunton. His obsessive struggle to hold on to the happiness of being alive and watching earth's beauty and savage mystery was intermittently compensated for by delusion's easier triumphs. But Clare's happiness was part of the "gift of joy" earliest, anonymous Celtic–Anglo-Saxon poets knew, sang about, bequeathed.

As well as this delight in earth, the conscious need for independence was implanted in him by having had to live through the devastating changes in the England of his youth. His early poetry is the fullest presentment we have of a pre-Enclosure English village. He saw village society disorganized and broken as village society had not been disrupted since the days of Norman overlords. In the name of Progress he and his fellow peasants were reduced to casual and frequently workless labourers subject to a servile dependence on parish relief or charity. This is why Clare looked on the Helpston life of his childhood as Eden and on childhood itself as a Golden Age. These myth-memories have been in us all since the half-millennium of peace in the late Bronze Age. Eden is the Christian interpretation. Totally ignorant of Classical myth, Clare used the term "Eden" from his Christian, Protestant upbringing, just as he used "Eternity", "Heaven" and "God" for Creation's mystery of Time and Being. Living when he did, being what he was, made Clare the spokesman for a class and an age as well as for humanity.

In the 1930s sociological research proved that the overall standard of living did rise in Britain after the distress and poverty of workers between 1800 and 1830. But books such as Edward Thompson's *The History of the Working Classes* have since shown not only that this fact cannot minimize the suffering before, but that J. L. and Barbara Hammond's contention that Enclosure helped to "destroy the spirit of a race" was not an overstatement.

Clare's suffering strengthened his need to escape, to see beyond. As Robert Waller wrote in 1964, the significance of Clare is not only that he lived and wrote during that cataclysmic change, but that he wrote "sensing the shadow of the future".[1] Clare's insight into man's interference with organic processes, Robert Waller adds, "was never more needed than it is today."

Clare's "failure" then, gives the measure, not of weakness, or lack of direction, but of odds against him and our society's lack of perception of those odds. Neither can such "failure" indicate a childlike intellect, as had been held. His poetic vitality and his independence, since he would not let them die, consumed part of his own mind for lack of other fuel. We grow further and further away from the England Clare knew and showed us. But it is well to remember that three-quarters of people still live outside cities and large towns, and perhaps always will. If the flame in Clare had died there would have been no 1835 poem-sequence, no "Child Harold", no later contemplative lyrics. He did not spend his life bewailing a past age.

He made many mistakes: a serious number of his longer poems, such as "Pleasures of Spring", "The Flitting", some of *The Shepherd's Calendar* months, are formless; as Edmund Blunden has said, he did not know when or where to stop; he was never to espy any "aesthetic economy", any "tyrannous judgement". He who could have found a precise word and phrase every time often used stale or worn ones; he repeats words and rhymes; he wrote not one flawless lyric. Yet on his life's output, which is what any artist must finally be judged by, he is a major poet. By a sacrifice which, half-unconsciously, he

1 "Enclosure and John Clare", *Journal of the Soil Association.*

made as early as 1824, of the man to the poet and thinker, Clare bought with madness his "freedom", his "liberty", to state, perhaps no more than to re-state, a few elemental truths "six thousand years" old.

Bibliographical Works

Poems Descriptive of Rural Life and Scenery. Printed for Taylor & Hessey, and E. Drury, London 1820. Second and third editions, 1820. Fourth edition, 1821.

The Village Minstrel, and Other Poems. Printed for Taylor & Hessey, and E. Drury, two volumes, London 1821. Second issue, 1823.

The Shepherd's Calendar; with Village Stories, and Other Poems. Published for John Taylor by James Duncan, London 1827.

The Rural Muse. Whittaker & Co., London 1835.

Selections, Biographies and Important Miscellanea

The Life of John Clare, by Frederick Martin (Macmillan & Co., London and Cambridge 1865).

The Life and Remains of John Clare, by J. L. Cherry (Frederick Warne & Co., London 1873; J. Taylor & Son, Northampton 1873). Issued in Chandos Classics, 1873–7.

Poems by John Clare, selected and introduced by Norman Gale, with a Bibliography by C. Ernest Smith (George E. Over, Rugby 1901).

Poems by John Clare, edited, with an introduction, by Arthur Symons (Henry Frowde, London 1908).

Northamptonshire Botanologia: John Clare, by G. Claridge Druce (no printer's name, vol. 16, no. 130, 1912). Reprinted in *Flora of Northamptonshire* (Arbroath 1930).

John Clare: Poems Chiefly from Manuscript, edited by Edmund Blunden and Alan Porter, with an Introduction by Edmund Blunden (Cobden-Sanderson, London 1920).

Madrigals and Chronicles: being newly found poems written by

John Clare, edited with a Preface and Commentary by Edmund Blunden (The Beaumont Press, London 1924).

Sketches in the Life of John Clare by Himself, with an Introduction, Notes and Additions by Edmund Blunden (Cobden-Sanderson, London 1931).

John Clare: A Life, by J. W. and Anne Tibble (Cobden-Sanderson, London 1932).

The Poems of John Clare, edited by J. W. Tibble (Dent, London 1935).

Poems of John Clare's Madness, edited by Geoffrey Grigson (Routledge & Kegan Paul, London 1949).

Selected Poems of John Clare, edited with an Introduction by Geoffrey Grigson (Routledge & Kegan Paul, London 1950).

The Letters of John Clare, edited by J. W. and Anne Tibble (Routledge & Kegan Paul, London 1951).

The Prose of John Clare, edited by J. W. and Anne Tibble (Routledge & Kegan Paul, London 1951).

Selected Poems of John Clare, edited with an Introduction by James Reeves (Heinemann, London 1954).

John Clare: His Life and Poetry, by J. W. and Anne Tibble (Heinemann, London 1956).

The Later Poems of John Clare, edited by Eric Robinson and Geoffrey Summerfield (Manchester University Press, 1964).

The Shepherd's Calendar, edited by Eric Robinson and Geoffrey Summerfield (Oxford University Press, 1964).

The John Clare Collection in Northampton Public Library, edited by David Powell (*The Library World*, vol. 65, no. 767, May 1964).

Clare: Selected Poems and Prose, edited by Eric Robinson and Geoffrey Summerfield (*New Oxford English Series*, Oxford University Press, 1966 and 1967).

John Clare: The Wood is Sweet. Poems for young readers, edited by David Powell (Bodley Head, London 1966).

Life and Works of John Clare, edited by C. Xenophonotos (the Philips Park Press, Manchester 1966).

John Clare: Selection of his Poetry, edited by J. H. Walsh (Chatto and Windus, London 1957 and 1967).

John Clare: Selected Poems, edited by Elaine Feinstein (University of London, Tutorial Press, 1968).

The Penguin Book of English Romantic Verse, edited by David Wright (1968).

Selected Poems: John Clare, chosen by Leonard Clark (Arnold, Leeds 1964).

John Clare, edited by Leonard Clark (Longmans).

John Clare, Northamptonshire Poet, 1793–1864, selected by J. L. Carr (Kettering 1968–70).

Reference Volumes

(with date of first publication)

Abbott, Claude Colleer *Life and Letters of George Darley* (Oxford University Press, 1928).

Abercrombie, Lascelles *The Theory of Poetry* (Secker, 1924).

Addison, William *Epping Forest. Its literary and historical associations* (Dent, 1945).

Baker, A. E. *Glossary of Northamptonshire Words and Phrases*, 2 vols. (John Russell Smith, London; Abel and Sons, Northampton 1854).

Bloom, Harold *The Visionary Company* (Faber and Faber, no date).

Blunden, Edmund *Keats's Publisher* (Jonathan Cape, 1936).

Boyle, Andrew *An Index to the Annuals* (Boyle, Worcester 1967).

Brain, Russell "Diagnosis of Genius", *The British Journal of Aesthetics*, vol. 3, no. 2 (1963).

Cary, H. *Memoir of H. F. Cary*, 2 vols. (Moxon, 1847).

Chambers, R. *Cyclopaedia of English Literature* (Chambers, Edinburgh 1861).

Dennis, J. *Studies in English Literature* (Stanford 1876).

De Quincey, T. *Works: London Reminiscences*, edited by D. Masson (A. and C. Black, 1890).

De Wilde, G. J. *Rambles Round About* (Dicey, Northampton 1872).

Dobell, B. *Sidelights on Charles Lamb* (Dobell, 1903).

Elton, Oliver *Survey of English Literature 1780–1830* (Edward Arnold, 1912).

Fisher, James *The Birds of John Clare*, Reprint from *A History of the Kettering and District Naturalists' Society* (East Midland Printing Co., Kettering 1956).

Forster, John *Life of Charles Dickens*, vol. III (Chapman and Hall, 1874).

Gosse, Edmund *Silhouettes* (Heinemann, 1925).

Grainger, Margaret *John Clare Collector of Ballads* (Peterborough Museum Society, 1964).

Graves, Robert *The Crowning Privilege* (Cassell, 1955).

Grigson, Geoffrey *Poets in their Pride* (Phoenix House, 1962).

The Mint, edited by Geoffrey Grigson, (Routledge and Kegan Paul, 1946).

Poems and Poets (Macmillan, 1969).

Hall, S. C. *The Book of Gems* (1838 and 1844).

Hall, S. T. *Biographical Sketches of Remarkable People* (Simpkin and Marshall, 1873).

Hammond, J. L. and Barbara *The Village Labourer 1780–1832*, fourth edition (Longmans, 1927).

Harrison, Thomas *Birds in the Poetry of John Clare* (Peterborough Museum Society, 1957).

Heath, R. *The English Peasant* (Unwin, 1893).

Hewlett, Maurice *Last Essays* (Heinemann, 1924).

Hone, W. *Every-Day Book*, 2 vols. (Tegg, London 1826–7).

Hood, E. P. *The Literature of Labour* (Partridge, 1851).

The Peerage of Poverty (Judd and Glass, 1859–1861).

Hood, T. *Hood's Own*, No. 12 (no publisher's name, 1893).

Jack, Ian *English Literature 1815–1832* (Clarendon Press, 1963).

Some British Romantics: "Poems of John Clare's Sanity", (Ohio State University Press, 1966).

James, T. MS. Lecture on Dryden and Clare (Northampton MSS., 1856).

Kent, Elizabeth *Flora Domestica* (John Taylor, London 1823).

Sylvan Sketches (John Taylor, London 1825).

King, R. W. *The Translator of Dante* (Secker, 1925).

Lamb, Charles *Letters*, edited by E. V. Lucas (Methuen, 1905).

Lewis, Cecil Day *The Lyric Impulse* (Chatto and Windus, 1965).

Lewis, Naomi *A Visit to Mrs Wilcox* (Cresset Press, 1957).

Lucas, E. V. *The Life of Charles Lamb*, 2 vols. (Methuen, 1905).

Lynd, Robert *Books and Authors* (Cobden-Sanderson, 1922).

Marsh, G. L. *John Hamilton Reynolds* (Humphrey Milford, 1928).

Martin, E. W. *The Secret People. English Village Life after 1750* (Phoenix House, 1954).

Mitford, M. R. *Recollections of a Literary Life* (no publisher's name, 1854).

Murry, J. Middleton *Countries of the Mind* (Collins, 1922, Oxford University Press, 1931).

John Clare and Other Studies (Peter Nevill, London 1950).

St Andrew's Hospital Case-books

Nisbet, J. F. *The Insanity of Genius* (Grant Richards, 1900).

Pike, E. Royston *Human Documents of the Industrial Revolution in Britain* (George Allen and Unwin, 1966).

Redding, Cyrus *Fifty Years' Recollections* (Charles Skeet, London 1858).

Past Celebrities Whom I Have Known, vol. II (Charles Skeet, London 1866).

Redfield, Robert *The Primitive World and its Transformations* (Cornell University Press, 1957).

Richmond, Kenneth *Poetry and the People* (Routledge and Kegan Paul, 1947).

Robinson, Henry C. MS. Journal (British Museum).

Sternberg, Thomas *The Dialect and Folk Lore of Northamptonshire* (Smith, London, Abel, Northampton 1851).

Strickland, Elizabeth *Life of Agnes Strickland, by her Sister* (no publisher's name, 1874).

Symons, Arthur *The Romantic Movement in English Poetry* (Constable, 1908).

Taylor, John *Bibliotheca Northantonensis* (Northampton 1869).

Thomas, Edward *Feminine Influence on the Poets* (Secker, 1910).

Unwin, Rayner *The Rural Muse* (George Allen and Unwin, 1954).

Walton, Robert *Random Recollections of the Midland Circuit* (Chiswicke Press, London 1869).

Wilson, John *Recreations of Christopher North*, 2 vols. (Blackwoods, 1864).

Wilson, June *Green Shadows: the Life of John Clare* (Hodder and Stoughton, 1951).

Young, Andrew *The Poet and the Landscape* (Rupert Hart-Davis, 1962).

Some Articles and Reviews

1820 *The London Magazine* (January and March).
—— *The Quarterly Review* (May).
1821 *The London Magazine* (November).
—— *The Monthly Review* (vol. 94).
1823 *The London Magazine* (January and February).
1835 *Blackwood's Edinburgh Magazine* (vol. 38, August).
1840 *The Athenaeum* (June).
—— *The London Saturday Journal* (July).
—— *Tait's Edinburgh Magazine* (December).
1841 *The English Journal* (vol. 1, May 15th and 29th).
1847–9 *The Bedford Times* (passim).
1858 *Notes and Queries* (second series, vol. 5, January to June).
1861 *Once a Week* (May).
1864 *The Athenaeum* (August and October).
—— *Gentleman's Magazine* (July).
1869 *Harper's New Monthly.*
1870 *The Literary World* (June).
1873 *The Manchester Guardian* (July).
—— *The Literary World* (January).
1886 *Northamptonshire Notes and Queries* (no. 97).
1890 *Notes and Queries* (September 6th).
1920 *The Athenaeum* (March, April, October and November).
—— *The London Mercury* (July).
—— *The Nation* (February 22nd).
—— *The Peterborough Citizen* (March, September and November).
1921 *The Athenaeum* (January).
—— *The Peterborough Citizen* (February 1st).
—— *The Times Literary Supplement* (January, June and July).
1922 *The Bookman* (October).
1924 *The Spectator* (August).
—— *The Times Literary Supplement* (August).

1925 *The London Mercury* (June and July).
1926 *More Footnotes to Literary History* (April).
1941 *The Times Literary Supplement* (December 27th).
1946 Geoffrey Grigson, "John Clare. Poems and Fragments", *The Mint*.
1947 *The Penguin New Writing* (no. 32).
1953 Dr. Thomas Tennent, "Insanity and Genius", *Journal of Mental Science* (January).
1955 Geoffrey Grigson, "Integrity and John Clare", *The Listener* (November 3).
1956 A. J. V. Chapple, "Some Unpublished Poetical Manuscripts of John Clare", *Yale University Library Gazette* (vol. 31, no. 1, July).
—— *The Observer* (April 8th).
—— *The Times Literary Supplement* (April 27th).
1957 *The Times Literary Supplement* (October 18th).
1958 *The Times Literary Supplement* (January 17th).
1961 J. M. Newbery, "John Clare—Captive Poet", *Westminster Hospital Gazette* (vol. R.18, no. 2, March).
—— James Fisher, "John Clare: Naturalist and Poet", *The Listener* (October 19th).
1962 Eric Robinson and Geoffrey Summerfield, *The Review of English Studies* (N. S. XII, 50, May).
1963 Eric Robinson and Geoffrey Summerfield, "John Taylor's Editing of *The Shepherd's Calendar*", *The Review of English Studies* (November).
1964 Naomi Lewis, "The Vanished Man", *Encounter* (December 23rd).
—— I. M. F. Hooker and N. Dermott Hunt, "Some Unpublished Documents of the Asylum Period", *Northamptonshire Past and Present* (vol. 3, no. 5).
—— Robert Waller, "Enclosure and John Clare", *Mother Earth: Journal of the Soil Association* (vol. 13, no. 3, July).
1965 Margaret C. Barnet, "Matthew Allen M.D. 1783–1845", *Medical History* (vol. 9, no. 1, January).
1966 David Bonnell Green, "John Clare, John Savage and the *Scientific Receptacle*", *Review of English Literature* (vol. 7, April).
1967 "Unpublished Poems by John Clare edited by Eric

Robinson and Geoffrey Summerfield." *The Malahat Review* (no. 2, April).

1967 David Bonnell Green, "New Letters of John Clare to Taylor and Hessey", *Studies in Philology* (vol. 64).

1968 David Bonnell Green, "Three early American Admirers of John Clare, Dean Dudley, Romeo Elton and Benjamin P. Avery", *Bulletin of the John Rylands Library* (vol. 50, no. 2, Spring).

1969 Mark Storey, "Letters of John Clare, 1821: Revised Datings", *Notes and Queries* (vol. 16, February).

—— G. Watson (ed.) *The New Cambridge Bibliography of English Literature* (vol. 3).

1970 David Powell, "Northamptonshire's Own Poet", *Northamptonshire Life* (February–March).

1971 Thomas R. Frosch, "The Descriptive Style of John Clare", *Studies in Romanticism*, Boston University (vol. 10, no. 2).

General Index

The initial C. represents John Clare

(Names from Introduction and Bibliography are not listed.)

Index of Clare's Poems